THE ARCTIC *GROẞRAUM*

How should the Arctic be viewed in the 21st century? In this book, a leading scholar assesses the competing players for the Arctic, looking at broad questions of governance and security.

The author challenges the view that the Arctic is a passive space which is the focus of competitive advances from superpowers, arguing that it is more correctly understood as a dynamic pluriverse. Drawing on international law, international relations and diplomacy, this is an important re-assessment of the Arctic and its position in geo-politics.

The Arctic *Großraum*

Geopolitics and the High North

Christopher R Rossi

•HART•

OXFORD • LONDON • NEW YORK • NEW DELHI • SYDNEY

HART PUBLISHING

Bloomsbury Publishing Plc

Kemp House, Chawley Park, Cumnor Hill, Oxford, OX2 9PH, UK

1385 Broadway, New York, NY 10018, USA

Bloomsbury Publishing Ireland Limited, 29 Earlsfort Terrace, Dublin 2, D02 AY28, Ireland

HART PUBLISHING, the Hart/Stag logo, BLOOMSBURY and the Diana logo are trademarks of Bloomsbury Publishing Plc

First published in Great Britain 2025

A catalogue record for this book is available from the British Library.

A catalogue record for this book is available from the Library of Congress.

Library of Congress Control Number: 2025937220

ISBN: HB: 978-1-50998-832-7
ePDF: 978-1-50998-834-1
ePub: 978-1-50998-833-4

Typeset by Compuscript Ltd, Shannon

For product safety related questions contact productsafety@bloomsbury.com

To find out more about our authors and books visit www.hartpublishing.co.uk. Here you will find extracts, author information, details of forthcoming events and the option to sign up for our newsletters.

For Monica

≈

Acknowledgements

PORTIONS OF THIS book were presented at the Maritime Security Dialogue in the Atlantic and Pacific Arctic, sponsored by the Stiftung Wissenschaft und Politik in Berlin, the Ocean Policy Research Institute at the Sasakawa Peace Foundation in Tokyo, the Ny Ålesund Research Station in Svalbard, the Pressclub Concordia Forum Journalismus und Medien in Vienna, the Peace Research Institute at Goethe University in Frankfurt, the Pax Slavica in Flux Research Group at The Arctic University of Norway in Tromsø, the Catholic University of Eichstätt-Ingolstat Center for Latin American Studies at the Xplanatorium Herrenhausen Palace in Hanover, at Leuphana University College of Law in Lüneburg, and at the Law Faculty of the University of Prishtina in Kosovo. Portions of this book appeared in 46 *University of Pennsylvania Journal of International Law (Online)*.

For helpful comments, discussions, assistance, and pointers, I thank Mathias Albert, Rasmus Gjedssø Bertelsen, Haley Boyd, Lothar Brock, Aidan Ross Caples, Claudia Cheng, Matthias Finger, Niklas Granholm, Pia Hansson, Alf Håkon Hoel, Jochen Kleinschmidt, Mariia Kobzeva, Fisnik Korenica, Karri Korhonen, Svalbard Museum archivist and historian, Haakon Unhammer Kvaale, Marc Lanteigne, Frédéric Lasserre, Willy Lyemaster, Giuseppe Nesi, Nick Onuf, Matthias Packeiser, Gunnar Rekvig, Andrei Rogatchevski, César F. Rosado Marzán, Christian Rossi, Sigrid Rossi, Bornholm Museum curator, Jakob Seerup, Jan Jakub Solski, Christopher Starheim, Mirjana Tomić, Apostolos Tsiouvalis, Ksenia Vakhrusheva, Miloš Vec, Ivan Vejvoda, Florian Vidal, Daniel Quiroga Villamarín, and Adrien K. Wing. I am most grateful to my editors at Hart Publishing and Bloomsbury Publishing, Sinead Moloney, Sasha Jawed, and Vicki Hillyard.

The maps were adapted from cartographs created under the gracious direction of Frédéric Lasserre and the Université Laval Faculté de foresterie, de géographie et de géomatiqe.

The University of Iowa College of Law generously sponsored me as a visiting scholar in 2025 and portions of this research resulted from a stint at the University of Trento Faculty of Jurisprudence as a senior Fulbright scholar.

Contents

Table of Cases

Aegean Sea Continental Shelf Case (Gr/Turk), 1978 ICJ Rep 3, 36 (December 19).
Calvin's Case (1608) 77 ER 377, 394 (KB).
Case Concerning Maritime Delimitation and Territorial Questions between Qatar and Bahrain (Qatar/Bahr) 2001 ICJ Rep 40, 97 (16 March).
Cherokee Nation v Georgia, 30 US (5 Pet) (1831).
Fisheries Case (UK v Norway), Judgment, ICJ Reports, 116, 127 (18 December 1951).
Island of Palmas Case (Netherlands/USA), II RIAA 839 (1928).
Johnson v M'Intosh, 21 US (8 Wheat) 543 (1823).
Maritime Delimitation in the Black Sea (Rom/Ukr), 2009 ICJ Rep. 61, 89 (3 February).
Maritime Delimitation in the Indian Ocean (Somalia v Kenya), Judgment, ICJ Rep 188 (2021).
North Sea Continental Shelf (FRG v Den; FRG v Neth), Judgment, 1969 ICJ Rep 47.
State v George Tassel, 1 Ga Rep Ann 478, 1 Dud 229 (1830).

Chapter One

The Liminal Arctic

PHYSICAL GEOGRAPHERS STUDY the natural world. Political geographers study the way humans configure the natural world. The essential features of political geography assess political society as affected by nature's frame, and how political organisations adjust to or conform physiographical conditions, international relations, and spatial variations.[1] According to Richard Hartshorne, once geographers untethered themselves from an 'unbalanced' study of earth's physical features in the nineteenth century, political geography began to concentrate on variations of political phenomena in relation to earth's features.[2]

Many political features and variations involve borders. Like natural borders, political borders are constructed. All borders are constructed. They often extend beyond the meaning of physical terrain and the simplistic but powerful billiard ball or spatial container-like caricatures of the state as found throughout theories of international relations.[3]

California State University professor and United States State Department Geographer, George Etzel Pearcy, once proposed a new map to replace what he believed to be the antiquated 50-state boundary system of the United States.[4] Western expansion, natural features such as rivers and mountain ranges, and simple line drawing recourse to latitude and longitude resulted in illogical divisions and distributions of political power across the country. Population centres such as Houston and Los Angeles sprawled across arbitrary frontiers. The desert communities of Las Vegas and Phoenix grew into urban complexes far removed from adequate water supply. The geo-deterministic flatline panhandles of

[1] See generally Jean Brunhes and Camile Vallaux, *La Géographie De L'historie: Géographie de la paix et de la guerre sur terre et sur mer* (1921); Hans W Weigert et al, *Principles of Political Geography* (1957); GE Pearcy and LM Alexander, 'Pattern of Air Service Availability in the Eastern Hemisphere', 29 *Econ Geog* 74 (1953); Richard Hartshorne, *The Nature of Geography: A Critical Survey of Current Thought in Light of the Past* (1939).

[2] See Richard Hartshorne, 'Political Geography in the Modern World', 4 *J Conf Res* 52 (1960) (discussing the development of the field).

[3] See generally Stuart Elden, 'Terrain, Politics, History', 11 *Dialogues in Human Geography* 170 (2020) (deploying the concept of 'terrain to analyze the political materiality of territory'); RBJ Walker, *Inside/Outside: International Relations as Political Theory* 125 ('billiard ball'), 127 ('spatial container') (1992).

[4] See generally George Etzel Pearcy, *A 38 States U.S.A.* (1973) (proposing a redrawn map of the US to correct for perceived misappropriations of federal tax dollars to states).

Idaho, Texas, Florida, and Maryland bore no sensible relation to populations, and primary population centres organically and stubbornly tended to rise far from the geographic centre of the state. Pearcy proposed reducing the number of states to 38 by intentionally considering the effects of human mobility while diminishing reliance on distorting natural features and simplistic straight-lining recourse to longitude and latitude. Neil Freeman proposed a more directly political redrawing of the map of the United States based on the fundamental imbalance of the Electoral College,[5] where the largest state was 66 times as populous as the smallest and yet had only 18 times as many electoral votes. His remedy proposed redrawing the 50 states with equal populations.[6]

Political geographers in the late twentieth century began to concentrate on geography's scale or perspective, which ranged from localities to world systems.[7] This research bore obvious similarities to the proliferation of theoretical research launched in international relations circles by J David Singer's now classic discussion of the levels of analysis problem, which explored the several ways phenomena may be 'sorted and arranged for purposes of systemic analysis'.[8] Earlier, Edith Ware made the connection between international relations and geography when she wrote in 1934 that 'the study of international relations is

[5] The Electoral College, as specified in Art II of the United States Constitution, ended a dispute about the form of US democracy and whether the president and vice president should be elected by direct popular vote of qualified citizens or by Congress. It established the process whereby selected electors meet every four years to vote for the president and the vice president.

[6] Neil Freeman, 'Electoral College Reform (Fifty States with Equal Population), Fake is the New Real' (2012), fakeisthenewreal.org/reform. See also Jason Fago, 'Neil Freeman's Alternative Geography', *The New Yorker* (25 March 2013), www.newyorker.com/culture/culture-desk/neil-freemans-alternative-geography (discussing Freeman's playfully artistic visualisations of geography for the purpose of highlighting the constructed absurdity of political divisions).

[7] See, eg, Peter J Taylor, 'Geographical Scales within the World-Economy Approach', 5 *Review* 3 (1981) (considering a trilogy of scales – global, national, and urban); Doreen Massey, 'Questions of Locality', 78 *Geography* 142 (1993) (renewing geography's emphasis on sense of place and locality); John Agnew, 'Representing Space: Space, Scale and Culture in Social Science', in *Place/Culture/Representation* 251 (James Duncan and David Lay eds, 1993) (broadening the discussion over how geographical space is regarded in contemporary social science); Colin Flint, 'Structure, Agency, and Context: The Contributions of Geography to World-Systems Analysis', 66 *Sociological Inquiry* 496 (1996) (illustrating the role of agency in conceptualising places of core, semiperiphery, and periphery as geographical scales); David Delaney and Helga Leitner, 'The Political Construction of Scale', 16 *Pol Geo* 93 (1997) (conceptualising geographic scale as 'socially constructed rather than ontologically pre-given, and that the geographic scales constructed are themselves implicated in the constitution social, economic and political processes'); Kevin R Cox, 'Rescaling the State' in question, 2 *Cambridge J Regions, Econ & Soc'y* 107 (2009) (critically assessing claims of decentralisation of state functions given globalisation); David Harvey, 'Reshaping Economic Geography: The World Development Report 2009', 40 *Development and Change* 1269 (2009) (discussing policy thinking operating at different scales of local, regional, and global levels), where what is important at one scale is not so at another); Yves Lacoste, 'Geography, Geopolitics, and Geographical Reasoning', 146–47 *Hérodote* 14 (2012) (classifying spatial sets by order of magnitude); Yann Calbérac, 'Close Reading Michel Foucault's and Yves Lacoste's Concepts of Space Through Spatial Metaphors', 7 *Le foucaldien* 1 (2021) (unfolding concepts and functions of space used by the philosopher and by geographers).

[8] J David Singer, 'The Level-of-Analysis Problem in International Relations', 14 *World Politics* 77 (1961).

no longer entirely a subject for political science or law', but needed to include geography and other social sciences in order to understand the international system.[9] And yet, as Daniel Lambach suggested, understanding this political space was 'too important to be left to the geographers'.[10] Many other disciplines predated and contributed to the discussion of place and politics, but the concept of scale as variously employed became a common denominator and important independent variable in the study of the international system.

This book adopts a spatial approach to understanding geopolitical and international legal events in the changing Arctic. It is sensitive to emerging securityscapes involving the Arctic and eschews interpreting the region as monolithic.[11] It is sensitive to scale, specifically the scalarity of the Arctic as variously interpreted by securityscapes, and indeed is a reaction to the pinpointed focus of security studies and its narrow orientation and idea about geopolitics. It agrees with a variety of authors who view the Arctic as a place where conflict 'cannot be disentangled from broader global realignments'.[12]

To better understand this snarl, this book deploys the problematic but helpful idea of *Großraum* as an analytical device to reinterpret the historico-scalar significance of large space thinking in the Arctic. This thinking currently weighs heavily toward the traditional perspectives linking security with physical territory, but the *Großraum* concept adds much more context. The concordant dynamics of traditional thinking overlook emotive, cultural, legal, and environmental factors that, taken together, add complexity to the understanding of Arctic geopolitics.

The melting Arctic is creating new tensions. The elision of the established conceptual notion of Arctic borders stirs passions about border security and the spatial foundations at the base of political identity and authority. The use of linear boundaries once helped to define membership with a polity, but this practice is now challenged by the rise of Arctic liminal space, a challenge that not only questions the eighteenth-century political house on which territorial sovereignty was built, but also challenges the liberal international order and its universalising global institutions.[13] We see a resurgence of Arctic challenges

[9] Ibid at 86 fn 15 (quoting Edith Ware, *The Study of International Relations in the United States* 174 (1934)).

[10] Daniel Lambach, 'Space, Scale, and Global Politics: Towards a Critical Approach to Space in International Relations', 48 *Rev Int'l Stud* 282 (2022).

[11] See Robert Albro et al, *Anthropologists in the Securityscape* (2012) (deploying the term to interpret the complex terrain variously linking anthropology to national security).

[12] Lambach, n 10, at 298. See also Lassi Heininen, '"Comprehensive Security" – A Prerequisite for Sustainable Development', in *Towards a Sustainable Arctic: International Security, Climate Change and Green Shipping* 25 (Michael Goodsite and Niklas Swanström eds, 2023) (advocating a comprehensive security approach to the Arctic).

[13] See generally Beth A Simmons and Hein E Goemans, 'Built on Borders: Tensions with the Institution Liberalism (Thought It) Left Behind', 75 *Int'l Org* 387 (2021) (noting the neglect in contemporary international relations scholarship with recrudescent concepts of borders and territoriality).

with recrudescent authoritarianism in Vladimir Putin's Russia, an authoritarianism that has renewed interest in Cold War confrontation and security studies.

The origin of security studies dates from the Cold War.[14] The passage of the monumental United States 1947 National Security Act reflected a transformation of scale and geopolitical thinking.[15] Allied concentration against fascist powers during World War II shifted to confront international communism in the post war world. This single omnibus bill, directly attributable to the coming Cold War, created the National Security Council, the Central Intelligence Agency, and a cabinet-level Secretary of Defense position. It merged the military departments into the National Military Establishment and within it created the Joint Chiefs of Staff. Most generally, it meshed science with industry to create a corporatist approach to diplomacy and geopolitics.[16] It situated the modern practice of international relations more centrally within the domain of security specialists, not diplomats or internationalists, and facilitated the academic study of geopolitics and foreign policy through the weighted lens of national security.[17] It led to a dominant narrative of international security studies as an Atlantic story, a Eurocentric story, and an independent field of study quickly absorbed as a sub-field of international relations.[18] These storylines predominantly apply to the study of the Arctic of today but not to the Arctic of tomorrow.

Fortified by NSC-68, the State Department's top-secret assessment of 'endemic' conflict against the Soviet Union's 'fanatic' quest for domination,[19] a massive military build-up ensued, prompted by the Soviet and Chinese-backed North Korean invasion of South Korea in June 1950. This transformation introduced a new mentality of defence and diplomacy that linked budgets and appropriations, used foreign aid for diplomatic purpose, and relied on a cadre of techno-managerial bureaucrats to permanently mobilise military preparedness and produce high-tech weaponry. The prosecution of geopolitical interests confronted both traditional American conservative views of anti-statist or

[14] See Arnold Wolfers, '"National Security" as an Ambiguous Symbol', 67 *Pol Sci Q* 481, 482 (1952) (locating national security in terms of Cold War threats and distinguishing security from welfare studies or the chimeric world community); David A Baldwin, 'Security Studies and the End of the Cold War', 48 *World Pol* 117, 119 (1995) (noting the commonplace association of 'the origins of security studies with the twin stimuli of nuclear weaponry and the Cold War, but mindful of pre-Cold War scholarship).

[15] 50 USC ch 15 § 401. See Douglas T Stuart, *Creating the National Security State: A History of the Law That That Transformed America* 1 (2008) (suggesting that the legislation is arguably second only to the 1964 Civil Rights Act in modern American legislative history).

[16] A leading presentation of the corporatist understanding of geopolitics is found in Michal J Hogan, *A Cross of Iron: Harry S. Truman and the Origins of the National Security State, 1945–1954* (1998).

[17] See Ali Muhammad and Sugeng Riyanto, 'International Security Studies: Origins, Development and Contending Approaches', 10 *Austral: Brazilian J Strategy & IR* 230, 230 (2021) (dating the emergence of international security studies as a sub-field of international relations to the end of World War II and the onset of the Cold War).

[18] See Barry Buzan and Lene Hansen, *The Evolution of International Security Studies* 1 (2009).

[19] United States Objectives and Programs for National Security [NSC-68]. For background and analyses, see *NSC-68: Forging the Strategy of Containment with Analyses by Paul H. Nitze* (S Nelson Drew ed, National Defense University, 1994).

limited government and domestic liberal values. It pitted the idea of the warfare state against the welfare state.[20] United States President Dwight D Eisenhower (1890–1969) reduced the tragic geopolitical competition with the Soviet Union to the burdensome drain of defence spending associated with the Cold War and the birth of the military-industrial complex, costs that left humanity 'hanging from a cross of iron'.[21]

Clinical divisions between peace and security, democracy and communism, and containment and deterrence, internalised the study of international relations and oriented it toward familiar tropes of territorialised competition. These tropes focused on the domestic economic, social, and political determinants of state building for purposes of national security. This became the important internal way the theorisation of security studies came to be reflected in geopolitics.[22] And now this domestic thinking is challenged not by a hanging cross of iron but by a melting cone of ice.

Robert Cox once noted that all theories are created 'for someone and for some purpose'.[23] The domestic/corporate view of security studies promoted the development of the national security state and took hold in the study of geopolitics. The meaning of the Arctic reduced to perceptions and purposes related to strategic competition. Moscow's sea-based nuclear forces in the Kola Peninsula, 'regarded as its most survivable nuclear asset', made the Arctic a priority in terms of NATO defence.[24] Harvard Belfer Center director Steven Miller sees a return of such thinking across the Arctic region due to Russia's aggression against Ukraine.[25] The reawakening of strategic Arctic concerns due to war in central Europe gives pause for consideration of the constructed and malleable scope of geopolitical boundaries.

The Cold War also ushered in a broader concern for spheres of influence. Saul Cohen argued that a three-fold geopolitical restructuration of great spaces resulted. Phase I (1945–1956) created two large worlds of containment involving the Eurasian continent and East Asia, which strategically attached to the Soviet Union, and the Trade-Dependent Maritime world of the Western powers, which included the extended Caribbean and Mediterranean basins, the Atlantic and Pacific regions, Maritime Europe and the Maghreb, and offshore Asia, Oceania, and South America.[26] Phase II (1957–1979) witnessed substan-

[20] See generally Hogan, n 16.

[21] Dwight D Eisenhower, Address to the American Society of Newspaper Editors, American Rhetoric (16 April 1953), www.americanrhetoric.com/speeches/dwighteisenhowercrossofiron.htm.

[22] See generally John Agnew, *Hidden Geopolitics: Governance in a Globalized World* (2023) (contesting how assemblages of networks and capital flows now affect territorial arrangements and challenge traditional geopolitical analysis).

[23] Robert W Cox, 'Social Forces, States and World Orders: Beyond International Relations Theory', 10 *Millennium: J Int'l Stud* 126, 128 (1981).

[24] Steven E Miller, 'The Return of the Strategic Arctic', *Arctic YB 2022*, at 1 (2023), arcticyearbook.com/images/yearbook/2022/Commentaries/6C_AY2022_Miller.pdf.

[25] See ibid.

[26] See Saul Bernard Cohen, *Geopolitics of the World System* 63–71 (2003) (discussing the period of nuclear stalemate, deterrence, and the drawing of the ring of containment).

tial changes to the geopolitical map as 'the Cold War leap-frogged Continental Eurasia's Near-Periphery and spread to the inner and outer reaches of the Maritime world'.[27] Here, Soviet incursions into the Maritime Realm created for Cohen three shatterbelts (the Middle East and the Horn of Africa, Sub-Saharan Africa, and Southeast Asia), which were 'regions torn by internal conflicts whose fragmentation is increased by the intervention of external major powers in contention over the region'.[28] Phase III (1980–1989) witnessed the waning of Soviet power and China's rise and separation from the Euroasian continental world 'to establish a separate East Asian geostrategic realm'.[29] Perhaps we are now in the midst of Phase IV, a phase brought on by Russia's aggression against Ukraine in 2022. This phase has infiltrated the liminal construction of Arctic great space, turned its perceived understanding as a sphere of confluence into a sphere of influence, and as derivatively affected by war in Ukraine, changed its staid hydrological status into a melting shatterbelt of great power competition, ever as much as affected by politics as by climate.

Central to Cohen's presentation was the important character of the natural environment. Ladis Kristof claimed that the modern geopolitician read from the map of nature's environment to draw certain conclusions about what nature influences in terms of decisions of modern politics and foreign policy.[30] Changes in nature and politics codetermine Arctic politics. Is the changing natural Arctic environment informing political calculations in ways akin to the human actions that now affect the environment?

THE ARCTIC PATHWAY OF THIS BOOK

There are many ways to interrogate hegemonic interests in the Arctic. Feminist, critical, postmodern, and Indigenous studies amplify alternative pathways to frame this securityscape. Disruptive meta-geographies may proffer explicit radical imaginaries that preference social and environmental justice (anti-geopolitics),[31] grassroots problems of indigeneity (alter-geopolitics)[32] and

[27] ibid at 71.
[28] ibid at 5.
[29] ibid at 82.
[30] Ladis KD Kristof, 'The Origins and Evolution of Geopolitics', 4 *J Conflict Res* 15, 19 (1960).
[31] See, eg, Paul Routledge, *Space Invaders: Radical Geographies of Protest* (2017); Simon Dalby, *Creating the Second Cold War: The Discourse of Politics* (1990); Anouar Abdel-Malek, 'Geopolitics and National Movements: An Essay on the Dialectics of Imperialism', 9 *Antipode* 28 (1977) (presenting counter approaches to geographical logic to interpret the significance of protest movements and pressure groups).
[32] See Klaus Dodds and Chih Yuan Woon, 'Triumphant Geopolitics? Making Space of and for Arctic Geopolitics in the Arctic Ocean', in *Arctic Triumph, Northern Innovation and Persistence* 163 (Nikolas Sellheim, Yulia V Zaika and Ilan Kelman eds, 2019); Sara Koopman, 'Alter-geopolitics: Other Securities are Happening', 42 *Geoforum* 274 (2011) (emphasising the kinetic action-politics of alternative, nonviolent geopolitical actors).

ethnographic participants (alternative geopolitics),[33] or they may seek 'new ways of putting peace(s) back together', perhaps orienting discussion toward the pawns rather than the kings and queens of the Arctic geopolitical game.[34] Reconceptualising the Arctic as a large and contested, but also consensual, space assists in this wide project of interrogation. However, the construction of this securityscape first necessitates a conceptual understanding of the securityscape.

This book interprets the securityscape in geopolitical terms, terms mindful of but broader than the mutable physical geography of its land and seascape. It begins in chapter two with an analysis of the idea of *Großraum*. This concept bears the unmistakable nineteenth-century association with imperialism and the twentieth-century imprint of the controversial international legal and geopolitical theorist, Carl Schmitt (1888–1985). Schmitt scripted a nationalist perspective of the concept and identified it with a large-scale international politico-economic presence, as exemplified by the Monroe Doctrine. While mindful of Schmitt's historico-legal analytical spin, this chapter and the one that follows it importantly separate the analytical attributes of the concept from Schmitt's dark political orientation. Schmitt did not simply contemplate the analytical features of the concept; he 'actively campaigned for one' modelled on a German-dominated *Mitteleuropa* in conformity with his explicit association with Nazism.[35] The seductive temptation to anoint Schmitt as a contemporary geopolitical theorist, not mindful of his 'deeply rooted' political views, has been appropriately condemned as a serious intellectual and political error.[36] Configuring the *Großraum* concept to the Arctic and applying it as an imperfect but usable tool help to illuminate the spatial boundaries of the Arctic, which extend beyond its physical, geographic frontiers and the limiting Westphalian vocabulary of territory.[37] The concept predates Schmitt's usage, but has not broken free of his dark and occluding presentation. Schmitt must be received with care.

Chapter three contextualises the historical significance of the *Großraum* concept apart from late nineteenth- and twentieth-century adulterations. It lifts the term out of its Schmittian framework and attempts to reclaim its association with the moral landscape of liberalism and its iterations in terms of wholes and parts. Detached from its dark adulterations, this reflection helps to conceptualise the Arctic and its components as *Großräume*, scalar representations

[33] See Nick Megoran, 'For Ethnography in Political Geography: Experiencing and Re-Imagining Ferghana Valley Boundary Closures', 25 *Pol Geo* 622 (2006) (contesting the political geographic focus on boundaries by suggesting ethnographic participant observation).

[34] Koopman, n 32, at 282.

[35] Stuart Elden, 'Reading Schmitt Geopolitically: *Nomos*, Territory and *Großraum*', 161 *Radical Philosophy* 18, 19 (2010).

[36] ibid at 24.

[37] Westphalian sovereignty is predicated on the *de jure* independence of the state and the relative de facto autonomy of the state to determine its own domestic character. For more detailed discussion, see Stephen D Krasner, *Problematic Sovereignty, in Problematic Sovereignty: Contested Rules and Political Possibilities* 10–11 (Stephen D Krasner ed, 2000).

distinct from its common singular or unitary presentation as a *Großraum*. Such distinctions allow for a more considered representation of the security interests affecting the Arctic in its various regional, geopolitical, and international legal constructions.

Chapter four addresses the historico-legal construction of the Arctic, processes that lent weighty emphasis to its caricature as an empty space or as a no man's land (*terra nullius*). Such vacuous portrayals facilitated colonial encroachment and territorialisation in ways that diminished Indigenous interests and promoted title to territory by fiat and the discovery doctrine. Interestingly, the territorialisation of the Arctic also accompanied attempts to comanage or classify portions of the Arctic as a common space (*res communis*), a space subject to a nascent condominium conversation that today implicates portions of the Arctic as a common resource and an exceptional space of cooperation and peace.

Chapter five specifically confronts the geopolitical problems of the Arctic great space given events caused by the Arctic's principal steward, Russia, and its 2022 aggression against Ukraine. The war has reconfigured the Arctic as a region now derivatively affected by Baltic–Arctic relations and specifically affected by Arctic Council stalemate. These intertwined developments lend support to reconceptualising the Arctic as a *Großraum*, as a Baltic–Arctic *Großraum*. The chapter also argues that Russia is isolated, that cooperative efforts to address major threats caused by the melting cryosphere are forestalled, and that Arctic environmental problems unrelentingly compound, producing security implications that will amount to additional geopolitical and international legal crises. The current crisis is muddled by a lack of temporal and spatial awareness of the strategic implications of the scope of Arctic concerns in a globalising world. It is also muddled by a concentrated tensions in the Arctic that obscure the nature of the security threat. NATO, fortified by the inclusion of Sweden and Finland, prepares for High North engagement with Russia. Sweden's Prime Minister spoke alarmingly about the need to prepare for homeland defence 'with weapons in hand and our lives on the line'.[38] If such a call for defence is realised, it will more likely take the form of responses to hybrid war, cyber intrusions, subsea fibre-optic and cable disruptions, and other expressions of grey zone attacks against the great landscape of the High North, including the Baltic region.

Chapter six addresses Russia's five-century engagement in the Arctic. The chapter investigates the geopolitical sense of insecurity bred by Russia's deep cultural and historical attachment to its Eurasian northland. This insecurity combines an understanding of Muscovy's dynamic expansion eastward over the Ural Mountains, the legacy of domination projected by the Soviets over

[38] Speech by Prime Minister Ulf Kristersson at Folk och Försvars Annual National Conference 2024, Gov of Sweden (8 January 2024), www.government.se/speeches/2024/01/speech-by-prime-minister-ulf-kristersson-at-folk-och-forsvars-annual-national-conference-2024.

Siberia, the civilisation continuum that now animates Russia's nationalistic Eurasianism project (fed by a Slavic Middle Kingdom sentiment), and the withering sense of insecurity that attaches to defending its peripheries, now further problematised by Finland's and Sweden's accession into NATO. This latter development forms the topic of chapter seven, which conjoins the histories of the Baltic Sea states and the Arctic circumpolar powers to assess the complex multilateral architecture of space and scale that connect the two regions geopolitically. Two historical island problems – Bornholm in the Baltic Sea and Svalbard in the Arctic Ocean – serve as examples to reinforce appreciation of Russia's diminishing sense of control over northern regions.

Chapter eight addresses Russia's proclaimed description of the Arctic as a Russian Mecca, its project of operationalising the Northern Sea Route as a major seafaring highway connecting Asian and European commerce, and the geopolitical and international legal implications of an evolving transpolar route, which in subtle ways may diminish the significance of Russia's Northern Sea Route project while simultaneously opening up new Arctic strategic frontiers involving Svalbard, Iceland, and Greenland. Chapter nine turns to China and other countries interested in globalising the Arctic, either as a common space for peaceful development or as a potential new source of great power competition. China's Polar Silk Road initiative, its hand's-length relationship with Russia, and its rhetorical support for a rules-based governance structure in the Arctic and over its resources are assessed before the concluding chapter of the book.

Chapter Two

The Return of the Großraum

WHAT IS MEANT by *Großraum*, and how or why should it apply to the Arctic? The term translated from German literally means 'great space'. This descriptor seems to appropriately project the Arctic's geographic immensity, which is often equated with spatial themes of emptiness and remoteness,[1] as well as with ineffable qualities of beauty.

Artefacts from the Heroic Age of Polar Exploration (roughly 1870s–1922) reflect this imagery and more. Sun-bleached timber huts, rail lines leading to nowhere, hulking conveyor belts, abandoned flensing camps, and desolate whalers' tombstones record forsaken attempts at human conquest – these ruins reflect epic tales of endurance, adventure, determination, privation, disaster, and intrigue.[2]

[1] See Oran R. Young, 'The Age of the Arctic', 61 *For Pol'y* 160 (1985–86) (noting the 'widespread tendency to dismiss the region as a remote, unimportant wasteland').

[2] See eg, Jessie Kratz, *Mystery of the Arctic Ice: Who Was First to the North Pole*, National Archives (6 April, 2022) (reviewing archival material involving Robert Peary's disputed claim that his party, not Frederick Cook's party, was the first to reach the North Pole): Paul Watson, *Ice Ghosts-The Epic Hunt for the Lost Franklin Expedition* (2018) (reconstructing the mystery surrounding the disappearance of Sir John Franklin's Canadian expedition to transit the Northwest Passage); Garth Cameron, *Umberto Nobile and the Arctic Search for the Airship Italia* (2017) (recounting the 1928 search for Italian airship designer Umberto Nobile and his crew aboard the airship, *Italia)*; Michael Pye, *The Edge of the World: How the North Sea Made Us What We Are* (2014) (discussing Christendom's engagement with the waters of its norther periphery); Jon Krakauer, *Into the Wild* (1996) (detailing the fated walk into the Alaskan wilderness by Chris McCandless, a person seeking solitude); Ejnar Mikkelsen, *Two Against the Ice* (1957) (presenting the Danish explorer's harrowing exploration of Greenland); Matthew Henson, *A Negro Explorer at the North Pole: The Autobiography of Matthew Henson* (2001)[1912] (presenting an account of Robert Peary's companion on the 1909 North Pole expedition): Fridtjof Nansen, *Farthest North: Being a Record of a Voyage of Exploration of the Ship 'Fram' 1893–1896 and of a Fifteen Months' Sleigh Journey With an Appendix in Two Volumes* (1897); Julius Payer, *Nie zurück!* (1892) (artistically imagining the incredible return of ill-fated Astro-Hungarian-led North Pole expedition after the fortuitous discovery of Franz Josef Land); 'The Latest Arctic Explorations – The Remarkable Escape of the Polaris Party', *Scientific American* (7 June 1873) (detailing the remarkable rescue mission of Commander Charles Francis Hall's fated expedition to reach the North Pole); Norwegian explorer Roald Amundsen gained use of Fridtjof Nansen's Fram under the pretence of a planned drift over the Arctic Ocean. Parry's announced conquest of the North Pole on 6 April 1909 motivated Amundsen to secretly amend his voyage and change his course toward the South Pole. He announced the deceit after setting sail, to the astonishment of most of his crew and to Nansen. His famously laconic telegram sent to rival, Robert Falcon Scott, read: 'Beg inform you Fram proceeding antarctic [sic]. Amundsen.' See 'Expeditions, Fram Polar' Exploration Museum, frammuseum.no/polar-history/expeditions/the-third-fram-expedition-1910-1914.

Polar depictions as inhospitable and unrelenting territory also appear among Antarctic venturers. No better presentation of these themes can be found than in Apsley Cherry-Garrard's masterpiece, *The Worst Journey in the World* (Paul Theroux intro, 1994)[1922] (presenting a first-person account

Reflecting on polar climes, the Antarctican Apsley Cherry-Garrard evocatively noted 'that Dante was right when he placed the circles of ice below the circles of fire'.[3] The Arctic's unrelenting harshness stokes a marooned sentiment of loneliness,[4] which belies its biodiverse natural geographies and stereotypes its Indigenous peoples.[5]

The term *Großraum* can also mean a sphere of influence or geopolitical space akin to Peter Uwe Hohendahl's description of an 'expanded territory'.[6] Within this sphere, great powers exert 'special prerogatives' that reflect their 'superior material power' as legitimised and recognised by international society.[7] This usage made an influential appearance in twentieth-century international circles principally due to the writings of Carl Schmitt (1888–1985).[8] No modern treatment of this term 'can avoid its adaptation – or adulteration – by Schmitt

of the three-person expedition to Cape Crozier in the dead of the Antarctic winter to recover Empire penguin eggs, and other accounts of Scott's ill-conceived attempt to reach and return from the South Pole); and Alfred Lansing's equally wonderful, *Endurance: Shackleton's Incredible Voyage* (1959). See also Roland Huntford, *The Last Place on Earth: Scott and Amundsen's Race to the South Pole* (intro by Paul Theroux, 1999) (presenting a controversial account of the bumblings of the Scott expedition to the South Pole); and Lennard Bickel, *Mawson's Will: The Greatest Polar Survival Story Ever Written* (2000) (detailing the Australian explorer's epic solo journey of survival).

[3] Cherry-Garrard, n 2, at 254.

[4] See generally Miloš Vec, 'The Last World: 150 Years of Franz Josef Land', Völkerrechtsblog (Englis trans, 14 July 2023), voelkerrechtsblog.org/the-last-world-150-years-of-franz-josef-land (expounding on Christoph Ransmayr's fictional account of the 1873 'discovery' of Franz Josef Land).

[5] See generally Gontran de Poncins, *Kabloona* (1941) (presenting an awakening account of Inuit life from stereotyped European impressions); Dawid Bunikowski, 'The Philosophy of Law in the Arctic', in *Philosophies of Polar Law* 30, 42–43 (Dawid Bunikowski and Alan D Hemmings eds, 2021) (noting the rejection of Arctic Indigenous cultures and customary laws in the Arctic).

[6] Peter Uwe Hohendahl, *Perilous Futures: On Carl Schmitt's Late Writings* 60 (2018). See also Christian Joerges, 'Europe a Großraum? Shifting Legal Conceptualisations of the Integration Project', in *Darker Legacies of Law in Europe: The Shadow of National Socialism and Fascism over Europe and Its Legal Traditions* 167 (Michael Stolleis and Navraj Singh Ghaleigh, eds, 2003) (noting 'sphere of influence' as Schmitt's more intended connotation).

[7] Alexander Wendt and Daniel Friedheim, 'Hierarchy under Anarchy: Informal Empire and the East German State', in *State Sovereignty as Social Construct* 240–41 (Thomas J Biersteker and Cynthia Weber eds, 1996).

[8] See generally Carl Schmitt, '*Großraum* versus Universalism: The International Legal Struggle over the Monroe Doctrine' ['Großraum gegen Universalismus: der völkerrechtliche Kampf um die Monroedoktrin'], in *Spatiality, Sovereignty and Carl Schmitt: Geographies of the Nomos* 46–54 (Stephen Legg ed, trans Matthew Hanna, 2011 [1939]) (introducing the concept of *Großraum* as a sphere of influence and linking it to the Monroe Doctrine); Carl Schmitt, *Writings on War* (Timothy Nunan trans and ed, 2011 [1941]); Carl Schmitt, *The* Nomos *of the Earth in the International Law of the* Jus Publicum Europaeum (2003 [1974]) (adapting the Monroe Doctrine sphere of influence idea to *Großräume* in Europe and Asia) [hereinafter Schmitt, Nomos *of the Earth*]; Roberto Orsi, 'On the Relevance of Carl Schmitt's Concept of Großraum in Contemporary International Relations', 17 *J Int'l Pol Theory* 295 (2019) (crediting Schmitt's influence); Lothar Gruchmann, *Nationalsozialistische Großraumordnung. Die Konstruktion einer 'deutschen Monroe-D.ktrin'* (1962) (crediting Schmitt). See also Elden, 'Reading Schmitt Geopolitically: *Nomos*, Territory and *Großraum*', 161 *Radical Philosophy*, 18, 19; See also Montserrat Herrero: *The Political Discourse of Carl Schmitt: A Mystic of Order* 127 (2015) ('sphere of organization'); William Hooker, *Carl Schmitt's International Thought: Order and Orientation* 4 (2009) (regarding the Grossraumordnung as 'a pluriverse of continental empires').

in his postwar reflection on world order'.[9] To Schmitt, the idea of *Großraum* meant more than 'an expanded minor space'. It presented a shift in the topography of scientific meaning, beyond an 'empty dimension of area' or the 'depth in which corporeal objects move'.[10] It embedded historical components derived from 'inner measures' that more appropriately represented the sphere of competence of the state, otherwise constricted by linear borders.[11]

The term is pregnant with implication, but Schmitt's primary geopolitical focus brought it closely into alignment with *Realpolitik* perspectives. Broadly, Schmitt theorised about the process of territorial acquisition (*Landnehmen*) in terms of geopolitical competition over new or emerging large spaces. As summarised by William Hooker,

> the great power (*Reich*) existed within this space not simply to acquire it, but to exercise political control over it. The great space itself was qualitatively different than the state, broader and less organic, but still of binding cultural relation to the state and subject to its political control.[12]

Schmitt's construction of the *Großraum* combined historiographic, geographic, spatial, telluric (soil-related), and political elements; however, it embedded dark racial understandings and intonations, as well.[13]

The Monroe Doctrine served as his template. This 1823 proclamation by the United States forewarned European powers against interfering in the political affairs of newborn American republics (or potential United States territories). Schmitt called it 'the first and … most successful example of a *Großraum* principle in the modern history of international law'.[14] The doctrine asserted separate spheres of influence for the Americas and Europe following the retreat of imperial powers and the independence of the Americas. It argued against recolonisation and for non-interference through a restructuring of the world into great regions.

It had a European analogue. The idea of a Greater Area in *Mitteleuropa* – with Germany at its core – dated from the mid-nineteenth-century economic

[9] Christopher R Rossi, 'The *Nomos* of Climate Change and the Sociological Refugee in a Sinking Century', 50 *GW Int'l LR* 613, 620 (2018) [hereinafter Rossi, '*Nomos* of Climate Change'].

[10] Carl Schmitt, 'The *Großraum* Order of International Law with a Ban on Intervention for Spatially Foreign Powers: A Contribution to the Concept of Reich in International Law (1939–1941)', in *Carl Schmitt: Writings on War* 75, 120 (2011) [hereinafter Schmitt, 'The *Großraum* Order of International Law'].

[11] ibid. In an antisemitic and counter-reformational broadside, Schmitt attributed the empty dimensional idea of space to Jewish influence, Occidental rationalism, the contemporary political-historical epoch germinating from the sixteenth and seventeenth centuries, the Renaissance, Reformation, Humanism and Baroque streams of thought, all of which culminated in Kantian philosophy. See ibid at 120–22.

[12] Hooker, n 8, at 4. See also ibid at 133–34.

[13] See Peter Stirk, 'Carl Schmitt's "Völkerrechtliche Grossraumordnung"', 20 *Hist Pol Thought* 357, 371 (1999) (noting criticisms that the political idea meant to 'radiate' from the leading power of the *Großraum* could be masked as indeterminate or explicitly racist).

[14] Schmitt, 'The *Großraum* Order of International Law', n 10, 75, 83.

concept of a German *Zollverein*.[15] This expansive free trade area grew from the Prussian tariff system of 1818. It formalised with treaties in 1834 and grew to include by 1888 the Baltic Sea free ports of Konigsberg, Danzig, and Lübeck, outlets to the North Sea in Neuwerk, Bremerhaven, and Hamburg, the House of Hanover, Luxembourg, Alsace-Lorraine, Baden, and Bavaria.[16]

This economic analogue also contained a geographic component. Prussia bordered on a dozen German neighbouring states (Austria bordered on three, France on four) and the externalities associated with a customs union, 'substantially influenced by geographic considerations',[17] logically motivated a consolidation of tariff schedules as part of a larger and ultimately incomplete project of Austro-Hungarian-German unification.[18] Contiguity and *Großraum* went hand-in-hand, as close as cartographic depictions of the spread of imperialism.[19]

The Monroe Doctrine *qua Großraum* developed from the European 'discovery' of the Western Hemisphere. Reworked by Schmitt, this discovery initiated a global demarcation of '*free space* … open to European occupation and extension'.[20] The waning of European rule over the Americas in the early part of the nineteenth century led to a reordering of the great space of the Americas in conjunction with the rise of republicanism. Schmitt's admixtures of global history, geography, spatiality, and soil constructed an organic idea of *Großraum* with peculiar emphasis on telluric considerations. This significance preferenced a *situatedness* or proximity to the lands of the earth in support or recognition of civilisation blocs. Like the *Zollverein*, it also implied contiguity and connectedness, which mapped the spread of economic language into Central European geographic space.[21] Each greater region of the world would be dominated by

[15] See Michael Heffernan, 'Fin de siècle, fin du monde? On the Origins of European Geopolitics, 1980–1920', in *Geopolitical Traditions: A Century of Geopolitical Thought* 27, 41 (Klaus Dodds and David Atkinson eds, 2000) (basing the idea of Mitteleuropa on the growth of Friedrich List's first espousal of a general Central European customs union during the 1830s and 1840s).

[16] For historical treatments on the development of the Zollverein, see Hans-Werner Hahn, *Wirschaftliche Integration im 19. Jahrundert: die hessichen Staaten und der Deutsche Zollverein* (1982); WO Henderson, *The Zollverein*, 2nd edn (1959).

[17] Florian Ploecki, 'A Novel Institution: The Zollverein and the Origins of the Customs Union', University of Adelaide Discussion Paper No 2019-05 (November 2019), at 20, iit.adelaide.edu.au/ua/media/390/Discussion%20Paper%202019-05%20Florian%20Ploeckl%20131119.pdf. See also ibid at 18 (noting that Prussia had more to gain from a 'widespread agreement' rather than from 'a small number of bilateral ones' due to the large number of bordering German states).

[18] Brendan Simms, *Die Rückkehr des Großraums?* 9 (2023) ('Die Ursprünge des Großraum-Konzepts, die Idee, dass Europa oder zumindest Mitteuropa um seinen deutschen Kern herum gruppiert werden sollte, scheinen bis ins frühe und mittlere 19. Jahrhundert zurückzureichen. Im Bereich der Wirtschaft war es die Vorstellung vom Zollverein, einer deutschen Freihandelszone, um die mitteleuropäische Großregion zu einer kompakten Mitteleuropäischen Wirtschaftszone zu erweitern').

[19] See generally James R Akerman ed, *The Imperial Map: Cartography and the Mastery of Empire* (2009) (interrogating maps in various historical contexts as a agents of empire).

[20] Schmitt, Nomos *of the Earth*, n 8, at 87.

[21] For a fascinating presentation of cartograms that resize world maps according to various subjects, each occupying great spaces, see World Mapper, worldmapper.org.

a proximate great power able to assert superior rights toward neighbouring countries. In the words of Peter Hilpold, the relative great power of a region 'could intervene to secure its prerogatives while being legitimised to impede interventions by exterior powers'.[22] Foreign powers ('*raumfremde Mächte*' in Schmittian terms) needed to remain within their own metropolitan area.[23] Schmitt claimed 'the Monroe Doctrine and the Western Hemisphere [were] linked together. They define[d] the sphere of the special interests of the United States. They encompass[ed] a space for exceeding the boundaries of the state proper – a *Großraum*.'[24]

To Schmitt, his Eurocentric reflection on the Monroe Doctrine would secure for Germany hegemonic control over continental Europe to counterbalance '"spatially alien" Anglo-American and Soviet incursions',[25] similar to German Chancellor Bismark's 1871 unification project to secure Central Europe from incursions by Russia in the East and France in the West.[26] Schmitt gave passing consideration to an evolving structuration of the earth into a 'new *nomos*', perhaps 'a combination of several independent *Großräume* or blocs' with mention of China and 'the new East Asia sphere rising in world history',[27] but his orientation clearly focused on his Western framework.

A new *nomos* would problematically intrigue Carl Schmitt as a distinctly political idea[28] and as a justification for territorial aggrandisement.[29] Schmitt redacted liberal constructs of an abstract, universal rule-ordered world from his understanding of *Großraum*. His idea of 'global human space was not based on an a priori abstract universe, as represented in physics or mathematics, but on a pluriverse of political-cultural, legal, and economic large spaces'.[30]

[22] Carl Schmitt, *Völkerrechtliche Großraumordnung mit Interventionsverbot für raumfremde Mächte. Ein Beitrag zum Reichsbegriff im Völkerrecht* (1941). Peter Hilpold, 'Justifying the Unjustifiable: Russia's Aggression against Ukraine, International Law, and Carl Schmitt's "Theory of the Greater Space" ('Großraumtheorie')', 22 *Chinese J Int'l L* 409, 426 (2019).

[23] Simms, *Die Rückkehr des Großraums?* at 23 ('Außenstehende Mächte – „raumfremde Mächte' in Schmitts Sprachgebrauch– dürften außerhalb ihres eigenen Großraums nicht eingreifen und sie sollten es auch nicht versuchen').

[24] Schmitt, Nomos *of the Earth*, n 8, at 281.

[25] Ryan Martinez Mitchell, 'Chinese Receptions of Carl Schmitt Since 1929', 8 *Penn State JL & Int'l Affs* 181, 262 (2020).

[26] Simms, n 23, at 10 ('Reichskanzler Otto von Bismarck entschied sich für eine österreichisch-deutsche Annäherung, durch die die vereinten Kräfte Mitteleuropas gegen Angriffe aus Ost und West zusammengefügt werden sollten.').

[27] Schmitt, Nomos *of the Earth*, n 8, at 352 ('new *nomos*'), 355 ('several independent *Großräume*), 292 ('new East Asia sphere').

[28] ibid at 252–53.

[29] See Joseph J Bendersky, *Carl Schmitt: Theorist for the Reich* 252 (1983).

[30] Werner Krawietz, 'Völkerrechtliche Großraumordnung mit Interventionsverbot für raumfremde Mächte', 34 *Rechtstheorie* 284, 285 (2004) ('Begreift man mit Schmitt den globalen menschlichen Raum nicht alse ein apriorisches abstraktes Universum, vie es sich der Physik oder Mathematik darstellen mag, sondern al sein Pluriversum von politisch-kulturellen, rechtlichen und wirtschaftlichen Großräumen, so erscheint die Vorstellung eines (und nur eines!) einheitlichen universalistischen Weltrechts'). See also Chantal Mouffe, 'Schmitt's Vision of a Multipolar World Order', 104 *South Atl Q*

LINES OF AMITY, LINES OF ENMITY

However, Schmitt was preoccupied by the rise of the United States and the occluding significance of its great space. Schmitt regarded *this* new *nomos* as a global linear expression of intervention.[31] It was founded on naval supremacy, which untethered the *rayas geográficas* (geo-spatial dividing lines) that provided spatial dimension and true meaning to the *publicum*.[32] The United States' world order did not stay within the lines of amity, and it strayed beyond the lines of enmity. This new global expression destroyed the international system's bounded lines of order.

In Schmittian terms, this new global order revealed itself to be a normless *nomos*[33] – a destructured (*raumlose*), borderless, groundless (telluric-less) exportation of spatially undifferentiated and free-floating political theology.[34] This normless *nomos* would not serve the bracketed ordering of his *publicum* as regulated by the dialectical conflict between friends and enemies, but rather the abstract political theology of techno-managerialism (*Technizität*), corporatism, Anglo-Saxon capitalism, and propagandism masquerading as liberalism, Good Neighbourly non-intervention,[35] free exchange, and rational choice. In Schmitt's political eschatology, his *jus publicum europaeum* represented the *katechon*, the last restraint against the nihilistic void that follows an international order based on liberalism. It could not be restored in its Westphalian, state-centric formulation, as 'this masterpiece of European form and occidental Rationalism' had been 'dethroned'.[36] As David Lewis concluded, the ruse of cosmopolitanism and

245, 247 (2005) (noting that, for Schmitt, 'the world was a "pluriverse", not a universe, and he was adamant that any attempt to impose one single model worldwide would have dire consequences').

[31] See Schmitt, Nomos *of the Earth*, n 8, at 100 ('This global line made it possible for the United States to upset the spatial order of the European world and to introduce a new concept of war into world history'). See also ibid at 354–55 (on new *nomos*).

[32] Gruchmann, n 8, at 121.

[33] Mark Antaki, 'Carl Schmitt's Nomos of the Earth', 42 *Osgood Hall LJ* 317, 322 (2004) (noting Schmitt's critique that 'Norms without a *nomos* do not constitute law proper').

[34] See Carl Schmitt, 'Groβraum versus Universalism: The International Legal Struggle over the Monroe Doctrine', in *Spatiality, Sovereignty and Carl Schmitt: Geographies of the Nomos* 46, 47 (Stephen Legg ed, Matthew Hannah trans, 2011) (discussing Woodrow Wilson's distortion of the Monroe Doctrine into a 'spatially undifferentiated [raumlose] and borderless extension of liberal democratic principles to the entire Earth and all of humanity').

[35] Schmitt attributed the US's shift from a passive, non-discriminating concept of neutrality to 'an interventionist stance that made the decision of justice and injustice for others' on the policies of US President Woodrow Wilson. Schmitt, 'The Turn to the Discriminating Concept of War (1937)', in Carl Schmitt, *Writings on War* 30, 37 (Timothy Nunan trans and ed, 2011 [1937]). US President Franklin D Roosevelt announced the Good Neighbor policy to 'resolutely respect[] the rights of others … and … the sanctity of … agreements in and with a world of neighbors' in his First Inaugural Address to Congress, 4 March 1933. See Avalon Project, Yale Law School, avalon.law.yale.edu/20th_century/froos1.asp. See also 'The *Groβraum* Order of International Law', n 10, 85 (referencing suspicions about good neighbourliness) and 125 (noting the 'shoreless universalism of the Anglo-Saxon rule of the seas').

[36] Marcus Llanque and Herfried Münkler, 'Vorwort von 1963', in *Carl Schmitt: Der Begriff des Politischen* 9, 19 (Reinhard Mehring ed, 2003) [*The Concept of the Political*, 1932] ('Die Epoche der Staatlichkeit geht jetzt zu Ende. Darüber ist kein Wort mehr zu verlieren. Mit ihr geht der ganze Überbau staatsbezogner Begriffe zu Ende, den eine europa-zentrische Staats-und Völkerrechtswissenschaft in vierhundertjähriger Gedankenarbeit errichtet hat. Der Staat als das

the failure of state sovereignty to stop it oriented Schmitt's mind toward a new spatiality, 'a multipolar world of regions dominated by hegemonic powers',[37] a world reduced to a single concept: *Großraum*.

Schmitt's intrigue with the Monroe Doctrine as an American *Großraum* became an essential component of his critique of nihilistic geopolitics.[38] He concentrated on this *Großraum* because it analogously inspired and usurped his theoretical attempt to frame one for Germany when he began writing *Nomos of the Earth* during World War II,[39] which drew from antecedents charted by Karl Haushofer's (1869–1946) analysis of the *Geopolitics of the Pacific Ocean* (1924).[40] Andrew Carty encapsulated the tensions in Schmitt's theoretical intrigue with the spheres of influence. He noted Schmitt's attack against liberalism's (and the League of Nations') 'globally enforced homogeneity' through its incoherent pursuit of a 'minority rights system'.[41] This incoherence violated his deeply rooted attachment to the German historicist concept of *Volk*, which 'reflect[ed] the popular will of a specific people in a specific place'.[42] It further exposed deficiencies in constitutional democracies' purported defence of individual rights, normalised military intervention as the means of securing international peace,

Model der politischen Einheit, der Staat als der Träger des erstaunlichsten aller Monopole, nämlich des Monopols der politischen Entscheidung, dieses Glanzstücks europäischer Form und occidentalen Rationalismus, wird entthront.').

[37] David G Lewis, *Russia's New Authoritarianism: Putin and the Politics of Order* 163 (2020).

[38] Schmitt separated the notion of nihilism from anarchy. He argued that anarchy need not be mutually exclusive of the application of law, for certain forms auto-interpretive resistance, such as self-defence, 'can be good law'. In contrast, nihilism destroyed 'every notion of resistance and self-defense'. Schmitt, Nomos *of the Earth*, n 8, 187. See also Schmitt, 'The *Großraum* Order of International Law', n 10, 86 (explaining the transition of the Monroe Doctrine from a principle of non-intervention to a justification for imperialistic interventions).

[39] See generally Carl Schmitt *Völkerrechtlische Grossraumordnung mit Interventionsverbot für Raumfremde Mächte: ein Beitrag zum Reichsbegriff im Völkerrecht* (1939); Andrew Carty, 'Carl Schmitt's Critique of Liberal International Legal Order Between 1933 and 1945', 14 *Leiden J Int'l L* 25 (2001). Schmitt also lectured on *Großraum* weeks after the 1938 Nazi invasion of Czechoslovakia, a lecture that 'contributed to his moniker as Kronjurist to the Third Reich'. Rossi, '*Nomos* of Climate Change', n 9, at 634 (referencing Charles E Frye). Schmitt had 'essentially' finished Nomos *of the Earth* before 1945, but it was not published until 1950. Hohendahl, n 6, at 61.

[40] See Karl Haushofer, *Geopolitik des Pazifischen Ozeans: Studien Über die Wechselbeziehungen zwischen Geographie und Geschichte* 27, 29, 68, 116, 259 (1924) (connecting the Monroe Doctrine to the development of U.S. spheres of influence in the Pacific).

[41] Carty, n 39, at 40. See also Thalin Zarmanian, 'Carl Schmitt and the Problem of Legal Order: From Domestic to International', 19 *Leiden J Int'l L* 41, 54 (2006) (describing Nomos *of the Earth*, n 8, as 'an obituary of modernism').

[42] Lewis, n 37, at 151. Although beyond the scope of this investigation, the idea of a geocultural or situationally specific development of law intrigued numerous followers and critics of the historical school. Chief among these proponents were Carl von Savigny and his idea of Volkgeist (the Spirt of the People), Sir Henry Maine's distillation of law's ontology as the movement from status to contract, Max Weber's idea of logical formal rationality, and Schmitt's loose adaptation in the form of the *ius publicum europaeum*. See generally GL Ulmen, 'The Sociology of the State: Carl Schmitt and Max Weber', 1 *State, Culture, and Society* 3 (1985). See also Frederick C Beiser, *The German Historicist Tradition* (2011) (presenting essays on important expositors of the German historicist tradition, including Meinecke, Ranke, Dilthey, Simmel, Herder, Weber, and more).

and ignored the liberal tradition's own colonialist heritage, which allowed France and Britain to extend amity lines beyond Europe over their colonial possessions while disqualifying Nazi Germany's translation of its colonialist imperialism over Central and Eastern Europe.[43]

Schmitt imparted normative significance to his notion of *Großraum*, but his derision of liberalism and the sustaining influence of his critique in critical and authoritarian circles eclipse a fuller appreciation of integrative, egalitarian, and historically informed aspects of the Monroe Doctrine, republican emphases that are commonly overlooked due to its turbulent affirmation as a justification for intervention.[44] Like many moderns, who critique liberalism as a 'spent force', bounded to overused themes of individualism, positivistic rules and rights-orientation,[45] Schmitt's revulsion of liberalism discounted if not ignored proto-republican elements geared toward Alexander Hamilton's (1757–1804) vision of the Americas as a region of futurity.[46] It overlooked sentiments expressed by *El Libertador*, Simón Bolívar's (1783–1830) *Jamaica Letter* (1815), which espoused a grand federated, republican union across the Isthmus of Panama.[47] It discounted the debate in the 1820s over attending the Panama Congress, a seminal foreign policy split in the early United States attempt to forge a consensus over the emerging nations of Latin America.[48] It diminished the conceptual foundation of Christian Wolff's (1679–1754) *Civitas Maxima* and Emmerich de Vattel's (1714–1767) 'unrivaled' influence on United States founders, which imbued 'governance by law in accord with higher purpose'.[49] Their influence sought to forge a link between commerce and diplomacy, and liberalism and republicanism. They 'affirmed the moral and legal equality of

[43] Carty, n 39, at 25, 41.

[44] See Mark T Gilderhus, 'The Monroe Doctrine: Meanings and Implications', 36 *Pres Stud Q* 5 (2006) (discussing the Monroe Doctrine's various meanings and implications, including its service as 'a cover for less ennobling purposes connected with the defense of [U.S] strategic and economic interests'); Christopher R Rossi, *Whiggish International Law: Elihu Root, the Monroe Doctrine, and International Law in the Americas* 101–09 (2019) (detailing the rise of the anti-liberal application of the Monroe Doctrine, dating the narrative from the annexation of Texas (1845) and the Mexican-American War (1846–1848) to the Roosevelt Administration's Caribbean policy, the Platt Amendment (1901) and Roosevelt and Lodge Corollaries (1904, 1912)).

[45] Nicholas Greenwood Onuf, *The Republican Legacy in International Thought* 118 (1998) [hereinafter Onuf, *Republican Legacy*].

[46] Alexander Hamilton, The Federalist Papers: No 11, Avalon Project [23 November 1787], avalon.law.yale.edu/18th_century/fed11.asp (conjecturing about 'regions of futurity' and noting the political division of the world into four political and geographic parts, Africa, Asia, America, and Europe, 'each having a distinct set of interests' and each 'unhappily' been subjected 'by force and by fraud' to Europe's 'dominion over them all').

[47] Simón Bolívar, 'Carta de Jamaica. Contestación de un Americano Meridional a un Caballero de esta Isla' (1815), web.seducoahuila.gob.mx/biblioweb/upload/carta_de_jamaica.pdf.

[48] Andrew RL Clayton, 'The Debate over the Panama Congress and the Origins of the Second American Party System', 47 *The Historian* 219 (1985) (noting the fragility and tenacity of ideological perspectives formed during the American Revolution 'in the debate over how to deal with the Latin Americans').

[49] Peter Onuf and Nicholas Onuf, *Federal Union, Modern World: The Law of Nations in an Age of Revolutions* 1776–1814, at 11 (1993) ('unrivaled'), 5 ('higher purpose').

nations no less than of people, whether small or large'.[50] This idea nurtured Thomas Jefferson's (1743–1826) idea of an *Empire of Liberty*[51] and Henry Clay's (1777–1852) 'human freedom league in America'.[52]

These sentiments also formed around republican strains connected to the Monroe Doctrine,[53] which at times pragmatically grounded political decisions in calculations of most immediate hemispheric threat. Jefferson had advocated an alliance with Britain in 1823 to protect the revolutionary hemisphere from the Holy Alliance.[54] Bolívar, an admirer of British parliamentarianism, applauded the Monroe Doctrine, as did numerous other Latins at that time, as a defence of newborn republicanism,[55] and as a catalyst for the spread of federated governance as a balance-of-power counterweight to the reconstituted European political order following the Napoleonic Wars.[56] Schmitt's revulsion of liberalism also ignored the long 'hidden history' of a distinctive idea of an international law of the Americas that animated hemispheric thoughts of solidarity,[57] and international foreign policy and organisational attempts to rearrange the hemispheric security structure with the International Union of American Republics (later renamed the Organization of American States), the 1947 Rio Pact on multilateral defense, and the 1948 Pact of Bogotá, the precursor to regional pacific settlement processes.

Schmitt's conceptual framework was decidedly antiliberal and conservative. It was void of spatial abstraction and universal appeal. It was grounded in concrete complexity and telluric metaphor. And it tilted around the unipole of state sovereignty, as correctly noted by Benno Teschke.[58] In contemporary colloquia, Schmitt's construction of *Großraum* has been labelled 'one of the most

[50] ibid at 15.

[51] Thomas Jefferson to George Rogers Clark, 25 December 1780, in *4 Papers of Thomas Jefferson: October 1780 to February 1781*, at 237–38 (Julian P Boyd ed, Lyman H Butterfield and Mina R Bryan, Assoc eds, 1951).

[52] International American Conference, Reports of Committees and Discussions Thereon. Vol. IV, Historical Appendix. The Congress of 1826, at Panama and Subsequent Movements Toward a Conference of American Nations, Ex Doc 232, pt 4, at 9 (1890), tile.loc.gov/storage-services/public/gdcmassbookdig/congressof1826at00inte/congressof1826at00inte.pdf.

[53] See Brita H Crandall and Russell C Crandall, *'Our Hemisphere'? The United States in Latin America, from 1776 to the Twenty-First Century* __ (2021).

[54] See Walter LeFeber, 'Jefferson and an American Foreign Policy', in *Jeffersonian Legacies* 370, 370–71 (Peter S Onuf, ed, 1993).

[55] See Samuel Guy Inman, 'The Monroe Doctrine and Hispanic America', 4 *Hispanic Am Hist Rev* 635, 640 (1921) (quoting Bolívar: 'England and the United States protect us. These two nations, which form today the only two powers in the world, will not permit that help be given to Spain.' For numerous other official Latin American expressions of support for the Monroe Doctrine's expression of republican virtue, see ibid at 640–43).

[56] Rossi, *Whiggish International Law*, n 44, at 77.

[57] See generally Juan Pablo Scarfi, *The Hidden History of International Law in the Americas: Empire and Legal Networks* (2017) (discussing the historical foundations of international law in the Americas and the rise of the Inter-American System).

[58] See Benno Gerhard Teschke, 'Fatal Attraction: A Critique of Carl Schmitt's International Political and Legal Theory', 3 *Int'l Theory* 179, 197 (2011) (noting Schmitt's focus on the territorial state) [hereinafter Teschke, 'Fatal Attraction'].

popular and effective keywords of the Nazi regime'. At the same time, it has been 'presented as a universal model for how continental spaces across the globe could be consolidated'; how 'global politics could be reconstructed as a … community of equals',[59] and how it can be used as an analytical tool to interpret geopolitical thinking post-February 2022, the start of Russia's invasion of Ukraine.[60]

Schmitt's idea of land appropriation drew from concepts of cultivation, provisioning, carving up, and parcelling out. He turned these demarcations into a narrative on geopolitics and international law.[61] Central to his lament was the breakdown of the great spatial *jus publicum europaeum*,[62] which provided for state equality and relative stability within continental Europe between the sixteenth and twentieth centuries. He viewed its greatest advantage as the bracketing of unconstrained violence to the competitive open spaces of the colonial world, which laid 'beyond the lines' of European amity.[63] However, the grand early-twentieth-century collapse of the *jus publicum europaeum* presented different spatial possibilities, perhaps none more porous than a suspect new form of world order, where, according to Jan-Werner Müller, 'morality seemed to have stealthily crossed the border between prudent statecraft and a reckless 'ethics of conviction'.[64]

Here, the idea of globalism, detached from territoriality,[65] or perhaps even the global commons, could instantiate hegemonic rule in the guise of a disingenuous, even nihilistic liberalism. This liberalism pursued the rhetoric of a free

[59] See colloquia sponsored by the Deutsche Gesellschaft für Geographie (DGfG) and Goethe University, '*Großraum* from Carl Schmitt to Aleksandr Dugin: Unpacking the Persistence of a Classical Geopolitical Trope' (20 September 2023) (paper abstract, Mark Bassin), dkg2023.de/papers/gro%C3%9Fraum-from-carl-schmitt-to-87862.

[60] See colloquia sponsored by the Deutsche Gesellschaft für Geographie (DGfG) and Goethe University, Greater Area and Border Fringe: Continuities and Breaks in Geopolitics after 1945 (20 September 2023), dkg2023.de/sitzungen/gro%C3%9Fraum-und-grenzsaum-kontinuit%C3%A4ten-und-90601 (paper abstracts of Niels Werber, Ulrike Jureit, and Patricia Chiantera).

[61] See Schmitt, Nomos *of the Earth*, n 8, Ch. 5. See also Anna Jurkevics, 'Hannah Arendt Reads Carl Schmitt's The Nomos *of the Earth*: A Dialogue on Law and Geopolitics from the Margins', 16 *Eur J Pol Theory* 345, 346 (2017).

[62] See Schmitt, Nomos *of the Earth*, n 8, at 227 (lamenting the decline of the *jus publicum europaeum* 'into a universal world law lacking distinctions …. replaced by an empty normativism of allegedly recognized rules'). See also Martti Koskenniemi, 'International Law as Political Theology: How to Read Nomos der Erde?', 11 *Constellations* 492, 495 (2004) ('Schmitt did not hide his admiration for the *jus publicum Europæum*').

[63] See Schmitt, Nomos *of the Earth*, n 8, at 93–94, and 97 ('beyond the line'); 99–100 (noting the 'rationalization, humanization, and legalization [bracketing]' of war). Schmitt regarded the bracketing of war as one of the great achievements of European international law. See ibid at 187 ('the essence of European international law'), 228; 'the highest form of order within the scope of human power,' ibid at 187. See also Claudio Minca and Rory Rowan, *On Schmitt and Space 222* (2016) (paraphrasing Schmitt's claim that the bracketing of European wars as 'the tremendous achievement' of the *jus publicum europæum*).

[64] Jan-Werner Müller, *A Dangerous Mind: Carl Schmitt in Post-War European Thought* 224 (2003).

[65] Schmitt referred to the prevailing concept of global universalism as 'lacking any spatial sense.' Schmitt, Nomos *of the Earth*, n 8, at 235.

economy, while normalising the protective tariff, most favoured nation status, and colonial treaties[66] – each an indirect method of exerting political influence.[67] To Schmitt, liberalism's *nomos* ignored territorial borders by supporting the rubric of universalism, while portaging the political triumph of the United States' *Großraum* – expressed as the Monroe Doctrine[68] – into the League of Nations Covenant.[69] Schmitt regarded this clause as an abandonment of the spatial relation between Europe and the Western Hemisphere and a nihilistic licence for the United States to determine solely its application. To Schmitt, 'this proviso [Article 21 of the League Covenant] constituted a symbol of the Western Hemisphere's triumph over Europe'; it 'abandoned the idea of a reciprocity of continents or hemispheres'; and it secured the 'paramount position of the American continent … which was neither specifically European nor consistently global … In so doing, it also renounced a clear spatial order.'[70] The concrete order and logic of a European international law based on sovereignty and territoriality then gave way to an American *imperium* based on the Open Door policy, which secured for the United States access to the open space and emporium of Asia.[71]

Schmitt's general idea of *Großraum* required demarcations to halt this metastatic spread. He noted in the first line of *The Concept of the Political* (1932) that the concept of the state 'presupposes the concept of the political'.[72] He expounded on the political as the natural organising condition of the person, who created telluric boundaries or actual physical carvings in the earth to actually take (*nehmen*) or appropriate land. This possessory attribute of *nomos* developed historically into the sovereign state, which conceptually formed after the cartographic disruption to the Ptolemaic world-view wrought by the discovery of the New World.

[66] See ibid (discussing economic liberalism).

[67] ibid at 255.

[68] See ibid at 281 (identifying the Monroe Doctrine in terms of the Western Hemisphere and declaring it a *Großraum* in the sense of international law).

[69] Article 21 of the League Covenant holds: 'Nothing in this Covenant shall be deemed to affect the validity of international engagements, such as … regional understandings like the Monroe Doctrine, for securing the maintenance of peace.' Schmitt regarded this clause as an abandonment of the spatial relation between Europe and the Western Hemisphere and a nihilistic licence for the US to determine solely its application. See ibid at 254.

[70] ibid at 254.

[71] Schmitt, Nomos *of the Earth*, n 8, at 292 (noting the 'antiquated Monroe Doctrine was replaced by a demand for the 'open door' to the wide-open spaces of Asia'). Through a similar Schmittian application, Renmin University's Liu Xiaofeng has argued: 'In today's international context, through the lens of Schmitt's interpretation of international law, the United States has every reason to worry about the relationship between itself and emerging East Asia. Just as old Europe was excluded from the Eastern Hemisphere after the rise of the", the United States could be squeezed out of Asia as a result of China's rise. China's arrival as a great power challenges the "free space" delineated by the United States.' Liu Xiaofeng, 'New China and the End of American "International Law"', 3 *Am Affs* (Fall 2019), americanaffairsjournal.org/2019/08/new-china-and-the-end-of-american-international-law/-.

[72] Carl Schmitt, *The Concept of the Political* 19 (2007).

In Schmitt's mind, the ordered world of states created boundary lines to demarcate friends and enemies. Hitherto, or *within* the demarcation line, was the pluralistic *nomos* of the friend and ally – who formed a community of shared values or, minimally, *understandings*, which managed the human instinct to dominate. Schmitt associated these shared values with the common code of European conduct (*inter gentes europaes*) to limit war.[73] Nether to, or *beyond*, the line was the primordial *nomos* of the Other – the enemy – who inhabited an unregulated or undistinguished space and to whom the rules and understandings did not apply. This was the lawlessly unlimited spatial order 'that denied the political and historical contemporaneity of regions beyond' the *jus publicum*.[74] Here, the unrestricted activities of Europeans resulted in the understood condition that there was 'No peace beyond the line'.[75] For Schmitt, his simplistic friend-enemy dialectic, like all political concepts, contained an inescapable and concrete tension that separated amity from enmity, good from bad, order from disorder, and dominance from servitude.[76]

Schmitt's almost obsessive interest in the Monroe Doctrine involved spatial and normative critiques of its line of demarcation. The spatial framework of this American *Großraum* decentred[77] the structured operation of his idea of the *jus publicum europaeum* and ended his wistfully C(c)atholic bracketing of civility and international order.[78] His international order had modelled the *jus publicum europaeum* in line with French and Spanish negotiated Peace of Cateau-Cambrésis (1559). Territories south of the Tropic of Cancer and west

[73] See Schmitt, Nomos *of the Earth*, n 8, at 97 ('The significance of amity lines in the 16th and 17th century international law was that great areas of freedom were designated as conflict zones in the struggle over the distribution of a new world. As a practical justification, … the designation of a conflict zone at once freed the area on this side of the line – a sphere of peace and order ruled by European public law – from the immediate threat of those events "beyond the line"'). See also Jochen von Bernstorff, 'The Use of Force in International Law before World War I: On Imperial Ordering and the Ontology of the Nation-State', 29 *Eur J Int'l L* 233, 240 (2018) (describing Schmitt's concept of war within the *jus publicum europaeum* as 'pragmatic and duel-like').

[74] Mark Netzloff, 'Lines of Amity: The Law of Nations in the Americas', in *Cultures of Diplomacy and Literary Writing in the Early Modern World* 54, 56 (Tracey A Sowerby and Joanna Craigwood eds, 2019).

[75] Schmitt took pains to note that the founding of the Congo Free State after the Berlin Conference also contributed to the demise of the traditional concept of European international law because of the disorder associated with exporting the idea of the publicum beyond the European line of amity. See Schmitt, Nomos *of the Earth*, n 8, 217–21.

[76] See Schmitt, *The Concept of the Political*, n 72, at 27.

[77] According to Schmitt: 'The new West claimed to be the true West, the true Occident, the true Europe. The new West, America, would supersede the old West, would reorient the old world historical order, would become the center of the earth.' Nomos *of the Earth*, n 8, 290.

[78] See generally Carl Schmitt, *Roman Catholicism and Political Form* (trans and annotated by GL Ulmen, 1996) (postulating the modern theory of the state as a secularised theological concept). For more on Schmitt's 'clerico-conservative' youth, see John P McCormick, 'Carl Schmitt's Europe: Cultural, Imperial and Spatial, Proposals for European Integration, 1923–1955', in *Darker Legacies of Law in Europe*, n 6, 133, 134ff. See also Andreas Koenen, *Der Fall Carl Schmitt: Sein Aufstieg zum 'Kronjuristen des Dritten Reiches* (1995) (connecting Schmitt's *Großraum* theory to *reichstheologischen* ideas).

of the prime meridian (the Azores) fell beyond the line(s) of European amity.[79] These divisions allowed for the 300-year imperial domination of the Indigenous peoples and landscapes of the Americas. It began to end in the early nineteenth century following the retreat of Metropolitan powers, principally Spain and France, then Britain and Russia.[80] By the end of the nineteenth century, the United States began to form a new, dangerous, and depersonalised *Raum* – a normative *nomos* framed by the emerging *jus publicum americanum.*

This new *publicum* promoted the United States' seductive creeds of republicanism, liberalism and internationalism, and it had turned the Monroe Doctrine inside-out. Although originally construed as a defensive shield against external hemispheric interference, its twentieth-century incarnation reworked the Monroe Doctrine into an adulterated nihilistic projection – a new *nomos* that eroded Schmitt's concept of the state, subdued the primacy of the political, and replaced his bracketed Eurocentric idea of the *publicum* with a spaceless Anglo-American universalism.[81] Rhetorically, the doctrine formed 'as a line of amity to defend fledgling American republics, uphold sovereign equality, and promote hemispheric fraternity'.[82] A blur of late-nineteenth and early-twentieth-century reworkings – the Olney Doctrine, the Cleveland Doctrine, the Roosevelt and Lodge corollaries, the Wilson Doctrine, the Meléndez Doctrine, the Calvo Clause, the Drago Doctrine – turned it inside-out, making it a self-deputised right of intervention and an elastic line of enmity.

Lines of amity and lines of enmity are essential characteristics of Schmitt's spatial *Großraum*. The order within the *rayas geográficas* of the Schmittian *Großraum* differed from the (dis)order beyond the line. Schmitt's lament about the displacement of the *jus publicum europaem* mirrors superintendency perspectives that only Arctic circumpolar powers can project. If there is a *jus publicum arcticum* – a *publicum* purportedly characterised by exceptionalism – can it be displaced or disrupted by states other than the spatially proximate circumpolar powers? The asserted superintendency of the Arctic proffered

[79] Garrett Mattingly, 'No Peace Beyond What Line?' 13 *Trans Royal Hist Soc* 145, 149 (1963) (discussing the history behind French and Spanish understanding as to the maritime limit of amity involving commerce and navigation in American waters).

[80] The demise of Spanish imperial rule in the Americas began with Simón Bolívar's widespread revolutionary independence movement in 1810. France's retreat from much of North America began with sale of the Louisiana Territory to the US in 1803. British interests in North and Central America waned after resolution of the Oregon Territory dispute in 1846 and between the periods marked by the Clayton-Bulwer Treaty 1850 and its abrogation with the Hay-Paunceforte Treaty in 1901. The period between these treaties marked intense suspicions about British regional and hemispheric intentions regarding its holdings in Central America, including its historical presence on the Mosquito Coast, its interests in British Honduras [Belize], the Bay Islands off the Atlantic coast of Honduras and control over the Isthmus of Panama, long identified as the likely pathway for a transoceanic concourse or waterway between the Atlantic and Pacific Oceans. Russia's imperial claims to the northern Pacific Coast in the Americas ended in 1867 with the sale of Alaska to the US.

[81] Teschke, 'Fatal Attraction', n 58, at 181.

[82] Rossi, *Whiggish International Law*, n 44, at 93.

by the spatially proximate few is now subject to changing circumstances and challenges.

GROßRAUM: AN IMPORTANT IF IMPERFECT FIT FOR ARCTIC DEBATES

At first blush, the concept's Arctic fit seems inappropriate. There is relatively little *free space* to fight over. Today, there are few politically significant maritime or territorial disputes in the Arctic. The last significant territorial dispute resolved peacefully in 2010 when Russia and Norway settled a Germany-sized 40-year boundary dispute between the states' Exclusive Economic Zones located in the Barents Sea.[83] In 2022, Canada and Denmark ended a 50-year pseudo-skirmish over uninhabited, bald-pated Hans Island (*Tartupaluk*) in the Lincoln Sea.[84] An ongoing pie-shaped boundary delimitation dispute in the Beaufort Sea separating Alaska from the Canadian Yukon engenders no concern of violent solution between such close allies.[85] Probable extended continental shelf disputes appear on the horizon, including the aforementioned Beaufort Sea dispute.[86] They involve vast projections of oil, gas, and mineral deposits such as nickel, cobalt, and manganese. A most likely dispute will involve Canadian, Russian, and Danish assertions that the Gargantuan underwater Lomonosov Ridge (in essence, an underwater mountain chain) extends naturally from each of their continental shelves, respectively. Because Article 76 of the United Nations

[83] Treaty between the Kingdom of Norway and the Russian Federation concerning Maritime Delimitation and Cooperation in the Barents Sea and the Arctic Ocean (15 September 2010). An English translation is available at www.regjeringen.no/en/dep/ud/campaign/delimitation/treaty.html?id=614006 (October 2010). Authentic Russian and Norwegian texts of the treaty are available at www.regjeringen.no/nb/dep/ud/kampanjer/delelinje/avtalen.html?id=614006 (October 2010).

[84] 'Canada and the Kingdom of Denmark, together with Greenland, reach historic agreement on long-standing boundary disputes', Global Affairs Canada, Government of Canada (14 June 2022), www.canada.ca/en/global-affairs/news/2022/06/canada-and-the-kingdom-of-denmark-together-with-greenland-reach-historic-agreement-on-long-standing-boundary-disputes.html. The agreement did recognise the historical significance of Tartupaluk for the Inughuit of Avanersuaq in Kalaallit Nunaat, Greenland and the Inuit of Nunavut, Canada given the legal implications of traditional fishing and hunting rights of the peoples inhabiting both sides of the division. See Apostolos Tsiouvalas and Endalew Lijalem Enyew, 'The Legal Implications of the 2022 Canada-Denmark/Greenland Agreement on Hans Island (Tartupaluk) for the Inuit Peoples of 'Greenland and Nunavut', Arctic Institute (24 January 2023), www.thearcticinstitute.org/legal-implications-2022-canada-denmark-greenland-agreement-hans-island-tartupaluk-inuit-peoples-greenland-nunavut.

[85] The US and Canada inherited this dispute from differing interpretations of an 1825 Anglo-Russian treaty. See J Breese, 'Interpretation of the Anglo-Russian Treaty of 1825 and Establishment of the Alaska-Canada Boundary', 33 *Survey Rev* 161 (2013). Canada claims the meridian line on both land and sea at 141°W longitude as the dividing line; the US claims the line should be drawn at a 90° angle from the shoreline. The Amerasian Basin is included in the disputed area and thought to probably hold up to 10 billion barrels of oil. See Bob Weber, 'Canada Pledges to Work with U.S. Over Competing Claims to Arctic Sea Floor', CBC News (3 January 2024), www.cbc.ca/news/canada/north/canada-work-with-us-artic-sea-floor-claims-1.7073547.

[86] University of Calgary securities studies professor Rob Heubert has noted, given the US's 2024 presentation of its extended continental shelf, that Canada now has jurisdictional overlap with all of its Arctic extended continental shelf neighbours. See Weber, n 85 (quoting Heubert).

Convention on the Law of the Sea (UNCLOS) grants coastal state authority over this extended seafloor, states need not *claim* ownership over the geospace that they already *technically* own. They merely must prove ownership. Scientific assessments of the geomorphological composition of the seabed will crucially help to establish what extended continental shelf areas belong to which country. Even though these and other Arctic extended continental shelf jurisdictional disputes are decades away from resolution, prospective solutions do not appear likely to result in war. There are simply too many rich rewards awaiting the five Arctic coastal states. Only they can actually assert title to extended continental shelves. What then would motivate the rise or intercession of a great power in the Arctic, and what great spatial order (*Großraumordnung*) would it seek to impose or control?

More problematic issues may arise over transit and passage through some or components of the seven major straits used for international navigation through the Arctic Ocean.[87] For decades, the United States and Canada have disputed the legal status of the waters of the Northwest Passage. Canada views these waters as historic internal waters and subject to full and exclusive Canadian authority.[88] The United States considers them an international strait, open for purposes of international navigation and subject to the international laws associated with the high seas and transit passage.[89] Thalassocracies seek to maximise the freedom of navigation and any concession with regard to Canadian assertions over the Northwest Passage may impede United States maritime interests elsewhere in the world. Ironically, opposing Canada's position may work against United States interests vis-à-vis an observant China, which could invoke the United States' understanding of the law of the sea to assert China's right to navigate the Northwest Passage, a result injurious to both Canada's and the United States' interests. Consequently, Suzanne Lalonde has suggested that Washington and Ottawa have settled on a more 'pragmatic approach – agreeing to disagree and getting on with the business of resolving issues of mutual interest and concern'.[90]

[87] The seven Arctic straits involved in international navigation include the Bering Strait, the Northeast Passage, the Northwest Passage, and the Nares, Davis, Fram and Denmark Straits. See J Ashley Roach, 'Freedom of the Seas in the Arctic Region' in *The Arctic and World Order*, at 231 (Kristina Spohr and Daniel S Hamilton eds, Jason C Moyer assoc ed, 2020) [hereinafter *The Arctic and World Order*].

[88] Suzanne Lalonde, 'The U.S.-Canada Northwest Passage Disagreement: Why Agreeing to Disagree Is More Important Than Ever', in *The Arctic and World Order* 267.

[89] See Roach, n 87, at 236.

[90] Lalonde, n 88, at 269. A general course of dealing between the US and Canada exists notwithstanding other disagreements over the status of the Dixon Entrance between Alaska and British Columbia, the Strait of Juan de Fuca between Vancouver Island and the State of Washington, and Machias Seal Island located in the Gulf of Maine.

GROßRAUM: AN IMPERFECT BUT USABLE ANALYTIC TOOL

Notwithstanding this seemingly unfit application, wrapped atop Schmitt's anachronistically occidental mindset,[91] his *Großraum* term is resurrected here because it serves as an important if imperfect analytical tool to investigate competing and converging interests in the Arctic – which itself is a multilayered region. These questions are central to strategic and geopolitical constructions of the idea of *Großraum*. Their predominance in topical discussions owe much to Schmitt and the power of his spatial and rhetorical legacy.

However, interpretations of the Arctic admit of a pluriverse of political, geographic, strategic, economic, legal, and communal considerations. They involve power complexes and their shifting spatial complexities. Reworking the *Großraum* idea certainly draws attention to entanglements between geopolitics and cartesian rationality, and between recrudescent biopolitics and virulent authoritarianism. However, it also draws attention to relationships beyond the state system, relationships that operate beyond the territorial trap of state-centric thinking and the snare of its spatial logic.[92]

The *Großraum* idea interrogates under-considered distinctions between large spaces and the dwindling universal commons. It suggests an awareness of spatial boundaries beyond their physical, geographic frontiers, which themselves are constructs.[93] It contemplates spatial interactions with adjoining frontiers and advertises an appreciation of the spaces in-between and beyond statist conceptualisation.[94] It suggests a scaffolding of latent and soft power spheres of influence – a scaffolding distinct from the spatial geography and geopolitics connected to concretised Schmittian influences. It suggests a liberal or republican conceptual framework separate from anti-liberal ideology – a sphere of confluence, not only a sphere of influence.[95]

[91] See Schmitt, Nomos *of the Earth*, n 8, 86 (noting Schmitt's historical review of the 'normal' meaning of 'European' between the sixteenth and nineteenth centuries as the creators and representatives of an order applicable to the whole earth).

[92] See Alexander B Murphy, 'National Claims to Territory in the Modern State System', 7 *Geopolitics* 193, 194 (2002) (noting 'how much of our ideas and actions are trapped in the spatial logic of the state system').

[93] See Ladis Kristof, 'The Origins and Evolution of Geopolitics', 4 *J Conflict Res* 33 (noting that geography admits of no universally accepted definition).

[94] See generally John Agnew, 'The Territorial Trap: The Geographical Assumptions of International Relations Theory', 1 *Rev Int'l Pol Econ* 53, 76–77 (1994) (introducing the trinity of geographical assumptions hampering international relations theory and creating the territorial trap: state sovereignty, the contrast of the domestic and the foreign, and the state as a social container); Norman JG Pounds, 'The Origin of the Idea of Natural Frontiers in France', 41 *Annals of the Assoc Am Geogr* 146 (1951) (discussing the non-natural nature of territorial state thinking); Stuart Elden, *The Birth of Territory* (2013) (critically interrogating the concept of territory and its historical development).

[95] I am obliged to Nick Onuf for his thoughts, vocabulary, and conceptualisation regarding these contrasting anti-liberal and liberal scaffoldings.

In-between spaces constitute the shadowland of interstitial space. This space disrupts the underexplored idea of 'fixity and spatial permanence' and contests the Westphalian conceit of sovereignty as presenting a closed, bounded, and tightly fitted set of jigsaw pieces called states.[96] Political geographer Saul Cohen interrogated these fragmented areas in contrast to his Shatterbelt theory and claimed that they lie within or between geopolitical regions as 'Compression Zones' that are lesser in scale and do not attract great power competition, although they nevertheless may be torn apart by conflict.[97] Halford Mackinder touched on the idea of this fringeland when he discussed the Inner and Marginal Crescent that ringed the core or pivot area of his Heartland thesis.[98] Nicholas Spykman inverted but complemented Mackinder's structural view of geopolitics by emphasising world power based on controlling the intermediate region of the Rimland, which included maritime Europe, the Middle East, and regions encircling Eurasia.[99] He viewed the Rimland as more important and dynamic than the Heartland due to its proximity to coastal regions and sea trade.[100] Ola Tunander sensed this hybrid quality of geospatial orientation (he referred to it as a 'double sovereignty') when he associated it with NATO, which to him created a peculiar kind of *Großraum* that was 'neither an alliance of sovereign states nor a true superstate but something in-between'.[101]

The interstitial complexity of *Großraum* pliably connects to the receding polar icecap, the dominant physical feature of the Arctic, and the emergent (if not turbid) implications of increasingly accessible polar resources, living and mineral. It broadens discussion about territorial units and territorial coordination beyond the bounded state, revives the analysis of geopolitics within a context of regionalism[102] and regional rivalries,[103] but also of precaution and

[96] See Christopher Rossi, 'Interstitial Space and the High Himalayan Dispute between China and India', 62 *Harv Int'l LJ* 429, 445–46 (2021).

[97] Saul Bernard Cohen, *Geopolitics of the World System* 5 (2003).

[98] HJ Mackinder, 'The Geographical Pivot of History', 23 *Geographical J* 421, 431 (1904) (discussing the Heartland–Marginal region distinction, marking the Heartland as insulated continental Eastern Europe space impregnable to attack and the inner and Marginal Crescent areas as constituting the World Islands of Europe, Asia and Africa, and the remaining periphery).

[99] Nicholas John Spykman, *The Geography of the Peace* 38 (1944) (introducing the concept of the Rimland and contrasting it with Mackinder's concept of the Inner Crescent).

[100] See ibid at 40–41.

[101] Ola Tunander, 'The Uneasy Imbrication of Nation-State and NATO: The Case of Sweden', 34 *Cooperation & Conflict* 169 (unified by US hegemonic ideas), 197 (neither … nor) (1999). His construction of NATO as 'something of a 'Greater USA' subjected him to criticism, both in terms of his critique of US hegemony in Europe and in terms of his invocation of the *Großraum* idea.

[102] See Carl Landauer, 'Regionalism, Geography, and the International Legal Imagination', 11 *Chicago J Int'l L* 557 (2011) (noting international law's lost vision of geographical specificity).

[103] See Anne Orford, 'Regional Orders, Geopolitics, and the Future of International Law', 74 *Current Legal Problems* 149, 179 (2021) (discussing rival regionalism and the rise of China); Daniel Bethlehem, 'The End of Geography: The Changing Nature of the International System and the Challenge to International Law', 25 *Eur J Int'l L* 9 (2014) (suggesting a movement in international law beyond the prism of Westphalian state-centric law).

mutual, reciprocated regard for sustainable use and economic association. It draws attention to the Arctic as a neighbourhood with extended suburbs.

Coordination and confluence suggest cooperation and coalition, as implied by the meaning of Arctic exceptionalism. It also implies competition and alliance, or calculated manoeuvring to create buffer zones that are similar to the so-called Great Game played between Britain and Russia to secure nineteenth-century imperial influence across Central Asia. The idea of *Großraum* also connects the perimeters of law to extended subjectivities of security and place, which Schmitt implicitly imagined. It problematises distinctions between legality and legitimacy and probes the elasticity of the rules or norms applicable to sovereignty and geospatial governance.[104] It adds complexity and coloration to Arctic discussions. It is usable.

Media magnate Henry Luce (1898–1967) once editorialised that the United States should helm the twentieth century, which he famously opined would become '*The American Century*'.[105] Guided by a principled internationalism, he urged the United States to set a course toward the worldwide promotion of freedom. He explicitly noted the ideological necessity of a *Großraum* to incubate this idea: 'Tyrannies may require a large amount of living space. But Freedom requires and will require *far* greater living space than Tyranny. Peace cannot endure unless it prevails over a very large part of the world.'[106]

Luce's construction of *Großraum* detached the term from Schmitt's emphases on geographical contiguity and physical proximity. It grew from Christian Wolff's imagined 'continental' construct of nature as presenting an ordered and purposive plan of human association, a *civitas maxima*, or *quasi pact* that formed above the sovereign state.[107] Vattel would famously reformulate this idea into what Nicholas Onuf referred to as an Atlantic variant of republicanism, which developed from the natural rights position anticipated by Hugo Grotius (1583–1645).[108] Luce's influential agglomeration of the European-inspired republican tradition carried forth Enlightenment constructs of public life, law, and diplomacy. It viewed the ideology of liberalism as the antidote to factionalism and partisanship. His interpretation – more universal than regional – attempted an ideological connection to *Landnehmen*. It suggested a broadening of the meaning of great space to include political governance based on propriety, representation, and reciprocity, ideas informed by a republican tradition tracing from Thomas Jefferson's *Empire of Liberty* and James Madison's (1751–1836) idea of representative government. In *The Federalist No 14*, Madison defended

[104] Eric A Posner and Adrian Vermeule, 'Demystifying Schmitt', in *The Oxford Handbook of Carl Schmitt* 612, 614 (Jens Meierhenrich and Oliver Simons eds, 2015) (noting Schmitt's argument in his last work before the collapse of the Weimar Republic, *Legality and Legitimacy* (1932), that equating legitimacy with legality 'is an impoverished account of legitimacy').

[105] Henry Luce, 'The American Century', *Life Magazine* (17 February 1941), at 61.

[106] ibid at 64.

[107] Onuf, *Republican Legacy*, n 49, 59–60 (1998).

[108] ibid at 60.

this construction because it was best suited to extend governance 'over a large region'.[109] Here, republicanism presented itself as a *Raumprinzip*.

The promotion of republicanism as a *Raumprinzip* idea would, of course, contest liberalism's emphasis on direct democracy. James Madison, in *The Federalist No 10* confronted this peril, arguing for the establishment of a republican government based on the promotion of the common good by a virtuous elite, who would be less likely to sacrifice justice to 'mischiefs of faction' and 'temporary or partial considerations'.[110] That idea would unravel in the wake of the Vietnam War, where in the United States, a clique of elites, for all of their upbringing at Groton, Yale, and Harvard, ended life in a campaign to justify the mistakes of Vietnam,[111] a war that liberal historian Henry Steele Commager deemed 'so deeply immoral that [it] must be lost'.[112]

CONCEPTUAL HISTORIES OF *GROßRAUM*

Shortly after the implosion of the Soviet Union, the idea of *Großraum* began to engage grand themes of world (dis)order, whether in terms of Francis Fukuyama's Hegelian-inspired *End of History* (1989), which touted the worldwide spread and supremacy of liberal democracy following the collapse of the Soviet Union;[113] Samuel Huntington's *Clash of Civilizations* (1993),[114] which described a future world of post-ideological conflict based on culture and religion, not economics and political philosophies; or Robert Kaplan's *Coming Anarchy* (1994), which foresaw global environmental disintegration and a dystopic political cartography of disease, water wars, stateless marauders, cartels, private armies, and Malthusian disaster.[115]

[109] James Madison, The Federalist Papers: No 14 (30 November 1787), Avalon Project, avalon.law.yale.edu/18th_century/fed14.asp.

[110] James Madison, The Federalist Papers: No 10 (23 November 1787), Avalon Project, avalon.law.yale.edu/18th_century/fed10.asp.

[111] See David Halberstam, *The Best and the Brightest* 47–54 (1972) (summarising the failures of the elite Establishment foreign policy experts and their decisions and failures leading to the Vietnam War).

[112] Henry Steele Commager, 'The Defeat of America', *The New York Rev* (5 October 1972), www-nybooks-com.mime.uit.no/articles/1972/10/05/the-defeat-of-america.

[113] Francis Fukuyama, 'The End of History?' 16 *National Interest* 3 (1989) (asserting at the end of the 20th century not 'an "end of ideology" … but to an unabashed victory of economic and political liberalism'); see also Francis Fukuyama, *The End of History and the Last Man* (2006).

[114] Samuel P Huntington, The Clash of Civilizations? 72 *For Affs* 22 (1993) (arguing 'the fundamental source of conflict in this new world will not be primarily ideological or primarily economic …. The fault lines between civilizations will be the battle lines of the future'); see also Samuel P Huntington, *The Clash of Civilizations and the Remaking of World Order* (1996). But see Peter Katzenstein, 'A World of Plural and Pluralist Civilizations: Multiple Actors, Traditions, and Practices', in *Civilizations in World Politics: Plural and Pluralist Perspectives* 1 (Peter J Katzenstein ed, 2010) (contending that Huntington's thesis greatly overstates the case and that evidence shows that clashes occur primarily within rather than between civilisations).

[115] Robert D Kaplan, 'The Coming Anarchy: How Scarcity, Crime, Overpopulation, Tribalism, and Disease are Rapidly Destroying the Social Fabric of our Planet', *The Atlantic* (February 1994); see also Robert D Kaplan, *The Coming Anarchy: Shattering the Dreams of the Post Cold War* (2001).

Geographers agreed that the idea of geopolitics needed reconceptualisation to reflect more than 'a continuation of Cold War themes',[116] or a corrupted 'form of geography' that had been 'conscripted to political service'.[117] Gearóid Ó Tuathail and Simon Dalby argued, 'In a world of perpetual speed and motion, convulsed by globalisation, saturated by information, and entranced by ephemeral media spectacles and hyperbole, geopolitics seems decidedly old-fashioned,' its 'mummified remains ... left for dead.'[118] They and others called for a critical updating of geopolitics in view of the concretised premises of iron-clad *Realpolitik* constructs as well as the fading away of so-called 'blockbuster visions' of global space, presented along the lines of Fukuyama, Huntington, and Kaplan.[119] To this, Mark Bassin argued in favour of a new *Geopolitik*, a break from the simple-minded moralism of the Cold War and its atonement for anti-communism.[120] Karl Schlögel, too, sought to deliver spatial studies from the iron grip of 'obsessive' geopolitical determinism, 'biological naturalism,' and the 'terminological repertoire' framed by 'blood and soil' (*Blut und Bodin*).[121] Ladis Kristof noted etymologically that geopolitics is about geographical 'politics and *not* geography'; it is about politics geographically 'analyzed for its geographical content'.[122]

Indeed, the conceptual history of the *Großraum* as an ideological and economic space has been reformulating since at least the advent of the Bretton Woods system (1944). Anne Orford argued that 'the narrative of the state' as the primary spatial form tended to mask the relevance and persistence of post-Cold War *regional* orders,[123] in essence new *Zollvereins*. The international liberal economy transformed as a great space into the functional and processual rules of the WTO, IMF, the Asian Development Bank, and the policy prescriptions of the Washington Consensus of the 1990s.[124] Counter-constructions now arise

[116] Simon Dalby, 'The Environment as Geopolitical Threat: Reading Robert Kaplan's "Coming Anarchy"', 3 *Ecumene* 472, 476 (1996).

[117] David Atkinson and Klaus Dodds, 'Introduction to Geopolitical Traditions: A Century of Geopolitical Thought', in *Geopolitical Traditions: A Century of Geopolitical Thought* 2 (Klaus Dodds and David Atkinson eds, 2000).

[118] Gearóid Ó Tuathail and Simon Dalby, 'Introduction: Rethinking Geopolitics: Towards a Critical Geopolitics', in *Rethinking Geopolitics* 1, 2 (Gearóid Ó Tuathail and Simon Dalby eds, 1998).

[119] ibid. For additional calls among geographers for a critical updating of the idea of geopolitics, see Dodds and Atkinson eds, *Geopolitical Traditions*, n 117.

[120] Mark Bassin, 'Between Realism and the "New Right": Geopolitics in Germany in the 1990s', 28 *Trans Inst Brit Geo* 350, 351 (2003).

[121] Karl Schlögel, *In Space We Read Time: On the History of Civilization and Geopolitics* (Gerrit Jackson trans, 2016) 32 (The German Case: Space as Obsession), 111 ('biological naturalism'), 32 ('terminological repertoire of German scholarly discourse'), 36 (blood and soil), (2003).

[122] Kristof, 'The Origins and Evolution of Geopolitic's, n 93, at 34.

[123] Orford, Regional Orders, Geopolitics, and the Future of International Law, n 103, at 149.

[124] The Washington Consensus was a term coined by economist John Williamson in 1989 to describe a purported consensus among Latin American policy makers, supported by Washington, DC international institutions, to deal with the persistent hemispheric debt problem. Ten recommended policy initiatives formed the consensus: reduced national budget deficits, redirected public spending, tax reform, financial sector liberalisation, market-driven exchange rates, reduced trade restrictions, increased foreign direct investment, privatisation of state-owned enterprises, stimulated competition, and stronger private property rights. See Douglas A Irwin and Oliver

with the Asian Infrastructure Investment Bank, the BRICS (Brazil, Russia, India, China, and South Africa), and the Communist Party of China's relativised idea of a 'democracy that works'.[125]

What lies beyond these great and newly emerging spaces? Cyberspace is commonly conceived of as a great space, although largely unregulated. The global environment presents itself as another great space, modulated by the United Nations Climate Change conferences (COP) and international initiatives to combat global warming. The COVID pandemic underscores the treatment of global health as a great space, functioning under World Health Organization attempts to stop the spread of disease and other incubating pathogens. And then there is the algorithmic age of the AI Spring, alternatively described as the advancement of disruptive technologies that circumvent statist barriers, spread (dis)information, disrupt businesses and markets, and generate images from text (stable diffusion). Already in formation, the vocabulary of this new space is creating large language models and privately owned ontologies powerful enough to manage national healthcare and transit systems, discrete enough to catch terrorists, cartel leaders, and Wall Street fraudsters, and effective enough to shape the nature and future of warfare in places such as Gaza, Lebanon, and Ukraine.[126] When this technology passes the Turing test, another great space across the Rubicon will unleash 'machines' ability to imitate human intelligence'.[127]

Kaplan predicted that the environment would become '*the* national security issue of the early twenty-first century'.[128] Ó Tuathail and Timothy W Luke

Ward, 'What is the "Washington Consensus?"', PIEE (8 September 2021), www.piie.com/blogs/realtime-economic-issues-watch/what-washington-consensus.

[125] See 'China: Democracy That Works', PRC St Council Info Off (4 December 2021), www.news.cn/english/2021-12/04/c_1310351231.htm (describing democracy as 'Rooted in history, culture and tradition [and taking] diverse forms … along the paths chosen by different peoples based on their exploration and innovation').

[126] See Mike Stone, 'White House Huddles with Industry on Tech Innovation for Ukraine', Reuters (8 January 2024), www.reuters.com/world/europe/white-house-huddles-with-industry-tech-innovation-ukraine-2024-01-08 (noting White House National Security Council meetings with private companies such as Palantir Technologies, Fortem Aerospace, and Anduril Industries to discuss security aid for Ukraine in the war against Russia and Israel's incursion into Gaza in its war against Hamas). Palantir actively and publicly has sided with Ukraine and Israel but forewarns of the need for the West to maintain supremacy in this emerging field. See Ginoy Kampmark, 'AI Giant Palantir on a Quest to Help the West', Green Left (31 December 2023), www.greenleft.org.au/content/ai-giant-palantir-quest-help-west; Tom Singleton, BBC News (8 June 2023), 'Stay Ahead in AI Race, Tech Boss Urges West' (noting Palantir CEO Alex Karp's admonishment: 'The race is on – the question is do we stay ahead or do we cede the lead? … Every country in the world – especially our adversaries – cannot afford for us to have this advantage'). Palantir's ability to mine massive data has been credited with pinpointing the location of Osama bin Laden, cartel leaders, and uncovering the Ponzi scheme of financial fraudster, Bernie Madoff. See Sabrina Kessler, 'A Secret Services' Darling Goes Public', DW (30 Sept. 2020), www.dw.com/en/palantir-the-darling-of-secret-services-goes-public/a-55107199.

[127] 'Top Risks 2023', Eurasia Group 9 (2023), www.eurasiagroup.net/files/upload/EurasiaGroup_TopRisks2023.pdf.

[128] Kaplan, 'The Coming Anarchy', n 115.

also foresaw a chaotic reterritorialisation of the post-Cold War environmental world, where 'contained … wild zones' of conflict would arise alongside 'tame' zones of peaceful prosperity.[129] They projected that this interplay would awaken a new 'sense of *Realpolitik*' and 'environmental worldwatching'.[130]

The French philosopher Jaques Derrida impugned Fukuyama's triumphal *End of History* thesis: he conjured up the spectre that comes back 'after the end of history'.[131] Derrida was referring to the first noun in Marx's famous opening to the *Manifesto of the Communist Party* (1848), the *spectre* of communism. However, he channelled postmodernity's association with Carl Schmitt elsewhere when he conjured up a 'phantom friend' of history, liberalism's 'naïve scansion' – democracy.[132] According to Derrida: how would liberalism reconstitute its need for enmity amid headlines touting 'the 'fall-of-the-Berlin-Wall, or … the "end of communism"'?[133] How would the 'parliamentary-democracies-of-the-capitalist-Western-World … find themselves without a principal enemy[?]'[134]

In this critique of friends needing enemies, Derrida questioned liberalism's naivety, which necessarily impugned Aristotle's idea of friendship. In the *Nichomachean Ethics*, Aristotle presented friendship as a virtuous bond among equals, a pleasantness formed by shared values and mutual goodwill.[135] This construction extended within the Western philosophical tradition to Immanuel Kant (1724–1804) and his liberal world-view, which Derrida also impugned. As expressed in *Perpetual Peace* (1795), Kant asserted in his Third Definitive Article that people were citizens of the world, and that universal hospitality extended to the stranger as a cosmopolitan right. According to Kant: 'so long as [the stranger] conducts himself peaceably, he must not be treated as an enemy …. This right to present themselves to society belongs to all mankind in virtue of our common right.'[136]

To Derrida, the *so long as* proviso obscured integral imbalances associated with disruptive differences and Otherness, just as the mystical foundation of law

[129] Gearóid Ó Tuathail, 'Present at the (Dis)integration: Deterritorialization and Reterritorialization in the New Wor(l)d Order', 84 *Annals of the Ass'n Am Geogr* 381, 394–95 (1994).

[130] ibid at 395.

[131] Jaques Derrida, *Specters of Marx: The State of the Debt, the Work of Mourning, and the New International* 10 (1994); see also Christopher R Rossi, 'Hauntings, Hegemony, and the Threatened African Exodus from the International Criminal Court', 40 *Human Rights Quarterly* 369, 383 (2018).

[132] Jacques Derrida, *The Politics of Friendship* 76 (George Collins trans, 2005) [1994].

[133] ibid at 76–77.

[134] ibid at 77.

[135] Aristotle, *Nichomachean Ethics*, bk 8.5 (holding: 'And in loving a friend men love what is good for themselves; for the good man in becoming a friend becomes a good to his friend. Each, then, both loves what is good for himself, and makes an equal return in goodwill and in pleasantness; for friendship is said to be equality, and both of these are found most in the friendship of the good').

[136] Immanuel Kant, *Perpetual Peace: A Philosophical Essay* (trans and introduction by M Campbell Smith, 1903) [1795].

obscured the relationship between justice and authority.[137] Aristotelian friendship suppressed fraternal tensions in favour of naïve homogeneity. Liberalism posed a false condition of equality as it scripted the rules of peaceable conduct, in ways that most certainly now isolate Russia from governance structures in the Arctic. In terms of hospitality, as noted by international relations theorist Nicholas Onuf, the condition of hospitality actually straddled the contradiction between absolute hospitality and the rules of the house.[138] A fundamental inequality exited between the guest and the householder, and only the latter can offer hospitality to the stranger.[139] A world without enemies would confuse a world among friends.[140] Schmitt saw friends and enemies as binary opposites. Derrida viewed them as commingled contaminants. Both of these antiliberal constructions of friendship abjured alternative constructions[141] and criticised liberalism's depoliticisation and false universalisation of fundamental orderings of life. From Russia's perspective, it is the *pater familias* of the Arctic geopolitical household. It has much to say about the Arctic house rules, and about hospitality in the Arctic regardless of those countries that seek shelter from its opinions and practices.

Derrida viewed the effects of this destructuralisation as an invitation for the liberal world order to reconstitute enmities, perhaps by multiplying 'little wars between nation-states', sustaining human rights campaigns against ethnic groups, or seeking repose through still identifiable adversaries such as China or radical Islam.[142] Here, we are marking the spectral revenant of the *Großraum* in the spatial realm of the Arctic.

And how might the hauntology of the *Großraum* return? Russia's exclusion from the Arctic Council is a subject of great concern. China has now drawn a

[137] Jacques Derrida, 'Force of Law: The 'Mystical Foundation of Authority', in *Deconstruction and the Possibility of Justice* 1, 12 (Drucilla Cornell, Michel Rosenfeld and David Gray Carlson eds, 1992) (quoting Montaigne: 'And so laws keep up their good standing, not because they are just, but because they are laws: that is the mystical foundation of their authority, they have no other').

[138] Nicholas Onuf, 'Relative Strangers: Reflections on Hospitality, Social Distance and Diplomacy', in *Hospitality and World Politics* 173 (G Baker ed, 2013).

[139] ibid, at 174. See also Nicholas Onuf, 'Friendship and Hospitality: Some Conceptual Preliminaries', 5 *J Int'l Pol Theory* 1 (2009) (rejecting anarchy's conceptual hegemony in describing relations among friends, rivals, and enemies) [hereinafter Onuf, *Friendship and Hospitality*].

[140] See Derrida, *The Politics of Friendship*, n 132, at 76 ('One would then have the time of a world without friends, the time of a world without enemies. … And anyone who would say 'O my friends, there are no friends', and again, or again' 'O enemies there is no enemy', would convince us … that he does not yet have a friend, but already no longer has an enemy. Or conversely …'). See also ibid at 1 (opening line). Both Derrida and Schmitt were influenced by Michel de Montaigne, *Essays*, Bk 1, ch. 28 (On Friendship), (Charles Cotton trans (1686), W Carew Hazlitt rev, 1877), hyperessays.net/essays/on-friendship, ('I was so grown and accustomed to be always his double in all places and in all things, that methinks I am no more than half myself [on mourning the loss of a friend]).

[141] See Onuf, *Friendship and Hospitality*, n 139, at 8. Onuf suggested that relations between friends and enemies are heteronomous. Friends and enemies may be autonomous agents, 'but their autonomy is limited by social conditions and the unintended consequences of their individual, autonomous choices.' ibid at 18, fn 7.

[142] Derrida, *The Politics of Friendship*, n 132, at 77.

capacious 10-dash U-shaped line around nearly 90 per cent of the South China Sea, the world's fifth largest body of water.[143] This dotted line is based on an oblique mixture of sovereignty assertions, treaty law, and historic rights.[144] Chinese scholars claim the historic right to this water spans millennia; opposing arguments date China's claim to 7 May 2009, based on a 1947 map drawn by the Nationalist Kuomintang Government.[145] The dispute over the South China Sea presents the non-negotiable assertion of another Sino Reich, on par with Beijing's claims to Hong Kong, Taiwan, Tibet, and Xinjiang.[146] Perhaps it represents the recrudescence of its culturally hierarchical dynastic and tributary traditions following in the wake of Admiral Zheng He's (c 1371–1433) seven voyages across the South China Sea and into the Indo-Pacific.[147]

What portion of President Xi Jingping's world-view will attach to the Arctic? His ideological recasting of Leninist vanguardism onto the global stage separates his foreign policy from Deng Xiaoping's reforms and Jiang Zemin's and Hu Jintao's moderation. How many dashed lines will appear in the Arctic, and asserted by which countries? Although not perceived as a peer competitor in the Arctic in ways recognised in the Indo-Pacific region, China asserts that it is an 'important stakeholder in Arctic affairs' (北极利益攸关者, *beiji liyi youguanzhe*) with the right to a greater role in Arctic governance. China refers to the region as a '*global commons* (全球公域, *quanqiu gongyu*) rather than a strictly regional space',[148] and as a space informed by the Belt and Road Initiative's idea of a 'community with a shared future for mankind'.[149] In its Fourteenth

[143] The line once had 11 dashes. It was then refashioned into a nine-dash line in 1953 to accommodate a spirit of 'comradeship and brotherhood' with Vietnam (ceding Bailonwei Island to Vietnam) before provocatively reconfiguring a disputed border and claiming 'new territory around Taiwan'. For a brief history of the old and new line, see Wei Pu, 'How the Eleven-Dash Line Became a Nine-Dash Line, and Other Stories', Radio Free Asia (16 July 2015), www.rfa.org/english/commentaries/line-07162015121333.html; Colin Clark, 'New Chinese 10-Dash Map Sparks Furor across Indo-Pacific: Vietnam, India, Philippines, Malaysia', Breaking Defense (1 September 2023), breakingdefense.com/2023/09/new-chinese-10-dash-map-sparks-furor-across-indo-pacific-vietnam-india-philippines-malaysia.

[144] See Zou Keyuan and Liu Xinchang, 'The U-Shaped Line and Historic Rights in the Philippines v. China Arbitration Case', in *Arbitration Concerning the South China Sea: Philippines versus China* 127, 132 (Wu Shicun and Zou Keyuan eds, 2016) (quoting Wu Shicun, the president of China's National Institute for South China Seas Studies).

[145] Christopher R Rossi, 'Treaty of Tordesillas Syndrome: Sovereignty ad Absurdum and the South China Sea Arbitration', 50 *Cornell Int'l LJ* 231, 243–44 (2017).

[146] ibid at 236–37. See also Charlotte Kroll, 'Reading the Temperature Curve: Sinophone Schmitt-fever in Context and Perspective', in *Carl Schmitt and Leo Strauss in the Chinese-Speaking World: Reorienting the Political* 103 (Kai Marchal and Carl KY Shaw eds, 2017).

[147] John Hobson and Shizhi Zhang, 'The Return of the Chinese Tribute System? Re-viewing the Belt and Road Initiative', 2 *Global Stud Q* 1 (2022) (interpreting China's Belt and Road Initiative as a neo-tribute system for world politics); Mark Cartwright, 'The Seven Voyages of Zheng He', *World Hist Encycl* (7 February 2019), www.worldhistory.org/article/1334/the-seven-voyages-of-zheng-he.

[148] P Whitney Lackenbauer, Adam Lajeunesse and Ryan Dean, 'Why China is not a Peer Competitor in the Arctic', *J Indo-Pac Affs* (3 October 2022), www.airuniversity.af.edu/JIPA/Display/Article/3172586/why-china-is-not-a-peer-competitor-in-the-arctic.

[149] See Liu et al, 'A Community of Shared Future for Mankind: A Study on the News Discourse of Environmental Cooperation in Countries Along the Belt and Road Initiative', Plos One (23 October 2023), pmc.ncbi.nlm.nih.gov/articles/PMC10593205/pdf/pone.0293296.pdf.

Five-Year Plan for Economic and Social Development (covering 2021–2025),[150] China included mention of the Arctic for the first time,[151] seeking to 'Actively expand the developmental space of the marine economy' in pursuit of the building of an 'Ice Silk Road' with Nordic countries at the western end.[152] The United States views China's modest scientific presence in the Arctic as partly legitimate, but regards with suspicion its dual-use 'intelligence or military application'.[153] China's Arctic fishing and energy extraction intentions have also generated concern, given China's lack of regard for environmental consequences.[154]

Russia's revanchist personification of the Motherland (*Мáтушка Россúя*), its splintering of Abkhazia and South Ossetia from Georgia (2008), its support of the breakaway statelet of Transnistria from Moldova, its annexation of Crimea (2014), incorporation of the Donetsk and Luhansk regions of Ukraine (2022), and its aggression against all of Ukraine (2022) have awakened Western concerns about Russian military improvements to the Arctic domain, not only with regard to preserving Russia's nuclear deterrent strategy, but with the intention of operationalising it as a 'tactical warfighting domain' against NATO.[155] The Biden Administration's elevated interest in updating the United States' 2013 National Strategy for the Arctic was 'relatively finished' when Russia launched its February 2022 aggression against Kiev. The invasion in Eastern Europe forced a 'long pause' in the National Security Council interagency process to formulate the United States' new Arctic strategy.[156] It also prompted the development of

[150] 'Outline of the People's Republic of China 14th Five-Year Plan for National Economic and Social Development and Long-Range Objectives for 2035', Xinhua News Agency (12 March 2021), reprinted and translated in CSET, cset.georgetown.edu/wp-content/uploads/t0284_14th_Five_Year_Plan_EN.pdf [hereinafter China's 14th Five-Year Plan].

[151] Trym Eiterjord, 'What the 14th Five-Year Plan Says About China's Arctic Interests', *Arctic Inst* (23 November 2023), www.thearcticinstitute.org/14th-five-year-plan-chinas-arctic-interests.

[152] See China's 14th Five-Year Plan, n 150, Art 33 ('Actively expand [maritime] space') and Art 33(3) ('We will participate in pragmatic cooperation in the Arctic and build the "Ice Silk Road"' ('冰上丝绸之路')); see also Guo Peiqing and Chen Huiwen, 'Chinese Perspective on the Arctic and Its Implication for Nordic Countries', Arctic Inst (20 June 2023), www.thearcticinstitute.org/chinese-perspective-arctic-implication-nordic-countries.

[153] 'National Strategy for the Arctic Region', White House (October 2022), at 6. China maintains four scientific projects in the Arctic, including the Yellow River Station at Ny-Ålesund, Svalbard, the China Iceland Arctic Research Observatory (CIAO) at Kárhóll, Iceland, the Esrange Space Center, Sweden, the Finnish Meteorological Institute and Chinese Academy of Science Joint Research Center for Arctic Space Observation and Data Sharing in Sodankylä, Finland (apparently suspended), and a proposed Chinese Satellite Receiving Ground Station in Nuuk, Greenland. See Michael Lipin, 'China Begins to Revive Arctic Scientific Ground Projects After Setbacks', VOA (5 December 2022), www.voanews.com/a/china-begins-to-revive-arctic-scientific-ground-projects-after-setbacks-/6860756.html.

[154] See 'Unpacking the 2022 US National Strategy for the Arctic Region', Wilson Center (25 October 2022), www.youtube.com/watch?v=B-gDTEuap48, time mark 43:58 (noting possible divergence with China's interest in Arctic fishing and hydrocarbon exploitation).

[155] Joseph S Bermudez Jr, 'Ice Curtain: Protecting the Arctic Motherland', CSIS (25 March 2020), www.csis.org/analysis/ice-curtain-protecting-arctic-motherland.

[156] Unpacking the 2022 US National Strategy for the Arctic Region, n 154, time mark 7:40 (recording comments from Devon Brennan, NSC director for maritime and Arctic security).

the 2024 Arctic Strategy.[157] Russia's 'hybrid tactics' of sabotage[158] and 'significant' militarisation of the Arctic, despite preoccupations with the war against Ukraine, prompted NATO's former Secretary General Jens Stoltenberg to remind Western audiences that 'The shortest way [line?] from Russia to North America is over the Arctic North Pole .... the strategic importance of these areas has not changed because of the war in Ukraine.'[159] This geopolitical construction of Arctic space remains sensitive to the 'revolutionary implications of air power' and the 'graphic projection of distance' based on polar azimuthal maps 'to highlight America's [and Russia's or China's] vulnerability to attack from the air'.[160] Critics of Western intentions would doubtless point to the Anglosphere's continuing democratisation projects in support of the *longue durée* of Henry Luce's *American Century*.

But why should the application of *Großraum* thinking in the Arctic sway so heavily in the direction of Schmittian vocabulary? Even as Schmitt observed, 'a nation is conquered first when it acquiesces to a foreign vocabulary',[161] and his vocabulary has infiltrated this discussion. Perhaps Arctic *Großraum* thinking need not exclusively conjure up sentiments of this hauntology. Could the great space of the Arctic contain within examples in support of the global commons, or of prospects of reciprocated respect for orderly regimes, the rule of law, and the equitable if not precautionary management of its resources? The Arctic pluriverse contains a land and sea of *Großräume*, opening up vistas for a new, perhaps not so heroic, age of geopolitical polar exploration.

[157] United States Department of Defense 2024 Arctic Strategy (21 June 2024), media.defense.gov/2024/Jul/22/2003507411/-1/-1/0/DOD-ARCTIC-STRATEGY-2024.PDF (directing the enhancement of Arctic capabilities, the deepening of engagement with Allies and partners, and the building of readiness and capabilities for high latitude operations).

[158] Colin Wall and Njord Wegge, 'The Russian Arctic Threat: Consequences of the Ukraine War', CSIS (25 January 2023), www.csis.org/analysis/russian-arctic-threat-consequences-ukraine-war.

[159] Nick Paton Walsh and Sarah Dean, 'Russia's Militarization of the Arctic Shows No Sign of Slowing Down', CNN (22 December 2023), edition.cnn.com/2022/12/21/europe/russia-arctic-military-intl/index.html.

[160] Douglas T Stuart, *Creating the National Security State: A History of the Law that Transformed America* 15 (2008).

[161] GL Ulmen, Translator's Introduction, Nomos *of the Earth*, n 8, 19 (2006) (quoting Schmitt).

Chapter Three

A Particularly Weighty Idiom

Lifting the term *Großraum* out of its Schmittian framework, or for that matter its sphere of influence connotation in conjunction with the Monroe Doctrine, requires careful and conscious consideration. Historians warn of the unconscious or improper lifting of concepts out of their own time and place, a feature they decry as the sin of anachronism.[1] Improper importations of concepts across time trigger spring-loaded debates about the uses and abuses of conceptual history.[2] Although the meaning of *Großraum* continues its travel through time, its association with Schmitt's *Realpolitik* and political theology remains a dominant construction. Consequently, the term *Großraum* must be received with indulgence or an awareness of Schmitt's temporal framework given his disturbing *orientations*.[3]

As the 'Crown Jurist' of the Third Reich,[4] Schmitt remains controversial in legal and political circles. Reading Schmitt presents academic hazards given his 'indelible' antisemitism and 'ideological conversion' to the Nazi party.[5] His authoritarian and antisemitic proclivities almost secured a place

[1] See Constantin Fasolt, *The Limits of History* 6 (2004) (complaining of chronological pollution). The intellectual historian Peter Uwe Hohendahl has specifically cautioned that 'scholars have frequently addressed Schmitt's theory of space [*Großraum*] as if it could be detached from its original purpose', which 'grew directly from his reading of German foreign policy between 1939 and 1941'. Peter Uwe Hohendahl, *Perilous Futures: On Carl Schmitt's Late Writings* 60–61 (2018).

[2] See, eg, Hersch Lauterpacht, 'The Grotian Tradition in International Law', 23 *Brit YB Int'l L* 1 (1946) (presenting an influential but heavily romanticised summary of the Grotian Tradition); Christopher R Rossi, *Broken Chain of Being: James Brown Scott and the Origins of Modern International Law* (1998) (discussing the Spanish Scholastic tradition of Francisco de Vitoria and the misguided attempt by James Brown Scott to establish his teachings as the fount of modern international law); Anne Orford, *International Law and the Politics of History* (2021) (focusing attention on what the proper use of law and history should be).

[3] See Olof Kronvall, et al, 'Comments on Ola Tunander's Article "The Uneasy Imbrication of Nation-State and NATO: The Case of Sweden"', 35 *Cooperation & Conflict* 417 (2000) (criticising the suggestion of NATO as a supranational network and a form of hegemony rather than consensus); Ola Tunander, 'A Criticism of Court Chroniclers: A Response from Tunander', 35 *Cooperation & Conflict* 431 (2000) (responding to association of his usage of the concept with Hitler's Third Reich).

[4] See Reinhard Mehring: *Carl Schmitt: A Biography* 391 (2014) (quoting Ernst Jünger's 1943 diary entry).

[5] Joseph Bendersky, 'The Expendable Kronjurist: Carl Schmitt and National Socialism, 1933–36', 14 *J Contemp Hist* 309, 321 (1979); Hubertus Buchstein, *Enduring Enmity: The Story of Otto*

for him in the dock at Nuremberg.[6] Following his release from detention in 1947, he was 'not allowed to teach, to publish, and to speak in public'.[7] For many years, post-war German higher education centres sequestered his writings under lock and key. His retreat to his birth village of Plettenberg after incarceration became a private pilgrimage destination and salon for intellectuals 'seeking shelter from the hostile intrusion of the new (liberal) state.'[8]

He first presented his concept of *Großraum* against the backdrop of the Austrian *Anschluß*.[9] His development of a so-called 'counter vocabulary to rewrite international history geopolitically as a series of "spatial revolutions"' attempted to 'insert[] Hitler's *Großraumpolitik* into a transhistoricized continuum of "land-appropriations"' and to 'mobilize[] this reconstructed history to ascribe historical legitimacy and direction to Nazi-Germany's wars of conquest'.[10]

Großraum is a particularly weighty idiom to employ in discussions of geospace. Achilles Skordas referred to it as 'a polyvalent but "dangerous" concept combining elements of international law and geopolitics', developed but not invented by Carl Schmitt.[11] It has a long, if not co-opted, history in the field of *Raum* (spatial) studies, beginning with classical geopoliticians such as Friedrich Ratzel (1844–1904), HJ Mackinder (1861–1947), Alfred Thayer Mahan (1840–1914), Rudolf Kjellén (1864–1922), Nicholas Spykman (1893–1943), and more contemporary expositors such as Henry Kissinger (1923–2023) in United States foreign policy circles, and Vladimir Zhirinovskii (1946–2022) in post-Soviet Russia.[12] The concept principally influenced Russian nationalist

Kirchheimer and Carl Schmitt, ch 10 (Sandra H Lustig trans, 2024) (explicating Schmitt's vocabulary and explicit and disguised antisemitic Nazi German usages); William Scheuerman, *Carl Schmitt: The End of Law* 152 (1999) (noting 'it would be a mistake to let Schmitt off the hook too easily even when his analysis seems most impressive'); Alex Schulman, 'Carl Schmitt and the Clash of Civilizations: The Missing Context', 17 *J Pol Ideologies* 147, 148 (2012) ('anyone who considers Schmitt a fascinating political theorist … must, one way or another, enquire into his relationship with Nazism').

[6] William Hooker, *Carl Schmitt's International Thought: Order and Orientation* 156 (2009) (noting his interrogation, nearly two-year detention, and eventual release by American authorities investigating war criminals).

[7] Hohendahl, n 1, at 35.

[8] ibid at 59.

[9] See Carl-Schmittt-Gesellschaft eV, ww.carl-schmitt.de/en/carl-schmitt/schmitt-chronik (undated) noting his writing against the background of the Austrian Anschluß: *Das Reich und die Krankheit der europäischen Kultur* (1938), his Kiel University lecture, *Der Reichsbegriff im Völkerrecht* (1939), and *Völkerrechtliche Großraumordnung mit Interventionsverbot für raumfremde Mächte* (1939)).

[10] Benno Gerhard Teschke, 'Fatal Attraction: A Critique of Carl Schmitt's International Political and Legal Theory', 3 *Int'l Theory* 187 (2011).

[11] Achilles Skordas, 'Russia's Eurasian *Großraum* and its Consequences', Verfassungsblog (31 March 2022), verfassungsblog.de/russias-eurasian-groraum-and-its-consequences/.

[12] Mark Bassim, 'Between Realism and the 'New Right': Geopolitics in Germany in the 1990s', 28 *Trans of the Inst Br Geogr* 259, at 350 (2003) (discussing the classical geopoliticians leading up to more contemporary examples). See also Friedrich Ratzel, *Politische Geographie* (1897); HJ Mackinder, *Britain and the British Seas* (1902); Alfred Thayer Mahan, *The Influence of Sea*

Aleksandr Dugin's *Foundations of Geopolitics* (1997) and his reactionary Eurasia political party.[13] Dugin's interpretation, in turn, has been linked to Putin's invasion of Crimea.[14]

A BRIEF ONTOLOGY OF *GROẞRAUM*

Ratzel began discussing a national conception of geography in the early 1880s, coining the term *anthropogeographie* in 1882,[15] from which continental geographers quickly began to adapt the idea of human geography (*la géographie humaine*, 1895).[16] This concept developed from a differentiation of the *Natural Regions of the World*[17] and a study of the *genius loci* of some [] human groups'.[18] Ratzel's 1897 work, *Political Geography*, explicitly construed the state as an organism connected to the soil, with metaphoric references to organic growth and biogeography.[19]

Central to geographers' fascination with *Raum* studies was the relationships of people and *milieu*, what Paul Vidal de la Blache (1845–1918) referred to as the *genre de vie*.[20] The human relationship to physical environment created not only spatial interdependencies but organic patterns of social interaction in a bid to

Power Upon History, 1660–1783 (1890); Rudolf Kjellén, 'Studier öfver Sveriges politiska gränser', 19 *Ymer* 183–331 (1899); Rudolf Kjellén, *Der Staat als Lebensform* (1917); Nicholas Spykman, *The Geography of the Peace* (Helen R Nicholl ed, 1944); Henry Kissinger, *Diplomacy* (1994); Rafael Kachaturian, 'The Specter of Russian Nationalism', 56 *Dissent* 19 (2009) (discussing Zhirinovskii, the populist demagogue and leader of the Liberal Democratic Party of Russia).

[13] A Dugin, *Foundations of Geopolitics* (1997) [in Russian]. For a partial translation in English, see Peter Nikolaevich Savitsky: 'Eurasia Middle Earth', agdugintranslate.gitbook.io/foundations-of-geopolitics/part-1-founding-founders-of-geopolitics/chapter-9-peter-nikolaevich-savitsky-eurasia-middle-earth.

[14] See Anton Barbashin and Hannah Thoburn, 'Putin's Brain: Alexander Dugin and the Philosophy Behind Putin's Invasion of Crimea', *For Affs* (31 March 2014), www.foreignaffairs.com/articles/russia-fsu/2014-03-31/putins-brain; Charles Clover, 'The Unlikely Origins of Russia's Manifest Destiny: How an Obscure Academic and a Marginalized Philosopher Captured the Minds of the Kremlin and Helped Forge the New Russian Nationalism', *For Pol'y* (27 July 2016), foreignpolicy.com/2016/07/27/geopolitics-russia-mackinder-eurasia-heartland-dugin-ukraine-eurasianism-manifest-destiny-putin.

[15] Friedrich Ratzel, *Anthropo-Geographie: Oder Grundzüge der Anwendung der Erdkunde Auf die Geschichte* (1882).

[16] See generally M-C Robic, 'Friedrich Ratzel, géographie et sciences sociales en France (1890–1918)–Centralité et distanciations', 78 *Geographica Helvetica* 157 (2023) (discussing the reception of Ratzel and the semantisation of Raum studies).

[17] P Claval, 'National Schools of Geography', in *International Encyclopedia of Human Geography* 236 (Nigel Thrift and Rob Kitchin eds, 2009). See also AJ Herbertson, 'The Natural Regions of the World', 3 *Geographical Teacher* 104 (1905).

[18] HJ Fleure, *Human Geography in Western Europe: A Study in Appreciation* (2022) [1918] (projecting a study of the genius loci of some human groups).

[19] Ratzel, *Politische Geographie* 4 ('Der Staat muß vom Boden leben').

[20] P Vidal de la Blache, 'Les genres de vie dans la géographie humaine', 20 (111) *Annales de Géographie* 193–212 (15 May 1911), www.jstor.org/stable/pdf/23440012.pdf?refreqid=excelsior%3A8cc817dfa12ce1cde5091792a7763a8f&ab_segments=&origin=&initiator=&acceptTC=1.

exert control over nature.[21] French geographers began broadening the pejorative adjectival association of the geopolitical with the German *Geopolitik* 'obsession with space', but modern connections between geography and human ecology did not significantly build on its Vidalian influence until the start of the 1960s.[22]

An earlier connection to Darwin temporalised this study of geography, adding a historical component that made the study of geographies of the past relevant to shaping the geographies of the present and of the future.[23] Ratzel drew from Darwin's *On the Origin of Species* (1860) and from the earlier work of Carl Ritter (1779–1859)[24] to emphasise a combined understanding of biological, geographical, and anthropological conditions that shaped the spatial needs of human populations.[25] In 1901, he would publish an essay and introduce the term *Lebensraum*, which would frame a state's natural needs for self-sufficiency in terms of evolutionary processes (*Lebensentwicklung*, *Lebensbewegung*, *Lebensprozesse*), social structures (*Lebensgemeinschaften*), living communities (*Lebensschichtung*), life stages (*Lebensstufe*), and the logical expansion of borders to accommodate living area or habitat (*Lebensgebiet*).[26] Ratzel's English language translator noted that the coinage of the term *Lebensraum*, translates as 'living space', but his original text presented a cluster of synonyms and compounds dealing with questions of life and space.[27] Swedish constitutional lawyer, Rudolf Kjellén, formalised Ratzel's teachings, coined the term 'geopolitics', and furthered the study of the state as a living organism rooted in soil.[28] He defined geopolitics as 'the theory of the state as a geographical organism or phenomenon in space'.[29]

Late nineteenth-century reactionary German scholarship would modify the dynamics and entanglements of biogeography and geopolitics.[30] By the early twentieth century Haushofer would systematise bio-organic attributes of statehood into 'a dualistic view of power determined by geographical position'.[31] To this, Walter Christaller (1893–1969) added considerations of 'high order'

[21] Katarina Vamvakeros, 'A Brief Description over Human Geography', 12 *J Geogr Nat Disast* 1 (2022).

[22] Paul Claval, *Hérodote and the French Left, in Geographical Traditions: Critical Histories of a Century of Geopolitical Thought* 239–40 (Klaus Dodds and David Atkinson eds., 2000).

[23] Mike Heffernan, *Historical Geography, Making History* (2008), archives.history.ac.uk/making-history/resources/articles/historical_geography.html.

[24] *Die Erdkunde im Verhältnis zur Natur und zure Geschichte des Menschen* (Berlin, 1817).

[25] See C Abrahamsson, 'On the Geneology of Lebensraum', 68 *Geogr Helv* 37, 39 (2013).

[26] Friedrich Ratzel, *Der Lebensraum: Eine biogeographishe Studie* (1901).

[27] Tul'si (Tuesday) Bhambry (trans), 'Friedrich Ratzel, Lebensraum: A Biogeographical Study' [1901], 61 *J Hist Geogr* 59 (2018).

[28] See Rudolf Kjellén, 'Studier ofver Sveriges politiska gränser', 19 *Ymer* 183–331 (1899); Rudolf Kjellén, *Staten som Lifsform* (1916).

[29] Kjellén, *Staten som Lifsform* 34–35, and 203.

[30] See generally Paolo Giaccaria and Claudio Minca eds, *Hitler's Geographies, The Spatialities of the Third Reich* (2016) (broadly interrogating the spatial vision of the Reich and complexity of key geographical ideas of Lebensraum, Groβraum and geopolitics) (hereinafter Giaccaria and Minca).

[31] Benno Teschke, 'Geopolitics', 14 *Hist Materialism* 327, 327 (2006); Karl Haushofer et al, *Bausteine zur Geopolitik* (1928) (presenting essays on the scope of geopolitics).

central place-based economies that revolved around market areas and *entrepôts* that would locate economic geographies in relation to the maximum distance consumers would travel to exchange goods.[32] The economist, August Lösch (1906–1945), 'Impressed by the accidental way in which states are created and smashed', forwarded 'a more natural and lasting spatial order of things' that treated regions as an 'organism rather than just as an organ'.[33] Through what became known as location theory,[34] Lösch gave expression to the complexity of clustered arrangements of economic activity. Far from haphazard, patterns of spatial hierarchies formed and grew to create core yet bounded communities. He went so far as to note that the hexagon formed '*the most economical shape*' for framing the limits of a core trading area.[35] Anthropological adaptations of the organic boundaries of living things also appear during this period and now form interdisciplinary pursuits on the subjects of place and space.[36]

Haushofer deeply suspected modernity's ability to supplant primordial organicist influences with liberal institutions such as the League of Nations.[37] The League Covenant prescribed 'just and honorable relations between nations', 'scrupulous respect for all treaty obligations', and 'the firm establishment of the understandings of international law as the actual rule of conduct among Governments'. To Haushofer, nothing here reflected the organic dynamic of spatial boundaries. Borders were not created by rule-of-law abstractions, nor were they created naturally by rivers, mountains, or forests. Instead, borders were fluid and dynamic political devices employed by nations to create 'elbow room', expand their sphere of influence and connect a people's living space to soil.[38] He and his mentee, Rudolf Hess (1894–1987),[39] would proffer a new, institutionalised *Großraumordnung*[40] based on biological racism and National Socialism's

[32] Walter Christaller, *Central Places in Southern Germany* 16 (Carlisle W Baskin trans, 1966 [1933]) (noting: 'All regions have some centers which are closer, yet their centers of a higher order are found in larger towns which satisfy those demands of the country and of the smaller towns with the little towns are not able to satisfy'). See also Trevor J Barnes and Claudio Minca, 'Nazi Spatial Theory: The Dark Geographies of Carl Schmitt and Walter Christaller', 103 *Annals of the Ass'n of Am Geogr* 669 (2013) (discussing Christaller's spatial imaginary, his employment of formal geometry to place-based study of empty space, and reactionary association with Schmitt).

[33] August Lösch, 'The Nature of Economic Regions', 5 *S Econ J* 71 ('smashed together') and 78 ('organism') (1938).

[34] For more on location theory, see Trevor J Barnes, 'A Morality Tale of Two Location Theorists in Hitler's Germany: Walter Christaller and August Lösch', in Giaccaria and Minca, n 30, 198ff.

[35] See Lösch, n 33, at 73.

[36] See, eg, Helmuth Plessner, *Levels of Organic Life and the Human: An Introduction to Philosophical Anthropology* (Millay Hyatt trans, 2019) [1928] (connecting human lives to complex boundary dynamics of the surrounding world); Bruce B Janz ed, *Place Space and Hermeneutics* (2017) (presenting essays on hermeneutics as an approach to place and space and important figures contributing to the field).

[37] Christopher R Rossi, 'The *Nomos* of Climate Change and the Sociological Refugee in a Sinking Century', 50 *GW Int'l LR* 613, 634 (2018).

[38] Holger H Herwig, *The Demon of Geopolitics: How Karl Haushofer Educated Hitler and Hess* 100 (2016) (noting also Haushofer's influence on Hitler's *Mein Kampf*).

[39] See ibid at xi (noting Haushofer counselled Hess and Hitler).

[40] Teschke, *Geopolitics*, n 31, at 327.

cooptation of the concept of *Lebensraum*. As advanced by other Nazis such as Reinhard Höhn, Werner Best, and Werner Baitz, the *Lebensraum* ideology would define *Großraum* exclusively with 'a biological essence, namely ties of common blood'.[41] Nazi 'contamination' of the concept would transmute to 'the entire vocabulary' of spatial study and impute 'territorial, military, and economic' dimensions to adjoining concepts such as *Ostraum* and *Großwirtschtsraum*[42]

Lebensraum implicitly connected to Schmitt's understanding of world order, which was framed by his concept of the political, not the biological. Schmitt explicitly reduced his concept of the political to the distinction between the friend and the enemy.[43] He regarded this distinction as fundamental to the human condition. The conflict it created featured as part of his ordered world. Conflict inescapably formed part of the political; it occupied 'a permanent presence … at the origin of order'.[44] He disconnected this distinction from 'other criteria' (antitheses) such as 'good and evil in the moral sphere'. He wrote that the realm of the political operated *independently* and 'can neither be based on any one antithesis or combination of other antitheses, nor can it be traced to these …. It can exist theoretically and practically [without having to draw upon moral distinctions].'[45]

Schmitt's *Großraum*, imbued with this clinical understanding, significantly qualified the likelihood of cooperative ventures, setting him apart from a major strand of Western philosophy and political theory. In the *Nicomachean Ethics* and *Politics*, Aristotle famously conceived of the person as a *zoon politikon*,[46] or a political animal who shared social and cooperative traits, even in conflictual situations. Schmitt starkly viewed the enemy as a blunt oppositional force, a force that fundamentally opposes your way of life:

> The political enemy need not be morally evil or aesthetically ugly; he need not appear as an economic competitor, and it may even be advantageous to engage with him in business transactions. But he is, nevertheless, the other, the stranger; and it is sufficient for his nature that he is … existentially something different and alien, so that in the extreme case conflicts with him are possible. These can neither be decided by a previously determined general norm nor by the judgment of a disinterested and therefore neutral third party.[47]

[41] Buchstein, *Enduring Enmity*, n 5, 302.

[42] Karl Schlögel, *In Space We Read Time: On the History of Civilization and Geopolitics* 32 (Gerrit Jackson trans, 2016).

[43] Carl Schmitt, *The Concept of the Political* (George Schwab trans and intro, 2007), at 26 (famously postulating: 'The specific political distinction to which political actions and motives can be reduced is that between friend and enemy').

[44] Carlo Galli and Elisabeth Fay, 'Carl Schmitt and the Global Age', 10 *New Centennial Rev* 1, 2, (2010).

[45] Schmitt, *The Concept of the Political*, n 43, 26.

[46] Aristotle, *Nichomachean Ethics* 1097b11, XI 9, 1169b18; *Politics* I, 2, 1253a; III 16, 1278b 20, quoted in António Rocha Martins, 'The Zoon Politikon: Medieval Aristotelian Interpretations', 75 *Revista Portuguesa de Filosofia* 1539, 1540 fn 2 (2019).

[47] Schmitt, *The Concept of the Political*, n 43, at 27.

Schmitt's binary distinction between friend and enemy as the fundamental basis for his concept of the political has been criticised as a *dicto simpliciter* for law and as a simulacrum too rudimentary to gain wide acceptance within international relations and international law circles.[48] Indeed, his revival in Western international legal circles challenges much of the Western legal project of associating the promotion of the good with the achievement of the just.

To Eric Posner and Adrian Vermeule, interpreting Schmitt also created translation challenges, not simply from German to other languages, but from continental jurisprudential traditions to social science frameworks beyond his 'feverish world' of mystical and jargonistic scholarship.[49] Decoding Schmitt's German through translation became much more than a mechanical process of transposing Wagnerian opera. Sandra Lustig noted that his reworkings of his pre-1933 oeuvre deliberately cultivated obscurantist linguistic techniques, not always well concealed, in support of a kind of encoded Nazi German writing intended to trigger emotions of the sociocultural context.[50] The para-logic language of Nazi German meant to instrumentalise social control, but its transcendental implications also created nuanced ambiguities that bordered on incoherence.[51] Beyond his 'largely silent' application of *Großraum* to Weimar Germany's divisive internal political order,[52] his concept of *Großraumordnung* has been criticised as an incoherent elision of the concepts of *nomos* ('the *measure* by which the land in a particular order is divided and situated'[53]) and of the technical-industrial networks that create totalitarian power over large spaces.[54] Teschke attributed this incoherence to his 'historiographically discredited' account of the rise of the state, which Schmitt construed as an absolutist creation.[55] According to Teschke, Schmitt's conceptual development of international

[48] Martti Koskenniemi, 'Carl Schmitt and International Law', in *The Oxford Handbook of Carl Schmitt* 592, 593 (Jens Meierhenrich and Oliver Simons eds, 2015) ('The booming Schmitt commentary of the past two decades has not spread into international law as much as one might have expected .... This may result from their ... activist role in precisely the international institutions that Schmitt would have indicated as parts of Anglo-American global hegemony.').

[49] Eric A Posner and Adrian Vermeule, 'Demystifying Schmitt', in *The Oxford Handbook of Carl Schmitt* 612, 613 (Jens Meierhenrich and Oliver Simons eds, 2015). Preserving Schmitt's 'tenor and tone' while translating his writing 'within the limits of readable English' has challenged other translators, as noted by Samuel Garrett Zeitlin, who translated Schmitt's *Land and Sea: A World-Historical Meditation* (2015) (Note on the Edition and Translation).

[50] Sandra H Lustig, 'Translator's Preface', in *Enduring Enmity* 15, 16–19.

[51] See ibid at 18 (referencing Heinz Paechter and others).

[52] Christian Joerges, 'Europe a *Großraum*? Shifting Legal Conceptualisations of the Integration Project', in *Darker Legacies of Law in Europe: The Shadow of National Socialism and Fascism over Europe and Its Legal Traditions* 171 (Michael Stolleis and Navraj Singh Ghaleigh, eds, 2003).

[53] Carl Schmitt, *The* Nomos *of the Earth in the International Law of the* Jus Publicum Europaeum 70 (2003 [1974]) [hereinafter Schmitt, Nomos *of the Earth*] ('it is also the form of political, social, and religious order determined by this process').

[54] Niels Werber, 'Zweimal *Großraum*: Netzwerke und Raumordnung bei Carl Schmitt', 61 *Archiv des Völkerrechts* 248 (2023).

[55] Teschke, *Fatal Attraction*, n 10, at 197.

law and the supra-territorial *jus gentium* lopsidedly revolved on only one concrete axis, the sovereign territorial state.[56]

Schmitt's conception of *Großraum* was also deeply rooted in interwar psychological and biogeographical interpretation due to rapid changes that decentred Europe's spatial identity. If not obvious, this point has connections to the Arctic given the accelerated reorientations relating to the global environment.

A CHANGING ARCTIC PANOPTICON?

The collapse of the Ottoman, Romanov, Hapsburg and Hohenzollern empires following World War I precipitated tremendous and enduring upheaval.[57] It introduced stateless classifications of *Heimatlosen* or *apatrides* who 'would not or could not assume the nationality of a successor state'.[58] The ensuing response to refugees, principally under the direction of Fridtjof Nansen (1861–1930), authenticated this concretised, enclosed spatial ordering through treaties on minorities administered by the League of Nations.[59] However, with seven new states and two free territories to accommodate Europe's new interwar map, in addition to 'inextricably intermingled' migrations that had taken place with various Slavic, German, and Magyar migrations over the preceding millennium, 'it proved impossible [for European framers] to draw any political frontier without creating a minority somewhere'.[60] Due to a massive spatial reordering of boundaries, Europe's predictably inadequate response to questions on minorities after the Great War lumped together about 30 per cent of its roughly 100 million inhabitants into the exceptional category of protection afforded by minorities treaties.[61] In accepting the 1938 Nobel Peace Prize for the work of the Nansen International Office for Refugees, the organisation's president, Michael Hansson, lamented that the massive European refugee problem relatively quickly resulted in 'restrictive policies … with practically impenetrable barriers. Now nobody wanted to accept refugees.'[62]

[56] ibid.

[57] Michael R Marrus, *The Unwanted: European Refugees in the Twentieth Century*, 52 (1985).

[58] ibid at 70.

[59] Nansen directed the League of Nations' High Commission for Refugees, established in 1921. It became the Nansen International Office for Refugees in 1931, an autonomous authority under the supervision of the League Secretariat. Its principal achievements included the creation of the passport for stateless persons and establishing the foundation for the League of Nations Refugee Convention and the Office of the High Commissioner for Refugees. Nansen was awarded the Nobel Peace Prize in 1922, the Nansen International Office for Refugees was awarded the Nobel Peace Prize in 1938. See Nansen International Office for Refugees, History. The Nobel Prize, www.nobelprize.org/prizes/peace/1938/nansen/history.

[60] Joseph B Schechtman, *European Population Transfers: 1939–1945*, 4 (1946).

[61] See Hannah Arendt, *Origins of Totalitarianism* 270, 271 (1966) [1951].

[62] Michael Hansson, *Nansen International Office for Refugees Nobel Lecture*, The Nobel Prize (10 December 1938), www.nobelprize.org/prizes/peace/1938/nansen/history.

Hannah Arendt forcefully connected this response to the *Origins of Totalitarianism* (1951).[63] Michael Marrus charted in *The Unwanted* (1985) the intersectional crisscrossing of nationalities dislodged by the postwar Versailles line-drawing. The implacable duration[64] and scale of normalising millions of people outside the full scope of statehood's protective shell presented new challenges in the history of Europe.[65] It also sparked one imaginative solution: Count Richard Coudenhove-Kalergi's (1894–1972) Pan-European Union, a movement of democratic unity for Europe fully 30 years ahead of Jean Monnet's (1888–1979) idea to form the European Coal and Steel Community, the forerunner of the spatial *Großraum* of the European Union.[66]

Schmitt's spatial orientation of international politics toward geopolitics attempted to fashion a new panopticon of protection for Europe and his disintegrating *jus publicum europaeum*. He conceived of the idea of *Großraum* as an integrated space, a space differentiated from the independent composition of the territorial state and 'coexist[ing] with other kinds of territories (such as protectorates and border states)' that fell within great power administration.[67] Anthropogenic machinations in the Arctic now create new biogeographical challenges. Political machinations now complicate the international administration of the Arctic. Given these Arctic challenges, questions arise over whether a new Arctic governance panopticon is needed.[68]

These challenges involve migrating pelagic resources due to warming waters, challenges to the extant Arctic regime complex and governance structure, rapidly reforming Arctic spatial conceptions given its diminishing ice wall, and the melting of Arctic exceptionalism, an idea once seemingly reflected by liberal tenets of coordinated and reciprocated management of the great space of the High North. Analogously, discussions of the global Arctic,[69] predicated either

[63] See generally Arendt, n 61, at 271.

[64] See Marrus, n 57, at 5 (noting the extraordinary duration of displacement in the post-1918 period).

[65] Arendt, n 61, at 275. Arendt noted, 'de jure [the minorities] belonged to some political body' but the special treaties and guarantees of displaced peoples set the stage for disputes over secondary rights such as language, culture, residence, and mobility, making stateless persons 'the most symptomatic group' in the contemporary politics of her time and the category a relentless European problem that could not be renormalised. ibid at 276–77.

[66] See generally Martyn Bond, *Hitler's Cosmopolitan Bastard: Count Richard Coudenhove-Kalergi and His Vision of Europe* (2021) (presenting a biography on the author of the manifesto Pan-Europa and the beginnings of the idea of European integration).

[67] Anne Orford, 'Regional Orders, Geopolitics, and the Future of International Law', 74 *Current Legal Problems* 149, 162 (2021).

[68] See, eg, Benjamin J Sacks, Marigold Black and Peter Dortmans, 'Arctic Governance Is In Trouble. The Antarctic Could Be Next, RandBlog (7 December 2022), www.rand.org/pubs/commentary/2022/12/arctic-governance-is-in-trouble-the-antarctic-could.html; Benjamin Chiacchia, 'The Case for an Arctic Treaty', 146 *US Naval Inst Proc* (2020), www.usni.org/magazines/proceedings/2020/may/case-arctic-treaty.

[69] Matthias Finger and Lassi Heininen eds, *The GlobalArctic Handbook* (2018).

on climate change or on an evolving 'form of "resource colonization"'[70] from a 'broadening spectrum of relevant Arctic actors'[71] create anxiety, certainly from a Russian mindset. This mindset is predicated on decades-old presumptions of primacy in and mastery over the Arctic, qualities built on a Russian panopticon of stability and predictability that seems to be crumbling on multiple fronts.[72] If maintaining this panopticon once relied on participating in the stewardship functions of the Arctic Council, its weakened status now prompts Russia to initiate cooperative ventures with other international Arctic actors, suggestively the BRICS (Brazil, Russia, India, China, and South Africa).[73]

Schmitt's vigorous critique of liberalism and its unmoored projection of universalist values stimulated numerous adaptations at the base of spatial studies. William Hooker reduced Schmitt's entire oeuvre to 'one pre-eminent theme': uncovering and tracing the specific 'failings of liberalism'.[74] It is quite correct to conclude that his thinking 'is internationally present in a variety of heterogeneous legal, political, and social debates', and that his ideas have added to these discourses in sometimes conflicting ways.[75] Teschke noted a 'surprising *complexio oppositorum*': Schmitt's 'double attraction' for the neo-Conservative Right, with his critique of the executive state, and the post-Marxist Left, with his revulsion of liberal universalism and Kantian cosmopolitanism.[76] Brendan Simms would doubtless extend his attraction to the authoritarian perspectives of Russian President Valdimir Putin, and Chinese General Secretary and President Xi Jinping. Beyond their embrace of Schmitt's hostility toward liberalism's democratisation project and 'Western universalism' is their shared and unsentimental binary distinction between the friend and the enemy, the elevation of the political over the social, and their recognition of 'cultural and civilizational diversity',[77] despite 'hav[ing] actually attempted to project their influence far beyond their traditional "space"'.[78]

[70] Matthias Finger and Gunnar Rekvig, 'Introduction', in *Global Arctic: An Introduction to the Multifaceted Dynamics of the Arctic* 1, 4 (Matthias Finger and Gunnar Rekvig eds, 2022).

[71] Lassi Heininen, 'The Post-Cold War Arctic', in *Global Arctic: An Introduction to the Multifaceted Dynamics of the Arctic* 109, 114 (Matthias Finger and Gunnar Rekvig eds, 2022).

[72] See Elizabeth Buchannan, 'Russia and China in the Arctic: Assumptions and Realities', *The Strategist* (25 September 2020) (noting concerns about Western misreadings of Russian relations in the Arctic).

[73] See 'Minister: Russia Will Develop International Scientific Station on Spitsbergen', Tass (6 April 2023), tass.com/economy/1600365 (announcing a proposed international Arctic science station in Russia's Barentsburg and Pyramiden with the BRICS).

[74] Hooker, n 6, at 126.

[75] Hohendahl, n 1, at 2.

[76] Teschke, *Fatal Attraction*, n 10, at 180. Louiza Odysseos and Fabio Petito, *The International Political Thought of Carl Schmitt: Terror, Liberal War and the Crisis of Global Order* (2007) (presenting critical essays on Schmitt's relevance to international relations); Danilo Zolo, *Invoking Humanity: War, Law and Global Order* (2002) (interpreting Western humanitarian intervention as a parochial political objective); Chantal Mouffe, ed, *The Challenge of Carl Schmitt* (1999) (presenting essays mindful of Schmitt's critique of liberalism's dangers).

[77] Brendan Simms, *Die Rückkehr des Großraums?* 9 (2023), at 49.

[78] ibid at 50.

Schmitt's revival has been influential in securitisation studies[79] and particularly significant in Chinese intellectual circles given his critique of liberalism,[80] his unsentimental and anti-Aristotelian notion of irremediable and existential threat,[81] his decisionist defence of the authoritarian and his scepticism of judicial review,[82] and China's new-found 'power to participate in global demarcation'.[83]

Schmitt regarded liberal internationalism's project as the 'transformation of a spatially conceived principle of non-interference into a spatially undifferentiated general system of interference'.[84] For this reason, he admired the 'earth-bound character of the partisan' who resisted rootless and ideological intrusion.[85] The historical geographer Michael Heffernan noted Schmitt's

[79] See Michael C Williams, 'Words, Images, Enemies: Securitization and International Politics', 47 *Int'l Stud Q* 511, 513 (2003) ('the specificity of 'security' as a particular kind of speech-act in the work of the Copenhagen School is underpinned by an understanding of the politics of enmity, decision, and emergency which has deep roots in Schmitt's understanding of the political order'). See also 'Carl Schmitt and Copenhagen School Security Studies', 4 *Western Balkans Security Observer* (2009) (presenting essays on Schmitt and the Copenhagen School).

[80] See Jiang Shigong, *Empire and World Order* (intro and trans David Ownby, 2019), www.readingthechinadream.com/jiang-shigong-empire-and-world-order.html (noting the nihilism of cultural liberalism); 'Carl Schmitt in China', *The China Story* (2015), www.thechinastory.org/cot/carl-schmitt-in-china/ (noting 'Schmitt's views have become influential in mainland Chinese scholarship').

[81] Schmitt, *The Concept of the Political*, n 43, 27 (discussing the existential threat posed by the enemy). Regarding the fractious issue of Taiwan and opposing, possibly existential differences between the United States and China (compare Chinese President Xi's 2024 New Year's address on the inevitability of reunification on both sides of the Taiwan strait, 'Full Text of President Xi Jinping's 2024 New Year Message', PRC Ministry of For Affs (31 December 2023), www.mfa.gov.cn/eng/zxxx_662805/202312/t20231231_11215608.html, with US pronouncements to defend Taiwan, see David Brunnstrom and Trevor Hunnicutt, 'Biden Says U.S. Forces Would Defend Taiwan in the Event of a Chinese Invasion', Reuters (19 September 2022), www.reuters.com/world/biden-says-us-forces-would-defend-taiwan-event-chinese-invasion-2022-09-18). Schmitt seemingly laid the theoretical foundation for China's position: 'Only the actual participants can correctly recognise, understand, and judge the concrete situation and settle the extreme case of conflict.' Schmitt, *Concept of the Political*, n 43, 27.

[82] See generally, Ryan Mitchell, *Carl Schmitt and the Development of Conservative State Theory in China*, YouTube (9 October 2020), www.youtube.com/watch?v=PBO9W5oqKK8, time mark 4:38 (on Schmitt's growing importance in China), time mark 34:06 (on Schmitt's decisionist view that 'The sovereign is the one who decides upon the state of exception'), time mark 1:00: 46 (rejection of Anglo-American juristocracy); Chen Duanhong, 'National Security and the Constitution', *Reading the China Dream* (intro and trans by David Ownby, 4 December 2020), www.readingthechinadream.com/chen-duanhong-national-security-and-the-constitution.html ('advocating the power and authority of the 'sovereign' over the formal law').

[83] Liu Xiaofeng, 'New China and the End of American "International Law"', 3 *Am Affs* (2019), americanaffairsjournal.org/2019/08/new-china-and-the-end-of-american-international-law; see also Xie Libin and Haig Patapan, 'Schmitt Fever: The Use and Abuse of Carl Schmitt in Contemporary China', 18 *Int'l J Const L* 130 (2020) (discussing the multiple influences of Schmitt in China based on his ideas relating to political legitimacy, sovereignty, and foreign affairs).

[84] Carl Schmitt, 'Großraum versus Universalism: The International Legal Struggle over the Monroe Doctrine', in *Spatiality, Sovereignty and Carl Schmitt: Geographies of the Nomos* 47–48 (Stephen Legg ed, 2011).

[85] Alberto Toscano, 'Carl Schmitt in Beijing: Partisanship, Geopolitics and the Demolition of the Eurocentric World', 11 *Postcolonial Stud* 417, 420 (2008) (referring to Schmitt's 'rich discussion of the anti-Napoleon guerrilleros' and their rear-guard guerrilla campaign during the Iberian Peninsular (1808–1814).

'prescient and perceptive observations that speak directly to the ironies' of the post-Cold War world,[86] perhaps none more problematic than liberalism's perpetual state of exception in dealing with the war on terror,[87] or even more recently, constitutional democracy's tumultuous weakness in reigning in the executive deceits of United States President Donald Trump.[88]

The critique of liberalism and its bruising imprint on themes of universality, internationalism, and by association, Arctic exceptionalism, owe much to Schmittian critique, making Schmitt's complex if contorted historico-political construction of the idea of *Großraum* of interest here. Construed as a regional construct, Schmitt proffered it in opposition to a 'normative or hegemonically defined world state'; construed as a universal construct, Schmitt regarded it as a 'pluralistic global order reliant on a balance of major powers'.[89] Cohabitating in each of these uses was Schmitt's 'aversion to moral ideas'.[90] Perhaps it is better to borrow the term *Großraum* from Schmitt rather than parse it, extend his usage rather than embrace it, and adapt it to contemporary circumstances rather than conform it to Schmitt's iron bed of Procrustean amoral reasoning.

GROßRAUM, *GROßRÄUME*, WHOLES, PARTS, AND LEVELS

Schmittian spatial imagery looms large in discussions of global politics and the Arctic. The theory contains wholes, parts, and levels, which suggests the plurality of meanings that now attaches to the Arctic. Can Mert Körkerer noted the grouping of these levels into four kinds of relations: 'first, between *Großräume as wholes …, second, inter-Reich relations between the leading Reichs of these*

[86] Michael Heffernan, 'Mapping Schmitt', in *Spatiality, Sovereignty and Carl Schmitt* 234, 234 (Stephen Legg ed., 2011). See also Jan-Werner Müller, *A Dangerous Mind: Carl Schmitt in Post-War European Thought*, at 2 (calling Schmitt one of the 'most notorious modern intellectuals' and yet recognising that his thoughts have meant so much to so many); Carlo Galli, *Janus's Gaze: Essays on Carl Schmitt* (Amanda Minervini trans, edited with an introduction by Adam Sitze, 2015) (assessing his contributions and faults).

[87] See generally Giorgio Agamben, *State of Exception* (2005) (problematising democratic rule versus government edicts suspending democratic rule due to the subjectivised need to deal with the threshold appearance of states of emergency); Jörg Friedrichs, 'Defining the International Public Enemy: The Political Struggle behind the Legal Debate on International Terrorism,' 19 *Leiden J Int'l L* 69 (2006) (discussing Schmitt's association of politics with the task of determining the international public enemy).

[88] See Yascha Mounk, 'After Trump, Is American Democracy Doomed by Populism?' Council For Rel (14 January 2021) (noting Trump's authoritarian populism and his ability 'to convince so many Americans of his lies'); Glenn Kessler, Salvador Rizzo and Meg Kelly, 'Trump's False or Misleading Claims Total 30,573 over 4 Years', *Wash Post* (24 January 2021), www.washingtonpost.com/politics/2021/01/24/trumps-false-or-misleading-claims-total-30573-over-four-years (tallying an average of 21 untruths per day of his presidency).

[89] Hohendahl, n 1, at 62.

[90] ibid.

Großräume; third, inter-popular relations inside of a *Großraum*; and finally … inter-popular relations between peoples of different *Großräume*'.[91]

In the hands of the technical disciplines such as mathematics, Schmitt recognised that geography and cartography are neutral devices.[92] He argued they can nevertheless be instrumentalised 'if they fall within the sphere of the political', for example the 200-year struggle between the English and French as to where to locate the prime meridian of the earth's cartographic grid (Greenwich versus Paris).[93] Schmitt forcefully applied geography to international law, admitting ('as every geographer knows') that cartography, when instrumentalised, can become 'highly political',[94] for instance in the context of the Monroe Doctrine 'with respect to the concept of the Western Hemisphere', or, as his critics would assert,[95] in the virulent context of the darker geography of the Nazi idea of *Lebensraum*.[96]

Especially important to Schmitt was the extension of the Monroe Doctrine *Großraum* beyond the continental landmass of the Western Hemisphere, formerly linked to the concrete parameters of 'mathematically and geographically determined spatial dimensions'.[97] The American *Großraum*'s 'displacement' to the sea, not only created a second sphere of influence, but made the concept of the Western Hemisphere 'even more abstract'.[98] Perhaps this concern manifested in World War II when in 1941 the Roosevelt Administration's Secretary of State Cordell Hull asserted that 'Greenland is within the area embraced by

[91] Can Mert Kökerer, 'The Sine Qua Non of Carl Schmitt's Political Thinking: The Issue of Interstate Relations', 47 *Phil & Soc Crit* 1137, 1147 (2020).

[92] Schmitt, Nomos *of the Earth*, n 53, 88.

[93] ibid (noting the establishment of 'the Greenwich prime meridian to be a symbol of the former English domination of the sea and the world'). The prime meridian is the line of 0° longitude. It is the starting point for measuring distances both east and west around the Earth. Britain, France, and China published cartographic maps that had the 0° longitude line running through their capitals (in England's case, the Royal Observatory in Greenwich), a relativisation that greatly problematised navigation and map reading, not unlike uncoordinated time zones. An international convention in 1884 standardised the meridian line and also set the standard for coordinated universal time. See 'Prime Meridian', *Nat'l Geo*, education.nationalgeographic.org/resource/prime-meridian.

[94] Schmitt, Nomos *of the Earth*, n 53, 88.

[95] See Jeffrey Herf, *Reactionary Modernism: Technology, Culture and Politics in Weimar and the Third Reich* 26 (on the politicisation of Le[b]ensphilosophie), 44–46 (on Schmitt's admiration of the authoritarian state and his contributions to reactionary modernism) (1984); Richard Wolin, 'Carl Schmitt: The Conservative Revolution and the Aesthetics of Horror', 20 *Pol Theory* 424 (1993).

[96] See Trevor J Barnes and Claudio Minca, 'Nazi Spatial Theory: The Dark Geographies of Carl Schmitt and Walter Christaller', 103 *Ann of the Ass'n of Am Geogr* 669–87 (2013).

[97] ibid at 283.

[98] ibid Schmitt was close to the mark with the Roosevelt Administration's contemplation of including Greenland and Iceland as part of the Western Hemisphere's Monroe Doctrine in response to Germany's invasion of Denmark. See 'Greenland Raises Hemisphere Issue; Monroe Doctrine to be Applied If It Is Necessary – Danish Envoy Sees Roosevelt', *New York Times* (11 April 1940), www.nytimes.com/1940/04/11/archives/greenland-raises-hemisphere-issue-monroe-doctrine-to-be-applied-if.html. In 2019, President Trump returned to the issue when floating up the idea that the United State should purchase the autonomous Danish territory,; see Vivian Salama et al, 'President Trump Eyes a New Real-Estate Purchase: Greenland', *Wall Street J* (16 August 2019), www.wsj.com/articles/trump-eyes-a-new-real-estate-purchase-greenland-11565904223, or trade Puerto Rico to Denmark in exchange for Greenland. See generally Peter Baker and Susan Glasser, *The Divider: Trump in the White House, 2017–2021* (2022).

the Monroe Doctrine'.[99] Schmitt attributed the significance of the American *Großraum* to the destructive Monroe Doctrine, which over time secured 'footholds, naval bases, refueling stations' and administrative outposts via treaties and legal agreements.[100] It destroyed the old order understanding of sovereignty and supplanted it with a controlling right of intervention and domination. According to Schmitt: 'Territorial sovereignty was transformed into an empty space for socio-economic processes.'[101] The external or linear boundaries of sovereignty were preserved, but not the substance within. The Monroe Doctrine projected a new kind of spatial sovereignty, where the controlling state maintained a freedom to intervene and thereby deprived the controlled state of its autonomy ('*cujus regio*, *ejus economia*').[102]

While it is doubtful that militarisation concerns and rapidly evolving spatial understandings of the Arctic have had a transformative effect on the understanding of sovereignty, a new kind of spatial sovereignty has seemingly infiltrated the workings of the Arctic Council, preserving its structure in form, but not its substantive workings from within. In view of the perceived shift in the balance of power of the Arctic Council, with formerly non-aligned Arctic Council members Sweden and Finland joining NATO, with globalising interests turning toward the Arctic, what will become of the Arctic stakeholder (*cujus regio*) and its control over the Arctic *ejus economia*?

Großraum presents a useful concept that allows us to concentrate on unit actors as parts or as wholes, their interactions, and 'decomposable systems'.[103] It has applicability to new Arctic spaces given rapidly receding ice, increasingly accessible resources, the awakening sense of an epochal merger of the Holocene and the Anthropocene, and the awareness that the Arctic is something more than a passive historical backdrop. The term is specific enough to interrogate parochial state interests and broad enough to cross-examine institutional players and normative influences, such as international law's idea of the global commons. Is the Arctic a *Großraum*? If it is, what do we make of it?

Aristotle's reflection of the whole being more than the sum of its parts, and parts themselves constituting some other kind of whole,[104] impliedly suggested

[99] Francis O Wilcox, 'The Monroe Doctrine and World War II', 36 *Am Pol Sci Rev* 433, 444 (1942) (quoting Hull).

[100] Schmitt, Nomos *of the Earth*, n 53, at 252.

[101] ibid.

[102] ibid at 253. *Cuius regio eius religio* coined the 17th-century outcome of the Peace of Augsburg (1555) that granted the Imperial estate-holder power to declare the presiding religion in his own territory. See Richard Potz, 'Cuius regio, eius religio', in *Encyclopedia of Early Modern History Online* (Graeme Dunphy and Andrew Gow eds, 2015), referenceworks.brillonline.com/entries/encyclopedia-of-early-modern-history-online/cuius-regio-eius-religio-SIM_018148. extends the imperial power to his household economy.

[103] Nicholas Onuf, 'Levels', 1 *Eur J Int'l Rel* 35, 40 (1995).

[104] Aristotle, *Metaphysics* 8.1045a, www.perseus.tufts.edu/hopper/text?doc=Perseus%3Atext%3A1999.01.0052%3Abook%3D8%3Asection%3D1045a ('In all things which have a plurality of parts, and which are not a total aggregate but a whole of some sort distinct from the parts, there is some cause').

that 'composition is never exactly what it seems'.[105] The idea of *Großraum* can frame the Arctic as one undifferentiated circumpolar whole, a Global Arctic, for purposes of macroanalysis, or as a diverse form of political spaces, a Global Ensemble, partitioned into taxonomic or political *Großräume* for sub-macro or regional inquiry.[106]

The aggregated components of Arctic *Großräume* reflect what J David Singer famously described as the 'level of analysis' problem in international politics.[107] Singer reduced these levels to the 'more common' systemic and sub-systemic or national level, but he noted the fruitful potential of 'many other' such schema.[108] RBJ Walker and Nicholas Onuf pointed out that 'levels of analysis' discourse (suggested here as *Großraum* versus *Großräume*) sometimes receives less 'critical appraisal' than required. The discourse on levels tends to reaffirm assumptions 'too easily taken for granted'.[109] The complexity of Arctic spheres of influence falls prey to casual generalisations, meshing independent and dependent variables, and causes and effects.[110]

Singer's main concern highlighted the tendency of theorists to mix systemic and sub-systemic levels or to shift their 'orientation in the midst of a study' unaware of having done so.[111] Singer's groundbreaking article spawned discussions relating to the number of levels,[112] the relationships between or among

[105] Onuf, *Levels*, n 103, at 53.

[106] Jochen Kleinschmidt, 'Politische Räume, Grossräume und Weltgesellschaft', in *Großraum-Denken: Carl Schmitts Kategorie der Großaumordnung* 71, 92 (Rudiger Voigt ed, 2008) ('Dies könnte man allenfalls dann behaupten, wenn man, 'Großraum' unbedingt as regionale Subdivision der Welt betrachten möchte. Vielmehr könnte der Sinn des Begriffs gerade darin bestehen, die Mannigfaltigkeit der Formen politischer Räume der Weltgesellschaft in ihrem Zusammenwirken als ein globales Ensemble zu beschreiben'). Kleinschmidt provides a taxonomy of the concept of space (*Raumbegriffs*) including functional differentiation, territorial borders, imperial borders, exclusion borders, and global society (*Weltgesellschaft*). See generally ibid Schmitt contemplated a future *nomos* of the earth in which 'an equilibrium of several independent Großräume' or blocs could exist. Schmitt, Nomos *of the Earth*, n 53, 355.

[107] J David Singer, 'The Level-of-Analysis Problem in International Relations', 14 *World Pol* 77 (1961) (introducing the concept and reducing level analysis to two possible levels, the systemic level and the national or sub-systemic level).

[108] ibid at 90 (concluding that there is no 'overriding case for one or another of the two models'). See also ibid at 80–82 (discussing the international systemic level) and 82–89 (discussing the national state level).

[109] RBJ Walker, *Inside/Outside: International Relations as Political Theory* 130–31 ('critical appraisal', 'taken for granted'); Onuf, n 103, at 36 (quoting Walker) and 35–36 (noting the 'all pervasive' language of levels with many writers not defining the term).

[110] See Stephen J Andriole, 'The Levels of Analysis Problems and the Study of Foreign International, and Global Affairs: A Review Critique, and Another Final Solution', 5 *Int'l Interactions* 113 (1979).

[111] ibid at 90.

[112] See generally Kenneth Waltz, *Man, the State, and War* (1959) (distinguishing three possible frameworks for the causes of war, human nature, the type of state, or Waltz's preferred theory relating to the structure of the system); Kenneth Waltz, *Theory of International Politics* (1979) (elaborating the theory of international anarchy, distribution of power among strong states, and structural realism); Bruce Russett and Harvey Starr, *World Politics: The Menu for Choice*, 3rd edn (1989) (introducing six levels of analysis: the global system, interstate relations, societal level, governmental level, roles, individual actors).

levels,[113] and their 'entanglements'.[114] Political geographer Elana Wilson Rowe conceptualised Arctic entanglements 'as a set of interlinked policy fields. … [arguing that] the same GPS coordinate in the Arctic Ocean could be mapped into a multitude of policy fields, some local, some national, some international'.[115]

Consider the many mixtures and understandings of the Arctic. Western security analysts focus on the North American Arctic of NORAD,[116] NATO's Northern Flank,[117] or on the strategic transit routes of the Bear Gap and GIUK Gap,[118] which connect Russia's Arctic Northern Fleet to the Atlantic Ocean. More specifically, the United States Arctic defense strategy adopts a multidomain approach, subdividing it into three geographic combatant commands: homeland security (USNORTHCOM), Europe (USEUCOM), and the Pacific (USINDOPACOM).[119] The Arctic's remoteness historically made its defence the province of the United States Navy and Air Force, but the Army has developed

[113] Peter Gourevitch, 'The Second Image Reversed: The International Sources of Domestic Politics', 32 *Int'l Org* 881 (1982) (critiquing the interaction of domestic politics as an independent and 'sometimes irrelevant' variable in the study of international relations).

[114] Robert D Putnam, 'Diplomacy and Domestic Politics: The Logic of Two-Level Games', 42 *Int'l Org* 427, 461 (1988).

[115] Elana Wilson Rowe, 'Analyzing Frenemies: An Arctic Repertoire of Cooperation and Rivaly', 76 *Pol Geo* 2 (2020).

[116] The North American Aerospace Defense Command (NORAD) is a US–Canada binational organisation created to detect, validate, and warn of aircraft, missile space vehicle, or maritime attack against North America. North American Aerospace Defense Command, www.norad.mil/About-NORAD. NORAD is commanded by USNORTHCOM, headquartered at Peterson Space Force Base in Colorado Springs, Colo. See 'Our Story', US Northern Command, www.northcom.mil/About.

[117] See, eg, Alexander B Gray, 'NATO's Northern Flank Has Too Many Weak Spots', *For Pol'y* (7 August 2023), foreignpolicy.com/2023/08/07/nato-arctic-greenland-svalbard-faroe-islands-defence-russia (signalling deficiencies in NATO's defence strategy in the Arctic and near-Arctic).

[118] Bathymetric studies of the topography of the ocean floor between Greenland and Iceland, and Iceland and the UK, reveal prominent rises. These rises constrict the width and raise the depth of the ocean floor of submarine traffic pathways leading to and from the Kola Peninsula, the home base of Russia's Northern Fleet. As a result, the GIUK Gap (an acronym for Greenland, Iceland, UK) presents a main strategic concern for anti-submarine warfare and monitoring for both NATO and Russia. See Gonzalo Vázquez, 'NATO Should Mind the Gap', Ctr for Mar. Strategy (28 March 2023), centerformaritimestrategy.org/publications/nato-should-mind-the-gap. NATO strategists also concentrate on the imaginary line connecting the southern tip of Svalbard to North Cape and separated by Bear Island (the Bear Gap). Russian submarines departing from their main base in Severomorsk encounter this area before reaching the GIUK Gap. See Silje Willassen, 'The Great Power Competition in the North Atlantic', Strategem (15 May 2021), www.stratagem.no/the-great-power-competition-in-the-north-atlantic. Here, 'the shallow Barents Sea meets the deeper Norwegian Sea'. Russia's Bastion Defence strategy seeks to control harder-to-defend (ie, shallower) submarine space east of the imaginary line in order to gain undetected access to deeper North Atlantic waters farther west and south of the line. See Thomas Nilsen, 'Russia Announces Multiple Missiles Towards Bear Gap as US Air Force Bombers Deploy to Norway for First Time', Barents Observer (17 February 2021), thebarentsobserver.com/en/security/2021/02/russia-announces-missile-shootings-towards-bear-gap-us-air-force-bombers-deploy.

[119] See Mark Grdovic and Marius Kristiansen, 'Why USSOCOM Should Develop an Arctic Strategy', *Strategem* (17 January 2022), www.stratagem.no/arctic-strategy.

its own operational procedures[120] and the Special Operations Command has enhanced high latitude operational capabilities.[121]

Scholarly and geographical formulations decline along lines of regional Arctic classifications, for instance, the North American Arctic,[122] the North Pacific Arctic,[123] the European Union Arctic,[124] the Red Arctic,[125] the United States Arctic (Alaska),[126] the Indo-Pacific United States Arctic Strategy Dimension,[127] the Canadian Arctic of the Northwest Passage,[128] the Eurasian Northeast Passage,[129] the Russian Northern Sea Route,[130] or the Asian-Pacific Arctic.[131] Even the European Union has now broadly

[120] See 'Regaining Arctic Dominance – The U.S. Army in the Arctic', Dep't of the Army, 2021, www.army.mil/e2/downloads/rv7/about/2021_army_arctic_strategy.pdf.

[121] See Socnorth (19 September 2023), www.socom.mil/socnorth/Pages/Special-Operations-Command-North-deploys-Special-Operations-Forces-to-the-Arctic-during-Operation-Polar-Dagger.aspx (executing Operation Noble Defender through Operation Polar Dagger).

[122] See eg, John Higginbotham and Jennifer Spence, *The North American Arctic: Energizing Regional Collaboration and Governance* (2018) (combining national and subnational jurisdictions of Greenland, Nunavut, the Northwest Territories, Yukon and Alaska).

[123] See eg, Oran R Young and Jong-Deog Kim eds, *North Pacific Perspectives on the Arctic* (2024).

[124] See eg, The EU in the Arctic, EEAS (2021), europa.eu (detailing day-to-day and strategic interests in the region); Nengye Liu, Elizabeth A Kirk and Tore Henriksen, *The European Union and the Arctic* (2017) (presenting views on the EU's roles in Arctic affairs).

[125] See eg, Elizabeth Buchanan, *Red Arctic: Russian Strategy Under Putin* (2023) (contesting the inevitability of a new Cold War); John McCannon, *Red Arctic: Polar Exploration and the Myth of the North in the Soviet Union, 1932–1939* (1998) (investigating the Stalinist development in the 1930s of its Northern territories).

[126] See eg, Michael J Forsyth, 'Why Alaska and the Arctic are Critical to the National Security of the United States', *Military Rev* 113, 114 (January–February 2018) (describing Alaska as 'the perfect power projection platform for the United States from a military standpoint').

[127] See eg, Rebecca Pincus, 'The Indo-Pacific Dimension in US Arctic Strategy', *J Indo-Pac Affs* (25 October 2021), www.airuniversity.af.edu/JIPA/Display/Article/2820744/the-indo-pacific-dimension-in-us-arctic-strategy; Marisol Maddox and Lyston Lea, 'The Intelligence Community Must Evolve To Meet the Reality of Arctic Change', 13 *Polar Perspectives* (2023) (describing the Arctic as 'a crucial link to U.S. interests in the Indo-Pacific' due to fighter jet deployments).

[128] See eg, Frédéric Lasserre, 'The Geopolitics of the Northwest Passage in an International Relations' Perspective, 170 *Relations internationals* 107 (2017) (contesting the classification of the Northwest Passage as an international strait and the application of the rules of innocent passage but noting cordial relations despite disagreement).

[129] See eg, Jens Petter Nielsen and Edwin Okhuizen eds, *From Northeast Passage to Northern Sea Route: A History of the Waterway North of Eurasia* (2022).

[130] See eg, Jędrzej Górski, 'Northern Sea Route: International Law Perspectives', in *International Collaboration, Economic Development, and Sustainability in the Arctic* 282 (Vasilii Erokhin, Gao Tianming and Zhang Xiuhua eds, 2018) (investigating Russian legitimate interests over control of the Northern Sea Route with the international community's interest in freedom of navigation in international waters).

[131] See eg, Christopher R Rossi, 'The Rotating Wheel: A New Cycle of Pacific Relations in the Emerging Arctic and the Role of the Middle Powers', in *The Global Arctic* (Matthias Finger and Gunnar Rekvig, eds, 2025) (updating Asian middle power perspectives on the Arctic post-Ukraine invasion); Calvin Heng and Eyck Freymann, 'Outsiders Wanting In: Asian States and Arctic Governance', Belfer Center (June 2023), www.belfercenter.org/sites/default/files/files/publication/Heng%20Freymann_Asian%20Arctic%20Observers_FINAL.pdf (discussing strategic interests of Asian countries in the arctic).

characterised Arctic regions as part of 'Europe's geopolitical interests'.[132] With the accession of Sweden and Finland into NATO, one might soon conjecture about the rise of a distinctly Nordic Arctic, a region aligned militarily and ideologically with Western interests but nevertheless capable of sounding a distinctly cultural perspective informed by commingled social democratic traditions and human geographic interconnections. A Nordic Arctic identity within the NATO structure will need to balance the abandonment cost of not fully embracing all that the 32-Member State alliance will demand against the entrapment cost of sacrificing sovereignty to the demands of military defence cooperation.[133]

According to Torbjørn Pedersen, the ability to frame High North security policies (*nordområdene*) around unresolved issues pertaining to a specific geographical point of reference, for instance the Barents region, *nordkalotten*, or fisheries jurisdiction, has served a useful purpose.[134] However, the term itself has been 'diluted and stretched in so many directions that it has become' an unhelpful analytical device, loaded more with regional and business development policy objectives than foreign and security policy concerns.[135] A similar problem afflicts the EU, where an inability to disassemble regional complexities results in an incoherent external policy based on a multitude of dispersed opinions.[136] Reframing intramural Nordic relations and also those relations with NATO (given its interest in joint and/or unrestricted access to host nations), will present even greater regional identity challenges. These challenges will more broadly implicate the Northern European security architecture. Rather than subdividing the analysis of Northern Europe's security structure, Matti Pesu argued in favour of a holistic approach, given the seamless interconnections and overlapping interests of the frontline countries (the Baltic states, Poland, and Finland, less so Norway), the hub nations (Sweden, Norway, Denmark), the security providers (Germany, UK) and the security guarantor (US).[137]

[132] Josep Borrell, 'The Arctic, A Key Region for the EU and Global Security', EU (3 February 2021), www.eeas.europa.eu/eeas/arctic-key-region-eu-and-global-security-0_en. See also Julien Lebel and Annika E Nilsson, 'EU Engagement in the Arctic: Challenges to Achieving Ambitions in an Area outside its Jurisdiction', 15 *Arctic Rev L&P* 47, 50 (2024) (noting the EU's European Green Deal engagement with the Arctic and its 'more assertive strategy result[ing] in broader coverage of its Arctic policy, including security issues').

[133] See Joel Linnainmäki, 'An Alliance of Strategic Divergencies: Contextualizing Northern Europe and Finland in Nato Decision-making, in Nato's New Northern Direction: The Evolving Role of the Alliance in Europe's North', *Finnish For Pol'y Paper* 11, at 28 (Matti Pesu ed, 2024) (discussing alliance dilemma).

[134] See Torbjørn Pedersen and Odd Gunnar Skagestad, 'Norway's Flawed Nordområdene Policy', in *Norway's Arctic Policy: Geopolitics, Security and Identity in the High North* 55, 60 (Andreas Østhagen ed, 2023).

[135] ibid.

[136] See generally Andreas Østhagen, 'The New Geopolitics of the Arctic: Russia, China and the EU', 18 *European View* 259 (2019) (criticising the EU's ability to communicate a long-term geopolitical strategy of engagement).

[137] Matti Pesu, 'NATO in the North: The Emerging Division of Labour in Northern European Security', FIAA Briefing Paper 370 (2023). Pesu acknowledged that the countries of 'Northern

POLYSEMOUS MEANINGS OF THE ARCTIC

International lawyers subdivide the Arctic into rule-oriented regimes relating to fisheries or jurisdictions. And then there are the bilateral Arctic frameworks, for instance between Russia and Alaska in the Bering Strait (the Arctic's only gateway to the North Pacific),[138] and between Norway and Russia in the Barents Sea.[139]

Soft law fora frame the Arctic around the Arctic Council, the commercial spheres of influence or quasi-legal consultative contributions of its Permanent Participants, Observer Non-Arctic states, intergovernmental and parliamentary organisations, or agenda-setting initiatives of non-governmental conferencing organisations such as Arctic Frontiers or the Arctic Circle Assembly.[140] Following Russia's invasion of Ukraine in 2022 and the accession of Finland and Sweden to NATO, the Arctic Council began to rebrand itself as the Arctic Seven,[141] adding another level to the structure of the Arctic Council and its core component, the Arctic Five.

The number of *Großräume* may also depend on the polysemous meanings of the Arctic. A common definition of the Arctic refers to the geospace above the Arctic Circle (approximately 66°33'N).[142] This land and sea area constitutes about 4.1 per cent of the Earth's surface, or about 8.14 million square miles.[143] Included in this area is the predominant feature, the Arctic Ocean, which covers

Europe are indeed distinctive .... However, the respective security situations of the Baltic Sea region, the European Arctic and the North Sea are also intimately interconnected [and that Russia] has not political constraints in dealing with the region as one strategic entity.' ibid at 5.

[138] See eg, Betsy Baker, 'Beyond the Northern Sea Route: Enhancing Russian-United States Cooperation in the Bering Strait Region', Polar Perspectives No. 8, at 3 (November 2021), www.wilsoncenter.org/sites/default/files/media/uploads/documents/Polar%20Perspectives%20No.%208_Beyond%20the%20Northern%20Sea%20Route.pdf (detailing Russian–US bilateral cooperation in the Bering Strait Region, noting as well that the Strait is merely 47nm wide (87 km) at its narrowest point and separates the US and Russia by 2 nm (3.7 km) between Little Diomede and Big Diomede islands).

[139] See eg, Pertti Joenniemi, 'The Barents Euro-Arctic Council', in *Subregional Cooperation in the New Europe: Building Security, Prosperity and Solidarity from the Barents to the Black Sea* 23–45 (Andrew Cottey ed, 1999) (discussing the post-Cold War flexible arrangements in Europe's High North).

[140] See generally Beate Steinveg, *Arctic Governance Through Conferencing: Actors, Agendas and Arenas* (2023) (investigating the function of conferencing organisations within the structures of Arctic governance).

[141] See Joint Statement by the Arctic 7 on the Limited Resumption of Arctic Council Cooperation – Without Russia!, Arctic Portal (9 June 2022), arcticportal.org/ap-library/news/2855-joint-statement-by-the-arctic-7-on-the-limited-resumption-of-arctic-council-cooperation-without-russia; Trine Jonassen, 'The Arctic Council: The Arctic 7 Resume Limited Work Without Russia', High North News (8 June 2022), www.highnorthnews.com/en/arctic-council-arctic-7-resume-limited-work-without-russia.

[142] Caitlin Dempsey, 'Arctic Circle', Geographyrealm (2022), www.geographyrealm.com/arctic-circle.

[143] See 'Changes in the Arctic: Background and Issues for Congress, Congressional Research Service' 1 (updated 5 July 2023), sgp.fas.org/crs/misc/R41153.pdf (reporting estimates of the Arctic polar region provided by the Geography and Map Division of the United States Library of Congress, and the National Geodetic Survey of the National Oceanic and Atmospheric Administration (NOAA)).

an area of about 6.01 million square miles, or about 4.3 per cent of the Earth's ocean area.[144]

The Arctic Council, unlike the functional foci of its Working Groups, eschews a geographic definition of the Arctic. Its biodiversity Working Group (CAFF) extends the definitional purview of the Arctic to six per cent of the Earth's surface.[145] The Arctic Monitoring and Assessment Program (AMAP), another of the six Working Groups of the Arctic Council, extends the High Arctic to include the sub-Arctic areas of Canada, Denmark (via Greenland and the Faroe Islands), Finland, Iceland, Norway, the Russian Federation, Sweden, the United States and associated marine areas. The AMAP's configuration of its circumpolar region includes northern seas that extend as far south as 51.1°N (James Bay, Canada) to better frame a geographical region 'intimately connected' to global environmental and pollution monitoring systems.[146] The United States defines the Arctic as the area above the Arctic Circle and including adjacent marine areas in the Arctic Ocean and the Beaufort, Bering, and Chukchi Seas.[147]

Certainly, a military mindset frames the Arctic around operational coordinates and set parameters. Generic definitions of the Arctic vary and depend on the mindset.[148] The common mindset may be less exacting, even sentimental, or focused on the politics of industrial development and resource extraction in the High North.[149]

Although diverse, all understandings of the Arctic tend to revolve around two common denominators, the Arctic Ocean and the Arctic Circle. Even here, there is variance. The position of the Arctic Circle hinges on the Earth's axial tilt, which fluctuates due to tidal influences and lunar orbit. Accordingly, the geographic position of the Arctic Circle is not fixed.[150] Meteorologists employ a climate-based definition that measures the 10°C average isothermic temperature line in July.[151] Oceanographers and hydrologists make distinctions based on fluid dynamics, patterns of marine circulation, and variances of permanent,

[144] ibid.

[145] CAFF (Conservation of Arctic Flora and Fauna) Arctic Biodiversity Report, Arctic Circle 2014, YouTube (time mark: 1:04), www.youtube.com/watch?v=MCXtLxIzqwE.

[146] Geographical Coverage, AMAP, www.amap.no/about/geographical-coverage (last accessed 15 November 2023).

[147] Arctic Research and Policy Act, 15 USC Ch 67 § 4111 (1984). Additionally, the Act claims the Arctic 'means US and foreign territory north of the Arctic Circle and all US territory north and west of the boundary formed by the Porcupine, Yukon, and Kuskokwim Rivers; all contiguous seas, including the Arctic Ocean and the Beaufort, Bering and Chukchi Seas, and the Aleutian Island chain.' Pub L 117–263, div E, title LIX, § 112, 31 July 1984, 98 Stat 1248.

[148] See 'What is the Arctic?', Barents Watch (1 October 2015) (noting the remark of Norwegian Polar institute advisor, Ellen Øseth), www.barentswatch.no/en/articles/what-is-the-arctic.

[149] See generally Hanna Lempinen and Marjo Lindroth, 'Fear and Hoping in the Arctic: Charting the Emotional Fabric of Resource Extraction', 8 *Extractive Industries & Soc'y* 100872 (2021) (noting the sidelined affective dimension of natural resource development in Greenland and the emotions involved with Arctic exploitation).

[150] See Changes in the Arctic, n 143, at 1 fn 2.

[151] See Paolo D'Odorico et al, 'Vegetation-Microclimate Feedbacks in Woodland-Grassland Ecotones', 22 *Global Ecol & Biogeography* 364 (2013).

seasonal, and marginal ice zones.[152] Although the smallest of the world oceans, the Arctic Ocean currents and water masses extend globally through a process of fluid mechanics or advective flows.[153] Advection makes the perimeters of the Arctic Ocean more blobular than circular. Environmentalists demarcate the Arctic as the sinuous boundary between tundra and boreal forest (the northern limit of tree growth) or as based on other vegetation or environmental determinants such as permafrost.[154] Indigenous peoples have 'their own mapping tools to narrate' the surrounding Arctic landscape, many of which have been impacted by colonisation, or as Schmitt might add, European cartographic technique.[155]

And then there is the notional idea of the 'political Arctic', which may decline around High, Low, and Subarctic separations,[156] and involve geopolitical interests and governance usages.[157] This idea would uniquely shape any Schmittian notion of the Arctic, with a sensitivity attached to the historical engagement of land and sea powers.[158]

Mindful of these variances, consider Russia's understanding of the Arctic – or its commanding geographic presence and control over its Arctic. Russia's Arctic coastline (the Arctic Zone of the Russian Federation) covers five million square kilometres and stretches over 24,140 kilometres,[159] or 53 per cent of the

[152] See eg, Samuel Brenner et al, 'The Evolution of a Shallow Front in the Arctic Marginal Ice Zone', 8 *Elem Sci Anth* 1 (2020) (discussing variability and Arctic ice zones).

[153] See Bert Rudels and Edy Carmack, 'Arctic Ocean Water Mass Structure and Circulation', 35 *Oceanography* 52 (2022) (examining the structure of the Arctic Ocean and the hydrological cycle of poleward water flow).

[154] See Arctic Tree Line, Polarpedia, polarpedia.eu/en/arctic-tree-line/ (last accessed 14 October 2023). Woodlike vegetation does not exist in the High Arctic, although non-contiguous flower plants, grass, sedges, moss, and lichen distinctions can grow. See generally 'What Is the Arctic?', BarentsWatch (21 January 2016), www.barentswatch.no/en/articles/Hva-er-Arktis. For graphic and scientific depictions of the perimeter of the Arctic Ocean and its sub-divisions, see generally 'Limits of Oceans and Seas' 189–215 (Draft 4th edn International Hydrographic Bureau, 1986), www.iho.int/mtg_docs/com_wg/S-23WG/S-23WG_Misc/Draft_1986/S-23_Draft_1986_Headings.pdf.

[155] Apostolos Tsiouvalas and Jan Jakub Solski, 'One Map to Rule Them All?' Revisiting Legalities Through Cartographic Representations of the Northwest Passage, 54 *Ocean Dev & Int'l L.* 93, 396 (2023). See also Apostolos Tsiouvalas, 'Law of the Sea in the Kinocene: Lessons from the Piniatorsuaq' (doctoral dissertation, UiT NCLOS, forthcoming) (mapping the spatial views of the seldom seen 'Great Hunters' of the Inughuit communities of Avanersuaq, Northwest Greenland, seldom seen because they are mostly out hunting on the ocean); Dalee Sambo Dorough, 'Our homeland: Arctic Indigenous Peoples' Perspectives on Non-Arctic States', in *Emerging Legal Orders in the Arctic: The Role of Non-Arctic Actors* 69, 88 (Akiho Shibata et al, eds, 2019) [hereinafter *Emerging Legal Orders in the Arctic*] (noting advances by Indigenous diplomats in Arctic discussions but recognising the need for recognition among non-Arctic communities of Indigenous conceptualisations for emerging Arctic legal orders); Thora Martina Herrmann and Thibault Martin eds, *Indigenous Peoples' Governance of Land and Protected Territories in the Arctic* (2016) (exploring perspectives on Indigenous knowledge and land governance practices in the Arctic).

[156] See generally 'What Is the Arctic?', n 154.

[157] Alf Håkon Hoel, 'Do We Need a New Legal Regime for the Arctic Ocean?' 24 *Int'l J Marine & Coastal L* 443, 444 (2009).

[158] See generally Carl Schmitt, (2015) [1942].

[159] Russia Facts / Figures, The Arctic Inst. (1 August 2022), www.thearcticinstitute.org/country-backgrounders/russia; Michael Paul and Göran Swistek, 'Russia in the Arctic: Development Plans, Military Potential, and Conflict Prevention', SWP Research Paper 3, at 7 (February 2022).

Arctic Ocean coastline. It covers the Barents Sea, the Kara Sea, the Laptev Sea, and the East Siberian Sea. It includes three major river systems – the Yenisei (Ienissei) River, which discharges into the Kara Sea; the Léna River, which empties in the Laptev Sea; and the Kolyma River, which debouches into the East Siberian Sea.

Four million people live in the Arctic and 2.5 million are Russian citizens, including 40 Indigenous peoples.[160] These peoples spread across the entire continental tier of North Russia, from the Vepsians of the Leningrad Oblast, to the 13 peoples living across the Central Siberian outstretches of the Krasnoyarsk and Sakha (Yakutia) regions, to the Aleuts and Chukchi of the Chukotka Autonomous Okrug and the Kamchatka Krai regions of Russia's Far Eastern Federal District.[161]

These peoples also spread across the 60 per cent of Russian territory covered by permafrost,[162] land that holds a tremendous amount of carbon 'locked up … as frozen organic matter'.[163] Worldwide estimates suggest that permafrost contains 800 gigatons of frozen carbon, 'roughly twice the amount … presently held in the atmosphere'.[164] As permafrost melts, carbon releases into the atmosphere, abetting higher concentrations of greenhouse gasses emitted through the burning of fossil fuels. This compounding effect of atmospheric carbon loading speeds up permafrost melting and creates a loop that physical geographers call permafrost carbon feedback.[165] Exacerbated by methane release, it presents a scenario for 'disaster',[166] a scenario with human geographic and geopolitical implications for Russia and well beyond.

This unfreezing tundra also entombs tremendous wealth. The Arctic accounts upwards to 15 per cent of Russia's GDP, 20 per cent of its exports, including 80 per cent of its gas and 17 per cent of its oil exports,[167] and 73 per cent of the Arctic's total economic activity.[168] Shortly after Russia's 2014 annexation of Crimea, in an announcement tinged with menace, Russia's

[160] The Russian Federation, Arctic Council, arctic-council.org/about/states/russian-federation.

[161] See Interactive Map, Association of Indigenous Peoples of the North, Siberia and the Far East, RAIPON, raipon.info (mapping the ethnographic distribution of Russia's Indigenous peoples of the North).

[162] Permafrost is any type of ground that has been frozen continuously for a minimum of two years. In the northern hemisphere, permafrost covers territory the size of the US, Canada, and China combined, although 'that footprint is rapidly shrinking'. 'Permafrost: Everything You Need to Know', NRDC (26 June 2018), www.nrdc.org/stories/permafrost-everything-you-need-know#sec-whatis. See also Atle Staalesen, 'More than 60% of Russian Territory is Permafrost. Now it is Melting', *Barents Observer* (14 May 2021), thebarentsobserver.com/en/climate-crisis/2021/05/more-60-russian-territory-permafrost-now-it-melting.

[163] Mark C Serreze, *Brave New Arctic: The Untold Story of the Melting North* 217 (2018).

[164] ibid at 218.

[165] ibid at 219.

[166] ibid.

[167] Nivedita Kapoor, 'Russia and the Future of the Arctic', ORF Occasional Paper No 336 (October 2021), www.orfonline.org/wp-content/uploads/2021/10/ORF_OccasionalPaper_336_Russia-Arctic.pdf.

[168] Lassi Heininen, Heather Exner-Pirot and Justin Barnes, 'Introduction – The Russian Arctic: Economic, Politics & Peoples,' *Arctic YB* 2023, arcticyearbook.com/arctic-yearbook/2022/52-yearbook/

deputy prime minister tweeted that 'the Arctic is a Russian Mecca'.[169] Although prone to hyperbole,[170] his announcement contained more than bluster. Russia's propinquity to the pole, together with its historical, economic, and emotional attachments to the region, have the clear markings of a *Großraum*.

2022-the-russian-arctic-economics-politics-peoples/451-introduction-the-russian-arctic-economic-politics-peoples.

[169] Dmitry Rogozin (@Rogozin) 19 April 2015.

[170] See Mike Wall, 'Russian Space Officials jettison the Bluster After Rogozin's Departure', Space.com (6 October 2022), www.space.com/russia-space-officials-tone-down-rhetoric (noting Rogozin's 'ramped up' 'combative statements' and 'famous bluster').

Chapter Four

Terra Nullius, *Arctic Exceptionalism, and the* Jus Publicum Arcticus

SITUATING THE IDEA of *Großraum* within its plurality of meanings necessitates a sensitivity to spatiality, which can be defined as 'the processual surface on which social phenomena interact'.[1] A continuum of natural philosophy from Lucretius (c 99 BCE) to Isaac Newton (1643–1727) viewed space as an objective void, a curious nothingness that nevertheless existed.[2] To Newton, space, like place, represented a physical feature. However, it was a physical feature of immovable hollowness, an objective fact, that had to exist in order to frame the relationship between particles.[3] In terms of sovereignty, this physical void attached to the idea of a no man's land – *terra nullius*. This was the *vacuum domicilium* that awaited possession by a sovereign imbued with recognised power or legal capacity to move into *unoccupied* space.[4]

International law has developed a number of factual frameworks to establish title to territorial vacuums. In the famous *Island of Palmas case* (1928), title to territory was based on 'an act of effective apprehension', such as occupation, conquest, or some tacit form of cession.[5] Sovereignty can also be asserted in terms of historical claims. In such cases, the claimant state must show an uninterrupted and public or notorious display of state authority as measured over a long period of time. Such acts constitute *à titre de souverain*, which means that

[1] Christopher R Rossi, *Remoteness Reconsidered: The Atacama Desert and International Law* 8 (2021).

[2] See Lucretius, *De Rerum Natura* (William Ellery Leonard trans, 1921); Isaac Newton, *Principia* 77 (Andrew Motte trans., 1846).

[3] See Newton, n 2, at 77 ('Absolute space in its own nature, without regard to anything external, remains always similar and immovable'). The 17th- and early-18th-century German polymath, Gottfried Wilhelm Leibniz famously contested this Newtonian view and modelled spatial studies around the idea of a continuum and a realm of inhabitance, which carried forth in the 20th century through writings of Henrì Lefebvre, Andreas Philippopoulos-Mihalopoulos and others. See Andreas Philippopoulos-Mihalopoulos, 'Spatial Justice in a World of Violence', in *Spaces of Justice, Peripheries, Passages, Appropriations* 9 (Chris Butler and Edward Mussawir eds, 2017).

[4] David Armitage, *The Ideological Origins of the British Empire* 97 (2000) (noting 'From the 1620s to the 1680s in Britain, and then in North America, Australia and Africa well into the nineteenth century, the argument from vacancy (*vacuum domicilium*) or absence of ownership (*terra nullius*) became a standard foundation for English and later, British dispossession of [I]ndigenous [P]eoples.').

[5] *Island of Palmas Case* (Netherlands/USA), II RIAA 839 (1928).

the title holder has exercised the functions of state authority on behalf of its own authority. Of course, if something is already owned, there is nothing left to claim. This rationale seems to inform international lawyers who are gearing up for debates about overlapping Arctic spaces relating to extended continental shelves. They eschew assertions of ownership as *claimants* because Article 76 of the United Nations Law of the Sea Convention details that these spaces already belong to the coastal states that can show dispositive evidence that the geomorphology of the continental shelf pertains to their land masses. To stake a claim harbours a degree of uncertainty as it can potentially beget a counterclaim. To negate that uncertainty, foreign ministry lawyers reject the usage of the term. Assertions of ownership are meant to seize the high legal ground and dispossess all others of good title. Owners need not stake claims to territory they already own.

THE DISCOVERY DOCTRINE

From modernity's perspective, unoccupied space crudely preoccupied the late-fifteenth-century European mindset given the *discovery* of the New World and the immediate encounter with aborigines. This discovery set off the threshold European debate of the sixteenth century between reason and faith: by what right could papal hierocratic authority occupy the newly discovered territories and command universal temporal authority over their peoples?[6] The conflict sparked a seminal debate among the Spanish Scholastics over the basis of papal temporal authority and served as a nodal point in natural law's centuries-long turn to natural rights.[7] The debate began to interrupt the association of original

[6] See Anthony Pagden, *The Fall of Natural Man: The American Indian and the Origins of Comparative Ethnology* 27 (1982) (noting: 'by what right had the crown of Castile occupied and enslaved the inhabitants of territories to which it could make no prior claims based on history?'). The debate catapulted the Dominican friar, Francisco de Vitoria, to the forefront of natural law's turn toward natural rights theory. Drawing from Roman law and Canon law, he lectured between 1537 and 1539: 'Now the rule of the law of nations is that what belongs to nobody is granted to the first occupant, as is expressly laid down in … the Institutes. And so, as the object in question was not without an owner, it does not fall under the title which we are discussing …. in and by itself [this title] gives no support to a seizure of the aboriginies any more than if [they] had discovered us.' Francisco de Vitoria, *De Indis et de Iure Belli Relectiones* 139 (intro Ernest Nys; trans John Pawley Bate (1917)).

[7] See Christopher R Rossi, *Broken Chain of Being: James Brown Scott and the Origins of Modern International Law* 120 (1998) (discussing the juridical reconstruction of the idea of natural law initiated by the Spanish scholastics). See also Francisco de Victoria, *De Indis et de ivre Belli Relectiones* (1557); Bartolomé de las Casas, *Brevísima relación de la destruición de las Indias* (1542); Bartolomé de las Casas, *Historia de las Indias*, posthumously published in 1875. The debate continues. See, eg, Antony Anghie, *Imperialism, Sovereignty and the Making of International Law* (2012); Martti Koskenniemi, 'Colonization of the "Indies": The Origin of International Law?', in *La idea de América en el pensamiento ius internacionalista del siglo XXI*; *Estudios a propósito de los bicentenarios de las independencies de las repúblicas latinoamericanas* 43 (Y Gamarra Chopo ed, 2010); Ignacio de la Rasilla del Moral, *In the Shadow of Vitoria: A History of International Law in Spain, 1770–1953* (2017); Liliana Obregón, 'Between Civilization and Barbarism: Creole Interventions in International Law', 27 *Third World Q* 815 (2006).

title with the concept of *terra nullius*, an association that in combination functioned as the basis for the traditional law of territory and as the unilateral justification for European colonisation.[8]

According to Kathryn Milun, the sovereign – in this case the Crown of Castile – negated Indigenous identities and translated Indigenous space into empty space. This translation informed 'an epistemic imaginary in the international law of the global commons'.[9] This imaginary conflated the meanings of *terra nullius* (no man's land) and *res nullius* (a thing that belongs to nobody) to project metaphors of vacant, empty space in fulfilment of twin Western colonial aims, namely: securing sovereignty, and dispossessing Indigenous peoples of title to the territory that they had occupied for millennia.[10] In several notorious juridical expressions, which developed from Lockean political theory and embraced in United States constitutional history, this rationale of Europe's inherent right of priority to such space drew from the application of the discovery doctrine.

In the 1823 ruling of *Johnson v M'Intosh*, United States Supreme Court Chief Justice John Marshall (1755–1835), often regarded as the most revered jurist in United States history, imparted dispositive importance to the discovery doctrine: It 'gave exclusive title *to those who made it*'.[11] Even Marshall sensed the absurdity of applying the discovery doctrine to an inhabited land. He labelled it an 'extravagant pretension', but one that could not be undone without attacking the very foundation of the United States.[12] His construction denominated Natives (specifically the people of the Cherokee Nation in what is now the State of Georgia) as tenants-at-will or 'domestic dependent[s]'.[13] It ascribed to them the character of infants in need of European guardianship,[14] and powerfully influenced the idea that settler nations owned the underlying title to tribal land.[15] In the spatial imaginary of the European descendants, Indigenous space

[8] Sookyeon Huh, 'Title to Territory in the Post-Colonial Era: Original Title and Terra Nullius in the ICJ Judgments on Cases Concerning Ligitan/Sipadan (2002) and Pedra Branca (2008)', 26 *Eur J Int'l L* 709 (2015).

[9] Kathryn Milun, *The Political Uncommons: The Cross-Cultural Logic of the Global Commons* 2 (2011).

[10] See ibid at 8 (2011).

[11] *Johnson v M'Intosh*, 21 US (8 Wheat). 543 (1823) (CJ Marshall) (meaning the European discoverers of the New World).

[12] ibid at 591. See also Christopher R Rossi, 'The Extravagant Pretension: Schmitt, Vitoria, the Discovery Doctrine, and the Trail of Tears', in *Francisco de Vitoria and the Shadow of Carl Schmitt in International Law: Crossroads in History and Political Theology* (José María Beneyto and Ignacio de la Rasilla eds, forthcoming).

[13] *Cherokee Nation v Georgia*, 30 US (5 Pet) 1, at 17 (1831) (CJ Marshall).

[14] See Christopher R Rossi, 'The Blind Eye: Jus Soli, and the "Pretended" Treaty of New Echota', 9 *Am Indian LJ* 402, 410 (2021) (discussing Marshall's characterisation of the Cherokee Nation as a 'domestic dependent' nation in need of tutelage and guardianship) [hereinafter Rossi, 'The Blind Eye']. In *Cherokee Nation v Georgia*, 30 US (5 Pet) 1 (1831), Marshall similarly reasoned for the Court that the Cherokee were not a foreign nation within the meaning of the US Constitution; they were 'something different'. ibid at 62. '[T]hey are in a state of pupilage. Their relations to the United States resemble that of a ward to his guardian.' ibid at 17.

[15] See ibid at 425 fn 169 (citing Felix Cohen's *Handbook of Federal Indian Law*).

was *pre-owned* by those who would come later to make (improve) it. Indigeneity conveyed merely a placeholder status. Marshall cited Locke, Grotius, Vattel, and Montequieu in support of the rational connection between Enlightenment values, Christianity, and civilisation:

> All the proprietary rights of civilized nations … are founded on this [discovery] principle. The right derived from discovery and conquest, can rest on no other basis, and all existing titles depend on the fundamental title of the occupancy of the natives, who were heathens, and, at the same time, admitting the prior title of any Christian people who may have made a previous discovery.[16]

This dispossession of Native interests could only be accomplished in the Western mindset by turning a blind eye to two ordering principles relating to nationality and citizenship. States developed such exclusionary principles after the modern principle of sovereignty began to take shape,[17] but they created anomalies too problematic to overcome in circumstances of Indigeneity. Consequently, they were simply ignored.[18]

The first principle was *jus soli*, which assigned nationality to a person born to the soil. The factor connecting citizenship to nationhood is the geographical place where the person is born, not the citizenship status of the parents.[19] The principle grew out of the early modern expression that based personal claims

[16] *Johnson v M'Intosh*, n 11, at 570 (citing Locke et al), and 576–77 ('heathens').

[17] The origins of citizenship have been well discussed in terms of ancient Greece and the centuries-long separation of religion from politics followed by the revolutionary Rights of Man period. The modern process referenced here relates to the 18th-century developments relating to the closing of frontier space in the Americas. For an excellent presentation of essays on the rise of the idea, see generally Richard Bellamy and Madeleine Kennedy-Macfoy, eds, *Citizenship* (2014).

[18] Marshall's reasoning in *Johnson v M'Intosh* created unanticipated problems of federalism. In *M'Intosh*, Marshall justified the discovery doctrine on the basis of title to territory that passed uninterrupted from the crown to the colonists. See *Johnson v M'Intosh*, 21 US (8 Wheat) at 570. In *State v George Tassel*, 1 Ga Rep Ann 478, 1 Dud 229 (1830), a Cherokee national named Corn Tassel, who had been accused of murdering another Cherokee in Cherokee Territory, argued that he could not be tried by the state court of Georgia. He obtained a writ in error granted by the United States Supreme Court, which the State of Georgia ignored, thereby executing Corn Tassel and marking a clear challenge to the United States Constitution's Supremacy Clause. The State of Georgia later boldly interpreted Marshall's reasoning in *M'Intosh* to mean that sovereign title passed to the states, not to the federal Government. This interpretation set up the Marshall Court's reconsideration of the discovery doctrine rationale in *Worcester* 31 US (6 Pet) 515 (1832), where the judgment asserted the sovereignty of Native American nations as separate from the US and 'completely separated from that of the states', ibid at 519. The Court held that the Cherokee Nation consisted of 'a distinct community occupying its own territory … in which the laws of Georgia can have no force', ibid at 561. Although construed as a victory for Indigenous rights, the underlying rationale perhaps had more to do with Antebellum struggles with federalism than with Native sovereignty and self-determination interests. See Guy C Charlton, 'Aboriginal Rights and Constitutional Conflict: The Marshall Court, State and Federal Sovereignty, and Native American Rights under the 1789 Constitution', 8 *Am Indian LJ* 149, 150 (2019).

[19] See, eg, the citizenship clause of the 14th Amendment to the United States Constitution ('All persons born … in the United States and subject to the jurisdiction thereof [which excludes children born to foreign diplomats] are citizens of the United States').

to land and inheritance on birthright connections to the sovereign domain.[20] A second principle, *jus sanguinis*, established nationality based on the nationality of the parents, usually the mother, through the bloodline relationship, not on the geographical place where the person is born. *Jus sanguinis* predominated throughout Europe due to the continent's more restrictive immigration practices,[21] which were influenced by definitions of race, ethnicity, and nationhood.[22] State practice in the Americas favoured *jus soli*, as it does today,[23] because it stimulated immigration and attracted population to abet territorial acquisition and expansion.[24] Neither principle, however, applied to Indigenous peoples. The dogmatic assertion of the discovery doctrine, based on conquest and the Christian entitlement to 'fill the earth and subdue it',[25] supported the proposition that the right of soil belonged to the *proper* inheritors of New World title, the beneficiaries of a metropolitan chain of title to empty space, which declined unassumingly to the progeny of the Christian Europeans themselves.[26] 'Their bloodline carried with it the pedigree, the permission, the capital, the charters, the subordinates, and the slaves to dominate' new space.[27] It supported also a 'blood-based elitism that spread an enduring pigmentocracy' across newly discovered territory.[28]

A report of the 1822 United States Indian Commission concluded that 'The right of soil, or the absolute property, belong[ed] to the Sovereign, or State under whose authority the discovery and settlement were made' and that aboriginal land was based on 'qualified' occupancy with 'no power to convey'.[29] In Lockean terms:

[20] *Calvin's Case* (1608) 77 ER 377, 394 (KB) (establishing in common law the *jus soli* (birthright citizenship) principle.

[21] Patrick Weil, 'Access to Citizenship: A Comparison of Twenty-Five Nationality Laws', in *Citizenship Today: Global Perspectives and Practices* 18, 19 (T Alexander Aleinikoff and Douglas Klusmeyer eds, 2001).

[22] See Christian Joppke, 'Citizenship between De- and Re-Ethnicization', 44 *Archives Européennes de Sociologie*, 429, 436 (2003).

[23] The second Trump administration promised to override the 14th Amendment citizenship clause through executive order, a bid likely to raise constitutional challenges. See Cody Wofsy and Hannah Schoen Steinberg, 'Trump's Remarks on Birthright Citizenship, Explained', ACLU (13 December 2024), www.aclu.org/news/immigrants-rights/trumps-remarks-on-birthright-citizenship-explained.

[24] In the context of US history, the citizenship clause was also specifically enacted following the Civil War to guarantee equal civil and political rights to formerly enslaved people. See *14th Amendment to the U.S. Constitution: Civil Rights (1868)*, Milestone Documents, National Archives, www.archives.gov/milestone-documents/14th-amendment#:~:text=No%20State%20shall%20make%20or,equal%20protection%20of%20the%20laws.

[25] *Genesis* 1:28 (New King James Version).

[26] See Rossi, 'The Blind Eye', n 14, at 426 and 432.

[27] ibid at 407.

[28] ibid.

[29] See Christopher R Rossi, *The Widening Gyre: Legal Formalism and International Law's Sense of Place*, 11 *Notre Dame J Int'l & Comp L* 107, 135 (2021) (quoting the 1822 *Report to the Secretary of War of the United States on Indian Affairs*).

> God, who hath given the world to men in common, hath also given them reason to make use of it the best advantage of life .... The Fruit, or venison, which nourishes the wild Indian, who knows no enclosure ... is still a tenant in common ...[30]

Schmitt advanced this notion with his emphasis on the telluric implications of land appropriation, which made land divisible, enclosable, and ownable, and the foundation of state-sovereignty.[31] The fundamental disjunction in the settler mindset, most pronounced in the United States, did not view Indigenous peoples as 'citizens to begin with even as sovereignty was claimed over them'.[32] They were 'not of the soil or the bloodline in the same way the European presentations of *jus soli* or *jus sanguinis* claimed to be. A nebulous category had to be constructed for them – domestic dependents.'[33]

In the New World of the Arctic, which began to entice European interest in the sixteenth century, the domiciled status of the Inuit and Métis of the Arctic archipelagos north of mainland Canada, the Unangax̂ and Aleut of the Aleutian Islands, and the Nenets of Novaya Zemlya mattered as much legally in the age of conquest as the historically uninhabited archipelagos of Severnaya Zemlya, Franz Josef Land, Spitzbergen and other uninhabited outcroppings large and small.[34] The discovery doctrine amounted to constructive and relatively uncontested ownership due to the general understanding of the Arctic as empty space.[35] This general understanding broadened into a political representation of particular national interests.[36] The commonsense physical features of geography transposed into social, economic, and legal considerations that shaped questions of political identity regardless of the interests of Indigenous peoples.[37] In Lockean terms, unbounded space presented a physical form of the mind's *tabula rasa* (blank slate), which could be filled in with proprietary appropriations secured through imaginary enclosures and cultivation.[38] In Schmittian

[30] See John Locke, *Second Treatise of Government*, ch V §26 (1690), www.gutenberg.org/cache/epub/7370/pg7370-images.html#CHAPTER_II.

[31] See Carl Schmitt, *Theory of the Partisan* 21 (2007) (discussing the important relationship between the telluric character of land and the 'autochthonous population').

[32] Kunal M Parker, *Making Foreigners: Immigration and Citizenship Law in America, 1600–2000*, 61 (2015).

[33] Rossi, 'The Blind Eye', n 14, at 410 ('nebulous'); *Cherokee Nation v Georgia*, 30 US (5 Pet), at 17 (referring to Natives as 'domestic dependent nations').

[34] For instance, the Strathcona Islands, Lavoie Islands.

[35] See S James Anaya, *Indigenous Peoples in International Law* 4 (1996) (noting due to relative isolation that 'Some indigenous groups [including Arctic Peoples] were not severely affected, if at all, by colonisation or its legacies until well into [the twentieth] century').

[36] Sybille Reinke de Buitrago, 'Risk Representations and Confrontational Actions in the Arctic', 12 *J Strat Stud* 13, 15 (2019).

[37] See John A Agnew and Luca Muscarà, *Making Political Geography* 1, (2nd edn, 2012).

[38] See John Locke, 'An Essay Concerning Human Understanding in Four Books', bk II, ch 1 (1690), www.gutenberg.org/files/10615/10615-h/10615-h.htm#chap2.01 (*tabula rasa*: 'Let us then suppose the mind to be, as we say, white paper, void of all characters ... How comes it to be furnished?'); John Locke, *Second Treatise of Government*, n 30, ch V §31 (articulating the labour theory of property, whereby a person is entitled to 'As much as anyone can make use of to any advantage of life before it spoils, so much he may by his labor fix a property in: whatever is beyond this, is more than his share, and belongs to others').

terms, 'the emerging new world did not appear' as presenting new enemies, 'but as *free space*'.[39]

TEMPORARY FREE SPACE, CONDOMINIUM, AND THE EXCEPTIONAL CASE OF SPITZBERGEN

The Arctic provides an interesting historical conception of free space: Spitzbergen.[40] The archipelago, located between 74° and 81°N latitudes had never been settled by humans. Early in the sixteenth century, Dutch East India Company sea rovers, searching for a northeast passage to Cathay (India), spotted pods of bowhead whales off the archipelago's north-west coast. Welsh harpooners called them right whales. They were the *right* whales to catch because they tended to live in shallower coastal waters and were easier to catch than deep-water sperm whales. Right whales were also thickly layered with blubber and fronted by an upper jaw of valuable comb-like baleen filter plates.[41]

By the end of the seventeenth century, flensing and rendering camps sprang up on Spitzbergen at places like Smeerenburg (Blubber Town) and Bellsund. The industry attracted hundreds of whaling ships and upwards of 12,000 men.[42] When whalers developed flensing techniques at sea using a complex system of ropes, pulleys and hooks, the Spitzbergen stock quickly depleted and has never significantly recovered.[43] The whalers then hunted pods all the way across the Greenland Sea, essentially abandoning Spitzbergen to its whaling history. A quiet period followed in the late-eighteenth to mid-nineteenth centuries, allowing Spitzbergen to return to its status as a de facto *terra nullus*,[44] until coal mining operations in 1899 ended once and for all Spitzbergen's province as a no man's land.

Oran Young once framed the Arctic as a 'distinctive region' borne out of a common belief that its sparse population and peripheral location from mainstream issues buffered it from 'political and socioeconomic matters'.[45] Juha

[39] Schmitt, *The* Nomos *of the Earth* 87 (2003).

[40] Spitzbergen is the historical name of the archipelago. It is also the name of the archipelago's largest island, home to its largest settlement, Longyearbyen, and the site of almost all human activity in Svalbard. The Spitzbergen Treaty was signed in 1920. When it came into effect in 1925, the King of Norway proclaimed that the islands shall be renamed Svalbard, an old Norsk name meaning 'cold coast'.

[41] See Christopher R Rossi, '"A Unique International Problem": The Svalbard Treaty, Equal Enjoyment, and Terra Nullius: Lessons of Territorial Temptation from History', 15 *Wash U Glob Stud LR* 93, 114–15 (2016).

[42] ibid at 113.

[43] See Kit M Kovacs et al, 'The Endangered Spitsbergen Bowhead Whales' Secrets Revealed After Hundreds of Years in Hiding', 16 *Biology Letters* (2020), royalsocietypublishing.org/doi/10.1098/rsbl.2020.0148 (noting difficulties preventing recovery of the population).

[44] Rossi, 'A Unique International Problem', n 41, at 118.

[45] Oran R Young, *Arctic Politics: Conflict and Cooperation in the Circumpolar North* 8 (1992).

Käpylä and Harri Mikkola noted romanticised visions of the Arctic due to its 'unique properties of physical, biological and human systems'.[46] A frontier mentality attached to Arctic imaginaries, as a place of 'bountiful resources awaiting exploitation'.[47] The Canadian-American-Icelandic ethnographer and Arctic explorer, Vilhjelmur Stefansson wrote of the 'The North That Never Was', a distortion formed from prejudicial and 'libelous' depictions of everlasting winter, lifeless, barren ground, and an 'eternal silence' that 'exists only in books'.[48] He viewed the 'Far North' as 'a greater frontier than the [American] West ever was'; a land of untapped commercial potential that 'will continue retreating till [colonised] far within the technical Arctic Circle as laid down by the mathematical astronomer and geodesist'.[49] Stefansson's view of the Arctic's commercial potential today seems prescient, far removed from the distorted criticism of Seward's Folly, which decried the United States' 1867 purchase of Alaska from Russia as nothing more than an unusable polar bear garden.[50] He also regarded this polar world as a great space, an '"Arctic Mediterranean", uniting Canada, the United States, and Russia in the same way that the "old World's lesser Mediterranean" had linked Europe, North Africa, and the Middle East'.[51]

P Whitney Lackenbauer and Ryan Dean claimed that scholarly treatments tended to exempt the Arctic from the normal drivers of international affairs and view Arctic exceptionalism as an observation of objective reality.[52] They treated Arctic exceptionalism as a polymorphic series of discursive invocations to explain the behaviours and relationships of actors.[53] As a separate space, Maria Ackren described the Arctic as a region of paradiplomacy, where functional interests of sub-state actors prevailed over competitive sovereign

[46] Juha Käpylä and Harri Mikkola, *On Arctic Exceptionalism: Critical Reflections in the Light of the Arctic Sunrise Case and the Crisis in Ukraine* 5 (2015).

[47] Richard C Powell and Klaus Dodds, 'Polar Geopolitics', in *Polar Geopolitics? Knowledges, Resources and Legal Regimes* 3, 4 (Richard C Powell and Klaus Dodds, eds, 2014).

[48] Vilhjalmur Stefansson, *The Friendly Arctic: The Story of Five Years in Polar Regions* 5 ('everlasting winter'), 7 ('The North That Never Was', 'lifeless'), 16 ('libelous', 'Barren Ground'), 74 ('eternal silence existing only in books') (1921). Stefansson's frontier (noting 'the Eskimos are honest and intelligent, but … they have a higher percentage of unfounded beliefs than any white people with whom I have associated').

[49] ibid at 74. Stefansson was prone to express racial beliefs common of his time and 'people', noting, for instance, that 'the Eskimos are honest and intelligent, but … they have a higher percentage of unfounded beliefs than any white people with whom I have associated.' ibid at 14).

[50] Milton O Gustafson, 'Seward's Bargain: The Alaska Purchase from Russia', 26 *Prologue Magazine, Nat'l Archives* (1994), www.archives.gov/publications/prologue/1994/winter/alaska-check (noting disputes over fair market value of the sale and the myth that the purchase was unpopular with the US public). See also 'U.S. Purchase of Alaska Ridiculed as "Seward's Folly"', *History* (3 March 2010), www.history.com/this-day-in-history/sewards-folly (recounting Republican criticisms of the Alaskan purchase as 'Seward's Folly', 'Seward's Icebox', and President Andrew Johnson's 'polar bear garden').

[51] Stuart, *Creating the National Security State* 15 (2008) (quoting Stefansson's article, 'The Logic of the Air', *Fortune* (April 1943).

[52] P Whitney Lackenbauer and Ryan Dean, 'Arctic Exceptionalism', in *The Arctic and World Order* 327 ('normal drivers), 344 ('objective reality').

[53] ibid at 344.

interests, where knowledge-based cooperation and science diplomacy nurtured a system of exchange, not competition, and where distinct sub-regional jurisdictions of the Faroe Islands, Greenland, Nunavut, and Svalbard constructed self-governing courses of dealing distinct from conventional channels of international diplomacy.[54] None of these depictions necessarily insulated the Arctic from geopolitical analysis. The political derision surrounding the purchase of Alaska overshadowed the 1867 United States State Department geopolitical assessment of 'obtaining ... Greenland, and probably Iceland also'.[55] Offers to purchase Greenland for its strategic value arose in the Truman administration[56] and repeatedly in the Trump administrations.[57] However, the idea of Arctic exceptionalism highlighted a geopolitical engagement that supported cooperative interests, or what Heather Exner-Pirot and Robert W Murray referred to as a conscious willingness to negotiate a regional order that minimised rivalry and competition.[58] Hans Mouritzen referred to this power configuration as a *Nordic balance*, whereby the 'less tense' relations between the bipolar power blocs depended on low profiles kept by Denmark and Norway in NATO in return for 'gentle' Soviet treatment of Finland.[59] This balance meant the

[54] Maria Ackrén, 'Diplomacy and Paradiplomacy in the North Atlantic and the Arctic – A Comparative Approach', in *The GlobalArctic Handbook* 235 (Matthias Finger and Lassi Heininen eds, 2019).

[55] See Polk Administration Treasury Secretary Robert J Walker's letter to William J Seward, 24 April 1868, in Benjamin Mills Peirce, *A Report on the Resources of Iceland and Greenland* 1 (1868) (referencing the suggestion of including Greenland and Iceland in US negotiations with Denmark involving the acquisition of St Thomas and St John for political and commercial reasons).

[56] See 'The Secretary of State to the Legation in Denmark, Washington', 2 January 1947, in *Foreign Relations of the United States*, 1947, *The British Commonwealth; Europe*, Volume III, 658 (referencing Secretary Byrnes' suggestion to Danish Foreign Minister Rasmussen of 'the outright purchase of Greenland by the United States' in a memorandum handed to the Foreign Minister on December 14).

[57] The First Trump administration offered to purchase Greenland in 2019. Shortly before commencing his second administration, Trump refused to assure reporters that he would not use military or economic coercion to obtain Greenland. See 'President-elect Trump on Greenland and Panama Canal', C-SPAN, 7 January 2025, www.c-span.org/video/?c5148065/president-elect-trump-greenland-panama-canal. See also 'Trump: "We Need Greenland for National Security Purposes"', Forbes Breaking News, YouTube (7 January 2025), www.youtube.com/watch?v=bQE8ADdjBck, time mark 0:14.

[58] Heather Exner-Pirot and Robert W Murray, 'Regional Order in the Arctic: Negotiated Exceptionalism', 20 *Politik* 47 (2017). For other depictions of Arctic exceptionalism, see Lassi Heininen, 'Special Features of Arctic Geopolitics – A Potential Asset for World Politics', in *The Global Arctic Handbook* 215–17 (Matthias Finger and Lassi Heininen eds, 2019) (differentiating classical international relations approaches based on zero-sum or Great-Game geopolitics from Arctic exceptionalism's emphasis on 'immaterial values' and 'environment matters'); Wilfrid Greaves, 'Arctic Break Up: Climate Change, Geopolitics, and the Fragmenting Arctic Security Region', *Arctic YB* 2 (2019) (noting but critiquing the rapid post-Cold War transformation of the Arctic); Käpylä and Mikkola, n 46, at 4 (describing the Arctic as 'a unique region detached ... from global political dynamics, and thus characterized primarily as an apolitical space of regional governance, functional cooperation, and peaceful co-existence').

[59] Hans Mouritzen, 'Security Communities in the Baltic Sea Region: Real and Imagined', 32 *Security Dialogue* 297–98 (2001).

> non-stationing of foreign troops or atomic weapons on the Danish and Norwegian mainlands, as well as reluctance towards NATO exercises in the vicinity of either the island of Bornholm in the Baltic Sea or the Soviet/Norwegian border to the north

in return for the Soviet abstention from invoking the Finnish-Soviet Treaty of Friendship and Cooperation, the militarisation of Finland, and the end of Finnish neutrality.[60] If the end of the Cold War served as a catalyst for cooperation, the Arctic presented a region of least resistance. It seemed to be without serious conflict and within the bounds of nature's amity lines formed by icecap and littoral states.

International legal history reveals some interesting examples of a willingness to negotiate a regional order in the form of a condominium arrangement. This form of shared sovereignty has a checkered history, but history provides a string of interesting examples. The Catalan Bihsop of Urgell and France administered rule over Andorra for 715 years. The United States and Great Britain established a loose condominium arrangement over the Oregon Territory between 1818 and 1846. Austria and Prussia maintained joint rule over Schleswig-Holstein and Lauenburg between 1864 and 1866. Egypt and Britain established, at least in name, a condominium over The Sudan (1898). Twentieth-century expressions of condominium arose with Austro-Hungarian rule over Bosnia and Herzegovina (1918–1919), the British and French joint rule over New Hebrides (Vanuatu, 1906–1914/1922[61]), and the tripartite rule among El Salvador, Honduras, and Nicaragua over the Gulf of Fonseca.[62]

Although not commonly preferred and historically rare, the idea of sharing sovereignty also informed part of the Arctic's history of exceptionalism, as in the case of Spitzbergen. As early as 1872, an exchange of notes between Russia and the Union of Sweden−Norway suggestively broached the idea that Spitzbergen could not be the object of exclusive possession by any state. In the interlude between the archipelago's whaling and mining periods, Spitzbergen had reverted to the status as a *terra nullius*, a place of no value except to stout Pomor, Norwegian, and Swedish fur trappers, whose numbers in the region had dwindled due to scurvy, murder, and privation.[63] It is interesting to note that Russia and the Union of Sweden−Norway, as two self-deputised Arctic stewards,

[60] ibid at 298.

[61] See 'Collection DOC 438-British Government Protocol Respecting New Hebrides: Signed at London on August 6, 1914, by representatives of the British and French Governments[Ratification]', Pacific Manuscripts Bureau, asiapacific.anu.edu.au/pambu/catalogue/index.php/british-government-protocol-respecting-new-hebrides-signed-at-london-on-august-6-1914-by-representatives-of-british-and-french-governments-ratification (signing the protocol modifying the condominium of 1906, with ratification in 1922).

[62] See Christopher R Rossi, 'The Gulf of Fonseca and International Law: Condominium or Anti-Colonial Imperialism?' 3 *Jus Gentium: J Int'l L Hist* 115 (2018). See also Jorge E Núñez, *Sovereignty Conflicts and International Law and Politics: A Distributive Justice* Issue 91−92 (2017) (differentiating condominium arrangements from shared sovereignty).

[63] Rossi, 'A Unique International Problem', n 41, at 116 (citing Vylegzhanin, Zilanov and Jasinski).

contemplated subjecting Spitzbergen to joint administration – an exceptional idea, except there was little if anything to administer.

Between 1899 and World War I, British-Norwegian, American-Norwegian, Russian, German, Swedish and Dutch mining communities began to prospect Spitzbergen for coal. Violence and labour strife quickly arose in Norwegian and English camps. The English petitioned support from the Royal Navy. The Americans briefly contemplated establishing Spitzbergen as a protectorate.[64] German mining companies appeared on the southernmost island of the archipelago, Bear Island, and claimed the island. In response, a Russia expedition hoisted its flag over Bear Island next to Pomor artefacts left over from the walrus and seal trade. A Norwegian company landed at the abandoned whaling station at Kvalrossbukta and set up operation from 1905 to 1908. Another Norwegian company created a settlement at Tunheim in 1915, and claimed all of the island.[65] Extending the bilateral diplomatic conversation initiated in 1872 to administer mining claims became impossible due to the number of additional states and commercial actors. The dissolution of the Union of Sweden−Norway and the founding of the modern Norwegian state in 1905 further complicated any such prospect. Any bilateral solution, as contemplated decades before, quickly encountered problems relating to the principle of *pacta tertiis*. How would such administrative agreement, based on what surely would be a contested assertion of sovereignty, be made opposable to third parties absent their consent? United States President Woodrow Wilson's (1856–1924) Secretary of State Robert Lansing (1864–1928), declared the situation 'so unusual … that comparisons and conclusions drawn from historical experience are entirely wanting'.[66]

An unlikely solution appeared in the making – condominium. Three international conferences convened in Christiania (renamed Oslo in 1924) in 1910, 1912, and 1914. Their purpose was to frame an international administration for the archipelago. By 1914, conference participants grew to include Germany, Belgium, the United States, Denmark, France, Great Britain, and the Netherlands. A flurry of administrative proposals surrounded joint management schemes for Spitsbergen. As variously presented, Norway first favoured an inclusive management among powers doing business in Spitsbergen. Sweden advanced a more limited proposal vesting authority with itself, Russia, and Norway. The United States supported Sweden's position but advanced a veto right regarding decisions that affected United States nationals' economic interests (which were after 1914 transferred to Norwegian interests). Germany insisted that it be included as part of the oversight commission. Sweden and Russia objected. Interestingly, the major sticking point seemed to have been the composition of Spitsbergen's oversight commission, not the idea of condominium itself. A fourth conference,

[64] ibid at 118–20.
[65] GCL Bertram and David Lack, 'Bear Island', 81 *Geo J* 43, 50 (1933).
[66] Robert Lansing, 'A Unique International Problem', 11 *Am J Int'l L* 763, 765 (1917).

scheduled for February 1915 never took place due to the advent of the Great War. Even as late as 1917, Lansing conceived in all but name of a condominium arrangement whereby with 'international unanimity of action', 'approached in the right spirit by the parties – in a spirit of conciliation and mutual purpose' a 'common government' with delegated political authority could 'ensure public control in the islands'.[67] However, he remained circumspect:

> Possibly the political situation which will arise after the Great War is ended will preclude any settlement along the lines of an international government. Possibly, in view of this, the nations of Northern Europe, now warring against one another, will prefer to abandon the principle of *terra nullius* and permit a neutral Scandinavian Power to assume territorial sovereignty over the archipelago, rather than attempt further to solve so complex a problem.[68]

Diplomatic manoeuvring at the Versailles peace conference, which excluded Russia and Germany and involved a secret plan developed in Norway's Storting, resulted in a settlement that established the Allies' 'neutral ally', Norway, as Spitsbergen's sovereign,[69] a point long remembered by Russia.

Today, Norway enjoys 'full and absolute sovereignty' over Svalbard, but not in a conventional understanding of the ordinary and plain meaning of the term. Norway's sovereignty is exceptional. The treaty kneads into the meaning of 'full and absolute' the condition that all citizens and companies of signatories receive equal enjoyment and liberty of access to Svalbard's *terra firma* and its territorial water. In other words, Norwegian nationality accords no preferential treatment to its citizens on this part of Norwegian territory, as compared to nonnational signatories to the treaty. Stitching together the oxymoronic implications of full and absolute sovereignty to Norway, and equal enjoyment to other signatories, presents an exceptional if imperfect concession to the idea of condominium. Oddly, the treaty requires that taxes assessed on Svalbard exclusively benefit Svalbard, with no remittance allowed to the mainland.[70] The taxes generated do not meet costs associated with the Norwegian Government policy decision to maintain the appearance of Svalbard (and principally Longyearbyen) as a predominantly Norwegian settlement. This fiscal deficit has led to persistent subsidies from the mainland in support of objectives to ally deep-seated security anxieties affecting Norway's assertion of sovereignty over Svalbard,[71] a point

[67] ibid at 770.
[68] ibid.
[69] See Rossi, n 41, at 127–32.
[70] See *Utvalgte Tableller of Figurer fra denne Statistikken, Offentlig Sektor på Svalbard*, Statistisk Sentralbyrå (17 October 2023), www.ssb.no/en/offentlig-sektor/offentlig-forvaltning/statistikk/offentlig-sektor-pa-svalbard (recording persistent deficits regarding the administration of Svalbard ranging from 105 million NOK between 2007 and 393 million NOK in 2022 save for 2012, a period of exceptionally high coal prices).
[71] Torbjørn Pedersen, 'The Politics of Presence: The Longyearbyen Dilemma', 8 *Arctic Rev L & Pol* 95, 96 (2017).

subliminally reflected by the requirement that Norwegians also present passports when travelling to this part of Norway.

The idea of Arctic exceptionalism grew out of a series of political events, including the end of the Cold War, Soviet leader Mikhail Gorbachev's 1987 Murmansk Speech on Arctic 'desecuritization',[72] the 1991 Rovaniemi Ministerial Conference,[73] which gave institutional voice to Arctic Indigenous peoples and the Arctic environment, the adoption of the first common Arctic Environmental Protection Strategy (1991),[74] and the Ottawa Declaration (1996),[75] which established the Arctic Council. The idea of Arctic exceptionalism alternatively characterised the Arctic as a 'Zone of Peace',[76] a 'pole of peace',[77] a 'Zone of Predictability',[78] a 'Territory of Dialogue',[79] and a region of 'High North-Low Tension'.[80]

Gorbachev's remarks initiated an intense period of formal and informal institution building in the Arctic, much of it predicated on 'the scaling down of military activity in the North as a whole'.[81] He specifically proposed a nuclear-free zone in Northern Europe, restricted naval activity in the Baltic, North, Norwegian, and Greenland Seas, and extended 'confidence building measures to these areas'.[82] He envisioned a rational and joint energy development program for the north of Europe, cooperative ventures to utilise the resources of the Kola Peninsula, scientific exchanges, discussions with sub-Arctic states, the creation of an Arctic Research Council, cooperative measures for protecting the marine environment, and the opening of the Northern Sea Route to foreign vessels. Four other components of his Murmansk initiative included energy, scientific, and

[72] Mikhail Gorbachev's Speech in Murmansk at the Ceremonial Meeting on the Occasion of the Presentation of the Order of Lenin and the Gold Star to the City of Murmansk, 1 Oct. 1987, reprinted in Barentsinfo.org, www.barentsinfo.fi/docs/Gorbachev_speech.pdf [hereinafter Gorbachev, Murmansk Speech].

[73] See 'The Rovaniemi Process: The Beginning of the Arctic Era', Arctic Finland, www.arcticfinland.fi/news/The-Rovaniemi-Process-The-Beginning-of-the-Arctic-Era/39969/15e81f13-69fe-4972-9668-a4d0b578318d (noting that the 1991 Rovaniemi Ministerial meeting originated with Finland's Arctic initiative in 1989).

[74] Arctic Environmental Protection Strategy (14 June 1991), library.arcticportal.org/1542/1/artic_environment.pdf.

[75] Declaration on the Establishment of the Arctic Council, *Joint Communique of the Government of the Arctic Countries on the Establishment of the Arctic Council*, Ottawa, Canada (19 September 1996), library.arcticportal.org/1270/1/ottawa_decl_1996-3.pdf [Ottawa Declaration].

[76] Gorbachev, Murmansk Speech, n 72.

[77] ibid.

[78] Elizabeth Buchanan, *Red Arctic: Russian Strategy Under Putin* 135 (2023).

[79] See, eg, Juha Käpylä and Harri Mikkola, 'Contemporary Arctic Meets World Politics: Rethinking Arctic Exceptionalism in the Age of Uncertainty', in *The GlobalArctic Handbook* 153 (Matthias Finger and Lassi Heininen eds, 2019); 'Putin Urges to Preserve Arctic as Territory of Dialogue, Tass (30 March 2017), tass.com/world/938424?utm_source=google.com&utm_medium=organic&utm_campaign=google.com&utm_referrer=google.com.

[80] See, eg, Arne O Holm, 'Barely Anyone Talks of Low Tension in the Arctic Anymore', High North News (17 March 2023) (discounting the veracity of the slogan).

[81] Gorbachev, Murmansk Speech, n 72.

[82] ibid.

environmental cooperation, special attention to and extended East–West cooperation among Indigenous peoples.[83]

ARCTIC COUNCIL EXCEPTIONALISM

The Arctic Council, widely regarded as the pre-eminent intergovernmental forum for circumpolar cooperation, contributed to this reputation of Arctic exceptionalism with its special status as an intergovernmental forum, not a treaty-based international organisation. Formed in 1996 and assisted by the biannual Rovaniemi Conferences beginning in 2013,[84] the Council cultivated an 'Arctic Spirit' of cooperation and respect for international law to address mutually beneficial objectives. This spirit – a *jus publicum arcticus* – provided a functional venue to advance discussions on sustainable development, the environment, and scientific cooperation while avoiding military security issues, which it expressly refused to consider, except incongruously, after the weight of Russia's invasion of Ukraine became too much for its members to bear.[85] The Ottawa Declaration explicitly excluded the Arctic Council from taking up matters of military security,[86] and circumpolar powers redirected those types of discussions to other forums, such as the Arctic Security Forces Roundtable (ASFR) and the Arctic Chiefs of Defense (ACHOD) forum.

The Arctic Council's insulation from military matters allowed it to pursue functional objectives and it has served as the venue for negotiating three international agreements on search and rescue,[87] marine oil pollution,[88] and scientific cooperation,[89] and as a catalyst for expanding knowledge on other important

[83] See Kristian Åtland, 'Mikhail Gorbachev, the Murmansk Initiative, and the Desecuritization of Interstate Relations in the Arctic', 43 *Cooperation & Conflict* 289, 295 (2008) (charting Gorbachev's seven policy initiatives contained in the Murmansk speech).

[84] See Rovaniemi Process, www.rovaniemiarcticspirit.fi/EN/Our-Story. See also Timo Koivurova, 'Is this the End of the Arctic Council and Arctic Governance as we Know it?' Polar Connection, Polar Connection (11 December 2019), polarconnection.org/arctic-council-governance-timo-koivurova (detecting 'grave uncertainties' and geopolitical fractures of the Arctic spirit at the Rovaniemi Ministerial meeting in 2019 given the Trump administration's concerns about Russian and Chinese Arctic intentions).

[85] See Ottawa Declaration, n 75.

[86] See ibid fn1 ('The Arctic Council should not deal with matters related to military security').

[87] See *generally* Agreement on Cooperation on Aeronautical and Maritime Search and Rescue in the Arctic, Search and Rescue Agreement, (12 May 2011), oaarchive.arctic-council.org/bitstream/handle/11374/531/EDOCS-3661-v1-ACMMDK07_Nuuk_2011_SAR_Search_and_Rescue_Agreement_signed_EN_FR_RU.PDF?sequence=5&isAllowed=y.

[88] See generally Agreement on Cooperation on Marine Oil Pollution Preparedness and Response in the Arctic (15 May 2013), oaarchive.arctic-council.org/bitstream/handle/11374/529/EDOCS-2068-v1-ACMMSE08_KIRUNA_2013_agreement_on_oil_pollution_preparedness_and_response_signedAppendices_Original_130510.PDF?sequence=6&isAllowed=y.

[89] See generally Agreement on Enhancing International Arctic Scientific Cooperation (11 May 2017), oaarchive.arctic-council.org/handle/11374/1916.

environmental agreements.[90] It contributed to the establishment of the Polar Code,[91] which promoted safe maritime transit, the IMO,[92] monitoring the status polar bears,[93] scientific cooperation,[94] fisheries and the Law of the Sea,[95] and the Barents Euro Arctic Council (BEAC).[96] Its soft power architecture enabled the Council to successfully navigate through the Russian invasions of Georgia in 2008 and Crimea in 2014, maintaining communication and important monitoring activity on matters such as organic pollutants, heavy metals, and the Central Arctic Ocean Agreement (CAO), which is the first multilateral agreement to legally implement the precautionary approach to sustainable resource management.[97]

Elements of cooperation remain due to mutual dependencies of circumpolar powers. Arctic states share deep jurisdictional interests that only an Arctic coastline can provide.[98] Important examples of ongoing collaboration include search and rescue missions,[99] the Arctic Coast Guard Forum,[100] and the Norwegian-Russian Fisheries Commission, which has adopted a precautionary

[90] See Kristina Spohr and Daniel S Hamilton, 'From Last Frontier to First Frontier: The Arctic and World Order' in *The Arctic and World Order* 6–7 (citing the Stockholm Convention on Persistent Organic Pollutants and the Minamata Convention on Mercury).

[91] See generally International Code for Ships Operating in Polar Waters (Polar Code), IMO (1 January 2017), www.imo.org/en/ourwork/safety/pages/polar-code.aspx.

[92] See IMO, www.imo.org.

[93] See 'Monitoring Polar Bears', Arctic Council (8 March 2011), arctic-council.org/news/monitoring-polar-bears (managed in accordance with the 1973 Agreement on the Conservation of Polar Bears via the Arctic Council Working Group CAFF), arctic-council.org/news/monitoring-polar-bears.

[94] See Agreement on Enhancing International Arctic Scientific Cooperation (2018) [Arctic Science Agreement], IASC, iasc.info/cooperations/arctic-science-agreement.

[95] See 'An Introduction To: The International Agreement to Prevent Unregulated High Seas of the Central Arctic Ocean', Arctic Council (25 June 2021), arctic-council.org/news/introduction-to-international-agreement-to-prevent-unregulated-fishing-in-the-high-seas-of-the-central-arctic-ocean; Vito De Lucia and Philipp Peter Nickels, 'Reflecting on the Role of the Arctic Council vis-à-vis a Future International Legally Binding Instrument on Biodiversity in Areas Beyond National Jurisdiction', 11 *Arctic Rev on L & Pol* 189 (2020).

[96] See 'The Barents Euro-Arctic Council', BEAC, barents-council.org/#:~:text=The%20Barents%20Euro%2DArctic%20Council&text=The%20Barents%20Council%20is%20the,by%20working%20on%20their%20own.

[97] See International Agreement to Prevent Unregulated Fishing in the High Seas of the Central Arctic Ocean (2018). See also Ed Struzik, 'How Tensions with Russia are Jeopardizing Key Arctic Research', YaleEnvironment360 (7 February 2023), e360.yale.edu/features/russia-ukraine-war-arctic-research.

[98] See Christopher R Rossi, 'The Club within the Club: The Challenge of a Soft Law Framework in a Global Arctic Context', 5 *Polar J* 11 (2015) (discussing the common denominators that circumpolar states share).

[99] Despite rapid deterioration in relations following the invasion of Ukraine, Norway's Rescue Coordination Center responded to a Russian request and conducted a spectacular medical evacuation of a Russian researcher icebound on the Russian drift station *Severny Polyus*, located at the 86°N (444km from the North Pole). See 'Russisk statsborger evakuert fra fartøy nær Nordpolen', NRK (7 June 2023), www.nrk.no/tromsogfinnmark/russisk-statsborger-evakuert-fra-fartoy-1.16436054.

[100] 'The Arctic Coast Guard Forum … is an independent, informal, operationally-driven organization, both bound by treaty, to foster safe, secure, and environmentally responsible maritime activity in the Arctic.' Russia held the chair throughout the period of the invasion of Ukraine, notwithstanding the fact that Russia's Coast Guard is a component of the Federal Security Service, as is Russia's border service. ACGF, 'About the ACGF', arcticcoastguardforum.com.

approach to the management of the world's largest stock of cod.[101] The three Arctic Council agreements (on search and rescue, oil pollution, and scientific cooperation), the Law of the Sea Convention, and shared coast guard services are expected to continue during this impaired time.[102] However the full-scale invasion of Ukraine abruptly halted and perhaps permanently damaged the spirit of cooperation that contributed to accomplishments of the Arctic Council and to the belief in the Arctic as an exceptional realm of cooperation.

ARCTIC INDIGENEITY AND ARCTIC COUNCIL RELATIONS

One must be careful not to narrowly construe the meaning of Arctic exceptionalism as an idea of modern international relations. This tendency lingers from the ascription of the region as a geopolitical zone of peace. The war in Ukraine doubtless complicated international relations with Russia, but the Arctic remains, perhaps not the exemplar of geopolitical exceptionalism, but an exceptional region of participation. An important measure of this participation arises with Indigenous peoples of the Arctic.[103]

Indigenous peoples have Permanent Participants status on the Arctic Council. This feature, unique to the Arctic Council,[104] affords the six organisations

[101] See Alf Håkon Hoel, 'Sea, Fish, and Resource Management in the High North', in *Norway's Arctic Policy: Geopolitics, Security and Identity in the High North* 65, 67 (Andreas Østhagen ed, 2023) (noting joint management of stocks of cod, haddock, Greenland halibut, redfish, and capelin, and allowing a portion of total annual quotas to be fished by select third countries and the EU). See also ibid at 71 (adopting a precautionary approach to quota levels). Russia and the US continue to cooperate in regulating sea traffic through the Bering Strait in the performance of the agreement in 2018. See 'Strategic Competition in the Arctic, Transportation and Maritime Security Subcommittee Hearing, Homeland Security Committee (comment of Mr O'Rourke)', www.youtube.com/live/hE8CGxMOR0I?app=desktop, 47:51 minute mark. See also Emily Russell, 'US, Russia Agree on Shipping Standards for Bering Strait', Alaska Public Media (6 June 2018), alaskapublic.org/2018/06/06/us-russia-agree-on-shipping-standards-for-bering-strait). See also Astri Edvardsen, 'Norway and Russia Reached a Fisheries Agreement for 2023', High North News (28 October 2022), www.highnorthnews.com/en/norway-and-russia-reached-fisheries-agreement-2023 (establishing fishing quotas for the Barents Sea). Russia's invasion of Ukraine resulted in restricted port access for Russian fishing vessel to three Norwegian ports, Kirkenes, Båtsfjord, and Tromsø. See Astri Edvardsen, 'Russian Fishing Vessels Now Only Allowed Access to Three Northern Norwegian Ports – And Will Be Controlled at Each Docking', High North News (7 October 2022), www.highnorthnews.com/en/russian-fishing-vessels-now-only-allowed-access-three-northern-norwegian-ports-and-will-be.

[102] See Troy J Bouffard, 'Overview of US Arctic Strategies: National and Geopolitical Perspectives', in *Navigating Breakup: Security Realities of Freezing Politics and Thawing Landscapes in the Arctic*, 37, 43 (Karsten Friis et al eds, 2023) (noting continued cooperation in these areas despite looming competition).

[103] See Sara Olsvig and Miriam Cullen, 'Arctic Indigenous Peoples and International Law', 93 *Nordic J Int'l L* 152, 154 (2024) (acknowledging gains of Indigenous peoples in the rules-based order of the Arctic but noting a system 'cloaked' in systemic failures to uphold those rights).

[104] The disputed Treaty of New Echota (1835), one of the 375 recognised agreements signed between the US and Tribal governments contained a unique provision: were the Cherokees to remove from their ancestral homelands in the Eastern United States to territory west of the Mississippi River (now the State of Oklahoma), the Cherokees would receive a delegate to the United States House of Representatives. The validity of the treaty, contested among factions of the Cherokees and persistently ignored by Congress, remains unfulfilled. See Rossi, 'The Blind Eye', n 14, at 410.

representing the Arctic Indigenous peoples with full consultation rights in connection with the Council's negotiations and decisions. The six recognised Indigenous peoples – the Arctic Athabaskan Council, the Aleut International Association, the Gwic'in Council International, the Inuit Circumpolar Council, the Russian Association of Indigenous Peoples of Siberia and the Far North (RAIPON), and the Saami Council – created through their 'own persistence'[105] an administrative secretariat that *predated* the Arctic Council and is granted standing in its organising document of the Arctic Council.[106] This status affords them full consultation rights in relation to negotiations and decisions while intentionally sidestepping any international legal recognition of their status as peoples.[107] Such a status contributes to a sense of self-determination within the modern human rights framework, but as James Anaya has argued, distorts alternative Native communal associations that did never 'organize[] around the state'.[108] This informal power nevertheless magnifies the significance of the consensus workings within the Council, as well as the institutional memory Native peoples bring to the shifting composition of Arctic Council delegations.[109]

This cohesiveness is remarkable enough, given the anthropology of most Arctic Indigenous peoples. Aside from the coastal dwellers of the Bering Strait, many Indigenous peoples preserved a cohesive sense of ethnic identity while migrating historically between the taiga margins and the tundra as hunters, trappers, fishers and herders, but not farmers. That they formed an association of self-governance before the rise of the Arctic Council is exceptional.[110] Domestic laws further instantiate largely autonomous rights to protect traditional life and primordial habitat, as found in Russian Federal Law guaranteeing the rights of

[105] Olsvig and Cullen, n 103, at 169 ('Arctic Indigenous Peoples have, through their own persistence, mastered and contributed to the development of the Western European legal norms in a system that once facilitated their colonisation').

[106] See Ottawa Declaration, n 75, 8 ('The Indigenous Peoples' Secretariat established under AEPS [the Arctic Environmental Protection Strategy in 1994] is to continue under the framework of the Arctic Council').

[107] See Ottawa Declaration, n 75, fn 2 ('The use of the term 'peoples' in this declaration shall not be construed as having any implications as regard the rights which may attach to the term under international law').

[108] Anaya, *Indigenous Rights in International Law*, n 35, at 81.

[109] See Olsvig and Cullen, n 103, at 167 (noting the 'significant informal power' held by Indigenous participants in the Arctic Council).

[110] Consider in contrast disruptions to the so-called Five Civilized Tribes of the Eastern United States – the Cherokee, Chickasaw, Choctaw, Creek (Muscogee), and Seminole – whose agriculture and land tenure practices conflicted with white settler farming interests, leading to their largely successful forced removal by the United States Government after 1832. Although variously described as heathens or child-like dependents, their attempted assimilations, no more pronounced than with the Cherokees, nevertheless ended with their forced expulsion. The Cherokees' attempted assimilation involved sedentary agricultural practices (raising corn). They created a constitution and a parliament in their capital city of New Echota (Georgia Territory). They alphabetised their language, created a syllabary, achieved mass literacy, published a national, bilingual newspaper, translated the Bible into Cherokee, and modeled legislative, judicial, and educational practices on American republicanism in support of separation of powers, bicameral legislative structure, agricultural technologies and sartorial styles of white settlers. See Rossi, 'The Blind Eye', n 14, at 422.

Indigenous small-numbered peoples,[111] the Canadian Nunavut Act (1993),[112] Norway's Finnmark Act[113] and the Sami Parliament at Karaskjok,[114] which are reflected in international legal documents that express customary norms.[115]

THE CLUB WITHIN THE CLUB

There is another understanding of exceptionalism, the exclusive 'unifying feature of Arctic Five engagement on Arctic futures'.[116] This unity, perhaps better described as a course of dealing, derives from the unusual geographical circumstance of the region. The Arctic is 'a pocket of international sea surrounded by territorial seas and long-resolved maritime delineations'.[117]

In 2008, five circumpolar states – Canada, Denmark, Norway, Russia, and the United States – issued the Ilulissat Declaration.[118] The document presented in eight short paragraphs a soft power approach to Arctic Ocean management with *Realpolitik* implications.[119] The declaration emphasised the 'unique position' of these coastal states – the so-called 'Arctic Five' – to safeguard issues affecting the Arctic.[120] The Arctic Five's self-professed stewardship made unnecessary the 'need to develop a new comprehensive international legal regime to govern the Arctic Ocean'.[121]

Although pledging strengthened trust, cooperation, and transparency, the rhetoric did not match public perceptions or private deliberations. Indigenous

[111] See Anna Sharapova et al, 'Indigenous Rights and Interests in a Changing Arctic Ocean', 13 *Arctic Rev L & Pol* 286, 290 (2022) (discussing Russian Federal Law No 82-FZ (1999)).

[112] See Nunavut Act SC 1993, c 28, Government of Canada, laws-lois.justice.gc.ca/eng/acts/n-28.6/FullText.html. (establishing the territory of Nunavut with Native Executive, Legislative, and Judicial power).

[113] *Lov om rettsforhold og forvaltning av grunn og naturressurser i Finnmark (Finnmarksloven)*, LOV-2005-06-17-85, Lovdata, lovdata.no/dokument/NL/lov/2005-06-17-85 (facilitating land management for the benefits of Finnmark residents and particularly as a benefit to Sami culture, reindeer husbandry and use of non-cultivated areas, commercial activity and social life).

[114] See *About the Sámi Parliament*, Sámediggi, sametinget.no/about-the-sami-parliament.

[115] See Shaugn Coggins, et al, 'Indigenous Peoples and Climate Justice in the Arctic', *Geo J Int Affs*, tbl 1 (23 Februar 2021), gjia.georgetown.edu/2021/02/23/indigenous-peoples-and-climate-justice-in-the-arctic (noting UNDRIP's regard for Indigenous distributional justice, well-being, and procedural justice). See also the Rio Declaration on Environment and Development (affirming in Principle 22 the 'vital role of Indigenous People) and Agenda 21 (acknowledging the relationship between the natural environment, sustainable development and the well-being of Indigenous Peoples); ILO Convention No 169 (1989) (sustaining the right of Indigenous peoples to further develop their culture); and Brit Fløistad and Lars Lothe, 'Indigenous Peoples Rights in the Arctic', Arctis, www.arctis-search.com/Indigenous+Peoples+Rights+in+the+Arctic (no date).

[116] Elizabeth Buchanan, *Red Arctic: Russian Strategy Under Putin* 150 (2023).

[117] ibid.

[118] Ilulissat Declaration, Arctic Ocean Conference, Ilulissat, Greenland (27–28 May 2008), arctic-portal.org/images/stories/pdf/Ilulissat-declaration.pdf.

[119] Christopher R Rossi, *The Club within the Club*, n 98, at 8.

[120] Ilulissat Declaration, n 118, at 1.

[121] ibid at 2.

communities, led by the Inuit Circumpolar Council (ICC), accused the Ilulissat signatories of 'neglect'.[122] Leaked classified diplomatic cables supported the view that the Arctic Five had turned into an informal niche governance association, an expedient for solving Arctic problems within the narrower group of littoral states.[123] When Canada hosted a second Arctic Five summit in late March 2010, Sweden, Finland, and Iceland again were excluded. Despite assurances of the Arctic Council's 'preeminence', overarching maritime jurisdiction and security issues prompted the coastal Arctic Five to initiate 'a dialogue among themselves regarding issues some deemed unsuitable for treatment within the setting' of the Arctic Council.[124]

> There is irony here. The Arctic Council has long been criticized for its own club-like behavior. It is the subject of a withering litany of complaints: Its membership is permanently limited to 'Arctic States,' defined in terms of geographic proximity to the Arctic Ocean; Indigenous groups are granted 'Permanent Participant' status – a neologism introduced in the Arctic Council's founding document – but are not allowed to outnumber the members; the Council permits secret meetings, with working groups and Senior Arctic Officials often meeting behind closed doors; the private sector complains of a lack of involvement; the Council tightly controls and accredits observers, but precludes their participation in discussions; major non-governmental environmental groups, such as Greenpeace, long have been denied observer status; and China's permanent observer applications were denied three times before being granted along with five others at the recent 2013 Kiruna ministerial meeting. Japan's application also had been held up, notwithstanding its 55-year history of polar research; Brazil's bid was recently turned down; and the Council continues to defer the EU's similar observer-status request due to Canadian objections over an EU import ban of Canadian seal products. European officials, with their developing interest in a 'Northern Dimension' policy, privately complain about the Arctic Council's resistance to broadening the forum, yet Greenland boycotted the Kiruna meeting when the Council's forum was further narrowed down: Denmark's commonwealth territories (Greenland and the Faroe Islands) were refused seats at the principals' table. Indigenous groups now voice concerns about *enhancing* the role of observers, leery aboriginal influence will dilute if weighty observers such as the EU are included. Now, cross-cutting influences inside and outside the Arctic Council, amplified by the *sui generis* implications of the Ilulissat declarants – given their self-professed 'unique position' to safeguard interests – call into question not only whether an Arctic forum's center will hold, but where will it be?[125]

In contrast to the kinetic machinations of Arctic climate change stands its static governance system, now hidebound by the politics and emotions of an irredentist Russia and its invasion of Ukraine. Keeping the Arctic Council door slightly

[122] Rossi, 'The Club within the Club', n 98, at 10.
[123] ibid.
[124] Paula Kankaanpää and Oran R Young, 'The Effectiveness of the Arctic Council', 31 *Polar Res* 17176 (2012).
[125] Rossi, 'The Club within the Club', n 98, at 12–14.

ajar instead of completely closed presents the current and modest diplomatic objective of members.[126] Although the Russian Arctic Ambassador expressed a future need for the forum, he expected that it would never reconstitute the level of trust achieved in terms of its former self. He warned that 'The risk of further fragmentation … is real and should not be underestimated.'[127]

To some observers, the Arctic Council's obituary has already been drafted;[128] they advance the claim that 'Russia no longer aspires to become integrated into the Western community.'[129] Others, such as Eda Ayaydin, have suggested that the concept of Arctic exceptionalism must now pivot away from the luminous pantheon projected by the Arctic Council. It must assume a more earthly, democratic, and decentralised profile as an Arctic agora, modelled on infra- and transnational civil society networks and discrete diplomatic workings of model organisations such as the Organization for Security and Co-operation in Europe.[130]

Before the crisis in Ukraine, Russian improvements in Arctic capabilities could be construed as legitimate investments in monitoring and securing its immense border, emergency features of which demanded reliance on the military; after the crisis 'increased Russian capability … has been read [] as a sign of aggressive and threatening behaviour in a conflictual geopolitical situation'.[131] Even if the latter assessment is premature, a decades-long desecuritisation process oriented towards making the cryosphere an exceptional region free of competition, territorial temptation, and militarisation is now at risk.[132] The full-scale invasion of Ukraine quickly compromised the rhetoric of Arctic exceptionalism and the Arctic as a pragmatic zone of peace, even more compromised than Russia's 2014 invasion of Crimea portended.[133]

[126] See Svein Vigeland Rottem, 'The Arctic Council in Danger', High North News (28 March 2023), www.highnorthnews.com/en/arctic-council-danger (opining on the limited options available for the Arctic Council given the absence of Russia).

[127] Astri Edvardsen, 'Russia: "The Risk of Weakening the Arctic Council Should Not Be Underestimated"' High North News (12 May 2023), www.highnorthnews.com/en/russia-risk-weakening-arctic-council-should-not-be-underestimated (quoting Russia's Arctic Ambassador, Nikolay Korchunov).

[128] See eg, Arne O Holm, 'The Arctic Council is Dead. Long Live the Arctic Council', High North News (28 March 2023); John Last, 'Future of Arctic Council in Doubt After End of Russian Chairship', CBC News (11 May 2023); Brett Simpson, 'The Rise and Sudden Fall of the Arctic Council', *For Pol'y* (31 May 2023).

[129] Yevgeny Aniskov, 'The Ice Is Not Broken', in *Environment & Rights, Bellona Arctic* 4, at 5 (2023).

[130] Eda Ayadin, 'The Arctic Council, A Strengthening Descent from Pantheon to Agora', High North News (22 May 2023), www.highnorthnews.com/en/arctic-council-strengthening-descent-pantheon-agora.

[131] Käpylä and Mikkola, n 46, at 12.

[132] See Bouffard, n 102, at 43 (referring to the Arctic's historical reputation 'as a region of exceptional cooperation').

[133] See Geir Hønneland, *Russia and the Arctic: Environment, Identity and Foreign Policy* 19, 2nd edn (2020) (noting 'widespread fear' in the West that the Crimea invasion upended the period of Russian pragmatism in the Arctic).

Attracted by the double pull of emerging access to trade and resources, and conditioned by Anthropogenic change and the mobile geological epoch of the Kinocene,[134] the globalising interest in the Arctic creates economic opportunities and strategic tensions that only further complicate the moribund Arctic governance structure currently frozen by war in Ukraine, and tinged by the clubbish reputation of the Arctic Five. The Arctic arises as a 'compression zone' amid the structural realms of the continental and the maritime, an emerging 'shatterbelt' of critical geographies created by the social–spatial stretches of the state.[135] The metaphoric significance of the frozen status of the Arctic Council belies a swirling undercurrent of activity as equally disturbing as the focus on climate change. This activity raises the question: is the Arctic becoming a contested sphere of influence among extant and emerging powers? Is the Arctic becoming a *Großraum*?

[134] Thomas Nail, 'The Climate Industrial Complex (November 2019), philosophyofmovementblog.com/2019/11/15/the-climate-industrial-complex (discussing the Kinocene as the geological mobility of our epoch as distinguished from the human-induced Anthropocene); Thomas Nail, 'Forum 1: Migrant Climate in the Kinocene', 14 *Mobilities* 375 (2019).

[135] Saul Bernard Cohen, *Geopolitics of the World System* 33 (2003).

Chapter Five

Actors and Actorless Threats: Russia and the Tectonic Shift in the Arctic

THE GEOPOLITICAL CONSEQUENCES of Russia's 2022 invasion of Ukraine reverberated quickly across the circumpolar world. Other members of the Arctic Council[1] suspended engagement with Russia, which chaired the Council.[2] The four-party Northern Dimension cooperative initiative (involving the European Union, Russia, Iceland, and Norway) also suspended activities,[3] as did the Barents Euro-Arctic Council.[4] A trans-Arctic telecom project connecting Asia and Europe across Russia's north coast, previously hampered by rising geopolitical tensions due Russia's 2014 annexation of Crimea, split into competing enterprises, potentially dividing Arctic cyberspace between Western powers and Russia in a coming digital divide.[5] Additionally, Scandinavian education ministries and the European Commission halted research and dialogue agreements with Russian institutions, as did the North Americans. The International Council for the Exploration of the Sea (ICES) suspended all Russian Federation associates from activities designed to advance

[1] The eight Arctic Council member states (the so-called Arctic Eight) are Canada, Denmark, Finland, Iceland, Norway, Russia, Sweden, and the US.

[2] Russia's Chairmanship of the Arctic Council 2021–2023, 'Responsible Governance for a Sustainable Arctic', arctic-council-russia.ru/en.

[3] Northern Dimension Policy: Joint Statement by the European Union, Iceland and Norway on Suspending Activities with Russia and Belarus (8 March 2022), www.eeas.europa.eu/eeas/northern-dimension-policy-joint-statement-european-union-iceland-and-norway-suspending_en. The Northern Dimension subsequently ended all activities in Autumn 2022 due to the termination of EC funding.

[4] Barents Euro-Arctic Cooperation: Joint Statement of the European Union, Finland, Denmark, Iceland, Norway and Sweden on suspending activities with Russia, European Union External Action (3 March 2022), www.eeas.europa.eu/eeas/barents-euro-arctic-cooperation-joint-statement-european-union-finland-denmark-iceland-norway_en (noting that the Arctic has warmed at about four times the global average over the last four decades and significantly faster that recently believed).

[5] See 'Data Capable Crossroad or Circumpolar Chokepoint: The Geopolitics of Subsea Infrastructure in the Arctic', *Polar Geopolitics* (10 November 2023), www.polargeopolitics.com/e/data-cable-crossroad-or-circumpolar-chokepoint-the-geopolitics-of-subsea-infrastructure-in-the-arctic (involving Eric Paglia's interview of Arctic Institute research associate, Nima Khorrami). See also Luca Bertuzzi, 'EU Eyes Arctic Internet Cable to Connect Europe to Asia via Alaska', Euractiv (14 October 2022), www.euractiv.com/section/digital/news/eu-eyes-arctic-internet-cable-to-connect-europe-to-asia-via-alaska (reconfiguring the Arctic digital cable through the Northwest Passage and bypassing the Northeast Passage).

and share scientific understanding of marine ecosystems.[6] The spillover effect silenced engagements protected by the 2017 Arctic Science Agreement,[7] which promotes open science practices on knowledge sharing and collaboration. These decisions resulted in a 'tectonic' interruption of multiple bilateral and multilateral education and science diplomacy initiatives.[8] The suspensions mirrored the severance in relations at the Arctic Security Forces Roundtable, which ended military-to-military contact with Russia following its illegal 2014 annexation of Crimea.[9]

Russia regarded the Arctic Council's suspension as illegitimate and violative of the organisation's commitment to consensus-based decision-making.[10] Anticipating its agenda setting mission as chair prior to the suspension, Russia had pledged to devote special attention to the Arctic Council's Strategic Plan for the coming decade.[11] This pledge had signalled a continuation of Russia's Basic Principles document, which outlined Russia's aims to preserve the Arctic as a region of peace, stability, and mutually beneficial partnerships to 2035.[12]

[6] See 'Statement from ICES Council', ICES (20 March 2022), www.ices.dk/news-and-events/news-archive/news/Pages/TemporarySuspension.aspx (announcing the suspension of the Russian Federation from activities involving the 20 coastal states that border the North Atlantic and Baltic Sea region).

[7] See Valery Konyshev, 'Arctic Science Diplomacy: With or Without Russia', GCSP 8 (September 2023). See also Agreement on Enhancing International Arctic Scientific Cooperation, reprinted in Arctic Council, oaarchive.arctic-council.org/bitstreams/e75076a2-4ff2-4de6-b08a-58034b991bf7/download (2023). Article 19 of the Agreement allows parties to withdraw but contains no provision allowing for suspension. See ibid.

[8] Warren Cornwall, '"We Are Cut off." Tensions with Russia are Hobbling Arctic Research', *Science* (3 May 2023), www.science.org/content/article/we-are-cut-tensions-russia-are-hobbling-arctic-research (quoting US Arctic Research Commission Chair, Mike Sfraga); Margaux Lisaerde, 'Scandinavian Universities to Suspend Ties with Russia', ResearchProfessional News (7 March 2022), www.researchprofessionalnews.com/rr-news-europe-nordics-2022-3-scandinavian-universities-to-suspend-ties-with-russia. The scientific disruption cut off Western information and data exchanges with Russia's main federal scientific authority for the Russian Federation Arctic Zone (the State Commission on the Development of the Arctic), with Russian federal-state institutions connected to the WMO, the UN Framework Convention on Climate Change, and the IPCC (Roshydromet), with Russia's Arctic and Antarctic Research Institute (which monitors ice environments in Severnaya Zemlya, Tiksi Bay and Svalbard), and with Russia's main Arctic education centres (including the Russian State Hydrometeorological University, the Northern Arctic Federal University, Saint Petersburg State University, and the Kola Science Center). See Konyshev, n 7, at 7.

[9] See 'Arctic Security Forces Roundtable', CASR (2022), www.uaf.edu/casr/projects/asfr.php. The 12 original members of the semi-annual gathering of military forces included Canada, Denmark, Finland, France, Germany, Iceland, the Netherlands, Norway, Russia, Sweden, the UK, and the US.

[10] See 'Russia to Quit Arctic Council in Case of West's Destructive Behavior – Diplomat', Tass (14 May 2023), tass.com/russia/1617119 (noting Russian Ambassador-at-Large Nikolay Korchunov's statement that Russia may quit the Arctic Council if Council members abandon 'collective approaches, which have always been a basis for the Council's work').

[11] Russia's Chairmanship of the Arctic Council 2021–2023, Responsible Governance for a Sustainable Arctic, n 2.

[12] Ekaterina Klimenko, 'Russia's New Arctic Policy Document Signals Continuity Rather than Change', SIPRI (6 April 2020), www.sipri.org/commentary/essay/2020/russias-new-arctic-policy-document-signals-continuity-rather-change.

In response to the Arctic Council's post-invasion action, Russia dramatically amended its Arctic pledges. It removed specific mention of the Arctic Council and the Barents Euro-Arctic Council from its Arctic policy statement; it excised mention of cooperation among the coastal Arctic Five (Canada, Denmark (Greenland), Norway, the United States, Russia) and with 'multilateral regional formats';[13] it characterised its national interests in the Arctic as a strategic priority and emphasised the development of bilateral relations,[14] quickly supplementing this readjustment to mean Arctic-related engagement with the BRICS (Brazil, Russia, India, China, and South Africa) and countries associated with the Shanghai Cooperation Organization.[15] The chairman of the Duma's Committee for the Development of the Far East and the Arctic incredulously noted that the Kremlin was studying whether to denounce the United Nations Convention on the Law of the Sea (UNCLOS),[16] a treaty deemed of great benefit to Russian interests. In February 2023, Russia suspended participation in New START, the last remaining nuclear arms control agreement between the United States and Russia.[17]

ACTORLESS THREATS: ENVIRONMENTAL PROBLEMS HELD IN ABEYANCE

The termination of almost every major form of cooperation with the Arctic's dominant coastal partner complicated policy promoting discussions on transglobal environmental issues, many of which the Arctic Council helped to identify in its sponsorship of the seminal Arctic Climate Impact Assessment report in 2004/2005.[18] These discussions cover impending environmental concerns, including nuclear waste, greenhouse gas emission, ocean acidification, and black carbon. The UN Intergovernmental Panel on Climate Change (IPCC) 2023 report enumerated multiple opportunities for scaling up mitigation and

[13] Malte Humpert, 'Russia Amends Arctic Policy Prioritizing 'National Interest' and Removing Cooperation Within Arctic Council', High North News (23 February 2023), www.highnorthnews.com/en/russia-amends-arctic-policy-prioritizing-national-interest-and-removing-cooperation-within-arctic.

[14] ibid (noting that 'the wording of the revised document now places the country's national interest in the Arctic ahead of the work towards economic, scientific and technological, and cultural cooperation').

[15] 'Russia to Engage BRICS, SCO Partners in Arctic Projects-Foreign Ministry', Tass (14 May 2023), tass.com/russia/1617145.

[16] See 'Russia is Considering Withdrawing from the UN Convention on the Law of the Sea in the Arctic', IZ (18 March 2024), iz.ru/1666954/2024-03-18/rossiia-izuchaet-vopros-vykhoda-iz-konventcii-oon-po-morskomu-pravu-v-chasti-arktiki (quoting Nikolai Kharitonov).

[17] Shannon Bugos, 'Russia Suspends New START', Arms Control Ass'n (March 2023), www.armscontrol.org/act/2023-03/news/russia-suspends-new-start (resulting in refusal to allow required 18 inspections per year and meetings with the treaty's implementation body, the Bilateral Consultative Commission).

[18] See 'Impacts of a Warming Arctic, Arctic Climate Impact Assessment' (2004); 'Arctic Climate Impact Assessment' Arctic Council (2005), oaarchive.arctic-council.org/handle/11374/2453?show=full.

adaptation options in response to climate change,[19] many Arctic components of which were put on hold by Russia's invasion of Ukraine.

Russia's chairship of the Arctic Council revolved around an ambitious 14-year project to clean up radioactive waste dumped in the Barents and Kara Seas during Soviet times.[20] This waste includes 1,000 objects that still produce high levels of gamma radiation.[21] The project requires the urgent removal of two sunken nuclear submarines (the B-159 in Andreyeva Bay near Russia's border with Norway, and the K-27 off the south-eastern coast of Novaya Zemlya), the reactor compartments from three others (the K-11, K-19, and K-140), and the reactor from the nuclear icebreaker, *Lenin* (scuttled off the Mideast coast of Novaya Zemlya).[22] The project also involves processing considerable nuclear and radiation hazards storage facilities on the Russian Arctic coastline.[23] However, the Ukraine invasion prompted Russia's Arctic Council peers to boycott future talks,[24] and discussions to lift the subs fell silent at the European Bank of Reconstruction and Development, which promised to help finance the clean-up.[25] The Bellona Expert Group, which has monitored the Russian Ministry for Nuclear Energy (Rosatom) for almost 20 years, concluded 'Russia will find it extremely difficult to solve the problem of accumulated environmental damage in the Arctic region on its own.'[26]

Mindful of the ticking environmental clock, non-governmental organisations such as the Geneva Center for Security Policy implemented high-level non-governmental talks to re-establish international collaboration in the Arctic.[27] In June 2023, the Arctic Council partially resumed activity without Russia's participation, pledging under the 2023–2025 Norwegian chairship a continuation of 'the historic and unique role of the Arctic Council for constructive cooperation, stability and dialogue between the people in the Arctic region'.[28]

[19] 'AR6 Synthesis Report', IPCC (2023), www.ipcc.ch/report/ar6/syr.

[20] Charles Digges, 'War Puts Cleanup of Russia's Radioactive Wrecks on Ice', *Bull of the Atomic Scientists* (28 November 2022), thebulletin.org/2022/11/war-puts-cleanup-of-russias-radioactive-wrecks-on-ice.

[21] ibid.

[22] 'From Moscow to the Very Outskirts: The Problems of Flooded Objects Were Discussed at an International Conference', Комплексная утилизация АПЛ (24 December 2019), nuclear-submarine-decommissioning.ru.

[23] 'The Nuclear Legacy of the Arctic: Cleaning It Up Without International Assistance Will Be Tough', in *Environment & Rights, Bellona Arctic* 30 (2023) [hereinafter 'The Nuclear Legacy of the Arctic'].

[24] See Gloria Dickie, 'Russian Officials Call Arctic Council Boycott "Regrettable"', Reuters (4 March 2022), www.reuters.com/world/europe/russian-officials-call-arctic-council-boycott-regrettable-2022-03-04.

[25] Digges, n 20.

[26] 'The Nuclear Legacy of the Arctic', n 23, at 33.

[27] The talks are part of the organisation's Diplomatic Dialogue series. For background, see 'Diplomatic Dialogue', GCSP, www.gcsp.ch/gcsp-activities#diplomatic-dialogue.

[28] 'Arctic States and Indigenous Permanent Participants Convened for the 13th Arctic Council Meeting and Issued Statement', Arctic Council (11 May 2023), arctic-council.org/news/13th-arctic-council-meeting-salekhard.

However, the Council's Senior Arctic Officials chair recognised that 'without functioning Working Groups', there is no Arctic Council, or discussions on emergency preparedness, sustainable development, or Arctic contaminants.[29] The Arctic Council Secretariat delicately began including the Russian Federation in discussions about guidelines to one day restart fully functioning Working Groups,[30] and reports from the Working Groups indicate 'considerable variation' in terms of their ability to operate effectively and universal 'uncertainty' about future prospects.[31] The move impliedly confirmed that little can be expected from a circumpolar forum that operates through consensus while excluding its dominant stakeholder.

ARCTIC AMPLIFICATION

The rupture in Arctic Council relations also muddled responses to the problem of the Arctic environment and so-called actorless threats. The Arctic has been heating up for decades and at a pace significantly faster than the global average. This pace, called 'Arctic Amplification', is now accelerating and it is creating multiple problems on land and at sea.[32] A Braudelian sense of temporal reconceptualisation,[33] marking geography's powerful agency over human affairs, now assigns multi-decade significance to the movement from the Holocene to the Anthropocene.[34] Although not a 'proper crisis', which is generally conceived of as a discrete event of short duration, an emerging paradigm of epochal change portends of a coming period of increasingly unmanageable environmental control over human affairs.[35] 'Actorless threats' in this sense refers to the human release of emissions into the atmosphere and not to natural causes. However,

[29] Eilís Quinn, 'Arctic Council Charting Way Forward to Resume Work Says Norwegian SAO', Barents Observer (6 September 2023), www.thebarentsobserver.com/arctic/arctic-council-charting-way-forward-to-resume-work-says-norwegian-sao/118300 (quoting Senior Arctic Officials chair, Morten Høglund).

[30] See ibid.

[31] Summary of Proceedings, Seminar on Arctic Cooperation in Difficult Times 2 (15–17 November 2023), www.svs.is/static/files/Arctic_Days_2023/arctic.impressions-and-participants.final.pdf.

[32] Chelsea Harvey, 'The Arctic Is Warming Four Times Faster Than the Rest of the Planet', *Scientific American* (12 August 2022), www.scientificamerican.com/article/the-arctic-is-warming-four-times-faster-than-the-rest-of-the-planet/#:~:text=It%20finds%20that%20the%20Arctic,over%20the%20last%2043%20years.

[33] Braudel treated time as a social construct, not as a simple chronological metre, better understood from the perspective of social analysis and the secular and cyclical patterns or structures observed over a longer period, hence a temporal reconceptualisation based on usage of the term *longue durée*. See generally Fernand Braudel, 'Histoire et Sciences sociales: La longue durée', 13 *Annales. Économies, Sociétés, Civilisations* 725 (1958).

[34] Eric Paglia regards Fernand Braudel as a forefather of environmental history, who considered physical geography as a powerful constraint on 'pathways for human development'. Eric Paglia, 'Not a Proper Crisis', 2 *Antropocene Rev* 247, 249 (2015).

[35] See ibid, at 258 (drawing conclusions about the new meaning of a proper crisis) and 255 (attributing the phrase 'proper crisis' to Hans Palmstierna).

as Marisol Maddox has clarified, 'actorless threats' refer to 'the specific acute events that occur because of climate change or that occur more intensely and more frequently because of climate change'. In this sense, they 'do not have a specific proximate actor associated with them'.[36]

Reconfiguring the Arctic as a proper crisis requires a shift in temporal and spatial awareness, particularly among scholars who have 'treated the environment simply as a silent and passive backdrop to their historical narratives'.[37] Dipesh Chakrabarty proposed a new view for historical understanding that 'collapse[s] the age-old humanist distinction between natural history and human history' in view of what anthropogenic explanations of climate change now portend.[38]

The 2023 report of the International Cryosphere concludes that 'Some degree of planetary-wide damage from Cryosphere loss is already locked in.' The 2015 Paris Agreement established an upper-limit 2°C target for global warming this century,[39] but the report now concludes that goal is far too high,[40] and its adjusted standard downward to 1.5°C already has been breached for the first time in human history across the entire year of 2024.[41] Permafrost is thawing and contributing to methane release, infrastructure degradation, and atmospheric exposure to long-dormant microbial threats.[42] The Russian Academy of Sciences estimated that as much as $250 billion-worth of physical infrastructure, spread over a permafrost area that covers more than 60 per cent of Russia's territory, is now at risk due to the thawing of permafrost.[43] Wetter and warmer snow climates destabilise landscapes and trigger increasing numbers of landslides and avalanches.[44] The unpredictability of geological activity has produced 'the

[36] Marisol Maddox, 'Arctic Security & the Urgency of Understanding Actorless Threats', Dickey Center for International Understanding, Dartmouth University, YouTube (1 April 2024), www.youtube.com/watch?v=WZrajuzT1tI, time mark: 13:37.

[37] Dipesh Chakrabarty, 'The Climate of History: Four Theses', 35 *Crit Inq* 197, 204 (2009).

[38] ibid, at 201.

[39] See 'Key Aspects of the Paris Agreement', UN, unfccc.int/most-requested/key-aspects-of-the-paris-agreement#:~:text=The%20Paris%20Agreement's%20central%20aim,further%20to%201.5%20degrees%20Celsius.

[40] 'State of the Cryosphere 2023: Two Degrees is Too High', International Cryosphere Climate Initiative (2023), drive.google.com/file/d/1QOqYHI0ezrmMCUrmCDV03rF-1aIYE6VB/view.

[41] Mark Poynting, World's First Year-Long Breach of Key 1.5C Warming Limit', BBC (8 February 2024), www.bbc.com/news/science-environment-68110310.

[42] See Katie Sipes et al, 'Permafrost Active Layer Microbes from Ny Ålesund, Svalbard (79°N) Show Autotrophic and Heterotrophic Metabolisms with Diverse Carbon-Degrading Enzymes', 12 *Frontiers in Microbiology* (2022), www.osti.gov/pages/biblio/1843517-permafrost-active-layer-microbes-from-ny-alesund-svalbard-show-autotrophic-heterotrophic-metabolisms-diverse-carbon-degrading-enzymes.

[43] Katarina Kertysova and Akash Ramnath, 'How Permafrost Thaw Puts the Russian Arctic at Risk', IPI Global Observatory (22 November 2021), theglobalobservatory.org/2021/11/how-permafrost-thaw-puts-the-russian-arctic-at-risk (noting as well that permafrost covers a quarter of the Northern Hemisphere's territory).

[44] Jiansheng Hao et al, 'Impacts of Climate Change on Snow Avalanche Activity Along a Transportation Corridor in the Tianshan Mountains', *Int'l J Disaster Risk Sci* (2023), doi.org/10.1007/s13753-023-00475-0; Nick Beake and Kate Vandy, 'Svalbard: The Race to Save the Fastest-Warming Place on Earth', BBC News (27 October 2022) (noting the growing risk of avalanches and mudslides in the Arctic community of Longyearbyen).

most *mobile* geological epoch of Earth's history', in what Thomas Nail calls the Kinocene.[45]

Old ice is shrinking and now covers less than 10 per cent of the Arctic Ocean, down from more than 40 per cent coverage in the 1980s.[46] Defined as ice at least five years old, old ice once provided a thicker base on which new ice forms to insulate against the summer melt season. Less and thinner old ice warms Arctic water and reduces temperature differentials between Arctic areas and lower latitudes. This reduction, which climate scientists claim is now too late to reverse,[47] destabilises the polar jet stream and makes weather swings as wobbly as a slowly peddled bicycle.[48]

Warming ocean temperatures have already disrupted marine ecosystems and have contributed to the secondary spread of non-native species. Red king crabs transplanted from the Bering Sea are now migrating into new stretches of the Barents Sea.[49] Snow crabs are crawling into colder waters surrounding Norway's Svalbard archipelago.[50] Omnivorous piscivores such as cod are moving northward and disrupting life of Arctic bottom-dwellers,[51] while Pacific salmon (*pukkellaks*) are migrating southward from their transplanted introduction in the Kola Peninsula and infesting rivers and streams in North Norway and as far away as Ireland.[52] Climate change and increasing coastal sea temperature will

[45] Thomas Nail, 'The Climate Industrial Complex', Baruch College Lecture (19 November 2019), philosophy-of-movement.com/2019/11/15/the-climate-industrial-complex. See also Thomas Nail, *Theory of the Earth* (2021) (constructing a philosophy of geology and movement based on ecological disruptions and kinetic ethics of the earth).

[46] 'Climate Change Indicators: Arctic Sea Ice', United States Environmental Protection Agency (July 2022), www.epa.gov/climate-indicators/climate-change-indicators-arctic-sea-ice#:~:text=The%20age%20of%20sea%20ice,ice%20cover%20is%20becoming%20thinner.

[47] Damian Carrington, 'Too Late Now to Save Arctic Summer Ice, Climate Scientists Find', *The Guardian* (6 June 2023), www.theguardian.com/environment/2023/jun/06/too-late-now-to-save-arctic-summer-ice-climate-scientists-find.

[48] Woosok Moon et al, 'Wavier Jet Streams Driven by Zonally Asymmetric Surface Thermal Forcing', 119 *PNAS* e2200890119 (2022), www.pnas.org/doi/pdf/10.1073/pnas.2200890119.

[49] Christopher R Rossi, 'Arctic Anadromy and Congested Regime Governance', 52 *Env't L Rep* 10193, 10209 (2022) [hereinafter Arctic Anadromy]. *But* See Jan H Sundet and Alf Håkon Hoel, 'The Norwegian Management of an Introduced Species: The Arctic Red King Crab Fishery', 72 *Mar Pol'y* 278, 282 (2016) (noting that the westward expansion of the red king crab fishery and the management regime created in response 'appears to work as intended'.

[50] Rossi, n 49, at 10209.

[51] See Gotje von Leesen et al, 'Temperature Exposure in Cod Driven by Changes in Abundance', 79 *Can J Fish Aquat* 587 (2022) (noting the movement of Northeast Arctic cod into colder waters due to thermal preferences related to climate change); Steven E Campana et al, 'Shifting Fish Distributions in Warming Sub-Arctic Oceans', 10 *Sci Repts*16448, 16449 (2020) (citing research indicating 'small bottom benthivores [seafloor fish] were being replaced by large motile generalist species like cod and haddock' in the Barents Sea).

[52] 'Mer pukkellaks kan skyldes høyere temperatur', Statsforvalteren.no (5 November 2021), www.statsforvalteren.no/troms-finnmark/miljo-klima/fiskeforvaltning/internasjonalt-pukkellaksseminar-pa-svanhovd (noting the extension and penetration of Pacific salmon into Irish and Scottish watercourses).

likely continue to push Atlantic acquaculture into the cooler fish-farming waters of the High North. This shift threatens to portage pathogens and novel parasites from warmer waters.[53] It risks homogenising portions of the ecosystem through escapes and interbreeding while creating a problem for management of wild northern fish stocks and estuaries.[54]

Over two decades ago, the UN Environmental Program Governing Council labelled the Arctic as the world's barometer of environmental change.[55] Currently, a Cambrian-like change in ecosystemic incubation portends of 'more invasive explosions to come'.[56] For climate and environmental scientists who depend on consistent data collection, Russia's exclusion amounts to a massive problem.[57] At no time has the Arctic Council's mission of promoting sustainable development been more relevant. And yet at no time has its future seemed more in doubt.

GEOECONOMIC AND GEOPOLITICAL IMPLICATIONS

The idea of an open polar sea beyond the ice pack atop the world has stimulated the imaginations of mariners, merchants, cartographers, and scientists for centuries. Renaissance cartographer Martin Waldseemüller's magnificent *Universalis Cosmographia* world map (1507) charted a round world with open water across 'America' and Eurasia.[58] Mercator's 1595 projection oriented high above the North Pole postulated a magnetic island surrounded by open water and a 'symmetrical arrangement of lands in the Arctic Basin'.[59]

Rapid ice loss is also opening traditionally constricted sea lanes and lengthening transit times across a still precariously fickle Arctic summer season. The

[53] Max Troell et al, 'Seafood from a Changing Arctic', 46(suppl 3) *Ambio* S368, S380 (2017) (noting environmental changes on aquaculture and increased risk of disease and pathogens).

[54] Rossi, Arctic Anadromy, n 49, at 10209.

[55] See Conference of Parliamentarians of the Arctic Region (intervention of Darcie Matthiessen), treaties.un.org/doc/source/events/PD/arctic_council.pdf (referencing UNEP's February 2003 resolution preceding release of the 2004 Arctic Climate Impact Assessment).

[56] Rossi, Arctic Anadromy, n 49, at 10209. See also 'Russland med I kampen mot fremmede arter i Arktis', Sysselmesteren på Svalbard (20 April 2021), www.sysselmesteren.no/nyheter/2021/04/russland-med-i-kampen-mot-fremmede-arter-i-arktis (noting a joint effort between Russia and the Norsk Institutt for Naturforskning to combat the spread of invasive species in the Arctic).

[57] See Brett Simpson, 'The Rise and Sudden Fall of the Arctic Council', *For Pol'y* (31 May 2023).

[58] See Martin Waldseemüller, 'Universalis Cosmographia secundum Ptholomaei traditionem et Americi Vespucii alioru[m]que lustrationes' (1507), Library of Congress, www.loc.gov/resource/g3200.ct000725/?r=-0.292,0.011,1.111,0.677,0. Waldseemüller's map contains many mysteries. He depicted a round world, astonishing markings of the New World (which he christened *America*), the Pacific Ocean (six years before the first 'credited' European discovery by Vasco Nuñez Balboa), images that suggest the Rocky Mountains and the Andes, and open water at Darién, precisely where the Panama Canal would be built 400 years later. See generally John W Hessler and Chet Van Duzer eds, *Seeing the World Anew: The Radical Vision of Martin Waldseemüller's 1507 & 1516 World Maps* (2012).

[59] John K Wright, 'The Open Polar Sea', 43 *Geo Rev* 338, 344 (1953).

freeing of sea ice has prompted scientific estimates of a completely ice-free Arctic September as early as the 2030s–2050,[60] predictions supported by the United States Navy's Arctic Roadmap projections.[61] The geoeconomic and geopolitical implications are profound.

The idea of an almost completely ice-free[62] polar season by this century's end stimulates thoughts about transforming the High Arctic into a viable economic and commercial geo-spatial region.[63] Studies indicate the region is surfeit of critical minerals necessary to improve supply chains needed in the green transition toward a climate neutral environment by 2050.[64] A much-cited study estimates that 22 per cent of the world's 'undiscovered, technically recoverable resources' exists in the area north of the Arctic Circle, including 13 per cent of undiscovered oil reserves, 30 per cent of undiscovered natural gas, and 20 per cent of undiscovered natural gas liquids.[65] The United States Bureau of Ocean Energy Management projected that Alaska's outer continental shelf alone contains perhaps 46.7 billion barrels of oil-equivalent resources.[66] The United States National Intelligence Council estimated that climate change will make more available $1 trillion worth of onshore precious metals and minerals.[67]

[60] Yeon-Hee Kim' et al, 'Observationally-Constrained Projections of an Ice-Free Arctic Even under a Low Emission Scenario', 14 *Nature Comm* 1, 5 (2023).

[61] See David W Titley and Courtney St John, 'Arctic Security Considerations and the US Navy's Roadmap for the Arctic', 63 *Naval War College Rev* 36 (2010).

[62] Scientific usage of the term 'ice-free' conditions do not necessitate complete lack of ice. For scientific definitions of varieties of sea ice, see 'Sea Ice', National Snow & Ice Data Center (2018), nsidc.org/cryosphere/seaice/characteristics/index.html.

[63] A geological survey of mineral resources in the Arctic, sponsored by the Geological Survey of Norway, specifically cited improved and longer-term opening of Arctic sea lanes as motivations to investigate the mineral potential of the Arctic. See 'Mineral Resources in the Arctic: An Introduction' 10 (2016), www.ngu.no/upload/Aktuelt/CircumArtic/Mineral_Resources_Arctic_Shortver_Eng.pdf.

[64] Statement of Arctic Economic Council executive director, Mads Qvist Frederiksen, International Relations and Defence Committee, House of Lords [UK], 7 June 2023, Q 76 ('the European Union has outlined in the Critical Raw Materials Act the critical raw materials needed in the green transition, and has found that most of them … can be found in the Arctic region. The question now is whether we want to continue getting rare earth elements from China or cobalt from the Democratic Republic of Congo or whether we would rather have it from northern Norway and northern Sweden. That is definitely a growing opportunity.'). The EU subscribes to the European Green Deal, which aims to make Europe climate neutral by 2050, meaning ensuring no net emissions of greenhouse gases. 'The European Green Deal', European Commission, commission.europa.eu/strategy-and-policy/priorities-2019-2024/european-green-deal_en.

[65] See '90 Billion Barrels of Oil and 1,670 Trillion Cubic Feet of Natural Gas Assessed in the Arctic', US Geological Survey (23 July 2008), archive.usgs.gov/archive/sites/www.usgs.gov/newsroom/article.asp-ID=1980.html (noting as well that 84% of the estimated resources are thought to be offshore).

[66] '2021 Assessment of Undiscovered Technically Recoverable Oil and Gas Resources of the Nation's Outer Continental Shelf Region', BOEM, at iii (October 2021), www.boem.gov/sites/default/files/documents/oil-gas-energy/resource-evaluation/2021%20Alaska%20OCS%20Assessment%20Report_0.pdf.

[67] 'National Intelligence Estimate, Climate Change and International Responses Increasing Challenges to US National Security Through 2040', National Intelligence Estimate, NIC-NIE2021-10030-A, at 8 (2021).

Already Norway has announced plans to mine mineral resources on the ocean floor of the Greenland, Norwegian, and Barents Seas, an underwater area slightly smaller than the UK and Ireland.[68] The European Community has funded a Blue Mining consortium of 19 companies and institutions to investigate the mineral content and environmental sustainability of deep sea mining in the Arctic.[69] Arctic Ocean coastal states (Canada, Denmark/Greenland, Norway, the United States, and Russia) have asserted claims to extended seabed jurisdiction in the Arctic Ocean, which are based on scientific measurements of the depth, shape, and geophysical characteristics of the seabed and subsoil. Together, these claims 'potentially territoraliz[e] huge swaths of Arctic Basin seabed and subsoil'.[70] The United States claim on its extended continental shelf adds approximately 1,000,000 km^2 to its territory.[71] Even assuming multiple and extensive overlapping claims can be resolved by the recommendations of the commission established by UNCLOS,[72] the remaining unclaimed area – the so-called Gakkel Ridge between Svalbard and the North Pole[73] – may tempt non-Arctic states to explore or exploit mineral resources in this area without consent.[74] Acknowledging the increasing accessibility and opportunity in the Arctic, Klaus Dodds nevertheless cautioned policy makers against undue optimism: 'Don't think that a warming Arctic makes the operating environment any easier, safer or somehow cheaper. That is simply not the case.'[75]

[68] Gwladys Fouche and Nerijus Adomaitis, 'Norway Moves To Open Its Waters to Deep-Sea mining', Reuters (20 June 2023), www.reuters.com/sustainability/climate-energy/norway-moves-open-its-waters-deep-sea-mining-2023-06-20. Norway postponed the first licensing round due to opposition from political and environmental groups expressing concern about the environmental impact of the seabed mineral operations. See Maia Davies, 'Norway Suspends Controversial Deep-Sea Mining Plans', BBC (2 December 2024), www.bbc.com/news/articles/c9wlj8l8kr7o.

[69] See generally 'Blue Mining', EU Commission (2023), bluemining.eu (detailing the background and objectives of the Blue Mining consortium).

[70] Christopher R Rossi, *Sovereignty and Territorial Temptation: The Grotian Tendency* 188 (2017).

[71] Announcement of U.S. Extended Continental Shelf Outer Limits, Department of State (19 December 2023), www.state.gov/announcement-of-u-s-extended-continental-shelf-outer-limits.

[72] See Art 76 of the 1982 UN Convention on the Law of the Sea (defining the continental shelf and setting for the rules for the Commission on the Limits of the Continental Shelf (CLCS), which is a scientific body created to assist coastal states finalise their continental shelf limits). The recommendations of the commission are non-binding, but Art 76(8) requires parties establish final and binding outer limits 'only after such recommendations are made'. Maritime Delimitation in the Indian Ocean (*Somalia v Kenya*), Judgment, ICJ Rep 188 (2021). See also Kevin A Baumert, 'Article 76 of the UN Convention on the Law of the Sea: Parties and Non-Parties', 99 *Int'l L Stud* 963, 964 (2022) (discussing the CLCS, the historical background leading to its creation, ambiguities relating to its function, and complexities associated with determining the outer limits of the continental shelf).

[73] See GoNorth Heads for the Gakkel Ridge in the Arctic Ocean, UiO, www.mn.uio.no/geo/english/research/news-and-events/news/2023/gonorth-norwegian-expedition-of-the-artic-ocean.html (detailing an expeditionary multi-year mission to explore the sea floor and subsea geology of the mid-Arctic Ocean Gakkel Ridge (aka Nansen Cordillera)).

[74] See Lars Kullerud and Oran R Young, 'Adding a Gakkel Ridge Regime to the Evolving Arctic Ocean Governance Complex', GRID (26 October 2020), www.grida.no/publications/527.

[75] Statement of Klaus Dodds, International Relations and Defence Committee, House of Lords [UK], 19 April 2023, Q3, committees.parliament.uk/oralevidence/13105/html.

EFFORTS TO MANAGE THE REMAINING GLOBAL COMMONS

When thinking about the ocean commons, a subtle distinction arises. The common spaces of the high seas and the Area are classified similarly in that they are beyond sovereign control. But they are treated differently.[76] The high seas are free and 'open to all states'.[77] They cannot be appropriated. The Area is 'owned' by humanity and can be managed and regulated in accordance with Part XI of UNCLOS subject to collective ownership and international management according to the principle of the Common Heritage of Humankind.[78]

Every incremental seaward extension of state control over the continental shelf amounts to a de facto reduction of the area of the deep seabed,[79] an area once thought to belong to everybody as part of the global commons (*res communis*), or perhaps to nobody (*terra nullius*). Indeed, this extension follows the general transformation of the law of the sea since World War II, which has resulted in the dramatic extension of territorial encroachments and state-sponsored appropriations.[80]

Efforts to manage the Arctic Ocean's remaining common space in accordance with the rule of law – an effort to forestall a pelagic 'land grab' – may benefit from two recent developments. In 2021, 10 countries with major distant-water fishing fleets agreed to implement the precautionary principle and establish a 16-year fishing moratorium in the Central Arctic Ocean (until 2037).[81] And in 2023, a treaty opened for signature to incorporate precaution and the ecosystem approach to conserve and sustain marine biological diversity beyond national jurisdiction (BBNJ Treaty).[82]

[76] UNCLOS details provisions relating to the high seas in Part VII. The high seas are all parts of the ocean that do not fall under the regimes of internal waters, the territorial sea, the EEZ or archipelagic waters. UNCLOS details provisions of the Area in Part XI and the 1994 Implementation Agreement. It is 'the seabed and ocean floor and subsoil thereof beyond the limits of national jurisdiction').

[77] UNCLOS Art 87.

[78] The concept of the Common Heritage of Humankind (formerly Common Heritage of Mankind) was introduced in an address to the UN General Assembly in 1967. See Official Records of the General Assembly, Twenty-Second Session, Agenda Item 92, Doc A./6695. See also Arvid Pardo, *The Common Heritage of Mankind: Selected Papers on Oceans and World Order 1967–1974* (1975).

[79] See Scott J Shackelford, 'Was Selden Right? The Expansion of Closed Seas and its Consequences', 47 *Stan J Int'l L* 3 (2011).

[80] Bernard H Oxman, *The Territorial Temptation: A Siren Song at Sea*, 100 *Am J Int'l L* 830, 832 (2006).

[81] See 'An Introduction to: The International Agreement to Prevent Unregulated Fishing in the High Seas of the Central Arctic Ocean', Arctic Council (25 June 2021), arctic-council.org/news/introduction-to-international-agreement-to-prevent-unregulated-fishing-in-the-high-seas-of-the-central-arctic-ocean.

[82] See Art 5 (b, common heritage principle), (d, precautionary principle/approach), (e, ecosystem approach), and (f, integrated approach), BBNJ Treaty, (opened for signature on 20 September 2023), www.un.org/bbnj/sites/www.un.org.bbnj/files/draft_agreement_advanced_unedited_for_posting_v1.pdf. The Convention, under UNCLOS's aegis, seeks to promote the conservation and sustainable use of marine biological diversity of areas beyond national jurisdiction. Its four substantive elements include Marine Genetic Resources, Area Based Management Tools, Environmental Impact Assessments, and Capacity Building and the Transfer of Marine Technology. See 'Intergovernmental Conference on Marine Biodiversity of Areas Beyond National Jurisdiction', UN, www.un.org/bbnj.

These major global treaties portend significant safeguards for Arctic governance. They aim to close governance gaps and provide integrative solutions to management frameworks for the high seas and marine biodiversity. With or without a fully functioning regional body such as the Arctic Council, Arctic states have historically abided by an array of functional agreements,[83] most of them bilateral.

Congratulatory pieties favouring the protection of the commons may be in order, but they are more likely to be premature. Numerous implementation failures make compliance the Achilles' heel of protected areas notwithstanding laudable global interest in protecting the remaining natural environment.[84] The ecosystem of the Central Arctic Ocean remains unknown, inaccessible, and unfished.[85] The practical details regarding the BBNJ's implementation (for instance, the meaning of its 'not undermine' clause) await future discussion.[86] Having signed but not ratified the treaty, Norway quickly began the race to the bottom by opening the process for simultaneous deep sea mining exploration and exploitation licenses for 281,200 km^2 mining areas in the Barents and Greenland seas.[87] The European Union and environmental organisations

[83] For instance, the Agreement on Cooperation on Aeronautical and Maritime Search and Rescue (2011), the Agreement on Cooperation on Maritime Oil Pollution Preparedness and Response in the Arctic (2013), the Agreement on Enhancing International Arctic Scientific Cooperation (2017), the Polar Code regulations on shipping (2017), and the UN Law of the Sea Convention (1982).

[84] See Brock Bergseth and Jon C Day, 'Compliance – The 'Achilles Heel' of Protected Areas', 155 *Mar Pol'y* 105728 (2023), doi.org/10.1016/j.marpol.2023.105728.

[85] Indeed, signatories recognise that 'commercial fishing is unlikely to become viable in the high seas portion of the [C]entral Arctic Ocean in the near future'. Lan Ngoc Nguyen, 'Principled Challenges: Between Collective Interest and Individual Freedom', in *International Law and Marine Areas Beyond National Jurisdiction: Reflections on Justice, Space, Knowledge and Power*, 114, at 122 (Vito De Lucia, Alex Oude Elferink and Lan Ngoc Nguyen eds, 2022) [hereinafter *International Law and Marine Areas*].

[86] BBNJ Treaty, Art 4(2) ('This Agreement shall be interpreted and applied in a manner that does not undermine *relevant* legal instruments and frameworks and relevant global, regional, subregional and sectoral bodies that promotes coherence and coordination with those instruments, frameworks and bodies') (emphasis added). The phrase has already been problematised as 'ambiguous' and having a possible 'chilling effect' as 'some States have used it as a device to limit the scope of the agreement'. Richard Barnes, 'The Construction of Ocean Space in Areas Beyond National Jurisdiction: A Fisheries Perspective', in *International Law and Marine Areas*, n 85, 275, at 306. '[A] multitude of existing [international organizations]' participated in the BBNJ negotiations, each with its own set of interests. Concerns relating to 'polycentric governance' within this fragmented and emerging regime complex gives rise to concerns relating to upholding the 'not undermine' clause. Arne Langlet and Alice BM Vadrot, 'Not "Undermining" Who? Unpacking the Emerging BBNJ Regime Complex', 147 *Mar Pol'y* 7, 8 (2023).

[87] See Frida Brembo, Sondre Skjelvik and Elvind Molde, 'Flertall for å lete etter mineraler på havbunnen', NRK (5 December 2023), www.nrk.no/nordland/flertall-pa-stortinget-for-a-apne-for-gruvedrift-pa-havbunnen-1.16663872 (reporting on the Storting's majority decision to open up extraction on parts of Norway's continental shelf for the deep seabed extraction permits). The Storting's decision became official on 9 January 2024. See also Karoline Andaur, 'Norway's Deep Sea Mining Plans Risk the Arctic's Future', The Circle (April 2023) (noting the massive size of the area opened by Norway's Storting for exploration and exploitation).

registered concern.[88] The devil in the details of both treaties obligate parties to negotiate future differences, but it does not obligate parties to agree.

As recognised by UNCLOS,[89] international law can only require that disputes over interpretation and implementation 'proceed expeditiously to an exchange of views regarding [their] settlement by negotiation or other peaceful means'.[90] International jurisprudence recognises that merely abiding by the formalities of a negotiation process is not sufficient proof that parties will proceed in good faith.[91] Yet every drafter of a treaty also knows that postponing agreement over substantive content also can 'provide much needed breathing space for "states to order their conduct on the basis of general agreements while adjusting details" as developing circumstances dictate'.[92] It is not clear whether the signatories promised to resolve future disagreements over the treaty's terms (creating a *pactum de contrahendo*), or simply promised to negotiate future disputes (engaging in a *pactum de negotiando*). At a base level, a fine line of distinction separates good faith from cosmetic façade,[93] and important international legal scholars have forewarned of the complications of international agreements enacted without appropriate implementing machinery in place.[94] Competition over resources remains suppressed at this time, making it easier for states to sublimate their appropriative interests as they jockey for position.

In Roman law, things that could not be contained or privately owned – things such as the air, flowing water, the sea, and the seashore – belonged to everybody (*res communis*).[95] Things that could be individually owned but had not been

[88] See EU Council 11508/24, 30 (25 June 2024) (noting 'with concern') Norway's seabed mining decision in light of the obligation to establish 'a thorough assessment process of the environmental impact of potential mining activities'); Jan Dusik, 'Norway Undermines the High Seas Treaty by Rushing Deep Sea Mining Authorization', WWF (28 June 2024), www.arcticwwf.org/newsroom/features/norway-undermines-the-high-seas-treaty-by-rushing-deep-sea-mining-authorization (noting criticisms from scientists, NGOs and others that practical allowances for significant expenses by the petroleum industry exploration cut short discussions of environmental concerns and additionally contending that Norway's environmental assessment 'was superficial and insufficient to assess' impacts on affected areas' biodiversity).

[89] 1833 UNTS 397 (10 December 1982).

[90] ibid, Art 283.

[91] North Sea Continental Shelf (*FRG v Den; FRG v Neth*), Judgment, 1969 ICJ Rep at 47, 85.

[92] Christopher R Rossi, 'A Case Ill Suited for Judgment: Constructing "A Sovereign Access to the Sea" in the Atacama Desert', 48 *U Miami Inter-Am L Rev* 28, 47 (2017) (quoting Stephen L Kass, 'Obligatory Negotiations in International Organizations', 1965 *Can YB Int'l L* 36, 39 (1965)).

[93] ibid, at 49.

[94] RR Baxter, 'International Law in "Her Infinite Variety"', 29 *Int'l & Comp LQ* 549, 552 (1980); IV Center for Oceans Policy, University of Virginia, 'UNCLOS 1982 Commentary' 668 (Myron H Nordquist et al eds, 1982) quoted in Gaetan Verhoosel, 'Beyond the Unsustainable Rhetoric of Sustainable Development: Transfering Environmentally Sound Technologies', 11 *Georgetown Int'l Env't L Rev* 49, 54 (1988) (quoting Nordquist).

[95] Stefano Cattelan, 'Mare Clausum in Legal Argumentation: Claiming the Seas in the Early Modern Age' (Dissertation, Aarhus University, 2020), 50 fn 58 (referencing A Watson's translation of Justinian's *Digest* 1,8,2: *Et quidem naturali iure omnia communia sunt illa: aer, aqua profluens, et mare, et hoc per litoras maris*) [hereinafter Cattelan, '*Mare Clausum* in Legal Argumentation'].

claimed belonged to the first finder or discoverer (*res nullius*).[96] As noted in the *Corpus Juris Civilis* (534 CE), Emperor Justinian's (482–565 CE) compilation of 1,000 years of Roman legal experience,[97] the idea of a commons, or *types* of commons, had legal significance, but the proprietary right deriving from it was too broad to imagine in terms of the law of nations (*jus gentium*). It was only understood in the context of the law that applied to Roman citizens.[98] Even by the beginning of the seventeenth century, the great Dutch polymath, Hugo Grotius (1583–1645) claimed that dominium over the sea, for instance, was impossible due to its immensity and also due to the fact that it returned to its natural condition once a boat's wake subsided. At best, the sea allowed for a particular kind of dominium, which granted a freedom of use but not a right of ownership or entitlement to trade (*extra commercium*).[99] At most, it could be regulated by public authority (*res publica*), but it could not be owned.[100] Today, spatial areas treated as *res communis*, or the slightly misnamed global commons, include: the high seas and the deep seabed (which are areas beyond national jurisdiction), the atmosphere, Antarctica, outer space, the moon,[101] and now perhaps cyberspace.[102]

Modern developments in the international law of the sea have markedly constricted humanity's understanding of the global commons since Grotius's time. Coastal countries now claim full territorial sovereignty over the fisheries and minerals in their territorial seas, a littoral belt that extends 12 nautical miles seaward from the low-tidal mark. Coastal countries also assert (as opposed to *claim*) exclusive fishing rights over their Exclusive Economic Zones (EEZs), which extend 200 nautical miles from their shores, and to the seabed and subsoil

[96] A thing that is *res communis* belongs in common to everybody. It cannot be individually owned or appropriated. A thing that belongs to nobody can be owned by the first finder (discovery doctrine) or the person who takes possession.

[97] Christopher R Rossi, *Equity and International Law* 27 (1991).

[98] Cattelan, '*Mare Clausum* in Legal Argumentation', n 95, at 49 fn 56 (noting in Justinan's *Institute* 2, *De rerum divisione*, four categories of *res publicæ*, *res universitatis*, *res nullius*, and *res communes*), and 50 (applied only to Roman citizens).

[99] See Hugo Grotius, *Mare Liberum 1609-2009*, at 81 (Robert Feenstra ed, with a general introduction by Jeroen Vervliet, 2009) [1609]. See also Christopher R Rossi, 'A Particular Kind of Dominium: The Grotian Tendency and the Global Commons in a Time of High Arctic Change', 11 *J Int'l L & Int'l Rel* 1 (2015).

[100] A grand debate arose in the early Modern Age when seafaring nations began to assert exclusive maritime rights in the Mediterranean Sea, the seas of northern Europe and parts of the oceans that were within a canon shot of the shore (about three nm). This debate contrasted the idea of freedom of the seas (*mare liberum*) with the idea of the closed sea (*mare clausum*) and sparked an epic doctrinal debate contrasting the views of Grotius (*Mare Liberum*, 1609), and the English jurist, John Selden (*Mare Clausum*, 1635). See generally Cattelan, '*Mare Clausum* in Legal Argumentation', n 95.

[101] Apostolos Tsiouvalas and Jen Evans, 'From "Common Pools" to "Fish Pools": Shifting Property Institutions in Traditional Waters of Norway and Canada', 54 *Ocean Dev & Int'l L* 135, 139 (2023); Rossi, *Sovereignty and Territorial Temptation*, n 70, at 33.

[102] Tara Murphy, 'Security Challenges in the 21st Century Global Commons', 5 *Yale J Int'l Affs* (20 July 2010), www.yalejournal.org/publications/security-challenges-in-the-21st-century-global-commons.

of their continental shelves, which can extend beyond 200 nautical miles to possibly as far as 350 nautical miles from their shores if the costal state can prove a scientifically continuous geological connection to its mainland.

The expansion of coastal state interest over the EEZ now partitions 57 per cent of the sea floor, leaving only 43 per cent 'unsecured' or subject to the shared interests of humanity.[103] While scientists have more readily live-streamed images from land rovers on Mars, oceanographers note that crushing pressure, extreme cold, and zero visibility have hindered the exploration of more than 80 per cent of the oceans.[104] Only about one-quarter of the Earth's blue surface has been mapped,[105] and these routes include 'very poorly chartered' waters of the Northern Sea Route and the Northwest Passage; indeed 'only six percent of Arctic waters [are] actually chartered to international standards and only 11 percent is even mapped'.[106] Notwithstanding twentieth-century enclosures, the remaining area of the high seas today covers almost half of the world's surface and 64 per cent of the oceans.[107] As the smallest and shallowest of the world's five oceans, the territorially ringed Arctic Ocean bears more the characteristics of a closed sea (*mare clausum*) and projects more the traits of a gigantic frozen lake rather than a high seas regime.[108] The diminishment of sea ice has attracted geopolitical competition in the Arctic, heightening concern about the region's future.

THE LURE OF COMMERCIAL REWARD

An open waterway across the top of the world presents exceptional commercial rewards beyond the obvious prospects of resource exploitation or deep-water port development in places such as Alaska, Greenland, Iceland, and Canada.[109] The Arctic also presents the fastest, most direct surface route between Asia

[103] 'Ocean Governance: Who Owns the Ocean', Heinrich Böll Stiftung, (2 June 2017), www.boell.de/en/2017/05/30/ocean-governance-who-owns-ocean.

[104] Emily Petsko, 'Why Does So Much of the Ocean Remain Unexplored and Unprotected?' Oceana (8 June 2020), oceana.org/blog/why-does-so-much-ocean-remain-unexplored-and-unprotected.

[105] 'About Us', Seabed 2030, seabed2030.org/about (noting the mapping of the seabed project initiated in 2017 by the Nippon Foundation and the General Bathymetry Chart of the Ocean).

[106] Elizabeth Nyman et al, 'The Svalbard Archipelago: An Exploratory Analysis of Port Investment in the Context of the New Arctic Routes', 19 *Mar Stud* 1, 3 (2020).

[107] 'The High Seas, An Undisclosed World', Océans Connectés, oceansconnectes.org/en/the-high-seas-an-undisclosed-world.

[108] See W Lakhtine, 'Rights over the Arctic', 24 *Am J Int'l L* 703, 713 (1930). See also Donald R Rothwell, *The Polar Regions and the Development of International Law* 288–89 (1996).

[109] See Marco Volpe, 'The Tortuous Path of China's Win-Win Strategy in Greenland', Arctic Institute (24 March 2020), www.thearcticinstitute.org/tortuous-path-china-win-win-strategy-greenland (citing geological studies supporting Greenland's massive proximity to possible hydrocarbon, natural gas, and critical mineral lodes); 'China's Expanding Investment in Global Ports, Iceland', Economist Intelligence (11 October 2017), country.eiu.com/article.aspx?articleid=925980476&Country=Iceland&topic=Economy&subtopic=R_9 (noting Chinese negotiations to secure deep-sea port access in a fjord in northern Iceland).

and Europe, the world's two largest regional trading blocs.[110] This route, were it reliably navigable, would save more than a week's transit time per voyage, thereby significantly reducing energy, environmental, and transportation costs as compared to more expensive southern routes through the Indian Ocean, Suez Canal, and Mediterranean Sea.[111] Although rife with safety and security problems of its own,[112] an Arctic route would avoid the politically roiled waters of the South China Sea and the Strait of Malacca, as well as the pirate-infested waters off the Horn of Africa.[113]

Not as easily avoided are the growing concerns of the four million inhabitants above the Polar Circle, 500,000 of whom are Indigenous peoples.[114] The commercialisation prospects of an opening Arctic, in conjunction with acquaculture development, threats to taiga ecosystems and climate change, have serious implications for inhabitants of the polar North, including the six Indigenous peoples' organisations that have Permanent Participants status at the Arctic Council.[115] Their collective political voice to address these implications

[110] See 'EU Position in World Trade', EU Communication (2 October 2014), ec.europa.eu/trade/policy/eu-position-in-world-trade.

[111] See Felix H Tschudi, 'Time Equals Money: Developing a Profitable Shipping System Using the Northern Sea Route', 70 *Proc* 17–18 (2013). Estimates indicate a trans-arctic route can shorten travel distances by as much as 60%, with up to $600,000 in fuel savings per trip. See Stan Jones, 'Northern Sea Route Beckons LNG Shippers', Alaska Natural Gas Transportation Projects Office of the Federal Coordinator (9 October 2013), www.arcticgas.gov/northern-sea-routebeckons-lng-shippers.

[112] Despite the landmark 2011 Arctic Search and Rescue Agreement, circumpolar capabilities to launch effective search and rescue responses to exigent circumstances remains 'far from robust'. Timothy William James Smith, 'Search and Rescue in the Arctic: Is the U.S. Prepared?' 1 (2017) (PhD dissertation, Pardee RAND Graduate School), www.rand.org/pubs/rgs_dissertations/RGSD382.html.

[113] See generally Jonathan Masters, 'The Thawing Arctic: Risks and Opportunities, Council on Foreign Relations', Council on Foreign Relations (17 December 2013), www.cfr.org/backgrounder/thawing-arctic-risks-and-opportunities; Tullio Treves, 'Piracy, Law of the Sea, and Use of Force: Developments off the Coast of Somalia', 20 *Eur J Int'l L* 399, 399–414 (2009).

[114] See 'Arctic Peoples', Arctic Council, arctic-council.org/explore/topics. Another definition of the Arctic yields a total population 'just over 10 million'. Timothy Heleniak, 'The Future of the Arctic Populations', 44 *Polar Geography* 136, 150 (2021).

[115] The six Indigenous peoples' organisations of the Arctic Council with Permanent Participants status are the Aleut International Association (of Alaska, Russian Federation, Pribilof Islands and Commander Islands (15,350 persons), the Arctic Athabaskan Council (of Alaska, Yukon and Northwest Territories of Canada (45,000 persons), the Gwich'in Council International (of Alaska, Yukon and Northwest Territories of Canada (9,000 persons), the Inuit Circumpolar Council (Alaska, Canada, Greenland, and Chukotka (180,000 persons), the Russian Association of Indigenous Peoples of the North (250,000 persons comprising 40 Indigenous peoples), and the Saami Council (of Finland, Russian Federation, Norway, and Sweden (over 100,000 persons)). See 'Permanent Participants', Arctic Council, arctic-council.org/about/permanent-participants. For a discussion about the changing notion of the ocean commons and the interplay between acquaculture development and Indigenous and local small-scale fisheries management, see Tsiouvalas and Evans, 'From "Common Pools" to "Fish Pools": Shifting Property Institutions in Traditional Waters of Norway and Canada', n 101.

has also been muted internationally and even split internally by the suspension of normal Arctic Council interactions due to war in Ukraine.[116]

STRATEGIC IMPLICATIONS OF A GLOBALISING ARCTIC

The prospect of an opening Arctic oceanscape, surfeit of untapped living and mineral resources, has stimulated re-evaluations of Arctic strategies. Updated White Papers abound from circumpolar powers and North Atlantic States,[117] the European Union,[118] Great Britain,[119] Japan,[120] China,[121] Russia,[122] and India.[123] Norway recently revamped its Svalbard White Paper due to climate change and other activity, including Russia's war against Ukraine.[124]

[116] See 'Cooperation with Russian Side on Hold', Sáámiráđđi (10 April 2022) www.saamicouncil.net/news-archive/cooperation-with-russian-side-on-hold (reporting on interruptions in communication across the four countries of Sámpi – Norway, Sweden, Finland, and Russia – and the Sámi Council's decision to put cooperation on hold with the Kola Sámi Association and the Association of Sámi in Murmansk Oblast due to Russian Sámi support for the Ukraine war); see also 'The Association of the Indigenous Minorities and the Far East of the Russian Federation Came Out in Support of the President of Our Country V.V. Putin', RAIPON (1 March 2022), raipon.info/press-tsentr/novosti/assotsiatsiya-kmnss-i-dv-rf-vystupila-v-podderzhku-prezidenta-nashey-strany-v-v-putina- (reprinting the text of the letter in support of Putin's invasion of Ukraine from the Association of Indigenous Peoples of the North, Siberia and the Far East). A report prepared by the North American and Arctic Defense and Security Network noted that although Putin loyalists had been placed in RAIPON's leadership around 2012, its support of the invasion of Ukraine 'demonstrate[ed] a new level of Russian state coercion and use of the [Permanent Participant of the Arctic Council position] as a proxy to advance its message through Arctic Council circles'. 'Effects of Recent Developments on Arctic Regional Governance', NAADSN (3 March 2022), at 2, www.naadsn.ca/wp-content/uploads/2022/03/Activity-Report-3-March-2022-Closed-Arctic-Etalks-Exec-Summary.pdf.

[117] See generally Njord Wegge, 'Arctic Security Strategies and the North Atlantic States', 11 *Arctic Rev L & Pol* 360–82 (2020) (reviewing Arctic security strategies among the US, Canada, Denmark, Norway, UK, Germany, and France). See also National Strategy for the Arctic Region, White House (2022), www.whitehouse.gov/wp-content/uploads/2022/10/National-Strategy-for-the-Arctic-Region.pdf; Arctic and Northern Policy Framework, Government of Canada (2019), www.rcaanc-cirnac.gc.ca/eng/1560523306861/1560523330587.

[118] See Joint Communication on a Stronger EU Engagement for a Peaceful, Sustainable and Prosperous Arctic, EU External Action (13 November 2021), at 1 [hereinafter Joint Communication on a Stronger EU].

[119] 'Our Friends in the North: UK Strategy Towards the Arctic', UK Parliament (29 November 2023), publications.parliament.uk/pa/ld5804/ldselect/ldintrel/8/8.pdf.

[120] Japan's Arctic Policy [Provisional Translation], Cabinet Office (16 October 2015), www8.cao.go.jp/ocean/policies/arcticpolicy/arcticpolicy.html.

[121] China's Arctic Policy, St Council, PRC (January 2018), english.www.gov.cn/archive/white_paper/2018/01/26/content_281476026660336.htm (describing China as 'an important stakeholder in arctic affairs' and, geographically, 'a Near-Arctic State').

[122] Decree on Approval of the Foreign Policy Concept of the Russian Federation (31 March 2023), www.kremlin.ru/events/president/news [English trans].

[123] India's Arctic Policy: Building a Partnership for Sustainable Development. Government of India 3 (2022), www.moes.gov.in/sites/default/files/2022-03/compressed-SINGLE-PAGE-ENGLISH.pdf.

[124] See Birgitte Annie Molid Martinussen, 'Researcher: "New Svalbard White Paper Affirms Norwegian Jurisdiction on Svalbard"', High North News (20 June 2024) (noting accelerated publication of the White Paper due to changing environmental and geopolitical factors).

The northernmost tip of the Shetland Islands is 400 km from the Arctic Circle,[125] making Great Britain 'the Arctic's closest neighbour' and developments in the Arctic of 'critical importance to the UK's security.'[126] Although 1,448 km from the Arctic region, China now proclaims itself to be a 'Near-Arctic' state,[127] a phrase nominalised as meaningless to some Western policy makers,[128] and weaponised as ominous to others.[129] The European Union calls itself an 'Arctic entity' and a geopolitical power with 'strategic and day-to-day interests [] both in the European Arctic and the broader Arctic region'.[130] These interests intermix fisheries, tourism, energy, biodiversity and conservation, and climate change.[131] Russia upgraded the Arctic to a region of top priority, no longer registering it as part of its Western policy, but as an 'organic extension of its domestic Arctic development policy'.[132] Accordingly, all mention of multilateral formats for international cooperation have been removed.[133] India directly links its food security and rural sector to Arctic climate change and its effect on what India refers to as the Third Pole, the Himalayas.[134] It maintains a research station (the Himadri Station) in Ny-Ålesund,[135] one of nine national stations 'operated by states that collectively represent almost half of humanity'.[136] Singapore,

[125] Adapting to Change: UK Policy Towards the Arctic, HM Government (2013), at ii.

[126] 'Our Friends in the North: UK Strategy Towards the Arctic', n 119, at 13 ('closest neighbor'), 3 ('critical importance').

[127] 'China's Arctic Policy', Xinhua News Agency (26 Jan. 2018), www.gov.cn/xinwen/2018-01/26/content_5260891.htm, 2 (noting that 'China is an important stakeholder in Arctic affairs. Geographically, China is a "near-Arctic country" and one of the countries closes to the Arctic Circle on Land').

[128] See eg, 'Introducing the New Director of the Polar Institute', Wilson Center (21 September 2022), www.wilsoncenter.org/video/introducing-new-director-polar-institute, time mark: 12:45 (quoting Rebecca Pincus: 'The term "near-arctic" … state, it has no meaning').

[129] See eg, P. Whitney Lackenbauer, Adam Lajeunesse and Ryan Dean, 'Why China Is Not a Peer Competitor in the Arctic', *J Indo-Pac Aff* (3 October 2022), www.airuniversity.af.edu/JIPA/Display/Article/3172586/why-china-is-not-a-peer-competitor-in-the-arctic (recognising but questioning narratives that China's 'near-Arctic state' claim portends its interest in undermining the sovereignty of Arctic states in ways connected to 'China's growing, informal, global empire').

[130] Joint Communication on a Stronger EU, n 118, at 1.

[131] See generally Julien Lebel and Annika E Nilsson, 'EU Engagement in the Arctic: Challenges to Achieving Ambitions in an Area outside its Jurisdiction', 15 *Arctic Rev L&P* 47, (2024).

[132] Nikita Lipunov and Pavel Devyatkin, 'The Arctic in the 2023 Russian Foreign Policy Concept', Arctic Institute (30 May 2023), www.thearcticinstitute.org/arctic-2023-russian-foreign-policy-concept.

[133] ibid.

[134] Kanagavalli Suryanarayanan, 'Third Pole's View on the North Pole – India's Arctic Policy', Polar Connection (12 April 2022), polarconnection.org/third-pole-india-arctic-policy. India's hydro-scientific connection to the Arctic is not far-fetched. Fluids-related problems involving Arctic snow and glacier melt inform water dynamics of the Himalayas, which feed the massive Indus and Brahmaputra-Ganges river basins. These basins stretch from Afghanistan to China and support the livelihood of 700 million people. Santosh Nepal and Arun Bhakta Shrestha, 'Impact of Climate Change on the Hydrological Regime of the Indus, Ganges and Brahmaputra River Basins: A Review of the Literature', 31 *Int'l J Water Res Dev* 201 (2015).

[135] 'Himadri Station', NCPOR, ncpor.res.in/app/webroot/pages/view/340-himadri-station (established in 2008).

[136] Eric Paglia, 'The Northward Course of the Anthropocene: Transformation, Temporality and Telecoupling in a Time of Environmental Crisis' 19 (doctoral dissertation (CRISMART), Swedish Defence University 2016).

China, and Japan have Arctic ambassadors. The United States announced its first Ambassador-at-Large for the Arctic Region in 2023. It reactivated the Arctic Executive Steering Committee to coordinate federal activities in the Arctic. Through the Department of Defense, it established the Ted Stevens Center to support the military's mission in the Arctic.[137] It also established a diplomatic presence post in Tromsø, Norway (situated at 69°N) after reopening its Cold War consulate in Nuuk, Greenland (population 17,635).

The geostrategic importance of access to Arctic resources and transit routes is already clear. Russia's Rosatom formed a partnership with the United Arab Emirates to develop a new class of maritime container transports along the Northern Sea Route.[138] South Korea's icebreaker *RV Araon* plies Arctic waters. Three of its chaebol megaconglomerates,[139] Daewoo, Hyundai, and Samsung, operate marine engineering shipyards to manufacture icebreaking liquefied natural gas (LNG) carriers to transport Yamal gas out of the Russian Arctic to global markets. As the world's largest importer of liquefied natural gas, Japan considers Russian Arctic gas a key component to securing its future energy needs. The Japan Bank for International Cooperation has invested substantially in the development of Russian oil and natural gas production along its Northern Sea Route, although many of its investments and loan agreements with Russia have also been suspended because of the war.[140] Western financial sanctions have also affected the French megacorporation, Total, Norway's Statoil, Italy's ENI, and the United States' Exxon-Mobile, Schlumberger, and Haliburton enterprises.[141]

Europe has consciously attempted to decouple energy imports from Russia since the aggression against Ukraine. This severance began 'less a consequence of European Union actions than of decisions taken by the Kremlin'.[142] Russia's energy blackmail has spurred an European Union effort to 'phase out … dependency on Russian energy imports as soon as possible'.[143] However, this rhetoric has exposed one irony and several problematic tensions. Europe's ill-

[137] See generally Ted Stevens Center for Arctic Security Studies, tedstevensarcticcenter.org (describing the collaborative security network of this United States Department of Defense regional centre).

[138] Malte Humpert, 'Russia Inks Deal with Dubai's DP World to Develop Arctic Container Shipping', High North News (23 October 2023), www.highnorthnews.com/en/russia-inks-deal-dubais-dp-world-develop-arctic-container-shipping.

[139] Chaebols are a group of mostly family-run vertically integrated business mega-conglomerates that have historically dominated South Korea's postwar economy due to the support of the Government. See Eleanor Albert, 'South Korea's Chaebol Challenge', Council on Foreign Relations (4 May 2018), www.cfr.org/backgrounder/south-koreas-chaebol-challenge.

[140] See Felix Thompson, 'JBIC Halts Financing for Russian LNG Project', *Global Trade Review* (14 June 2022), www.gtreview.com/news/global/jbic-halts-financing-for-russian-lng-project.

[141] See Juha Käpylä and Harri Mikkola, *On Arctic Exceptionalism* at 16 (2015).

[142] Szymon Kardaś, 'Conscious Uncoupling: Europeans' Russian Gas Challenge in 2023', European Council on Foreign Relations (13 February 2023), ecfr.eu/article/conscious-uncoupling-europeans-russian-gas-challenge-in-2023/#:~:text=Before%20Russia%20invaded%20Ukraine%2C%20the,cent%20of%20total%20gas%20imports (noting Russian efforts to pressure European countries by withholding gas).

[143] REPowerEU Plan, SWD(2022) 230 final, EUR-Lex (18 May 2022), eur-lex.europa.eu/legal-content/EN/TXT/?uri=COM%3A2022%3A230%3AFIN&qid=1653033742483.

fated dependency on Russian energy has bolstered the ruble and diluted the effect of Western sanctions aimed at pressuring Russia to end the invasion.[144] It portends inflation, unemployment, and supply-chain interruptions in chemical, steel, and automotive sectors of industrial Europe.[145]

It has also promoted the perception of a strengthened lock and key relationship with China. China expanded its 2013 Belt and Road Initiative in 2017 to include a Polar Silk Road component.[146] Russia stands as the Gatekeeper of the Arctic for China, and China serves as Russia's 'main potential foreign benefactor'.[147] The Northern Sea Route provides China with access via the Bering Sea to Siberian minerals and gas. China's import demand provides crucial revenue for the greatly distressed ruble. 'Chinese and Russian geoeconomic strategies around energy and transportation are aligning' in the Arctic,[148] and at the expense of Western capital influx, energy demands, and bottom-line interests of Western corporations. Chinese President Xi Jingping and Russian President Vladimir Putin coyly suggested that their countries' aligning friendship has 'no limits' and 'no "forbidden" areas of cooperation',[149] suggesting a deepening military cooperation against the West as well.[150] That much appears to be true with regard to 'unprecedented' collaboration in fields of science, undersea technologies, civil–military relations, energy, and space and satellite information.[151] While the two countries commonly seek to disrupt a US-led Western World, and while China is becoming the most important post-Ukraine-invasion partner for Russia in the Arctic, there is little evidence to suggest that

[144] See Malte Humpert, 'EU Received 300 Shipments of LNG from Russia Since Beginning of Ukraine War', High North News (29 June 2023), www.highnorthnews.com/en/eu-received-300-shipments-lng-russia-beginning-ukraine-war (discussing the $20 bllion in payments to Russia from Belgium, France, Spain, Portugal, and the Netherlands for LNG exports in the year following the full-scale invasion of Ukraine).

[145] Sebastian Dullien, 'Wer ein Energieembargo fordert, muss die Gefahren kennen', Spiegel Wirtschaft (12 March 2022), www.spiegel.de/wirtschaft/russland-sanktionen-wer-ein-energie-embargo-fordert-muss-die-gefahren-kennen-gastbeitrag-a-aac5290a-5791-423e-9f83-a7cc398bc9ca ('Dieses Szenario könnte sich leicht beim Importembargo gegen russische Energie wiederholen. Besonders betroffen von solchen Effekten wären dann die Produktion und Arbeitsplätze in der Chemie-, Stahl- und Autoindustrie').

[146] Jan Jakub Solski, 'The Northern Sea Route in the 2010s: Development and Implementation of Relevant Law', 11 *Arctic Rev L & Pol* 383, 401 (2020).

[147] ibid.

[148] Rasmus Gjedssø Bertelsen, 'Jackie Fisher's Missing Key: The Northern Sea Route in Geoeconomics and Geostrategy', in *Konfliktraum Arktis: Die Großmächte und der Hohe Norden* 43, 54 (Joachim Weber ed, 2021).

[149] Joint Statement of the Russian Federation and the People's Republic of China on the International Relations Entering a New Era and the Global Sustainable Development, President of Russia (4 February 2022), www.en.kremlin.ru/supplement/5770.

[150] Joint Statement between the People's Republic of China and the Russian Federation on Deepening the Comprehensive Strategic Partnership of Coordination for a New Era on the Occasion of the 75th Anniversary of the Establishment of Diplomatic Relations between the Two Countries (Full Text), Xinhua News Agency (16 May 2024) (emphasising the developing China-Russia comprehensive strategic partnership and regarding 'each other as priority partners').

[151] Heather A Conley et al, 'A New Era of Arctic Geopolitics', GMF Report (18 July 2024).

diverging long- and medium-term interests in the Far East, the post-Soviet space of Central Asia, and the rapidly evolving region of the northern cryosphere will abate in terms of projected policies vis-à-vis NATO, the US, and the West.[152] As evidence, Yu Jie noted that the 2024 Joint Communique issued by Beijing and Moscow following Putin's state visit to China replaced the 'no limits' partnership with a language affirming a 'confluence of interests', a switch that 'almost certainly displays some sense of agonising on Beijing's part about its bilateral ties with Moscow'.[153] Moscow and Beijing share a commitment to create a post-Western world order, but they will never agree on what that order should look like apart from its autocratic veneer.

The nostalgia intentionally suggested by invocation of a Polar Silk Road engenders problematic calculations regarding the geopolitical costs needed to finance its development. These costs are measured not only in terms of establishing dual Chinese and Russian capacities for icebreaker fleets, but also in terms of developing feeder lines into the Euro-Asian sea transport corridor from coastal and offshore oil and gas fields in the Timan-Pechora province, the gas condensate fields of the Kara and Barents Seas, the Yamal gas project, and in terms of infrastructure developments to the expansive basins of the Ob and Yenisei rivers. The scale of China's investment in these projects do not match the scope of the political rhetoric nor the unease generated in Russian domestic circles by financing Chinese infrastructural investments that weaken Russian industrial capabilities.[154] Additionally, China maintains a 'carefully vague' position regarding Russia's legal,[155] as opposed to de facto claims to the Northern Sea Route. Russia, itself, has relied on 'ambiguous policy tools' regarding the seaward limits of its sovereign control over the Northern Sea Route as a means of 'discourage[ing] independent use' and 'navigational rights and freedoms by foreigners'.[156]

The Arctic Ocean also represents the shortest distance between Asia and Europe for purposes of data accumulation, dissemination, and fibre optic undersea cable development. None of the 380 underwater cables in operation

[152] See Margarete Klein, 'Myths and Misconceptions Around Russian Military Intent', Chatham House (14 July 2022), www.chathamhouse.org/2022/07/myths-and-misconceptions-around-russian-military-intent/myth-10-russia-and-china-are (Myth 10: 'Russia and China are Joining Forces Militarily Against the West').

[153] Yu Ji, 'China's Alignment with Putin is Uneasy. But Its Rivalry with the US Makes Him Too Useful to Abandon', Chatham House (17 May 2024), www.chathamhouse.org/2024/05/chinas-alignment-putin-uneasy-its-rivalry-us-makes-him-too-useful-abandon.

[154] Geopolitical and geoeconomic strategists have noted that the rhetoric associated with the polar silk road in Russian waters is poorly correlated with economic outlays, suggestive of the possibility that following a Chinese-financed string of pearls might be replaced by the loop of the Anaconda See Yu N Gladkiy et al, '"Polar Silk Road": Project Implementation and Geo-Economic Interest of Russia and China', IOP Conference Series: Earth and Environmental Science 5–6 (2021), https://iopscience.iop.org/article/10.1088/1755-1315/434/1/012009.

[155] Solski, n 146, at 401.

[156] ibid, at 402.

around the world has been laid in the Arctic Ocean,[157] although plans for the first Pan-Arctic connectivity route are rapidly progressing, with the prospect of reducing the round-trip signal delay between Japan and Western Europe to 142 milliseconds.[158] This burgeoning subsea infrastructure creates critical transatlantic cyberattack and hacking security issues for governments heavily dependent on such communications.[159]

THE RISE OF ASIAN ARCTIC INFLUENCE

Despite the potentially devastating effects of climate change on all Asian Pacific Economic Council (APEC) countries, Arctic energy security benefits appear substantial.[160] These potential rewards animate increasing engagement among Asian countries in Arctic institutions and dialogues.[161] The economic throw-weight of APEC countries active in the Arctic leverages more than the foothold implied by their observer status in the Arctic Council.[162] It indicates an emerging Asian ability to influence the discourse on Arctic Ocean sovereignty.[163]

Already, an Asia Arctic Five network has arisen through an amalgam of multi- and mini-lateral initiatives, including the Arctic Science Ministerial, the International Arctic Science Committee, the mostly entrepreneurial and private

[157] See Alan Cuningham, 'Underneath the Ice: Undersea Cables, the Arctic Circle, and International Security', Arctic Institute (29 March 2022), www.thearcticinstitute.org/underneath-ice-undersea-cables-arctic-circle-international-security (noting the advancement of public and private submarine internet cable schemes to connect the Atlantic and Pacific Oceans).

[158] See 'Unrivaled Speed, Security, And Diversity Linking Asia, North America and Europe through the Arctic', Far North Fiber (detailing the public–private initiative to provided connectivity to Japan, Iceland, Iceland, and Finland/Norway via Alaska). Cinia Oy Finland, American Far North Digital, and Japan's ARTERIA Networks Corporation are principally involved in developing this 15,000 km cable system, with funding from the EU's Connecting Europe Facility and mapping services provided by the Cable Route Study. The route runs entirely through international waters and within the maritime boundaries of Japan, the US, Canada, the EU and Norway. See Trine Jonassen, 'Far North Fiber One Step Closer to Pan-Arctic Connectivity', High North News (12 April 2023), www.highnorthnews.com/en/far-north-fiber-one-step-closer-pan-arctic-connectivity.

[159] See generally Colin Wall, 'Invisible and Vital: Undersea Cables and Translatlantic Security', CSIS (11 June 2021), www.csis.org/analysis/invisible-and-vital-undersea-cables-and-transatlantic-security (noting that undersea cables carry over 95 percent of international data).

[160] Hooman Peimani, 'Melting of the Arctic Sea Ice: Significance for the APEC Economies' Energy Security' 4 (APEC Oil and Gas Security Studies, Series 6, November 2015), www.apec.org/-/media/APEC/Publications/2015/12/Melting-of-the-Arctic-Sea-Ice---Significance-for-the-APEC-Economies-Energy-Security/Melting_of_the_Arctic_Sea_Ice_-_Significance_for_the_APEC_Economies__Energy_Security.pdf.

[161] See Calvin Heng and Eyck Freymann, 'Outsiders Wanting In: Asian States and Arctic Governance', Belfer Center (June 2023), at 14, www.belfercenter.org/sites/default/files/files/publication/Heng%20Freymann_Asian%20Arctic%20Observers_FINAL.pdf14 (noting 'Asian states have re-centered Arctic affairs in their post-pandemic national priorities').

[162] See Young Kil Park, 'South Korea's Interests in the Arctic', 18 *Asia Pol'y* 59, 63 (2014).

[163] See Li Xing and Rasmus Gjedssø Bertelsen, 'The Drivers of Chinese Arctic Interests: Political Stability and Energy and Transportation Security', in *China's Arctic Engagement: Following the Polar Silk Road to Greenland and Russia* 15, 26 (Justin Barns et al, eds, 2021).

Arctic Economic Council, the Asia Forum for Polar Sciences, the Trilateral High-Level Dialogue on the Arctic, and China's, Japan's, and South Korea's accession to the Agreement to Prevent Unregulated High Seas Fisheries in the Central Arctic Ocean (CAO Treaty).[164]

The Central Arctic Ocean represents the 'last unexploited fishery on Earth'.[165] It bobs like an enticing lure atop the world. Although commercial fishing has yet to take place in this inaccessible high-seas area, the CAO Treaty represents a sea of anticipation tempered by a still out-of-reach ability to secure its resources, and by a temporary agreement of 'historic' forbearance.[166] The treaty provides a 16-year moratorium on fishing in this vast Arctic area beyond national jurisdiction.[167] It recognises the need for knowledge-based decision-making to support fisheries management decisions in this remotest of areas. It also represents a fragile precautionary reprieve from the ever-expanding reach of distant-water fleets.[168] A 'prominent knowledge gap regarding' nutrient concentrations and 'the pelagic food web beneath the permanent pack ice' stir suspicions that the Central Arctic Ocean may be relatively fish-less.[169] And yet this knowledge-based assessment is precisely the kind of open science data collection now held in abeyance by the Western Arctic Seven allies of the Arctic Council. Concerns have already arisen that the CAO Treaty will not likely 'prove either sufficiently strong or sufficiently well-coordinated to manage increasing human activity there in the coming years'.[170] Consequently, Asian participation in the fisheries management regime in Central Arctic waters and elsewhere[171] is

[164] See www.mofa.go.jp/files/000449233.pdf [CAO Fisheries Agreement]. The 10 signatories to the convention include the so-called Arctic Five littoral countries plus China, Japan, South Korea, the EU and Iceland (the so-called A5+5).

[165] Hannah Hoag, 'Sea Ice Retreat Could Lead to Rapid Overfishing in the Arctic', *The Atlantic* (17 March 2017), www.theatlantic.com/science/archive/2017/03/fishing-at-the-top-of-the-world/519639.

[166] See 'Arctic: Agreement to Prevent Unregulated Fishing Enters into Force', European Commission (25 June 2021), oceans-and-fisheries.ec.europa.eu/news/arctic-agreement-prevent-unregulated-fishing-enters-force-2021-06-25_en (quoting EU Commissioner for Environment, Oceans and Fisheries, Virginijus Sinkevičius).

[167] CAO Agreement, Art 31(1). The treaty provides that it may conclude in 2037 or be extended for five-year periods unless a party objects. See ibid, Art 13(2).

[168] The treaty provides that it may conclude in 2037 or be extended for five-year periods unless a party objects. See ibid, Art 13(2).

[169] See Pauline Snoeijs-Leijonmalm et al, 'Unexpected Fish and Squid in the Central Arctic Deep Scattering Layer', 8 *Sci Adv* 1, 12 (2022), www.science.org/doi/pdf/10.1126/sciadv.abj7536 (noting also that 'the capacity of the CAO ecosystem to support larger fish stocks is without doubt rather limited.' ibid, at 13).

[170] David Balton, 'Advancing US Diplomacy in the Arctic', *For Service J* (May 2021), afsa.org/advancing-us-diplomacy-arctic.

[171] Principal regional fishery management organizations regulate tuna and other highly migratory species. They include the Commission for the Conservation of Southern Bluefin Tuna (CCSBT covering Southern Hemisphere waters between 30°S and 50°S; the Inter-American Tropical Tuna Commission, IATTC, off the coasts of the Western Hemisphere; the International Commission for the Conservation of Atlantic Tunas (ICCAT); the Indian Ocean Tuna Commission (IOTC); and the Western and Central Pacific Fisheries Commission (WCPFC).

too crucial to exclude, and perhaps too elusive to secure.[172] By either measure, the world's distant-water fishing fleets present an inclusive challenge to Arctic governance and to the circumpolar powers' desire to keep their hands on the helm of Arctic decision-making and on Arctic science as a lever for diplomacy.

China, Japan, and South Korea together engage in 58 per cent of the global distant-water fisheries trade.[173] Four of the seven largest subsidised long-distance water fleets[174] originate in Asia,[175] with substantial long-distance fishing fleets emerging also in India, Vietnam,[176] and Taiwan.[177] China's distant-water fleet, by far the largest in the world,[178] has expanded due to depletions of domestic fish stocks.[179] Since 1950, heavily subsidised fishing fleets of the world have 'increased the total fished area from 60 per cent to more than 90 per cent of the world's oceans, doubling the average distance traveled from home ports but catching only one-third of the historical amount per kilometer traveled'.[180]

[172] See Lyle J Goldstein, 'What Does China Want with the Arctic?' National Interest (2 September 2019), nationalinterest.org/feature/what-does-china-want-arctic-78731 (projecting general concerns of endangerment to delicate Arctic fishing and ecosystems due to reckless Chinese resource extraction); Miki Okuyama, Nikkei (1 August 2021), asia.nikkei.com/Politics/International-relations/International-research-planned-to-manage-Arctic-fish-stocks.

[173] See generally Heng and Freymann, n 161 (detailing Asian state engagement with Arctic affairs).

[174] 'Distant-water fishing fleets are the fishing vessels that operate within the 200-mile Exclusive Economic Zones (EEZs) of other countries, and less often further offshore, in what is known as the high seas.' 'Ask Dr. Pauly: What Are Distant Water Fleets, and How Do They Affect Overfishing?' Oceana (21 October 2013), usa.oceana.org/blog/ask-dr-pauly-what-are-distant-water-fishing-fleets-and-how-do-they-affect-overfishing/#:~:text=Distant%2Dwater%20fishing%20fleets%20are,known%20as%20the%20high%20seas.

[175] Isabel Jarrett, 'Most Long-Distance Fishing in Foreign Waters Dominated by Only a Few Governments', Pew (27 May 2022), www.pewtrusts.org/en/research-and-analysis/issue-briefs/2022/05/most-long-distance-fishing-in-foreign-waters-dominated-by-only-a-few-governments (noting that two-thirds of harmful fisheries subsidies, which enable vessels to travel farther and stay at sea longer, thus contributing to overfishing and overcapacity, are supported by China, Japan, South Korea, and Thailand, with other major subsidised fleets originating in Russia, the US, and EU).

[176] See Nicole Covey, 'Legitimization of the Arctic Coastal States (A5) through the Central Arctic Ocean (CAO) Fisheries Agreement', *NAADSN Pol'y Primer* 8 (28 October 2021) (advising that the CAO Agreement should expand signatories to include Vietnam, Thailand, India, and Chile).

[177] See 'Taiwan's Distant-Water Fleet Still on Troubled Waters', European Values Center for Security Policy (19 September 2023), europeanvalues.cz/en/taiwans-distant-water-fleet-still-on-troubled-waters/#:~:text=Taiwan%20owns%20one%20of%20the,tuna%20suppliers%20to%20global%20markets (estimating Taiwan's distant-water fishing fleet to number 2000 vessels).

[178] Estimates of China's distant-water fleet vary considerably, from about 10,000 (see Edward White, 'China's Fishing Fleet Embroiled in rising Tensions with US', *Financial Times* (23 May 2023), www.ft.com/content/5b3cc3a1-0c42-4679-81ca-be0ca7f448d1) to 16,996 vessels, with 'at least 183 vessels … suspected of involvement in IUU fishing'. Miren Guiterrez and Guy Jobbins, 'China's Distant-Water Fishing Fleet: Scale, Impact and Governance', ODI Global (2 June 2020), odi.org/en/publications/chinas-distant-water-fishing-fleet-scale-impact-and-governance.

[179] Ian Urbina, 'How China's Expanding Fishing Fleet Is Depleting the World's Oceans', YaleEnvironment360 (17 August 2020), e360.yale.edu/features/how-chinas-expanding-fishing-fleet-is-depleting-worlds-oceans (noting: 'Having depleted the seas close to home, the Chinese fishing fleet has been sailing farther afield to exploit the waters of other countries').

[180] David Tickler et al, 'Far From Home: Distance Patterns of Global Fishing Fleets', 4 *Science Advances* 1 (2018), www.science.org/doi/pdf/10.1126/sciadv.aar3279.

Such diminishing marginal returns threaten commercially valuable fish stocks and entice fishing fleet extensions into pristine polar waters.[181] China has been accused of tacitly engaging in illegal, unreported, and unregulated fishing (IUU),[182] raising a national security concern in the United States and around the world.[183] Together these fleets stimulate rising geopolitical and geoeconomic Asian food security interests with implications for Arctic waters. Japan and South Korea have taken measures through Regional Fisheries Management Organizations (RFMOs) to combat IUU fishing and by signing on to the Port State Measures to Prevent, Deter and Eliminate IUU Fishing (PSMA).[184] This treaty acts as a form of border patrol and inspection of foreign vessels attempting to land their illegal catches. Taiwan has directed government agencies to domestically incorporate the PSMA,[185] although it has repeatedly been cited for violations.[186] China has not signed the agreement; Russia has.[187] Together, however, concerns about their lack of compliance with this emerging norm place them among the leading high-risk fleets in terms of fleet size, catch volumes, vessel entries into foreign ports, and foreign vessels into home ports.[188]

[181] See ibid, at 4 (corroborating diminishing global fishing returns and the extension of distance fishing into 'all but the polar extremes of the global oceans').

[182] See Bruce Vaughn et al, *China's Role in the exploitation of Global Fisheries*, CRS (12 April 2022), 12, crsreports.congress.gov/product/pdf/R/R47065/1 (noting also that one study 'identified China as the overall worst-scoring coastal country (out of 152 total countries) with regard to IUU fishing practices. … [b] a wide measure'); Gilles Hosch et al, 'IUU Safe Havens or PSMA Ports: A Global Assessment of Port State Performance and Risk', 155 *Marine Policy* 10 (2023), www.sciencedirect.com/science/article/pii/S0308597X23002841?via%3Dihub (noting that China and Russia lead in terms of overall risk).

[183] White, n 178 (quoting Pacific Forum policy researcher Elizabeth Freund Larus' claim that 'Washington had determined that … (IUU) fishing by Chinese boats was a "national security concern"'); Isabella Montecalvo et al, 'Ocean Predators: Squids, Chinese Fleets and the Geopolitics of High Seas Fishing', 152 *Marine Policy* 1 (2023) (discussing predatory distant water fishing by Chinese vessels of concern to Argentina, Chile, Peru, and Ecuador); Henry Wilkins, 'Gulf of Guinea Countries Agree to Stop Illegal Chinese Fishing', VOA (9 December 2022), www.voanews.com/a/gulf-of-guinea-countries-agree-to-stop-illegal-chinese-fishing-/6869807.html (detailing the decimation of West African fishing stocks due to illegal fishing mainly from Chinese-owned boats); Overfishing Fuels South China Sea Tensions, Risks Armed Conflict, Researcher Says, RFA (5 January 2022) www.rfa.org/english/news/china/southchinasea-fisheries-01052022141237.html.

[184] See generally Agreement on Port State Measures (PSMA), FAO www.fao.org/port-state-measures/en. For the full text of the agreement, see www.fao.org/3/i5469t/I5469T.pdf.

[185] See 'Taiwan Supports Global Treaty Against Illegal Fishing', Department of Information Services, (29 July 2016), english.ey.gov.tw/Page/61BF20C3E89B856/ae6b9717-e389-49ce-8364-635fdda9d70a.

[186] See generally 2023 Report to Congress: Improving International Fisheries Management, NOAA Fisheries (2023), www.fisheries.noaa.gov/s3/2023-08/2023RTC-ImprovingIFManagement.pdf.

[187] See Agreement on Port State Measures (PSMA), UN FAO (2020), www.fao.org/port-state-measures/background/parties-psma/en. See also Agreement on Port State Measures to Prevent, Deter and Eliminate Illegal, Unreported and Unregulated Fishing, Ratification by the Russian Federation FAO 13/IV/2021, faolex.fao.org/treaty/docs/csl000263.pdf.

[188] Hosch et al, n 182, at 18.

A NEW REALITY

Rising Asian Pacific interest in the High North, rapidly receding ice, emerging resources, submerging shorelines, disappearing ocean features, the growing need for cyber-resilient underwater digital communication cables and energy pipelines, distant-water fishing fleets, and the shrinking commons contribute to the new reality of a global Arctic in the Kenocene. This new reality challenges the established binary separating human history and natural history. It reframes the human being as a 'geological force', not simply a 'biological agent'.[189] It widens or at least fogs the lens through which the High North is viewed, meshing geological, human, environmental, and political considerations.

In international law, regime analysis has long been predicated on the thesis that the 'land dominates the sea'.[190] The once presumed *exclusive* ambit of circumpolar powers is now transposing into the *inclusive* claims of other states.[191] This new reality undercuts the jurisdictional assertion that 'There are only Arctic States and Non-Arctic States.'[192] It undercuts the five circumpolar countries'[193] contention that their propinquity to the pole grants them 'unique' (exclusive?) stewardship rights that obviate any other need for a new Arctic governance structure.[194] And it calls into question the theme of Arctic exceptionalism. Was it ever so?

[189] Chakrabarty, n 37, at 206.

[190] See *North Sea Continental Shelf Cases (Ger/Den; Ger/Neth)*, 1969 ICJ Rep. 3, 51 (20 February); *Aegean Sea Continental Shelf Case (Gr/Turk)*, 1978 ICJ Rep 3, 36 (19 December); *Case Concerning Maritime Delimitation and Territorial Questions between Qatar and Bahrain (Qatar/Bahr)*, 2001 ICJ Rep. 40, 97 (16 March); *Maritime Delimitation in the Black Sea (Rom/Ukr)*, 2009 ICJ Rep. 61, 89 (3 February). For doctrinal discussion, see Irini Papanicolopulu, 'The Land Dominates the Sea (Dominates the Land Dominates the Sea)', 47 *Q Int'l L* 39 (2018).

[191] See generally Gershon Hasin, 'Ocean Governance in the 21st Century: A 'New Package-Deal' to Balance Mare Liberum and Mare Clausum', 48 *Yale J Int'l L* 223–87 (2023).

[192] Michael R Pompeo, *Looking North: Sharpening America's Arctic Focus*, US Department of State (6 May 2019), 2017-2021.state.gov/looking-north-sharpening-americas-arctic-focus (speech by the United States Secretary of State at the Arctic Council Ministerial meeting in Rovaniemi, Finland).

[193] The so-called Arctic Five circumpolar coastal states are Canada, Denmark (via self-governing, autonomous Greenland), Norway, Russia, and the US.

[194] Illulissat Declaration, Arctic Ocean Conference, Illulissat, Greenland (28 May 2008), reprinted in cil.nus.edu.sg/wp-content/uploads/2017/07/2008-Ilulissat-Declaration.pdf (asserting 'By virtue of their sovereignty … [that] the five coastal states [rimming the Arctic Ocean] are in a unique position to address [Arctic] possibilities and challenges').

Chapter Six

Russia and Eurasia

FOLLOWING THE UKRAINE invasion, two members of the Arctic Council, Finland and Sweden, joined the North Atlantic Treaty Organization (NATO).[1] Finland had been neutral since 1948. Sweden had adopted this posture after disastrous territorial losses to Russia during the Napoleonic wars and had shaped its removal from partisanship into an activist foreign policy of mediation, moderation, and soft power diplomacy. Both countries bring to NATO recalibrated capabilities given their substantial military arsenals, as adapted to high north latitudes, and deep cultural and geopolitical ties to the Baltic region. Finland has Western Europe's strongest artillery and 280,000 troops at the ready from 870,000 reserves who engage in regular training.[2] Sweden has an established and technologically advanced military-industrial complex, more than 100 advanced fighter planes, and a modern navy.[3]

Seven of the eight circumpolar Arctic stakeholder states now align militarily against Russia. This shift in the political orientation of the Council has an impact that cannot be ignored. Arguments now arise that Russia's longstanding paranoia about Western ideological and geographical encirclement – what George Kennan influentially described as its 'traditional and instinctive … sense of insecurity'[4] – have fuelled a self-fulfilling prophecy about its need to secure Crimea and Ukraine.[5] What implication does this prophecy hold for the Arctic space?

[1] *Finland and Sweden Submit Applications to Join Nation*, NATO (18 May 2022), www.nato.int/cps/en/natohq/news_195468.htm. Finland deposited its instrument of accession and formally joined NATO on 4 April 2023. Sweden's application has been blocked by Turkey (over Sweden's alleged harbouring of Kurdish militants) and Hungary (due to Sweden's criticisms of Hungary's commitment to the rule of law).

[2] Anne Kauranen, 'What Can Finland's Armed Forces and Arsenal Offer NATO?' Reuters (4 April 2023), www.reuters.com/world/europe/what-can-finlands-armed-forces-arsenal-offer-nato-2023-04-04.

[3] Lucia Mackenzie, with Joshua Posaner, Hanne Cokelaere and Giovanna Coi, 'What Sweden brings to NATO' Politico (7 March 2024), www.politico.eu/article/sweden-nato-membership-military-power.

[4] 861.00/2–2246: Telegram, The Charg[é] in the Soviet Union (Kennan) to the Secretary of State (22 February 1946), nsarchive2.gwu.edu/coldwar/documents/episode-1/kennan.htm [the Long Telegram].

[5] Indeed, Polish–Russian hostility dates to 981. See Oscar Halecki, 'Polish-Russian Relations–Past and Present', 5 *Rev of Pol* 322, 323 (1943) (noting beginning of the centuries-long frontier dispute over the castle Przemysl). Russo-Swedish wars erupted throughout the 17th and 18th centuries (note the Treaty of Stolbovo (1617), with Swedish armies reaching Moscow, the Great Northern War of 1700–1721 (launching the anti-Swedish coalition and rise of Russian influence in the Baltic), the Treaty of Åbo (concluding the Russo-Swedish War of 1741–1743, which ceded southern Finland to Russia), the Anjala League war of 1788–1790 (over Sweden's failed attempt to recapture lost Finnish

Critics of liberalism's 'flawed theory of world politics' and its wishful 'illusions',[6] even 'delusions',[7] seemingly affirmed liberalism's nihilistic penchant to 'divide[] the world into "good states" … and "bad states".'[8] Stephen Walt claimed that the presumption of NATO's 'benign intentions' to creation of a '"vast zone of peace" across all of Europe' reflected naivety 'in the extreme'.[9] From the perspective of an emerging Russian endeavour to create a Eurasian Economic Union (EaU) homologous with the European Union (EU), Richard Sakwa wrote

> just at the moment when the peaceful unification of the [Eurasian] continent was in prospect for the first time in history …. The Atlantic community rejected … the substantive engagement with Eurasian institutions, let alone any putative greater Asian complex.[10]

John Mearsheimer went so far as to identify the United States and its European allies as the 'taproot of the trouble', pinpointing NATO's eastern expansion and its 'larger strategy to move Ukraine out of Russia's orbit and integrate it into the West'.[11] He further articulated the theory of 'offensive realism', whereby great powers (determined 'on the basis of their relative military capability') – fundamentally insecure about the status quo – 'look for opportunities to gain power at each others' expense'.[12] They 'defend the balance of power when looming change favors another state [and] … undermine the balance when the direction of change is in [their] own favor.'[13]

Mearsheimer claimed that the structure of the international system 'force[d]' states to act aggressively. He based this view on the system's absence of central authority, the relative or situationally specific offensive capability harboured by each state, and the overlaying condition of uncertainty as to other states' intentions, which creates an international system based on fear.[14] The theme of fear is fundamental to this realist perspective and as old as the writings of Thucydides (c 460–400 BCE).[15]

provinces), the war of 1808–1809 (resulting in Sweden's loss of Finland to Russia), Napoleon's march through Poland to Moscow (1812), the US Army occupation of Archangel and military engagement against the Bolsheviks (1918–1919), and Operation Barbarossa (1941), Hitler's march to within 30 km of the Kremlin.

[6] Stephen Walt, 'Liberal Illusions Caused the Ukraine Crisis', *Foreign Pol'y* (19 January 2022), foreignpolicy.com/2022/01/19/ukraine-russia-nato-crisis-liberal-illusions.

[7] John J Mersheimer, 'Why the Ukraine Crisis Is the West's Fault: The Liberal Delusions That Provoked Putin', *For Affs* (September–October 2014).

[8] Walt, n 6.

[9] ibid.

[10] Richard Sakwa, 'The Age of Eurasia?', in *The Politics of Eurasianism: Identity, Popular Culture and Russia's Foreign Policy* 201, at 205 (Mark Bassin and Gonzalo Pozo eds, 2017) (hereinafter Bassin and Pozo).

[11] Mersheimer, n 7.

[12] John J Mearsheimer, *The Tragedy of Great Power Politics* 5 (2001).

[13] ibid, at 3.

[14] ibid.

[15] See *Thucydides: The War of the Peloponnesians and the Athenians* I.23.6 [16] (Jeremy Mynott ed, 2013) ('I consider the truest cause, though the one lease openly stated, to be this: the Athenians

Similarly, Carl Schmitt maintained that the essence of the political reduced to the relationship between friend and enemy, which could not be confused with the binary distinction between good and evil. Enemies posed existential threats and needed to be dealt with; evil could perhaps be avoided or sequestered to its own realm '*beyond the line of amity*'. On a grand scale, Schmitt attempted to defend if not preserve the internal order of Europe as a civilisation unit, a *jus publicum europaeum*. Consequently, the friend–enemy antithesis stood alone as 'a distinct new domain'. Schmitt thought it was independent from other normative counterpositions, and 'must even less be confused with or mistaken for the others'.[16] As much as he focused on nihilistic liberalism as the existential enemy of his conservative Eurocentric worldview, he kept an eye on Bolshevism. His antagonistic regard for Marxism reduced to its displacement of the political for the totalising importance of the material or economic.[17] Nevertheless, he clinically endorsed the infamous Molotov–Ribbentrop Pact of non-aggression (1939) because it 'establish[ed] in the sharpest terms the principle of [non-intervention] and at the same time speaks of 'the mutual state interests' … of the peoples on both sides' of the line.[18]

Schmitt's simple binomial construction of the political comports with the revival of polarity discussions and the logic embedded in its spatial emphasis. Modern critics of liberalism also argue that international politics must focus on oppositional forces that pose existential threats, not on normative assessments of morality, or what is good and bad. In classical realist terms, order and security override justice. Maintaining the spatial order minimises perceptions of violence-inducing threats and instability.

There is of course variance here. According to Kenneth Waltz, balance-of-power theory fostered defensive realignments in order to minimise hegemonic security threats in 'closely competitive' systems.[19] While war remained a 'normal'

were becoming powerful and inspired fear in the Spartans and so forced them into war'). On the timeless application of the theme, see Robert Gilpin (noting 'everything that the new realists find intriguing in the interaction of international politics can be found in The History of Thucydides'. Robert Gilpin, *War and Change in World Politics* 292 (1981); Kenneth N Waltz, *Theory of International Politics* 66 (1979) (noting 'the striking sameness of the quality of international life throughout the millennia').

[16] Carl Schmitt, *The Concept of the Political* 26 (George Schwab trans and intro, 2007).

[17] Alex Schulman, 'Carl Schmitt and the Clash of Civilizations: The Missing Context', 17 *J Pol Ideologies* 148 (2012) (noting 'Schmitt's critique of Marxism as a totalizing philosophy where economics trumps politics').

[18] David G Lewis, *Russia's New Authoritarianism: Putin and the Politics of Order* 162 (2020) (quoting Schmitt's 1940 lecture).

[19] See Kennith N Waltz, 'The Origins of War in Neorealist Theory', 18 *J Interdisciplinary Hist* 615 616 and 628 ('closely competitive' systems) (1988) (contending: 'Because power is a possibly useful means, sensible statesmen try to have an appropriate amount of it. In crucial situations, however, the ultimate concern of states is not for power but for security'). See also Waltz, *Theory of International Politics* 118 (1979) (explicating assumptions about state behaviour and noting that 'Fear of … unwanted consequences stimulates states to behave in ways that tend toward the creation of balance of power'). For a discussion of the constellation of problems associated with security maximisation, see John H Herz, 'Idealist Internationalism and the Security Dilemma', 2 *World Pol* 157 (1950)

occurrence,[20] 'potentially destabilizing' imbalances elicited calculated and flexible responses to offset the accumulation of power. Even Waltz's defensive power balancing schematic harboured offensive implications: 'an alliance that in the interest of defense moves to increase cohesion among its members and add to its ranks inadvertently imperils an opposing alliance and provokes countermeasures.'[21]

European unionisation, NATO enlargement, market liberalisation, and economic interdependence projected liberalism's mutually reciprocated norms of peaceful engagement across Europe following the demise of the Soviet Union. The liberal Arctic order flourished during this period and allowed for a recalibration (or perhaps suspension) of the West's Arctic focus while maintaining strategic interests in Alaska, Greenland (the Pituffik Space Base, formerly Thule Air Base), and in easternmost Vardø, Norway (to surveil the Barents Sea and Russia's Spetsnaz special marine forces).[22] The Arctic again assumed its peripheral status as projected for centuries atop Gerardus Mercator's influential planisphere (1569).[23] For states proximate to the High North, the region never stopped evoking strong political and emotional interests, notwithstanding the fact that no Arctic state locates its capital in the Arctic.

From Russian President Vladimir Putin's historical perspective, liberalism's chimeras presented a toxic pharmakon of illusion intended to diminish Russia's primacy in Europe and, by implication, in the Arctic. They awakened longstanding Russian sentiments of Western betrayal tracing from the punishing 1918 Brest–Litovsk Treaty[24] and the 1919 Versailles Treaty,[25] where the fate of Russia's

(noting the 'vicious circle' of insecurity caused by one state acquiring more power and the impact of that acquisition on the drive of others to acquire more power).

[20] Waltz, n 19 at 620.

[21] ibid, at 619.

[22] Jackie Northam, 'In a Remote Arctic Outpost, Norway Keeps Watch on Russia's Military Buildup', NPR (3 November 2019), www.keranews.org/2019-11-03/in-a-remote-arctic-outpost-norway-keeps-watch-on-russias-military-buildup (noting also the Norwegian build-up of its northernmost military camp at Porsangermoen in Finnmark, a training ground for winter warfighting).

[23] See Gerardus Mercator, 'Nova et Aucta Orbis Terrae Descriptio ad Usum Navigantium Emendate Accommodata' (1569), gallica.bnf.fr/ark:/12148/btv1b7200344k/f14.item.zoom.

[24] See Peace Treaty of Brest Litovsk (30 March; 2 April 1918), Avalon Project, avalon.law.yale.edu/20th_century/bl34.asp. The Brest–Litovsk Treaty created a separate peace between the Bolsheviks in Russia and the Central Powers (Germany, Austria-Hungary, Bulgaria, and the Ottoman Empire). The treaty ended Soviet Russia's participation alongside allied powers in World War I and effectively ceded Russian control over part of Transcaucasia, the Baltic governorates, and Ukraine. Russia ceded about 780,000 km^2 and ultimately agreed to pay war indemnity of 6,000,000 marks. See generally Simon Hinrichsen, *When Nations Can't Default: A History of War Reparations and Sovereign Debt* (2023). Soviet historical narratives regarded the Brest–Litovsk Treaty as an encirclement campaign and ultimately shifted war blame onto the Entente and specifically the USA for forcing Lenin to sue for peace on such terms. See 'When Did the First World War End for Russia? Marking the Centenary of the Treaty of Brest-Litovsk', RIAC (5 March 2018), russiancouncil.ru/en/analytics-and-comments/analytics/when-did-the-first-world-war-end-for-russia-marking-the-centenary-of-the-treaty-of-brest-litovsk (noting Soviet historical narratives of western encirclement and Entente responsibility).

[25] See generally Peter Rudolf, 'The Sino-American World Conflict' SWP (2020), www.swp-berlin.org/10.18449/2020RP03 (discussing the rising adversarial relationship between the US and China, and the increasing globalisation of regional competitions).

historical interests in the Arctic archipelago of Spitzbergen and Bear Island lost out to diplomatic machinations of Norway and its status as a 'neutral ally' of the Americans, French and British.[26] From Putin's post-Soviet perspective, liberalism constructed its own hegemonic security sphere. It stoked the militarisation of the Arctic, contributed to the diaspora of 25 million Russians now sprawled across 14 borderland states of the former Soviet Union, and imposed economic policies reminiscent of Tsarist imperial interests to maintain Moscow's periphery as a pool of historical stagnation.[27]

Michael Paul and Göran Swistek have emphasised Russia's geopolitical sense of insecurity fed by the difficulty of defending its vast borders, its proximity to other great powers, its demand to be regarded as a coequal world power, and a narrative of NATO deceit, which Putin persistently and inaccurately frames as a breach of a NATO promise not to expand eastward.[28] These factors form the basis of Russia's centuries-old strategy of engagement with the outside world, making the peaceful period of the 1990s, when the idea of Arctic exceptionalism took hold, the truly exceptional deviation from 'the rule of structural geopolitical competition between great powers in Eurasia'.[29]

Structural changes to the post-Cold War environment now project geopolitical considerations beyond liberalism's 'unipolar moment',[30] which purportedly highlighted the United States' unchallenged hegemonic status following 1991. Debates abound about when this moment ended and what structure replaced it. Scholars and analysts continue to nuance the nature of power, the meaning of great power status, and the structure of international relations, variously described as multipolar, bipolar, (still) unipolar, or some hybrid mix.[31] Criticisms

[26] Although only observers at the Versailles peace conference, Norwegian attendees executed a secret plan hatched at the Storting to leverage Norway's wartime status as a 'neutral ally' of the Americans, French, and British to secure sovereignty over Spitzbergen. Norwegian diplomacy, deftly pursued by Helmer Bryn (1865–1933) and Fritz Wedel Jarlsberg (1855–1942) resulted in an agreement facilitated by US Secretary of State Robert Lansing (1864–1928) that secured for Norway the archipelago, a result that expanded 'neutral' Norway's territory by 20% more than it had before the outset of the Great War. Norway's territorial gain of Spitzbergen came at the expense of Germany as a vanquished power, Russia, having sued for an earlier separate peace with Germany, and Sweden See generally Christopher R Rossi, '"A Unique International Problem", The Svalbard Treaty, Equal Enjoyment, and Terra Nullius: Lessons of Territorial Temptation from History', 15 *Wash U Global Stud LR* 93 (2016).

[27] See Charles Emmerson, *The Future History of the Arctic* 35–42 (2010).

[28] Michael Paul and Göran Swistek, 'Russia in the Arctic: Development Plans, Military Potential and Conflict Prevention', Stiftung Wissenschaft und Politik Research Paper 3 (February 2022) 24–25

[29] ibid, at 25.

[30] The phrase was coined by Charles Krauthammer, 'The Unipolar Moment', 70 *For Affs* 2 (1990/1991) (holding: 'The most striking feature of the post-Cold War world is its unipolarity. No doubt, multipolarity will come in time').

[31] For a variety of informed perspectives on the question of unipolarity and its purported demise see 'Did the Unipolar Moment Ever End? Foreign Affairs Asks the Experts', *For Affs* (23 May 2023) www.foreignaffairs.com/ask-the-experts/did-unipolar-moment-ever-end.

of liberalism's globalisation strategy[32] and thin extension to the regions of the Third World[33] and China's rise as a global power now suggest the emergence of a new bipolar arrangement based on Sino-American rather than Soviet–American competition,[34] or perhaps a 'multiplex' of crosscutting international orders in the great Arctic space and elsewhere.[35] Where will Russia and its historical hold on the Arctic fit in?

RUSSIA'S FIVE-CENTURY ENGAGEMENT IN THE ARCTIC

Russia's presence in the Arctic dates from the Pomors (sea people). They were traders who populated the region of the White Sea beginning in the fourteenth century following a migration northward from their ancestral homeland in Veliky Novgorod.[36] The important Russian ethnographer, Ivan M Durov wrote of the Novgorodians' displacement of a succession of inhabitants in the area, including Sámi, Finns, Swedes and then Karelians, and of their fishing, trapping, boat-building, and salt-making prowess.[37] Arctic historian John McCannon wrote that their expanded trade network made them 'provisional' members of the Hanseatic League after the mid-1400s.[38] Sixteenth- and early-seventeenth-century English and Dutch merchant fleets encountered Pomor traders in White Sea waters and shared tales of large Arctic whale and walrus pods around Spitzbergen, then thought to be part of Greenland,[39] and of pelagic passageways eastward along Russia's north coast. Russian whalers and Pomor walrus hunters began appearing around Spitsbergen, and English and Dutch explorers began entering the Kara Sea.[40] A leading Russian narrative credits the Pomors with discovering the uninhabited Spitzbergen archipelago, which they called

[32] See David Harvey, *Spaces of Global Capitalism* 71 (2006) (noting neo-liberalism's promised outcomes have not materialised).

[33] See Ayşe Zarakol, *After Defeat: How the East Learned to Live with the West* (2011) (exploring responses to outsider stigmatisation of polities and cultures falling outside the social hierarchies of modernity).

[34] See Jennifer Lind, 'Back to Bipolarity: How China's Rise Transformed the Balance of Power', 49 *Int'l Sec* 7, 9 (2024) ('If the USSR was a superpower then, China is one today. The world is bipolar').

[35] Amitav Acharya, 'After Liberal Hegemony: The Advent of a Multiplex World Order', 31 *Ethics & Int'l Affs* 271 (2017).

[36] Anna Sorokina, 'Who Are the Pomors and How Did They Create the Civilization of the Russian North?', Russia Beyond (17 November 2022), www.rbth.com/travel/335597-who-are-pomors-russian-north.

[37] ibid. See also IM Durov, The Dictionary of the Living Pomor Language in its Everyday and Ethnographic Use, Slovar' zhivogo pomorskogo yazyka v ego bytovom i etnograficheskom primenenii (2011) [*Dictionary of the Living Pomor language in its Everyday and Ethnographic Application*].

[38] John McCannon, *A History of the Arctic: Nature, Exploration and Exploitation* 70 (2012).

[39] 'The Pomors', Svalbard Musuem, svalbardmuseum.no/en/the-pomors.

[40] See Nils Storå, 'Russian Walrus Hunting in Spitsbergen', 11 *Études/Inuit/Studies* 117, 119–20 (1987); McCannon, n 38, at 91 (noting captain Stephen Burrough's penetration of the Kara Sea in the *Searchthrift* vessel of the Muscovy Company (1556), and Willem Barents' two ice-blocked voyages to the edge of the Kara Sea in 1594 and 1595).

Grumant.[41] Competing claims of Spitzbergen's first finder also spring from Viking accounts in the Icelandic sagas (the *Landnámabók*, c 1200 BCE), and Danish, Dutch, and English maritime explorations.[42]

The Pomors also developed maritime trade routes that penetrated East of the Ural Mountains into northwest Siberia. They developed in all but name the cabotage system in the Western portion of what would become the Northern Sea Route and connected it to the great central Siberian tributaries and headwaters of the Ob, Taz, and Yenisei river systems. They were expert 'soft gold' hunters, trading squirrel, fox, marten and sable pelts, in addition to sealskin, bearskin and ivory taken from walruses and narwhals.[43] They bartered goods with the local Ostyak and Samoyed peoples who had engaged with 'middlemen' to connect to Central Asian and Chinese markets.[44] Their maritime pathways helped to create the outpost of Mangazyea ('a virtual Baghdad of Siberia'), which 'Perhaps more than any other settlement … lent luster to Siberia's name' and impetus to the mid-seventeenth century Russian domination of its vast interior.[45]

Peter the Great's (1672–1725) interest in seafaring and naval power led to the establishment of private trading companies under state protection, which promoted Arctic hunting and trapping from the coast of Finnmark up to Spitzbergen.[46] Pomor commercial activity through the White Sea port of Archangel initiated Russia's only pelagic 'window on Europe' until the establishment of St Petersburg in 1703. St Petersburg then linked Russia to the West via the Gulf of Finland and the Baltic Sea,[47] and spurred the construction of the Russian navy. By the time of Peter the Great's death, Russia's navy had grown to include 28,000 mariners and an accompaniment of 49 ships and 800 smaller vessels.[48]

Foreign penetration began with Ivan IV (Ivan the Terrible, 1530–1584)'s agreement to open up northern trade. The Muscovy Trading Company, an English concern chartered in 1555, formed to find a north-east waterway to Cathay and the Spice Islands.[49] Its administrative headquarter building in

[41] See AN Vylegzhanin and VK Zilanov, *Spitsbergen: Legal Regime of Adjacent Maritime Areas* 1–2 (WE Butler ed and trans, 2007).

[42] See Rossi, n 26, at 112–13 (selectively reviewing various discovery claims of the Spitzbergen archipelago).

[43] McCannon, n 38, at 71.

[44] Benson Bobrick, *East of the Sun: The Epic Conquest and Tragic History of Siberia* 56 (1992).

[45] ibid, at 56–57.

[46] 'The Pomors', n 39. The Pomors also established late-16th-century overwintering stations in Spitsbergen in order to capture fur-bearing pelts 'at a time when their furs were most valuable. Storå, n 40, at 119.

[47] See Joost van Baak, *The House in Russian Literature: A Mythopoetic Exploration* 83 (2009) (attributing the phrase to Pushkin and the Italian traveller, Algarotti before him).

[48] Wayne L Chadick, 'Naval Tradition–A Russian Heritage', 22 *Naval War College Rev* 26, 2[illegible] (1969) (noting as well his founding of the Russian Naval Academy in 1715); 'Peter the Great', Royal Museums Greenwich, www.rmg.co.uk/stories/topics/peter-great.

[49] See Nicholas Casimir and Baron de Bogoushevsky, 'The English in Muscovy During the Sixteenth Century', 7 *Transactions of the Royal Hist Soc'y* 58 (1878) (noting the exploits of English mariners to find a direct passage through the polar seas to Cathay and India).

Archangel was established in 1584. The company monopolised trade between the two countries along the Volga River, unsuccessfully attempted to monopolise the blubber and whaling industry around Spitzbergen's waters,[50] and 'initiat[ed] the first direct commercial and diplomatic relations between England and Iran through the northern seas and Russia'.[51] One of the company's fabled sea captains, Sir Hugh Willoughby (d 1554), allegedly sighted Spitzbergen in 1553, fully 43 years before the Dutch explorer Willem Barents (1550–1597) spied the land, which he named because of its mountains and pointed peaks.[52]

Foreign intrusion stimulated Tsarist anxiety about Russia's relationship to Europe throughout the sixteenth and seventeenth centuries, as mariners and cartographers honed in on the area east of Moscow called Tartary. Important cartographers such as Abraham Ortelius (1527–1598), Herman Moll (1654–1732), and Guillaume de L'Isle (1675–1726) began mapping north-east passageways connecting Asia and North America.[53] Fearful of foreign penetration, the Tsar closed the sea route in 1619,[54] an act that at once caused the decline of Mangazeya, facilitated the rise of Russia's geopolitical awareness of the Northern seas, and signalled Russia's determination to control adjacent territories of Siberia.

Russian frontier settlers (*zemleprokhodtsy*) and commercial venturers (*promyshlenniki*) followed Pomor maritime routes from the North into Siberia's vast interior.[55] They established military and trade outposts along the river systems,[56] and also ventured across Ural Mountain gaps onto the Perm Krai and the southerly steppe frontier. Complex nativised Russian communities spread across the tundra zones to the Bering Sea, surprising Russian ethnographers

[50] For a brief history, see 'The Muscovy Company: World's First Joint Stock Company', *Bus Standard* (25 July 2021), www.tbsnews.net/features/panorama/muscovy-company-worlds-first-joint-stock-company-278674. For dynamics on Russian blubber trade, see Alexei Kraikovski, 'Profits from Under the Water: The International Blubber Market, Russian Monopolistic Companies and the Idea of Whaling Development in the Eighteenth Century', 31 *Int'l J Mar Hist* 34 (2019).

[51] On the Muscovy Company's trade with Iran and competitions with Turks, Armenians and Venetians for the Iranian market, see Hamid Hajianpour and Khalil Salehi, 'Investigating the Causes and Failure of the English Company of Muscovy in Safavid Iran', 15 *Hist Sciences Stud* 23 (2023), hss.ut.ac.ir/article_91300.html?lang=en.

[52] Rossi, n 26, at 113 (referencing VF Starkov).

[53] See Abraham Ortelius, *Tartariae sive Magni Chami Regni tÿpus* (1603); Herman Moll, *A New and Correct Map of the Whole World* (1719); Guillaume de L'Isle, *Carte de Tartarie* (1706), available at The Russian Discovery of Siberia, Library of Congress Digital Collections, www.loc.gov/collections/meeting-of-frontiers/articles-and-essays/exploration/russian-discovery-of-siberia.

[54] Bobrick, n 44, at 56–57.

[55] On the Russian colonisation of Siberia and the violent wars against indigenous populations of Turkic-Mongols, Kazakhs, and Oirats, see James Forsyth, 'The Siberian Native Peoples Before and After the Russian Conquest', in *The History of Siberia: From Russian Conquest to Revolution* 69, 69–79 (Alan Wood ed, 1991) (hereinafter Wood, *The History of Siberia*).

[56] See Basil Dmytryshyn, 'The Administrative Apparatus of the Russian Colony in Siberia and Northern Asia, 1581–1700', in Wood, *The History of Siberia*, n 55, 17, 23 (discussing the *zemleprokhodtsy* penetration of Siberia's great rivers).

who later studied the sub-ethnos of this 'turnaround in assimilation'.[57] Their two-pronged rapid ascent into inner Asia compared analogously to the conquest of the Americas,[58] and bore resemblance to the Spanish Viceroyalty system, with its administrative high courts (*audencias*), magistrates (*alcaldías mayors*) and governorates (*gobernaciónes*).[59] As the Russians pushed eastward against the vestiges of the Mongolian Golden Horde, a central agency, the *Siberian Prikaz* developed to administer colonial expansion and collect taxes through a network of sub-administrative secretariats (*diaks*) and clerks (*pod'iacheis*).[60] The *Prikazes* attained jurisdictional recognition as permanent departments of Muscovy administration by the late fifteenth century.[61] Russian historian Alan Wood equated Muscovy's expansion toward the Pacific Ocean with the institutional consolidation of political power within the Russian autocratic state.[62]

Historians note the 'remarkable speed' in which Muscovy expanded suzerainty over an area four times its own size.[63]

> One hundred and twenty-five years after Spaniards had discovered the Pacific from the east, Russians had discovered it from the west; and in just fifty-five years, while American colonists were still east of the Appalachians, Russians had crossed the whole of northern Asia.[64]

It would take almost twice as long for Russians to cross the strait separating Asia and America (the Bering Strait) and set up frontier posts on the Far North Pacific Unalaska and Kodiak Islands.[65]

Russia's colonisation of Siberia eventually brought it into conflict with the Qing Dynasty in the Far East area south of the Stanovoy Mountains down to the Amur River Basin, where the Russians located frontier forts at Albazin and Nerchinsk.[66] The Treaty of Nerchinsk (1689), which ambiguously demarcated

[57] Willard Sunderland, 'Russians into Iakuts? "Going Native" and Problems of Russian National Identity in the Siberian North, 1870s–1914', 55 *Slavic Rev* 806, 807 (1996).

[58] George V Lantzeff, *Siberia in the Seventeenth Century: A Study of the Colonial Administration* v (1943) (noting 'wave after wave' of adventurers and colonists, 'very much in the same way as … empire builders of the American continent').

[59] For more on the Spanish colonial administration system of the Americas, See Christopher R Rossi, *Remoteness Reconsidered: The Atacama Desert and International Law* 18–21 (2021).

[60] Lantzeff, n 58, at 2.

[61] ibid, at 3. The 'long, complex and highly controversial' process of incorporating Siberia into Russia as 'a single administrative unit' occurred only after the 1820s. See Viacheslav Shevtsov, Iraida Nam, and Elena Khakhalkina, 'Siberian Identity in the Historical Perspective and at Present', 28 *SHS Web of Conferences* 1, 2 (2015), www.shs-conferences.org/articles/shsconf/pdf/2016/06/shsconf_rptss2016_01092.pdf.

[62] Alan Wood, *Introduction: Siberia's Role in Russian History*, in Wood, *The History of Siberia* n 55, 1, 4.

[63] JL Black, *Opening up Siberia: Russia's 'Window on the East'*, in Wood, *The History of Siberia* n 55, 57, 58.

[64] Bobrick, n 44, at 59.

[65] James R Gibson, 'Russian Expansion in Siberia and America', 70 *Geographical Rev* 127, 128–29 (1980).

[66] Peter C Perdue, 'Boundaries and Trade in the Early Modern World: Negotiations at Nerchinsk and Beijing', 43 *Eighteenth-Century Stud* 341, 345 (2010).

e boundary along the Amur River Basin according to disputed mountain nges, nevertheless kept a tenuous peace between the two empires for the :xt 160 years.[67] The treaty marked the first ever signed by the Qing empire with Western nation.[68]

THE CULTURAL CONSTRUCTION OF THE RUSSIAN ARCTIC

ıssia's cultural construction of Siberia up to the late imperial period involved omplex … anxieties about culture, race, colonisation, and the meaning of ıssianness'.[69] Russian national identity conjoined 'highly contrasting and latile images of Siberia', projecting it as a 'terra incognita', a 'promised land', ıd a 'mercantile colony'.[70] Mark Bassin noted that this frontier represented Russians what the American West meant to frontier settlers.[71] By the early neteenth century, Siberia's economic significance waned with the declining r trade. Its lack of infrastructure and development oriented Russian interests ward Western Europe.[72] Perceptions arose of Siberia as a 'stagnant Asiatic vironment' and a place of exile,[73] except among nationalists, who embraced e expanse with a 'radically de-Europeanized vision'.[74]

While Russia's Tsars turned Russia into the world's largest country, its ɔlshevik successors had the improbable task of harnessing the great Siberian ndscape. This landscape amounted to over 13,000,000 km^2, fully 77 per cent Russia's *terra firma*.[75] Even today, its population of 40,000,000 people, spread er eight of Russia's 11 time zones, subdivides into 'three inhabitants per square ile, making it one of the most sparsely populated areas in the world'.[76]

[67] See VS Frank, 'The Territorial Terms of the Sino-Russian Treaty of Nerchinsk', 1689, 16 *Pac st Rev* 265 (1947) (referring to the treaty as 'extremely ambiguous' and containing 'a number of anslation] discrepancies').

[68] Perdue, n 66, at 341.

[69] Sunderland, n 57, at 808.

[70] Mark Bassin, 'Inventing Siberia: Visions of the Russian East in the Early Nineteenth Century', *The Am Hist Rev* 763, 765–67 (1991). On the rise of Siberian regionalist resistance to Russian lonisation, see Aleksandr Korobeinikov, 'Non-Russian Intellectuals of Siberia: Regionalism the Transformation of the Russian Empire', Peripheral Histories (1 December 2021), www.ripheralhistories.co.uk/post/non-russian-intellectuals-of-siberia-regionalism-the-transformation--the-russian-empire (noting leading Siberian advocates of Siberian self-government or autonomy, :luding Girgory Nikolaevich Potanin, Afanasy Shchapov, Alexander Adrianov,and others); Nikolai ikhailovich Yadrintsev, *Siberia as a Colony* (1882), www.prlib.ru/en/node/365755 [in Russian].

[71] See Bassin, n 70, at 766.

[72] See ibid, at 770–71.

[73] ibid, at 772.

[74] ibid, at 784.

[75] Ségolène Allemandou, 'The Chilling Global Impact of Siberia's Record Heatwave', France24 5 July 2020), www.france24.com/en/20200716-the-chilling-global-impact-of-siberia-s-record-atwave.

[76] Elizabeth Peet, 'The Rise of Siberian Nationalism', *Wilson Q*, www.wilsonquarterly.com/arterly/_/the-rise-of-siberian-nationalism.

The Soviets created large-scale settlements and urbanised areas across the interior, but in doing so, they produced 'a supremely distorted economic geography'.[77] Marxist geographer David Harvey noted questions of scale presented 'a generally neglected arena in economic thinking' and that they were complicated by a priori central planning decision making when geographical literature suggested that they would better defined by processes.[78] Such an 'erroneous spatial planning practice[]' accompanied the Soviet Union's attempt to industrialise Siberia, which contributed 'to the downfall of communism'.[79]

Indeed, the Soviet development model magnified centre–periphery gradients and contributed to a significant inertia pertaining to Russia's internal processes of spatial development.[80] Even the impressive engineering accomplishment of the 9,289 km Trans-Siberian Railway, which connected Moscow to the Pacific Ocean port of Vladivostok in1904, created uneven North–South developments. This economic artery contributed to poorly diversified local economies, delayed development of infrastructure and community connectivity away from the tracks, drained peripheral populations of skilled and highly educated workers among a growing population base and contributed to the spread of multiple shadow and shadowy economies throughout Central Asia.[81]

The paradoxes of Central Asia's resource-rich yet uneven geographical development remain problematic today, as evidenced by deficient rail networks that poorly integrate with the Trans-Siberian railway. At the time of its completion, the railway also provoked the alarm of the Japanese, who viewed it as a transmission belt of Russia's imperial interests toward North-East Asia and as encroachments on the Japanese regions of influence and interest, namely Korea and Manchuria.[82] Its construction helped to spark the Russo-Japanese War in 1904–1905, with a disastrous outcome for Russia, its Pacific fleet, and Far East Asian ambitions.[83] Fiona Hill and Clifford Gaddy concluded that Siberia's vast unwieldiness eclipsed Russia's supreme strength of size, turning Russia's greatest

[77] See Fiona Hill and Clifford G Gaddy, *The Siberian Curse: How Communist Planners Left Russia Out in the Cold* 3 (2003).

[78] David Harvey, 'Reshaping Economic Geography: The World Development Report 2009' (2009) davidharvey.org/2009/12/reshaping-economic-geography-the-world-development-report-2009.

[79] ibid.

[80] TG Nefedova, AI Treivish and AV Sheludkov, 'Spatially Uneven Development in Russia', 12 *Reg Res Rus* 4 (2022), www.ncbi.nlm.nih.gov/pmc/articles/PMC9244343.

[81] Artem Dankov, 'The Paradoxes of Social and Economic Development in Central Asia', Russian International Affairs Council (31 January 2020), russiancouncil.ru/en/analytics-and-comments/analytics/the-paradoxes-of-social-and-economic-development-in-central-asia.

[82] See generally Felix Patrideeff and Harold Shukman, *Railways and the Russo-Japanese War: Transporting War* (2007).

[83] Bruce Menning noted that the 'hastily constructed and ill-financed Trans-Siberian Railroad and its Far Eastern branches' simply could not transport mobilised Russian ground forces quickly enough to confront Japanese troops estimates. The low carrying capacity and the great distances fostered reliance on Admiral Alekseev's Pacific Squadron, 'a very slender reed upon which to construct a Mahan-like premise for command of the sea.' Bruce W Menning, 'Neither Mahan nor Moltke: Strategy in the War', in *The Russo-Japanese War in Global Perspective: World War Zero* 129, 145–4 (John W Steinberg et al. eds, 2005).

asset into its greatest liability. Only coercion, centralised planning, and massive financial outlays could bring a semblance of conquest over Siberia.[84]

THE EURASIAN MIDDLE EARTH THESIS: RUSSIA, THE MIDDLE KINGDOM

And yet a Eurasian Middle Earth thesis began to develop among disaffected Soviet exiles in the 1920s.[85] The thesis was rooted in the idea that Russia and its Siberian torso formed a civilisation empire of nativist Russian, Slavic, Turkic-Mongol steppe people. It had connections to the Prague Circle of structural linguists,[86] which systematically catalogued connections between Russian, Slavic, and Indo-European languages and their peoples.[87] Its predominant Russian member was the phonologist NS Trubetzkoy, who 'embedded linguistics' into a much larger geographic and cultural context with his articulation of *Sprachbund* (language union) theory.[88] This theory found patterns of mutual assimilation of historically unrelated languages in a given geographic area.[89] According to Sergi Glebov, 'Eurasianism attempted to reinvent the Russian Empire as a cultural, political, and geographic unity, and to reconcile a particularly illiberal vision of modernity with ethnic and cultural diversity of a multinational state.'[90] Old geography conceived of the interstice between European Russian and Asia as a void. The Eurasian construction regarded it as a civilisation continuum, linking 'into an organic whole … the diverse cultures of the Old Continent and remov[ing] the confrontation between East and West'. Russian cultural historians have described this geospatial image as a colossal sub-global cultural circle, a complex intermingling of Hyperborean archetypes that form an inner part of Russian identity 'from which the ancestors of ancient world civilizations came'.[91]

[84] Nefedova, Treivish and Sheludkov, n 80, at 80 (holding: 'Only the Soviet Union – a totalitarian state with coercion at its core, with is highly centralized control of production and redistribution of resources, and with absolutely no sense of cost – could really conquer Siberia').

[85] Shahzada Rahim Abbas, 'Russia's Eurasian Union Dream: A Way Forward Towards Multipolar World Order', 9 *J Glob Faultlines* 33 2022). See also Richard Sakwa, 'The Age of Eurasia?', in Bassin and Pozo, n 70, at 207 (noting the classic Eurasianism of the 1920s had roots in the 19th-century writings of Nikolai Danielevskii and Konstantin Leontyev).

[86] For more on the heterogeneous group of Czech, Russian, Ukrainian, and German scholars who formed in Prague to study the basis of language, see Jindřich Toman, *The Magic of a Common Language, Jakobsen, Mathesius, Trubetzkoy, and the Prague Linguistic Circle* (2003).

[87] See David Chioni Moore, 'Colonialism, Eurasianism, Orientalism: N.S. Trubetzkoy's Russian Vision', 41 *SEEJ* 321 (1997).

[88] Toman, n 86, at 186 (noting *Sprachbund* theory led to the 'embedding of linguistics into a wider cultural and ideological context').

[89] ibid.

[90] Sergei Glebov, 'A Life with Imperial Dreams: Petr Nikolaevich Savitsky, Eurasianism, and the Invention of "Structural" Geography', 3 *Ab Imperio* 299 (2005).

[91] VD Sukhorukov, Yu N Gladkiy and SV Kulik, 'The Russian Arctic World as a "Cultural Circle" and an Object of Development', 816 *IOP Conf Series: Earth & Environ. Sci* 1 (2021), iopscience.iop.org/article/10.1088/1755-1315/816/1/012010/pdf.

This thought was expressed in the early 1930s by Petr Savitsky (1895–1968), who advanced the thesis that 'There are significantly more grounds for calling Russia the "middle state" … rather than China.'[92] Russia's Eurasianist centricity offered a 'spiritual synthesis of Eastern and Western elements'; without its unifying location, 'the system of continental margins (Europe, Western Asia, Iran, India, Indochina, China, and Japan) become but a mere "scattered temple"'. As for the Urals, which old-order theories posited as the division of Europe and Asia, Savitsky labelled this distinction as a 'divisive' and orographically unsupported 'geographical cliché[]'.[93]

According to Charles Clover, the thesis drew renewed sustenance from historian Lev Gumilev's 14 allegorical histories of the steppe tribes, which tended to 'de-emphasize[] Russia's links to European culture' while presenting the nomads as 'frequent Russian allies'.[94] Trubetzkoy regarded the 'so-called European "cosmopolitanism" as simply *pan-Romano-Germanic chauvinism*'.[95] Like Trubetzkoy, Gumilev projected a similar vision of nationhood over an expanded Eurasian space – a *super-etnos* or agglomeration of ethnic units – albeit not as distinctly demarcated and geographically bounded as Trubetskoy's vision.[96] Clover also associated Eurasianism with a convoluted reading of Halford Mackinder's famous Heartland thesis: 'Who rules East Europe commands the Heartland; Who rules the Heartland commands the World Island; Who rules the World Island commands the World.'[97] Mackinder had suggested the Heartland thesis in 1919 to convince Britain of the need to create a *cordon sanitaire* around communism.[98] Repurposed by Russian nationalists, Eurasia's appeal sought to mollify generations affected by war and repression, first in terms of the displacements caused by the Bolshevik revolution, then due to the tyrannies of the Stalinist gulag repression, and finally by the surreal collapse of the Soviet Union.[99]

[92] Petr Savitsky, 'The Geographical and Geopolitical Foundation of Eurasianism', 17 *Orient und Occident* (1934), in Eurasianist-Archive.com (Jafe Arnold and John Stachelski trans, 2016), eurasianist-archive.com/2016/10/10/the-geographical-and-geopolitical-foundations-of-eurasianism.

[93] ibid.

[94] Charles Clover, *Black Wind, White Snow: The Rise of Russia's New Nationalism* 10–11 (2016). See also Mark Bassin, 'Eurasian Visions of Russian Nationhood in Space', in *Mastering Russian Spaces: Raum und Raumbewältigung als Probleme der Russichen Geschichte*, 47, 54 (Karl Schlögel ed, 2011) (noting Lev Gumilev's 'reanimation of the Eurasian legacy') (hereinafter Bassin, 'Eurasian Visions').

[95] Nikolai Sergeyevich Trubetzkoy, *Europe and Mankind* (Alexandr (Sasha) Trubetskoy trans, 2023 [1920]), sashamaps.net/docs/writings/europe-and-mankind.

[96] Bassin, 'Eurasian Visions', n 94, at 58 (noting 'Gumilev's Eurasia, by contrast, was at once a much larger, more inclusive, and altogether more nebulous entity'). See also ibid at 63 (summarising Trubetskoy's and Gumilev's understanding of *super-etnos*).

[97] Clover, n 94, at 233.

[98] ibid.

[99] See ibid at 19. A modern incarnation of the Eurasia movement arose in 2013 with Kazakh President Nazabayev's proposed establishment of a Eurasian Union, modelled after the EU. See Abbas, n 85, at 33.

In Schmittian-like tone, Eurasionists also emphasised the telluric significance of latitudinal 'soil zones' connecting Russia from east to west.[100] This measure purportedly supported the autarkic rise of an expansive Eurasian civilisation, or 'territorial complex' reflected in the German geographical tradition which influenced Russian Eurasianists.[101] Savitsky's Eurasian mindset created a geographical *Großraum* 'North of the Tibeto-Iranian mountains ... of the desert steppes ..., which extend in an uninterrupted strip from the Wall of China to Galicia'.[102] Marlene Laurelle noted Eurasianists further subdivided this region into Chinese or Confucian-Buddhist, Indian or Buddhist-Brahmanist, and Iranian or Islamo-Mazdean subspaces, with interstitial competitions over overlapping Mongolia, Xinjiang, and Tibet.[103]

Russia's new authoritarianism,[104] expressed in the writings of Alexander Dugin, Gennady Zyuganov, Alexander Prokhanov[105] and the worldview of Vladimir Putin, draws sustenance from Gumilev's reanimation of the Eurasian thesis in the 1960s and 1970s.[106] Dugin made Schmitt an explicit feature of his vision of Eurasianism and his screed against the West,[107] a vision certainly complicated by Russia's recent history with Chechnya and the Transcaucuses, and perturbations across Central Asia.[108] Here, Eurasianism presented a 'continental logic' for the restoration of the 'organic, native ethni' of lands (and

[100] Glebov, n 90, at 315 (connecting Savitsky theory regarding regularities of 'the territorial structure of Eurasia' to the soil zone thesis of Vasilii Dokuchaev).

[101] See ibid at 314 (referencing Ratzel's *Anthropogeographie*). See also Mark Bassin and Gonzalo Pozo, 'Introduction', in Bassin and Pozo, n 70, 1, at 4 (associating Eurasianism's Russian progenitors with the 'vision of Russia as an autonomous world civilization').

[102] Marlene Laruelle, 'When Eurasia Looks East: Is Eurasianism Sinophile or Sinophobe?', in Bassin and Poso, n 70, 145, at 146. (quoting Savitsky's definition of Eurasia).

[103] ibid.

[104] See generally Thomas Parland, *The Extreme Nationalist Threat in Russia: The Growing Influence of Western Rightist Ideas* (2005) (discussing variants of new Russian Eurasionist nationalism).

[105] See generally Alexander Dugin, 'Carl Schmitt's 5 Lessons for Russia', Eurasianist-Archimve.com (Jafe Arnold trans, 12 October 2016), eurasianist-archive.com/2016/10/12/carl-schmitts-5-lessons-for-russia; Aleksandr Dugin, *The Fourth Political Theory* (Nina Kurpianova et al, trans, 2012). See also Alan Ingram, 'Alexander Dugin: Geopolitics and Neo-Fascism in Post-Soviet Russia', 20 *Pol Geo* 1029 (2001); Grant Scott Fellows, 'The Foundations of Alexandr Dugin's Geopolitics: Montage Fascism and Eurasianism as Blowback' (MA thesis, Josef Korbel School of International Studies, University of Denver, 2018 (including author's appendixes translating selections of Dugin's *Foundations of Geopolitics*).

[106] See Bassin, 'Eurasian Visions', n 94, at 54; David Martin Jones, 'Putin's Geopolitical Brain', CIEO (23 August 2022), www.cieo.org.uk/research/putins-geopolitical-brain.

[107] On Schmitt's influence on Dugin, see Jones, 'Putin's Geopolitical Brain', n 106; Lewis, n 18, ch 8; 'Heidegger, Schmitt, Dugin: Exploring Intellectual Sources of Illiberalism', Institute for European, Russian, and Eurasian Studies, George Washington University (20 October 2023), YouTube, ieres.elliott.gwu.edu/project/heidegger-schmitt-dugin-exploring-intellectual-sources-of-illiberalism; Jussi Backman, 'A Russian Radical Conservative Challenge to the Liberal Global Order: Aleksandr Dugin', in *Contestations of Liberal Order: The West in Crisis?*, 298 (Marko Lehti, Henna-Riikka Pennanen and Jukka Jouhki eds, 2020).

[108] See Craig Oliphant, 'Russia's Role and Interests in Central Asia', *Saferworld* 1 (2013) (noting the reality of Russia's 'diminished influence' in Central Asia).

identity) lost with the collapse of the Soviet's federated empire.[109] It extended the friend–enemy thesis to peripheralised areas to justify internal repressions, external aggression,[110] and a suggested a 'concrete implementation' plan to 'defeat the maritime world exemplified by the United States'.[111] It would restore the *rayas geográficas* (or what Dugin referred to as the 'radiation of power') of Russia's historical memory project to 'those additional territories which are rapidly losing their ethno-state identities' of the 'unnatural geopolitical situation since the collapse of the USSR'.[112] It would feed on the recollection of the colonisation of Siberia in the seventeenth century, the movement into Alaska in the eighteenth century, the conquest of Finland in the nineteenth century, and renewed Soviet supremacy across the Northern Sea Route and Central Asia in the twentieth century. Mark Lilla interrogated the reckless penchant among intellectuals such as Schmitt (and perhaps Dugin) to intermix the Messianic theology of their message with a constructed nihilistic threat arising within their own time.[113] Alexander Etkind associated this counter-modernist project with the historical sentimentality of Russian nationalism and the imperial stop-gap feature of Russia as the *katechon* interdicting humanity's demise.[114]

More complicated for Russian authoritarian elites has been the projection of Schmitt's *Großraum* thesis, which has attempted to recover political space from the double-pull of emerging *Großräume* since the collapse of the Soviet Union. As noted by Richard Sakwa, Russian 'Eurasian integration [is] now caught between the hammer of a resurgent Atlanticism and the anvil of new Asian power, pre-eminent among which is China.'[115] It is also caught between reckless intellectual formulations of politics.

SOVIET SIBERIA

Karl Schlögel noted that every social order presented its own spatial order, which was certainly true of Russian authoritarianism's predecessor, the Soviet Union. The 'Sovietization of space' immediately began with a construction of the Arctic.[116] Its legacy continues to today. Aleksandr Solzhenitsyn, in *The Gulag*

[109] Dugin, 'Carl Schmitt's 5 Lessons for Russia', n 105.

[110] Stefan Auer, 'What Carl Schmitt Reveals About Putin', UnHerd (27 August 2022), unherd.com/newsroom/what-carl-schmitt-reveals-about-vladimir-putin.

[111] Marlene Laurell, 'Alexander Dugin and Eurasianism', in *Key Thinkers of the Radical Right* 60 (Mark Sedgwick ed, 2019).

[112] Dugin, 'Carl Schmitt's 5 Lessons for Russia', n 105.

[113] See generally Mark Lilla, *The Reckless Mind: Intellectuals in Politics* (2001).

[114] Alexander Etkind, *Russia Against Modernity* 79 (2023).

[115] Richard Sakwa, 'The Age of Eurasia?', in Bassin and Pozo, n 70, 201, at 203.

[116] Karl Schlögel, 'Raum und Raumbewältigung als Probleme der russischen Geschichte, Zur Einführung', in *Mastering Russian Spaces: Raum und Raumbewältigung als Probleme der russischen Geschichte* 1, 7 (Karl Schlögel, ed, 2011) ('*Man kann fraglos von einer "Sowjetisierung des Raumes", … sprechen. Jede soziale Ordnung gibt sich ihren eigenen,je spezifischen Raum. Das gilt auch für die Sowjetunion.*').

Archipelago (1973), credited Lenin, not Stalin, for undertaking the initiative.[117] The 'labour camp' became the first and indelible metonym for the Sovietisation of Siberia.[118]

However, it was Stalin's 1932 policy of *Glavsevmorput* (the Main Administration of the Northern Sea Route) that created a gigantic commissariat to consolidate Arctic agencies, develop the region economically, and quickly thereafter, to lay claim to Wrangle Island and Franz Josef Land before the Norwegians did.[119] Building on Pomor seafaring knowledge, the Russian icebreaker *Sibiryakov*, piloted by Otto Schmidt, plowed a route from Archangel to the Bering Strait in the single summer season of 1932,[120] establishing the feasibility of the Northern Sea Route atop Eurasia. Assimilating this route into the Soviet enterprise became the *sine qua non* for Arctic industrial development.[121] It also would become, like its space programme, the emblem of the Soviet mastery of nature through use of science and technology. It would manifest the Soviet intention to 'dominate its vast Arctic interior, civilize its economic geography, and rebrand Siberia as the engine of Russia's prosperous future rather than the gulag-region of its notorious past.'[122] According to Wilson Center Polar Institute Director, Rebecca Pincus, the Russian Arctic identity forms 'a central part of Russia's sense of place and sense of self … [it forms] a core part of their place in the world'.[123]

Glavsevmorput proved far more unwieldy in practice. It imposed a Soviet-styled bureaucracy onto Russia's northern latitudes that could not bear the weight of its own superstructure. Its jurisdiction pertained to all Arctic islands and Soviet territory east of the Urals and north of the 62nd parallel, excepting operations involving gold mining, the military, and the Gulag system.[124] Using

> hundreds of thousands of slave laborers, and 'tried and true' industrial practices better fitted to the climate of the southern Urals, where Soviet steel production had

[117] Aleksandr I Solzhenitsyn, *The Gulag Archipelago 1918–1956: An Experiment in Literary Investigation* 209 (Thomas P. Whitney trans, 2007 (discussing 'a new type of prison' and writing: 'What new could the proletarian state contribute here? Lenin was feeling out [by December 1917] new paths. … Thus we can observe that the leading idea of the Archipelago – *forced labor* – had been advanced in the first month after the October Revolution').

[118] For a particularly harsh view of Lenin, see the fictional Solzhenitsyn's fictional account, *Lenin in Zürich* (HT Willotts trans, 1976); for his Dante-esque treatment of Stalin, see *The First Circle* (1968). McCannon, n 38, at 207 (noting Lenin established the first labour camp in 1923 at the Solovetsky Monastery on the Arctic Islands of the White Sea).

[119] Paul R Josephson, *The Conquest of the Russian Arctic* 70 (2014).

[120] 'Sailing Through the Ice', Arctic Russia (16 March 2022) arctic-russia.ru/en/article/sailing-through-the-ice/ (recounting the impressive accomplishment of the icebreaking steamer's single-season transit from Archangel to the Pacific Ocean).

[121] 'A Trillion-Rouble Plan', Arctic Russia (11 Dec. 2022), arctic-russia.ru/en/article/a-trillion-rouble-plan.

[122] Christopher R Rossi, 'Russian Arctic Straits and the Temptation of Uti Possidetis', 24 *Trans L & Contemp Pblms* 19, 24 (2014).

[123] Rebecca Pincus, 'Points of Clarity: US-Russian Arctic Identities', Wilson Centre (29 January 2024), www.wilsoncenter.org/video/points-clarity-us-russia-arctic-identities (time mark 0:29).

[124] McCannon, n 38, at 206.

spawned the 'hero' city of Magnitogorsk, Stalin attempted to create a 'utopian vision of a fully 'Soviet' Arctic.[125]

McCannon called it 'a fiefdom', 'a semiautonomous republic, and one of the 'most unusual' and 'greatest experiments in [Soviet] hypercentralisation'.[126] It came to include fisheries, reindeer farms, forestry operations, mining and metallurgy, communication and transport, inland waterways, shipping, icebreaking and shipbuilding, polar aviation, oceanographic exploration, research and education, geology and meteorology.[127] The conglomerate became too large, even by Soviet standards. Following purges and some spectacular failures, the Soviet Council of Ministers reorganised and downscaled its operations in 1953, subsuming its remaining parts within the Soviet Navy.[128]

The historical significance of its Pomor people, the Siberian expanse, *Glavsevmorput* the Northern Sea Route, and the Eurasian narrative contributed greatly to Russia's construction and contestation of its great borderland expanses. McCannon regarded the narrative to be of 'vital significance' to Stalinist culture of the 1930s.[129] Robert Ištok and Dominika Plavčanová noted that the reclamation of Russian spatial identity was central to its practical geopolitical thinking 'after the trauma' following the Soviet collapse.[130] This grand narrative includes the mythos and mastery of the Arctic and the geopolitical anxieties associated with centring the Arctic Middle Europe thesis around modern Muscovy and a self-informed mythos of a Russian 'Arctic genotype'.[131] Russian authoritarian memory politics now weaponise the North and elevate its peripheral status to a position of primacy. Its Arctic *Großraum* is a chip to be used at geopolitical bargaining tables elsewhere.

[125] Josephson, n 119, at 19 (slave labour), 11 (hero city of Magnitogorsk; utopian vision).

[126] John McCannon, *Red Arctic* 6 (1998) (and over time employing as many as 200,000 people).

[127] See generally Josephson, n 119, at 19.

[128] See ibid at 114. For the CIA's declassified assessment of *Glavsevmorput's* history and Cold War activities leading up to its reorganisation, see generally Recent Developments in the Arctic, CIA/SC/RR 82 (13 October 1954), www.cia.gov/readingroom/docs/DOC_0000496064.pdf.

[129] McCannon, n 38, at 178.

[130] Robert Ištok and Dominika Plavčanová, 'Russian Geopolitics and Geopolitics of Russia. Phenomena of Space' 1 *Eur J Geopolitics* 61, 64 (2013).

[131] Sukhorukov et al, n 91, at 6.

Chapter Seven

The NATO Lake and the Baltic–Arctic Galaxy

CONTROL OVER THE seas has been a dominant theme of empire and a major cause of war. Ancient Greek historians wrote of the Minoan (c 1600–1400 BCE) and Athenian (c 500–400 BCE) rule over the Aegean Sea. The Romans asserted the Mediterranean Sea as their *mare nostrum*. Italian city-states laid claim to the Tyrrhenian Sea, the Ligurian Sea, and the Adriatic Sea. The United States rose to empire through control of the Caribbean Sea. China has suggestively drawn a 10-dotted line around the South China Sea, completely enveloping Taiwan and shunting off claims of the Philippines, Brunei, and Malaysia over Exclusive Economic Zones and continental shelves westward and northward of their coastlines.[1]

Attempts to control the Baltic Sea also are hardly new. However, waterway traffic around Denmark had been among Europe's busiest since the medieval period.[2] Superintending the competing commercial, political, and security interests proved difficult and generated much conflict. Hanseatic League merchants patrolled Baltic trade to combat piracy between the fourteenth and seventeenth centuries. From the mid-sixteenth century to the end of the Great Northern War (1720), Denmark–Norway and Sweden–Finland fought to establish a *dominium maris Baltici*.[3] Denmark's strategically situated Bornholm Island, fortified by Hammershus Castle, preoccupied Hanseatic interests and served for 50 years as a hub for the former capital and Queen City of the Hanseatic League, Lübeck (1525–1575). English Kings James I (reign: 1603–1625) and Charles I (reign: 1625–1649) proclaimed a *mare nostrum* over the 'narrow sea' leading to the Baltic. In turn, the Hanseatic League forced English merchants out of Scania. The Danes made claims over the Skagerrak Strait, and Sweden and Poland also

[1] See Peter Suciu, 'Why China's 10-Dash Line Map is a Clear Threat', *National Interest* (16 November 2023), nationalinterest.org/blog/buzz/why-china%E2%80%99s-10-dash-line-map-clear-threat-207302 (noting protests as well from Vietnam over maritime claims and India, which protested China's map that also claimed parts of Arunachal Pradesh and Aksai Chin).

[2] Jens E Olesen, 'The Struggle for Supremacy in the Baltic between Denmark and Sweden, 1563–1721', in *The Cambridge History of Scandinavia*, Vol II, 1520–1870, at 246 (EI Kouri and Jens E Olesen eds, 2016).

[3] ibid.

laid claim to the Baltic with Sweden additionally regarding the Gulf of Bothnia as a *mare clausum*.[4]

President Vladimir Putin's irredentist aggression in Ukraine prompted Poland to rename the Russian Oblast of Kaliningrad, the exclave adjacent to the Baltic Sea surrounded by NATO countries (Poland and Lithuania), Obwód Królewiecki. This is the name of the territory when it was ruled by the Kingdom of Poland in the fifteenth and sixteenth centuries.[5] Poland's place-renaming of the strategically vital home port of the Russian Baltic Fleet, a military instillation of particular sensitivity to Russia and to NATO,[6] infuriated Moscow,[7] as doubtless did Finnish and Estonian assessments that the Baltic Sea is now a NATO lake.[8]

The inclusion of Finland and Sweden into NATO made NATO the dominant military actor in the Baltic Sea. It enhanced the defences of the Baltic states and doubled the length of Russia's border with NATO states. It consolidated realist and normative perspectives regarding 'communities of shared practice' and helped to create a NATO 'security community' derived in important ways from a 'Nordic core',[9] as represented spatially by Baltic and Arctic heritage. This geostrategic result represented 'the exact opposite of Moscow's original intention to halt the alliance's expansion' with its invasion of Ukraine.[10] Alexander Etkind noted the irony: NATO is now 'much closer to Russia's vital centers than it would have been had Ukraine ever succeeded with its application to join the alliance'.[11]

The Baltic Sea and the Arctic Ocean have a conjoined history, less attenuated and more politically charged than geography and historical neutrality suggest.

[4] Christopher R Rossi, *Sovereignty and Territorial Temptation: The Grotian Tendency* 40 (2017) (noting as well multiple other claims by state to control seas). See also Jürgen Sarnowsky, 'The "Golden Age" of the Hanseatic League', in *A Companion to the Hanseatic League* 64, 81 (Donald J Harreld ed, 2015) (discussing attempts to close the Baltic Sea to English merchants).

[5] See 'Kremlin calls Poland's Decision to Rename Kaliningrad a "Hostile Act"', *The Guardian* (10 May 2023), www.theguardian.com/world/2023/may/10/kremlin-calls-polands-decision-to-rename-kaliningrad-a-hostile-act#:~:text=On%20Wednesday%2C%20Poland's%20development%20minister,the%2015th%20and%2016th%20centuries.

[6] See Vaidas Saldžiūnas, 'Kaliningrad: A Useless Sliver of Russia or the Cause of a New Fulda Gap?', ICDS (12 February 2016), icds.ee/en/kaliningrad-a-useless-sliver-of-russia-or-the-cause-of-a-new-fulda-gap.

[7] Adam Easton and Tom Spender, 'Kaliningrad: Russian Fury as Poland Body Recommends Renaming Exclave', BBC News (10 May 2023), www.bbc.com/news/world-europe-65545636.

[8] See '"The Baltic Sea Will Become a NATO Lake" – Interview with Gen. Major Pekka Toveri, Former Intelligence Chief of the General Staff of the Finnish Defense Forces', Georgia Today (19 May 2022), georgiatoday.ge/the-baltic-sea-will-become-a-nato-lake-interview-with-gen-major-pekka-toveri-former-intelligence-chief-of-the-general-staff-of-the-finnish-defense-forces; David Brenna, '"NATO Lake" Vital in Long-Term Russia Conflict: Estonia FM', Newsweek (14 May 2023), www.newsweek.com/nato-lake-baltic-vital-russia-conflict-ukraine-estonia-foreign-minister-margus-tsahkna-1800155.

[9] Steve Wood, 'Change in the Baltic Sea Region: Geopolitics, Identity, and the Russian Negative Integration Factor', 32 J *Contemp Eur Stud* 787, 796 (2024).

[10] Michael Paul, 'Arctic Repercussions of Russia's Invasion', SWP (10 June 2022), www.swp-berlin.org/publikation/arctic-repercussions-of-russias-invasion.

[11] Alexander Etkind, *Russia Against Modernity* 107 (2023).

Indeed, the Arctic continues to serve as a receptacle for geopolitical spillover emanating from the Baltic region, and certainly from Russia's war against Ukraine.[12] Barry Buzan and Ole Wæver theorised that the logical relationship between geography and adjacency define complex regional security relationships that interlink 'durable patterns of amity and enmity' amid subglobal regional clusters.[13] However, the Arctic appears to be the 'highly unlikely' situs for the beginning of major power conflict.[14] In Andrea Charron's view, major power conflict will most likely arise in the seams between the West and East, perhaps in the interstitial areas of Eastern Europe or wherever NATO, the North American Aerospace Defense Command, the United States Northern Command or other Western-oriented defence organisations front opposing great power influences.[15] Vulnerabilities within these gaps create exploitable threats that, in turn, expose credibility gaps elsewhere, such as in the Arctic. According to Andreas Østhagen and Svein Vigeland Rottem, the spillover effect arising from tensions elsewhere in the world poses the greatest threat to Arctic security, not the relatively calm Arctic environment itself.[16] Consequently, conveying 'to Russia that the Arctic cannot be threatened and exploited relative to a conflict elsewhere is vital'.[17]

Discussing Arctic geopolitical issues without contemplating Baltic influences or effects, and vice-versa, results in a partial understanding of strategic consequences. Regional Baltic organisations have created a complex multilateral architecture that supports a more holistic perspective than securitisation analysis indicates. 'A plurality of institutions and instruments' now weaves together connections between the Baltic and the Arctic regions.[18] These connections create regime complexes that evolve in line with interest-based actors, but like galaxies, the totality of this Arctic regime complex may not rotate at the same speed as its lesser-included components.[19]

[12] See Brett Simpson, 'Scandinavia Is Preparing for War', *For Pol'y* (9 February 2024) (interpreting Russia's invasion of Ukraine as a wake-up call to the Scandinavian Peninsula and Finland).

[13] Barry Buzan and Ole Wæver, *Regions and Powers: The Structure of International Security* 45 (2003).

[14] Andrea Charron, 'NATO and the Geopolitical Future of the Arctic', *Arctic YB* (2020), arcticyearbook.com/arctic-yearbook/2020/2020-briefing-notes/363-nato-and-the-geopolitical-future-of-the-arctic.

[15] See ibid.

[16] Andreas Østhagen and Svein Vigeland Rottem, 'Geopolitics and Increased Tension? Differentiating between Political Dynamics in the Arctic', in *Norway's Arctic Policy: Geopolitics, Security and Identity in the High North* 23, 27 and 30 (Andreas Østhagen ed, 2023). See also Andreas Østhagen and P Whitney Lackenbauer, 'Security Dynamics In, Through, and Over the Arctic "Region"', in *Towards a Sustainable Arctic* 1, 17 (contending that 'the core drivers of Arctic 'militarization' are only partially (and minimally) linked to drivers and changes *in* the Arctic').

[17] Charron, n 14.

[18] Luca Cinciripini, 'The Arctic within EU Strategies: A Renewed Centrality', IAI (28 July 2023), www.iai.it/en/pubblicazioni/arctic-within-eu-strategies-renewed-centrality.

[19] Amandine Orsini, Jean-Frédéric Morin and Oran Young, 'Regime complexes: A Buzz, a Boom, or a Boost for Global Governance?' 19 *Global Gov* 27 (galaxies), 36 (interest-based actors) (2013).

Notwithstanding analytic properties that may inure specifically to the Arctic or the Baltic, a confluence of regime interconnections informs policy planning in this galaxy. For instance, the CPMR Baltic Sea Commission, an independent organisation of regional authorities, includes the Arctic within its jurisdiction and maintains an Arctic Task Force to coordinate Baltic Sea issues with the European Union.[20] The Northen Dimension Policy Framework, a partnership among the European Union, Iceland, Norway and the Russian Federation, defines the Northern Dimension as the area from the European Arctic to the southern shores of the Baltic Sea.[21] Its mandate is 'broadly similar' to the Arctic Council mandate, but provides more means for the European Union to promote a common strategic framing of Arctic and Baltic issues.[22] The European Parliament developed its Baltic Sea strategy via the Northern Dimension and the Arctic 'has always had a reference' therein since its first Action Plan (2000–2003).[23] The Arctic Council itself includes two Baltic Member States with no adjacent Arctic coastline (Finland and Sweden), two as permanent observers (Germany and Poland), and expressions of interest in aspiring Arctic Council observers from Estonia and Latvia.[24] The Barents Euro-Arctic Region coordinates relevant activities with the Council of Baltic Sea States,[25] and the latter organisation fosters multilateral intergovernmental regional cooperation at the foreign ministerial level and includes Iceland and Norway.[26] Both organisations take up Arctic programmes involving contaminants, conservation, resources, industry, infrastructure, education and research, culture, and health.[27] Six countries serving the International Arctic Science Committee Council draw from Baltic countries.[28] Taken together, there is a 'common conceptualisation of the Arctic and the Baltic',[29] and its roots are spatial, organisational, and geopolitical but not always consciously framed

[20] Arctic Task Force, CPMR [Conference of Peripheral and Maritime Regions] Baltic Sea Commission, cpmr-baltic.org/policy-work/arctic.

[21] Northern Dimension Policy Framework, 1, www.europarl.europa.eu/cmsdata/124360/nd_framework_document_2006_en.pdf.

[22] Cinciripini, n 18.

[23] Diana Wallis and Stewart Arnold, 'Governing Common Seas: From a Baltic Strategy to an Arctic Policy', 42 *J Baltic Stud*, 103, 104 (2011).

[24] 'Estonia as an Aspiring Arctic Council Observer State: The Arctic's Inventive Neighbour', Embassy of Estonia (Oslo) (1 January 2025), oslo.dev.mfa.ee/events/estonia-as-an-aspiring-arctic-council-observer-state-the-arctics-inventive-neighbour; 'Minister of Foreign Affairs: In 2022, Latvia is Preparing to Apply for the Role of an Observer in the Arctic Council', Ministry of Foreign Affairs Republic of Latvia (11 November 2021), www.mfa.gov.lv/en/article/minister-foreign-affairs-2022-latvia-preparing-apply-role-observer-arctic-council?utm_source=https%3A%2F%2Fwww.google.com%2F.

[25] 'Cooperation in the Barents Euro-Arctic Region', Barents Euro-Arctic Region, barents-council.org/about-us/cooperation-in-the-barents-euro-arctic-region.

[26] See generally 'About Us', Council of the Baltic Sea States, cbss.org.

[27] Pekka Haavisto, 'Review of the Arctic Council Structures', Finnish Institute of International Affairs 10 (2001).

[28] 'IASC Council', IASC, iasc.info/about/organisation/council (including Denmark, Finland, Poland, Sweden, and Russia).

[29] Cinciripini, n 18.

or understood as such. The geopolitics of the Arctic are much better framed by a sensitivity and review of the Arctic's historical entanglement with the Baltic, a point under appreciated by security and policy analysts.

THE BALTIC–ARCTIC HISTORICAL GEOPOLITICAL CONNECTION

Denmark's Bornholm Island historically served as the gatekeeper connecting the Baltic Sea to the North Sea through the Danish straits of Kattegat and Skagerrak. Controlling the Danish Sound and its Belts equated with mastery over the Baltic Sea.[30] The Nazis made the capture of Bornholm a central focus of their early Eastern Front war efforts and constructed foundations for a massive gun battery on the island's southern tip to control all traffic from the east, a decision aborted in 1941 with the move of fortifications to Vara and Hanstholm to control the Kattegat Strait and seaborne traffic in the west.[31] The Soviets occupied the island for 11 months after the end of World War II, casting a pall over Danish post-war security, territorial integrity, and sovereignty. Soviet diplomatic correspondence dating from 1942 and 1944 projected Baltic security interests that would bring the Åland Islands under Soviet control and establish a straits regime that would close the Baltic Sea to warships of non-littoral countries, a prospect that ultimately strained Soviet diplomatic credulity but factored into concerns over the occupation of Bornholm.[32]

[30] Olesen, n 2, at 247 ('mastery'). Any such mastery obviously would implicate control over the Kiel Canal, which linked the North Sea and the Baltic Sea, as opposed to traversing the Jutland Peninsula.

[31] 'Gun Battery Dueodde', Battlefieldsww2.com, www.battlefieldsww2.com/gun-battery-dueodde.html (noting the Nazi decision halt production, build another gun battery near Danzig, and ship the big guns to Kristiansand, Norway); 'Naval Gun Battery Vara', Battlefieldsww2.com. www.battlefieldsww2.com/coastal-gun-battery-vara.html (detailing the construction of batteries at Vara and Hanstholm to control the Kattegat Strait).

[32] Sven G Holtsmark, *The Limits to Soviet Influence: Soviet Strategic Interests in Norway and Denmark 1944–1947*, at 8 (1994) (noting the Litvinov Commission (Komissila Litvinova) and Soviet diplomat Litvinov's scepticism about 'the chances of achieving a straits regime which would close the Baltic Sea to the navies of the Western great powers'. A Danish diplomatic note dated 5 March 1946 informed Soviet Foreign Commissar Molotov that British troops were departing Denmark. The Soviets informed that they, too, would decamp from Bornholm, although no mention of Bornholm' s demilitarised status is contained in the note. See also Miłosz Jeromin Cordes, 'Bornholm, Russia and the Politics of Memory', Lossi 36 (8 May 2022), lossi36.com/2022/05/08/bornholm-russia-and-the-politics-of-memory. The note from foreign minister Molotov read: 'If Denmark is now capable of occupying Bornholm with its own forces and of setting up on Bornholm its own administration without any participation whatsoever of foreign troops or foreign administrators, the Soviet government will withdraw its troops …'. Holtsmark, at 11. The Danish reply from Thomas Døssing on 8 March read: 'at Danmark vil umiddelbart være klar til at indtage øen Bornholm meg egen kræfter uden udenlandske styrkers nogen som helst deltagelse, og udøve fuldt sine beføjelser på den' ['that Denmark will immediately be ready to occupy the island of Bornholm with its own forces without any foreign troops whatsoever participating, and fully exercise its powers on it.']. See Christian Wenande, 'Russia Alarmed about Foreign Troops on Bornholm', *Copenhagen Post* (18 February 2022), cphpost.dk/wp-content/uploads/2022/02/FLu7eBlXwAIGgd_-scaled.jpg (reprinting the 1946 correspondence).

Geographically, Denmark's key position in the Baltic and its self-governing autonomous Arctic islands of Greenland and the Faroes secured this connection.[33] However, extant and historical High North policies of Norway, Sweden and Finland, and certainly Russia, also connected their Arctic domains to the Baltic directly or through the North Atlantic.

Denmark, Sweden, Norway, and Finland started World War II as neutrals, which for all but Sweden proved too slender a reed on which to hang claims of territorial integrity. Their geographic station, wedged between Allied and Axis interests in both the Arctic and the Baltic, would require cautious and discreet small power diplomacy over issues such as Svalbard, Finnmark, Petsamo, and Bornholm.[34] When diplomacy failed, occupation, resistance, complicity, and territorial concessions followed.

The Soviet aggression against Finland during the Winter War (1939–1940) secured portions of the Baltic Sea's northern littoral across the Karelia Isthmus (the Mannerheim Line).[35] It also secured the key Southwestern naval base on the Hanko Peninsula, which 'dominated the entrance to the Gulf of Finland' and served as a means 'to move westward into the Baltic'.[36] The Soviets conjoined these Baltic coastal gains with land grabs specifically mindful of Baltic and Arctic interests. They took land from Finland around the northern tier of Karelia (Lake Ladoga), around Finland's upper-midsection (near Suomussaimi and Salia), and captured and later annexed the Finnish Arctic port of Petsamo.[37] Defeated in the Winter War against the Soviets and defeated again in the Continuation War (1941–1944), Finland suffered the fate of small powers. It lost over 12 per cent of its territory to the Soviets[38] – more territory than the Soviets had taken originally in the Winter War – including direct access to the Arctic Ocean and its Baltic port city of Viipuri (now Vyborg).[39]

[33] Politically, it is interesting to note that serious Danish divisions arise over prioritising Arctic verses Baltic defence policy and what any shift in policy and military spending would mean in terms of Greenlandic and Faroese cooperation. See Hilde-Gunn Bye, 'Denmark Wants to Prioritize Arctic Defense and Put the Baltic Sea Second', High North News (3 May 2023), www.highnorthnews.com/en/denmark-wants-prioritize-arctic-defense-and-put-baltic-sea-second.

[34] See Karl Molin, 'Winning the Peace: Vision and Disappointment in Nordic Security Policy, 1945–1949', in *Scandinavia During the Second World War* 324, 378 (Henrik S Nissen ed, Thomas Munch-Petersen trans, 1983) (discussing Nordic adaptiveness and diplomatic prowess).

[35] For a discussion of the failed diplomatic efforts for the Soviet Union to secure security needs for 'an exit from the Baltic Sea,' see Jonathan Haslam, *The Spectre of War: International Communism and the Origin of World War II* 337 (2021) (quoting Molotov).

[36] Cris Whetton, 'Remember Bengtskar!', 125 *US Naval Inst Proc* 86 (1999), www-proquest-com.mime.uit.no/docview/205994780?parentSessionId=03QaL18K2seZokBWfdeJK%2FFlw0KpkcR83WIxzepFk3M%3D&pq-origsite=primo&accountid=17260&sourcetype=Trade%20Journals.

[37] See Jarosław Suchoples, 'In the Shadow of the Eastern Neighbor. Finland in the Security Policy of Russia and the Soviet Union from Peter the Great to Contemporary Times', 26 *Stud in Eur Affs* 9, 22 (2022) (noting Soviet territorial gains against Finland in the Winter War).

[38] Alan J Day, 'Back to the Finland Station', *IBRU Boundary and Security Bulletin* 60 (1993).

[39] After defeat in the Winter War, Finland made better relations with Germany a priority. In September 1940, Finland allowed German troop transfers through Finland to fortify Germany's occupation of northern Norway. When Germany attacked the Soviet Union in June 1941 (Operation

The Yalta Conference in February 1945 had settled on the Elbe River as the post-war dividing line between East and West. However, shifting undercurrents of suspicion eroded the public projection of unity among the Big Three Yalta powers (led by Roosevelt, Churchill, and Stalin). Practical considerations and a shared Allied belief in the need to secure Russian participation in the war in the Pacific lessened Allied Supreme Commander interest in pushing toward Berlin, Prague, and Vienna ahead of the Soviets.[40] The Big Three omitted reference in their public statement at Yalta that allowed Stalin to annex parts of Japanese-controlled Manchuria as an inducement for entering the Pacific Theatre.[41] The Soviets, pursuant to the non-aggression pact and secret protocols signed with the Nazis in 1939,[42] had already secured swaths of the southern littoral of the Gulf of Finland, including Estonia, Latvia, Lithuania, and Eastern Poland to protect Leningrad,[43] and the Allies were wary of Soviet westward intentions.[44] The impending

Barbarossa), Finland joined forces with Germany as a co-belligerent (as opposed to an ally) to regain land taken by the Soviets in the Winter War. However, by September 1941, 'Finland had reached its previous borders. In eastern Karelia, it crossed the pre-war borders and occupied areas that had never been part of the Finnish territory, but were populated by peoples linguistically related to the Finns.' Public sentiment began to wane for the Finns and the Moscow Armistice of September 1944, ending the Continuation War, resulted in Finland's loss of territories to the Soviets that was greater than the 1940 peace treaty that ended the Winter War. Immi Tallgren, 'The Finnish War-Responsibility Trial in 1945–6: The Limits of Ad Hoc Criminal Justice?', in *The Hidden Histories of War Crimes Trials* 432–33 (Kevin John Heller and Gerry Simpson eds, 2013). For discussion regarding loss of access to the Arctic and of the Baltic port city of Viipuri, see Lauri Hannikainen, 'Finland's Continuation War (1941-1944): War of Aggression or Defence? War of Alliance or Separate War', 17 *Baltic YB Int'l L Online* 77(2020).

[40] Luis R Martinez, Jonas Jessen and Guo Xu, 'A Glimpse of Freedom: Allied Occupation and Political Resistance in East Germany', DIW Berlin 5 (2020) (noting Allied commander Dwight Eisenhower's decision that advancing on Berlin would be excessively costly and 'given the ongoing war against Japan in the Pacific').

[41] No 1417, Communiqué Issued at the End of the Yalta Conference, *For Rel of the United States Diplomatic Papers, The Conference of Berlin (The Potsdam Conference), 1945*, Volume II, 740.0011 EW/2–1145 (declaring that 'Nazi Germany is doomed' and setting out agreements on reparation by Germany, the need for a United Nations, the establishment of free and fair elections in Europe, and specific references to Poland and Yugoslavia). See also Melvyn P Leffler, 'Adherence to Agreements: Yalta and the Experiences of the Early Cold War', 11 *Int'l Sec* 88, 107 (1986) (noting secret negotiations between Roosevelt and Stalin regarding a 'Far Eastern protocol' involving a Soviet promise to war against Japan after Germany's surrender).

[42] Treaty of Non-Aggression between Germany and the Union of Soviet Socialist Republics [Molotov-Ribbentrop Pact/ Hitler-Stalin Pact], avalon.law.yale.edu/20th_century/nonagres.asp.

[43] See Romuald J Misiunas and Rein Taagepera, *The Baltic States: Years of Dependence: 1940–1990*, at 15 (1993) (noting that a secret additional protocol to the Molotov-Ribbentrop Pact had originally left Lithuania to Germany but subsequent modification after the collapse of Poland 'placed most of Lithuania in the Soviet sphere as well').

[44] The question of Allied naiveté of Stalin's intentions and of the historical significance of the Yalta conference is the subject of much historical debate. The notable historian Arthur Schlesinger Jr opined that history vindicated Roosevelt's shrewdness in dealing with Stalin. Some of Roosevelt's closest advisors, including Charles (Chip) Bohlen, and Averell Harriman, both with Roosevelt at Yalta, and Loy Henderson and George Kennan presented stark assessments of Stalin's credibility and trustworthiness. Days before he died, Rosevelt noted 'Averell is right. We can't do business with Stalin. He has broken every one of the promises he made at Yalta.' Arnold Beichman, 'Roosevelt's Failure at Yalta', *Hoover Digest* (6 October 2004), www.hoover.org/research/roosevelts-failure-yalta.

post-war division of Europe into segmented spheres of influence presented overlapping Scandinavian problems. Both problems connected the Arctic to the Baltic region: the first involved Denmark, the second involved Norway.

ISLAND PROBLEMS: BORNHOLM AND SVALBARD

The 1940 Nazi invasion and occupation of the Danish mainland threatened the status of Denmark's two territories of Greenland and the Faroe Islands. Britain occupied the Faroe Islands in April 1940, and the Americans, still neutral at that time, but suspicious of Nazi intentions involving Greenland, declared it as part of the Western Hemisphere pursuant to the Monroe Doctrine.[45] An agreement, signed by the Danish minister (Kauffmann),[46] made Greenland a United States protectorate and the Americans established a consulate at Godthåb (now Nuuk).[47] In addition to securing this territorial portion of Denmark's dwindling monarchy from Nazi control, the move preemptively protected strategic access to the cryolite mine at Ivigtut, a rare earth mineral important for the production of aluminum and aircrafts. It also secured access to European weather monitoring information. Much of the weather originating in the Arctic regions of Greenland drifted eastward toward northern Europe. Predicting this weather pattern crucially informed the timing and movements of military operations.[48]

The Nazi invasion of Norway, part of the same Operation Weserübung involving the attack against Denmark, sought to secure access to another vital mineral – the iron-ore lode mined in Sweden's northernmost city, Kiruna. The Swedish port at Luleå, on the Gulf of Bothnia, froze during winter, leaving the rail line to the North Norwegian port at Narvik, and Norway's coastal waters as the most reliable year-round cargo route for export of the mineral to

[45] The Secretary of State [Hull] to the Consul at Gothaab (Penfield) (17 February 1941), *For Rel of the United States Diplomatic Papers, 1941, Europe*, Volume II, 859B.7962/3: Telegram (claiming 'the United States considers Greenland to be in the Western Hemisphere and therefore included within the general scope of the Monroe Doctrine').

[46] See Danish Minister (Kauffmann) to the Secretary of State (13 April 1941), *For Rel of the United States Diplomatic Papers, 1941, Europe*, Vol II, 859B.7962/123 (informing the US of his actions and of his recall by Denmark's occupying Government, which 'disapproves the fact that you, without authorization … and contrary to the constitution, have concluded an agreement with the Government of the United States regarding the defense of Greenland').

[47] See Memorandum of Conversation, by the Assistant Secretary of State (Berle) (20 April 1940), *For Rel of the United States Diplomatic Papers, 1940, General and Europe*, Vol II, B59B.01/152 (discussing 'the proposed request from the Greenland councils to the United States to give protection [notwithstanding the United States recognition] that protection was a word which had acquired an unpleasant meaning … [and] that any request they might make for consideration of their special situation would receive sympathetic attention [in Washington]).

[48] 'Protecting Greenland: The American Consulate at Godthab', 1940–42, ADST (2024), adst.org/2017/07/protecting-greenland-american-consulate-godthab-1940-42.

smelting plants in Germany.[49] Ships laden with iron ore could snake through the Norwegian *skjægaard* leading from above the Arctic Circle almost down to the 'mouth of the Baltic Sea without leaving Norwegian waters'.[50]

By the war's end, Britain possessed the Danish mainland and the Americans controlled Greenland (and Iceland[51]). However, German troops still controlled the Danish Baltic island of Bornholm, well east of Yalta's Elbe River demarcation line, but with Soviet forces fast approaching. The German commander at Bornholm had strict orders to surrender only to the British or Americans,[52] as Bornholm provided an escape route to the West for surrendering forces.[53] When the Soviets seized Bornholm on 10 May, shortly after the 4 May announcement of the liberation of the Danish mainland, concerns arose about a divided post-war Denmark, and the establishment of a Soviet foothold in Scandinavia with implications for the Jutland peninsula. Anticipating such a scramble, Britain's Second Army seized Lübeck on 2 May, cutting off Soviet westward Baltic (Pomeranian coast) advancement and stunting Soviet post-war prospects in Scandinavia.[54] The manoeuvre proved successful in terms of ultimately preserving a unified Denmark, but the Soviets then overtook and occupied Bornholm for the next 11 months. Their presence there presented an ominous political lever that could be used to pry open territorial concessions elsewhere.

The Norwegians fretted privately about the Soviets linking Svalbard discussions specifically to the complicated geopolitical movement of Soviet warships

[49] See Richard Petrow, *The Bitter Years: The Invasion and Occupation of Denmark and Norway, April 1940–May 1945*, at 11 (1974). As described by the International Court of Justice, this coastline, extends from 'north of the Arctic Circle, and it includes the coast of the mainland of Norway and all the islands, islets, rocks and reef, known by the name of the *skjærgaard* (literally, rock rampart), together with all Norwegian internal and territorial waters.' *Fisheries Case (UK v Norway)*, Judgment, ICJ Reports, 116, 127 (18 December 1951).

[50] ibid at 10. Norway's *skjærgaard* served as the backdrop for the famous *Altmark* incident during WWII. The *Altmark* serviced its companion ship, the German battleship, *Graf Spee*, which was scuttled in South America in December 1939. The *Altmark*, with British prisoners of war on board, attempted to return to Germany and after zig-zagging across the Atlantic Ocean entered Norway's territorial *skjærgaard* and charted a course southward toward the Baltic Sea. British intelligence sighted the vessel near Bergen and British naval forces intercepted the vessel after a complicated cat-and-mouse pursuit (also involving an alarmed Norwegian navy), establishing an important international legal precedent regarding the right of intervention regarding the inability or unwillingness of a neutral state to uphold principles of neutrality. For an account of the incident, see Petrow, n 49, 18–30.

[51] The British had originally occupied Iceland in May 1940 for fear that the Germans were about to do the same. The Americans replaced the British in July 1941, who could no longer maintain troops there given Germany's move toward the English Channel. See Gunnar Karlsson, *The History of Iceland* 314–15 (2000).

[52] See Caroline Kennedy-Pipe and Chris Bellamy, 'Stalin's Danish Mystery', Hist Today (5 March 2020), www.historytoday.com/miscellanies/stalin%E2%80%99s-danish-mystery.

[53] 'The Final Liberation of Bornholm', Det KGL.Bibliotek, www.kb.dk/en/inspiration/liberation/final-liberation-bornholm ('With its location in the Baltic Sea, Bornholm was strategically important for the Germans, who transported German refugees and soldiers across the Baltic Sea and to the west').

[54] See Ed Storey, 'Bolting for the Baltic', Legion (3 May 2022) (detailing the British (Canadian) capture of Lübeck, which 'effectively blocked a Soviet advance into Denmark').

through the Dardanelles.[55] The Danish Ambassador in Washington 'drew attention' to Bornholm's occupation in connection with United States bases on Greenland and Iceland, and the possibility that the Soviets might raise the question of a trade-off or some sort of 'compensation' for its withdrawal from Bornholm.[56] Neither possibility resulted, possibly because Moscow sought advantages elsewhere over more important objectives.[57] However, in his famous Long Telegram, United States diplomat George Kennan specifically noted Bornholm as a possible and immediate 'strategic necessity' of the Soviets in terms of establishing a base.[58]

Suspicions about Soviet intentions in Scandinavia already stirred with its Winter War invasion of Finland in 1939. There, Russia reclaimed portions of Finland ceded as a consequence of Finnish independence shortly before the end of World War I. As a lead up to the invasion, Russia had ruled over Finland for nearly a century (1809–1917), but Soviet security concerns about the Nazi takeover of Poland, and Finland's rebuff of Soviet proposals for a lease of the Hanko port and a land swap to better insulate Leningrad, prompted the invasion.[59] The Soviets had contemplated strategic interests in Denmark and the Baltic as early as the fall of 1940.[60] As their forces advanced westward across the Pomeranian coast and ultimately toward Bornholm in 1945, they already had set into motion another interest lost to the Russian Revolution and the Bolshevik egress from World War I – Svalbard.

[55] See The Ambassador in Norway (Bay) to the Secretary of State (28 March 1947), *For Rel of the United States, 1947, The British Commonwealth; Europe*, Vol III, at 1018 (summarising the Norwegian Ambassador's private communication that Svalbard discussions were linked to other issues, specifically speculating on the strictures surrounding the Dardanelles).

[56] Erling Bjøl, 'NATO and Denmark', 3 *Cooperation & Conflict* 93, 95 (1968) (discussing Danish Ambassador Kauffmann's concern about Soviet occupation of Bornholm as a lever for American occupation of Greenland), 99 (noting withdrawal from Bornholm as an argument for withdrawal from Greenland and Iceland).

[57] Bent Jensen, 'Soviet Occupation of a New Type: The Long Liberation of the Danish Island of Bornholm 1944–1946', 25 *Scandinavian J Hist* 219, 236 (2000) (referencing Stalin's view that 'by withdrawing from certain areas of minor importance, Moscow could put pressure on London and Washington to withdraw from other points of more importance for the Soviet Union'). See generally Bent Jensen, *Den Lange Befrielse: Bornholm Besat og Befriet 1945–1946* (2020).

[58] Telegram from George Kennan Charge d'Affaires at United States Embassy in Moscow to the Secretary of State: The Long Telegram (22 February 1946), National Archives Catalogue, catalog.archives.gov/id/2642322?objectPage=2 (page 9 of 24: 'Wherever it is considered timely and promising, efforts will be made to advance official limits of Soviet power. For the moment, these efforts are restricted to certain neighboring points conceived of here as being of immediate strategic necessity, such as Northern Iran, Turkey, possibly Bornholm').

[59] See eg, Albin T Anderson, 'Origins of the Winter War: A Study of Russo-Finnish Diplomacy', 6 *World Politics* 188–89 (1954) (suggesting long-range security interests). See also DW Spring, 'The Soviet Decision for War against Finland', 30 November 1939, 38 *Soviet Stud* 207 (1986) (discussing the emergence of the revolutionary element in Soviet foreign policy).

[60] See Holtsmark, n 32, at 7 (noting a 1940 Soviet memorandum explaining that 'Denmark's strategic significance is defined by its rôle as a country which [has] the real control over the shipping through the Straits, which are an important link in the general strategic situation in the Baltic theatre of war').

In Autumn 1944, the Soviets approached the Norwegian Government in exile with a proposal to revise the 1920 Spitzbergen Treaty.[61] That agreement had been concluded without Russian participation due to the separate peace signed with Germany, the Brest–Litovsk Treaty (1918).[62] This treaty allowed the Bolsheviks to exit the war and turn attention to their civil war with the Mensheviks and the White Russians. Their repudiation of international debts and nationalisation of Western investments cast long shadows over any return to historical discussions about establishing a condominium or coparcener sovereign relationship over the long indeterminant status of Svalbard.

The treaty is a remarkable historical refraction of current Arctic–Baltic geopolitical concerns. Article 5 of the treaty framed security interests in the Arctic Ocean but also paid close attention to demilitarised mine-sweeps in the Baltic Sea. Article 6 dealt with security implications involving Finland and the Åland Islands, countries bordering the Baltic Sea (specifically Esthonia [Estonia] and Livonia [Latvia]; Lithuania existed as part of Russia at this time), and any prospective fortification of Baltic islands, with specific mention of the Åland Islands.[63] The treaty particularly inveighed against Russian interests but internecine civil strife on the home front precluded extraction of any more favourable treatment from the Central Powers. Even so, Germany and Russia had inserted a mutually beneficial placeholder provision in the treaty involving the Arctic islands of Spitzbergen. It mandated that 'both parties shall be placed on an equal footing' for purposes of resolving the indeterminate status of Spitsbergen.[64] The treaty charged Norway with the responsibility of convoking 'as soon as possible after the conclusion of [World War I]' a continuation of negotiations over the archipelago that had taken place in [1872, 1910, 1912, and] 1914.[65] With buyer's remorse, the Soviets expressed resentment of the Svalbard Treaty, which was negotiated at Versailles without Russian participation: They variously claimed it inappropriately altered the 'no man's land' status of Spitzbergen, altered the status of Bear Island (part of the Spitzbergen Archipelago) – which 'was actually [a] Russia island' – failed to take into consideration 'exceptionally important' USSR security interests, negated the economic significance of Spitzbergen coal in relation to northern regions of the USSR and the Soviet northern fleet, and, in the face of Germany's attempted placeholder rights to Spitzbergen, granted the convenor, Norway, with 'full and unqualified' sovereignty over the islands.[66]

[61] The Ambassador in Norway (Bay) to the Secretary of State (10 January 1947), *Foreign Relations of the United States, 1947, The British Commonwealth; Europe*, Vol III, at 1006.

[62] The Peace Treaty of Brest–Litovsk (3 March 1918), avalon.law.yale.edu/20th_century/brest.asp.

[63] ibid.

[64] ibid, Art 33.

[65] ibid.

[66] Ambassador in the Soviet Union (Smith) to the Secretary of State (16 January 1947), *Foreign Relations of the United States, 1947 The British Commonwealth; Europe*, Vol III, at 1008 (translating Tass report). Norway proposed in Art 10 of the treaty that Russian citizens be given the same rights as citizens of contracting states – until such time as Russia could accede to the treaty. Sven Holtsmark claimed this was done to avoid making Spitzbergen a source of conflict with Russia.

The Soviet solution in the early 1940s favoured bilateral negotiations with Norway, abrogation of the treaty, and the establishment of a new agreement mindful of Norway's and the Soviet Union's 'common defense interests'.[67] Informed beyond its own means via Norwegian and British information, United States assessments reduced the Soviet–Norwegian discussions to the elimination of the demilitarised status of Spitsbergen, to be replaced by a joint Soviet–Norwegian defence installation, special economic privileges with respect to fishing and the exploitation of coal, and a new treaty organised as a regional defence agreement under Article 43 of the UN Charter.[68]

In a 1944 meeting in Moscow between Norwegian foreign minister Trygve Lie and his Soviet counterpart Viacheslav Molotov, Molotov presented a map and emphasised emerging geopolitical constraints that ran counter to the Soviets' exceptional interests. He pointed to strictures confining Soviet access through the Dardenelles and between Denmark and Sweden, the latter obviously involving Bornhom. Molotov then drew attention to a third stricture – Nordkalotten, or the cap of the Arctic North (meaning the Norwegian provinces of Finnmark, Nordland, and Troms, the Swedish province of Norrbotten, and Finnish Lapland). He stressed that the Soviets could not accept blockage around this Arctic tier, which in his mind necessitated the conversion of the Svalbard Treaty into a Soviet–Norwegian condominium agreement with Bear Island escheating to the Soviets.[69]

The war underscored the importance of supply routes in the Arctic Ocean. Diplomatic correspondence noted the regular and heavy losses to Norwegian and Allied ships in Arctic waters, a point reminiscent of World War I losses, where Norway lost thousands of mariners and half the tonnage of its merchant fleet in the North Atlantic.[70] The meetings between the Norwegians and Soviets over Svalbard made clear that 'powerful political interests' were

Russia protested the treaty three days after its signature in 1920, asserting later that same year that the archipelago was 'neutral territory'. Nevertheless, Russia used the issue of its accession to the treaty as a bargaining chip in 1924 to secure Norway's recognition of the Soviet Government in Moscow as the only de facto and *de jure* government. High politics precluded the US's recognition of the Soviet Union until 1933 (the US broke off diplomatic recognition of Russia in 1917 after the October Revolution and Bolshevik overthrow of the Tsarist regime), but the Soviet Union did formally accede to the treaty in May 1935. Sven G Holtsmar, 'Russia and the Svalbard Treaty', Artica, www.articasvalbard.no/artica-writings-2019/russia-and-the-svalbard-treaty.

[67] Ambassador in Norway (Bay) to the Secretary of State (17 January 1947), *Foreign Relations of the United States, 1947, The British Commonwealth; Europe*, Vol III, at 1009–10 (translating Norwegian Foreign Office communiqué on Spitzbergen).

[68] Memorandum by the Director of the Office of European Affairs (Matthews) to the Secretary of State (23 December 1946), *Foreign Relations of the United States, 1947, The British Commonwealth; Europe*, Vol III, 1004–05 (1947).

[69] Molin, n 34, at 333 (*Nordkalotten* discussion) and 336 (proposed condominium agreement with Bear Island passing to Russia). See also Holtsmark, n 32, at 13.

[70] See Jan Normann Knutsen, 'Norway in the First World War', 5 *Folia Scandinavica Poznan* 43, 57 (1999).

at work on Norway.[71] Norway threaded the diplomatic needle by 'declaring itself willing to consider … possibilities of agreement between Norway and [the] Soviet Union on the military utilization' of Spitzbergen provided other signatory powers and a reconstituted Storting in Oslo agreed.[72] The United States characterised the proviso as a fatal non-starter[73] although apparently had also contemplated a 're-study [of the treaty] in light of [the] recent Iceland Agreement' and dealings with Denmark with regard to Greenland.[74] The United States Secretary of State George Marshall confirmed that 'if the Soviet Union pursues its apparent objectives in Spitsbergen the possession of military rights in Greenland and Iceland will become correspondingly more essential to our national defense'.[75]

NATO'S *DOMINIUM MARIS BALTICI*?

The inclusion of Finland and Sweden in NATO now encloses the northern gap of Baltic coastline within a United States-led military alliance.[76] Finland's addition to NATO adds 1,340 km to Russia's border with NATO and will significantly enhance air, ground, and sea defence systems. As indicated by NATO's comprehensive Nordic Response 2024 exercise, the alliance mustered over 20,000 soldiers from 13 nations, with active participation from Finland and Sweden. The large-scale operation included 50 submarines, frigates, corvettes, aircraft carriers and amphibious vessels, along with 110 fighter jets, helicopters and air transport accompaniments. Although conducted in northern Norway, Sweden, and Finland, the exercise closely integrated NATO's Steadfast Defender operations taking place in the belt of Germany–Poland–Baltic region and the British-led Joint Warrior exercises held in the seas between Scotland, Norway,

[71] See *Ambassador in Norway (Bay) to the Secretary of State* (17 January 1947), n 67, at 1010.

[72] See ibid. See also Ambassador in Norway (Bay) to the Secretary of State (11 March 1947), *Foreign Relations of the United States, 1947, The British Commonwealth; Europe*, Vol III, at 1017 (noting after meeting with Norwegian Secretary General of the Foreign Office Rolf Andvord, 'He made it clear that Norway would not initiate a request for revision of [the Svalbard] treaty, but would be willing to join such a request if USSR should initiate request. My conclusion is that Norway desires to reject USSR proposal for treaty revision, but wishes to do so as graciously as possible').

[73] Secretary of War (Patterson) and the Secretary of the Navy (Forrestal) to the Secretary of State (4 February 1947), *Foreign Relations of the United States, 1947, The British Commonwealth; Europe*, Vol III, at 1012.

[74] Memorandum by the Director of the Office of European Affairs (Matthews) to the Secretary of State (23 December 1946), *Foreign Relations of the United States, 1947, The British Commonwealth; Europe*, Vol III, at 1004–05.

[75] Secretary of State [Marshall] to the Secretary of the Navy (Forrestal) (18 February 1947), *Foreign Relations of the United States, 1947, The British Commonwealth; Europe*, Vol III, at 1014.

[76] See generally Wesley Clark et al, 'Closing Nato's Baltic Gap', International Centre for Defense & Security (2016), icds.ee/wp-content/uploads/2015/ICDS_Report-Closing_NATO_s_Baltic_Gap.pdf (noting 'Without a robust and adequately postured forward-based conventional force [in the Baltic States] NATO is … unprepared to prevent or counter … incursion').

and Iceland.[77] NATO's intense focus on sea defence served as a response to Russia's 2022 announcement of its new maritime doctrine,[78] which reshuffled regional priorities and placed the Arctic as Russia's first priority. However, Russia's goal of establishing naval combat capabilities worldwide appears severely compromised given NATO's northern expansion and Russian maritime debacles against Ukraine in the Black Sea,[79] developments that severely call into question the feasibility of Russia's new naval doctrine, except in terms of reinforcing the utility of hybrid warfare and covert activity in places like the Baltic Sea.[80]

According to former Swedish Prime Minister, Carl Bildt, the two countries' inclusion in NATO turns all of northern Europe 'from Narva to Nuuk east-west, and Kirkenes to Kraków north-south' into 'one big region'.[81] Certainly, Bildt's declaration of the region as a whole has been the object of historical, strategic, and diplomatic attention. Enclosing it within an Arctic–Baltic sphere of influence is also not a new idea, but perhaps only recently reconceptualised as possible given Finland's and Sweden's rejection of neutrality.

If Bildt's intention was to characterise the region as a NATO *Großraum*, it more productively should be considered in terms of its parts rather than as a whole. The North Atlantic and the Baltic regions project different security profiles, and certainly Russia's specialised naval assets have been much better maintained within its Murmansk-based Northern Fleet than its Kaliningrad-based Baltic Fleet.[82] The latter now numbers 52 surface warships, one Kilo-class submarine, numerous support vessels,[83] and 'at least two squadrons of Su-24 attack and Su-27 fighter aircraft'.[84] However, NATO's

[77] 'Nordic Response 2024', Forsvaret (5 March 2024), www.forsvaret.no/en/exercises-and-operations/exercises/nr24.

[78] Russian Federation Naval Doctrine Approved, President of Russia (31 July 2022), en.kremlin.ru/events/president/news/69084.

[79] See 'Ukrainian Attacks Increasingly Sap the Power of Russia's Black Sea Fleet', AP/ABCNews (5 March 2024), abcnews.go.com/International/wireStory/ukrainian-attacks-increasingly-sap-power-russias-black-sea-107818567 (detailing the April 2022 sinking of the *Moskva*, the Russian Black Sea fleet's flagship missile cruiser, the attack against the fleet's headquarters in the port of Sevastopol, and the use of Magura V5 remote-controlled drone boats and cruise missiles to destroy about 20% of the Russian Black Sea fleet).

[80] See John R Deni, 'Is the Baltic Sea a NATO Lake?' Carnegie Endowment for International Peace (18 December 2023), carnegieendowment.org/2023/12/18/is-baltic-sea-nato-lake-pub-91263 (noting that chronic underfunding since the end of the Cold War particularly in Russia's once dominant naval realm of the Baltic will likely shift Russia's military posture in the region toward hybrid threat activities).

[81] Richard Milne and Max Seddon, 'Sweden Joins "NATO Lake" on Moscow's Doorstep', *Financial Times* (7 March 2024) (quoting Bildt).

[82] Deni, n 80.

[83] Steve Wills, 'Kaliningrad: Impregnable Fortress or "Russian Alamo"'?, CNA in depth (15 May 2023), www.cna.org/our-media/indepth/2023/05/kaliningrad-impregnable-fortress-or-russian-alamo.

[84] Felix K Chang, 'Crowded Pond: NATO and Russian Maritime Power in the Baltic Sea', Foreign Policy Research Institute (14 December 2021), www.fpri.org/article/2021/12/crowded-pond-nato-and-russian-maritime-power-in-the-baltic-sea.

capture of this enlarged economy of scale reaps security rewards beyond the interoperability of already established NATO-standard weapons systems employed by Finnish and Swedish armed forces. Such a foreshadowing of alliance expansion, decades in the making,[85] at least must have been within the contemplation of Moscow.

The strictures of the Skagerrak and Kattegat straits, ringed by Sweden, Norway, Denmark, and nearby Germany diminish the strategic importance of Bornholm. The straits, which are slightly wider than 200 km, are now 'well within the range of most modern anti-ship missiles'.[86] Cold War strategies of defending or penetrating the eastern approaches to the Kattegat Strait have now shifted deeper into the inland sea. Russia's fortification of Kaliningrad depends now on denying NATO access to the Baltic Sea port long enough for Russia to establish ground force dominance in connection with the seizure of Estonia, Latvia, and Lithuania through the Suwałki Gap, a strategy known as anti-access area denial capability.[87] In response, NATO has shifted toward an enhanced forward presence in the Baltic Sea,[88] and development of capabilities to overrun or circumvent Russia's Kaliningrad Oblast to bolster support for the Baltic States, should such an exigency arise. Procurement strategies for NATO Baltic states orient toward expanding Poland's fleet of diesel-electric attack submarines, fortifying Baltic state high-frequency communications and mine warfare systems (both to choke off Russian passage through Estonia's Hari Kurk, Soela, Suur, and Väike Straits and to preserve ally seaborne reinforcement routes), upgrading the German Navy's Baden-Württemberg-class frigate anti-missile defences, and adding to the complement of speedier corvettes and preparatory assault and escort vessels, as well as roll-on-roll-off transports to facilitate fast sealift of cargo and troops.[89] The Baltic integration of NATO countries will doubtless enhance the cooperative approach to security; however, it adds complexity to NATO's continental

[85] NATO's Adaptation and Partnership system has been in development for over three decades. It covers about 1,500 projects in almost 40 areas of miliary education, consultation, and exercises. Its Interoperability Platform enables high-level consultations. Its Enhanced Opportunity Parter Program (which included Finland and Sweden) allows for widest access to NATO exercises 'to adapt … armed forces to Alliance standards'. The Enhanced Opportunity Partner Program, given perceptions of threats 'so deep and … so similar that they could provide practical support to NATO collective-defense missions in the regions of the Baltic (Sweden and Finland) and Black Sea (Ukraine, Georgia)'. 'Evolution of NATO Cooperation with Its Partners: Opportunities and Challenges', PISM (21 August 2020), pism.pl/publications/Evolution_of_NATO_Cooperation_with_Its_Partners_Opportunities_and_Challenges.

[86] Chang, n 84.

[87] See Chang, n 84.

[88] 'NATO's Forward Presence', NATO (2022), www.nato.int/nato_static_fl2014/assets/pdf/2022/6/pdf/2206-factsheet_efp_en.pdf.

[89] Chang, n 84. See also Tim Fish, 'Eastern European Navies Expand as Russian Occupation of Ukraine Drags On', USNI News (20 July 2023), news.usni.org/2023/07/20/eastern-european-navies-expand-as-russian-occupation-of-ukraine-drags-on (noting upgrades in the Baltic and Black Seas to amphibious warships and high-frequency ship-to-shore communications systems).

dialogue and the priorities listed in its seminal Harmel Report (1967),[90] namely: military defence first, political dialogue second.[91]

Characterising the Baltic region now as a NATO lake implies that the region is a *mare clausum*, or as once possessively suggested by the European Parliament's Vice President, an European Union *mare nostrum*.[92] Such descriptions seriously undervalue Russia's militarised lakefront exclave of Kaliningrad (its only year-round ice-free Baltic Fleet port) and naval bases near St Petersburg (Kronstadt and Leningrad stations) in the easternmost Gulf of Finland. They also discount inventive means available to Russia to reframe its posture in the Baltic. The terms have psychological importance, and they are not without descriptive value, but they diminish the strategic challenges associated with patrolling such seascape, to say nothing of the adjacent landscape, which has long presented the Western alliance with military mobility, storage, and logistical challenges.[93]

Baltic waters are shallow. They have rocky bottoms and hard sound profiles. This combination makes mines easy to plant and hard to detect. It presents an environment already conducive to a host of hybrid warfare activities and unaccounted for sub-surface and electronic vulnerabilities that multiply Russia's anti-access/area-denial capabilities. With the world's largest sea mine stockpile – estimated at 250,000 munitions – Russia could achieve asymmetric threat advantages against Eastern Baltic nations, which are heavily dependent on seaborne energy imports.[94] Russian strategic planners doubtless are aware of potential costs of such activity, as 57 per cent of Russia's total oil exports ship from its Baltic Sea ports.[95]

[90] 'The Future Tasks of the Alliance', NATO (14 December 1967), www.nato.int/cps/en/natohq/official_texts_26700.htm. The report bears the informal name of the Harmel Report, named after the Foreign Minister of Belgium, who initiated the report to 'study the future tasks which face the Alliance, and its procedures for fulfilling them in order to strengthen the Alliance as a factor for durable peace'. ibid 1.

[91] See ibid 5 ('The Atlantic Alliance has two main functions. Its first function is to maintain adequate military strength … to deter aggression …. its second function, to pursue the search for progress towards a more stable relationship in which the underlying political issues can be solved').

[92] Wallis and Arnold, n 23, at 104 (noting 'The Baltic Sea is now effectively a mare nostrum and is covered by existing EU regional and environmental policies').

[93] See 'Baltic Countries to Build Defensive Installations on their Borders', Ministry of Defence, Republic of Estonia (19 January 2024), www.kaitseministeerium.ee/en/news/baltic-countries-build-defensive-installations-their-borders (responding to NATO's Madrid Summit spotlighting the need for Baltic countries to upgrade the building of anti-mobility defensive installations on borders with Russia and Belarus); Jan Van Tol et al, Deterrence and Defense in the Baltic Region: New Realities vii (2022), csbaonline.org/uploads/documents/CSBA8312_(Deterrence_Defense_Baltic)_web.pdf (emphasising the need for hardened storage sites and stocks of munitions).

[94] Victor Duenow, 'Baltic Sea Mining as an Extension of the Russian Gray Zone', Foreign Policy Research Institute (18 April 2022), www.fpri.org/article/2022/04/baltic-sea-mining-as-an-extension-of-the-russian-gray-zone.

[95] Katrine Westgaard, 'The Baltic Sea Region: A Laboratory for Overcoming European Security Challenges', Carnegie Endowment for International Peace (21 December 2023), carnegieendowment.org/2023/12/21/baltic-sea-region-laboratory-for-overcoming-european-security-challenges-pub-91312.

The war in Ukraine has further heightened Arctic and Baltic island tensions. More recent Russian complications have centred on the status of Svalbard's adjacent maritime zones (some extensions also contested by NATO members), fishing rights around Svalbard,[96] and potential NATO HIMARS artillery installation on Bornholm.[97] The invasion of Ukraine renewed a focus on the Arctic as a competitive strategic domain. The archipelago's proximity to the Kola Peninsula and Russia's strategic Northern Fleet, and Norway's interpretation of Article 9 of the Treaty (which prohibits Norway from fortifying the archipelago 'for warlike purposes,' or establishing 'any naval base') raised somnambulant Cold War concerns that renews examination of Russia's High North bastion defence. This stratagem asserts the primacy of Russia's strategic nuclear submarine capability and asserts a two-tiered protection system in the High North. A bastion of surface combat vessels and a large submarine force attempts to *deny* NATO penetration into SSBN (ballistic missile submarine) launch point areas in the Barents Sea. An extended bastion defence ring contests NATO maritime power in the Atlantic by controlling passageway through the Norwegian Sea and the Greenland–Iceland–United Kingdon (GIUK) gap to North Atlantic sea lanes. As explained by Stephen Miller, NATO has a 'parallel but inverse set of interests'.[98] It seeks to keep the Soviet threat to NATO sea lanes bottled up north of the GIUK gap and is 'determine[ed] to break into the bastion and vigorously pursue' Russia's SSBNs. The renewed strategic focus around Iceland, Greenland, and Svalbard evidences the importance both Russia and NATO regard as the metaphorical cork in the bottle.[99]

Western authorities suspect that Russia's Mir 1 and Mir 2 submersibles sabotaged underwater cable connections linking mainland Norway with its Svalbard and Lofoten archipelagoes.[100] Western governments and Russian

[96] See Astri Edvardsen, 'Svalbard Gets Exemptions from New Sanctions against Russia', High North News (5 May 2022), www.highnorthnews.com/en/svalbard-gets-exemptions-new-sanctions-against-russia (noting Norway's adapted version of the EU's sanction package against Russia stemming from the Ukraine invasion, with certain exemptions for Russian fishing, search and rescue, coal and humanitarian supplies, Russia's official view that Norway's so-called fishing protection zone surrounding Svalbard is international water, and questioning whether fisheries cooperation between the two countries might be 'hanging by a thin thread' due to geopolitics and Ukraine).

[97] 'Deploying US Rocket System at Bornholm to Lead to Escalation with Russia, Envoy Says', Tass (2 June 2022), tass.com/politics/1459349 (warning the US and its satellites that any such installation, which could strike targets in the Kaliningrad region, 'will lead to an unacceptable escalation of the [Ukraine] conflict').

[98] Steven. Miller, 'The Return of the Strategic Arctic', *Arctic YB* 2 (2023).

[99] ibid.

[100] See Atle Staalesen, '"Human Activity" Behind Svalbard Cable Disruption', Barents Observer (11 February 2022), thebarentsobserver.com/en/security/2022/02/unknown-human-activity-behind-svalbard-cable-disruption (discussing the unnatural disruption of Norwegian cables). See also Malte Humpert, 'Nord Stream Pipeline Sabotage Mirrors Svalbard Cable Incident', High North News (29 September 2022), www.highnorthnews.com/en/nord-stream-pipeline-sabotage-mirrors-svalbard-cable-incident (suggesting a connection between the sabotage of the Nord Stream 1 and 2

authorities traded accusations over the 2022 Nord Stream gas pipeline explosions impeding delivery of Russian gas to energy-dependent Europe. The breach resulted in the largest methane greenhouse gas release in history.[101] The finger-pointing exposed not so much the perpetrator of this subterfuge as the plausible motivation that each accusing state had to disrupt the flow. Sabotage incidents against the Nord Stream pipelines and damage to cable and gas pipeline links between Finland and Estonia in October 2023, possibly involving a Chinese cargo ship,[102] misapply placid inland sea-like descriptions of the Baltic and the free-reign operations of its purported NATO suzerains.[103] One certainty emerging in the wake of the explosions is the vulnerability of Europe's underwater energy and communication networks to future attacks.[104] The total length of the Norwegian gas pipeline network alone, concentrated mostly on the Norwegian continental shelf off Stavanger to Tronheim, but extending from Zeebrugge, Belgium to Niechorze, Poland and into the Arctic Ocean, covers a distance from Oslo to Bangkok.[105] The cutting of subsurface fibre-optic cables between mainland Norway and Svalbard, and near the Faroe and Shetland Islands, 'point to a pattern fitting the traits of hybrid warfare'.[106] In November 2024, submarine telecommunication cables connecting Sweden and Lithuania were cut. The next day, another

pipelines in the Baltic Sea, the cutting of the two Norwegian communication cables off Svalbard and Lofoten, and Russia's advanced subsea capabilities).

[101] Laura Benshoff, 'The Nord Stream Pipelines Have Stopped Leaking. But the Methane Emitted Broke Records', NPR (4 October 2022), www.npr.org/2022/10/04/1126562195/the-nord-stream-pipelines-have-stopped-leaking-but-the-methane-emitted-broke-rec (noting the release was equivalent to 'a day or two of regular ethane emissions from the fossil fuel industry').

[102] Claudia Chiappa and Pierre Emmanuel Ngendakumana, '"Everything Indicates" Chines Ship Damaged Baltic Pipeline on Purpose, Finland Says', Politico (1 December 2023), www.politico.eu/article/balticconnector-damage-likely-to-be-intentional-finnish-minister-says-china-estonia (discussing the opinion of Finland's Minister of European Affairs regarding the damage to the 77 km Balticconnector gas pipeline and noting also damage to two telecom cables connecting Estonia to Finland and Sweden occurring around the same time). See also Essi Lehto and Andrius Sytas, 'Finland Boards Oil Tanker Suspected of Causing Internet, Power Cable Outages', Reuters (26 December 2024), www.reuters.com/world/europe/finland-police-investigate-role-foreign-ship-after-power-cable-outage-2024-12-26 (regarding suspected sabotage of the 170 km Eastlink 2 interconnector between Finland and Estonia and the taking of control of a Cook Islands-registered ship suspected of belonging to Russia's shadow fleet).

[103] Julian Pawlak, 'No, Don't Call the Baltic a "NATO Lake"', RUSI (5 September 2022), rusi.org/explore-our-research/publications/commentary/no-dont-call-baltic-nato-lake.

[104] See Sergey Vakulenko, 'Shock and Awe: Who Attacked the Nord Stream Pipelines?' Carnegie Endowment for International Peace (30 September 2022), carnegieendowment.org/politika/88062 (suggesting that the greater signaling threat to the West was that the rest of its marine energy infrastructure was susceptible to attack).

[105] 'Gas Pipelines on the Norwegian Continental Shelf', Arkiv for utskrift, Norwegianpetroleum.no, www.norskpetroleum.no/en/utskrift (noting that the gas transport infrastructure system is a natural monopoly, as opposed to the oil transport system, which is deemed a less important part of the value chain) (updated 22 September 2022).

[106] Colin Wall and Njord Wegge, 'The Russian Arctic Threat: Consequences of the Ukraine War', CSIS (25 January 2023), www.csis.org/analysis/russian-arctic-threat-consequences-ukraine-war.

telecommunications link between Finland and Germany was cut, prompting the German Defence Minister to suspect sabotage involving a Chinese bulk carrier.[107]

Göran Swistek and Michael Paul identified another connection between the Baltic and the Arctic: 'Today, the Baltic and North Seas are part of the larger geostrategic Arctic–North Atlantic space, which stretches as far as the Black Sea as an area of operations.'[108] Sweden's Gotland Island in the centre of the Baltic Sea, a demilitarised zone before Russia's annexation of Crimea, now constrains Russia's defence of Kaliningrad. It provides NATO with reactivated and forward-based Swedish air defence installations 330 km from Kaliningrad. Its defences now include a mechanised battalion,[109] and serves as a chokepoint for resupply from the Gulf of Finland to the Russian mainland.[110] It also constricts Russian access to the Suwałki corridor through Kaliningrad, should Russia seek to isolate the Baltic countries of Lithuania, Latvia, and Estonia from the NATO mainland by severing this narrow strip of Lithuania's border with Poland.[111] Gotland also provides NATO with sea links to the Baltic states should supply lines through the Suwałki corridor become compromised. The countries are connected by only two highways and a rail line.[112] Importantly, Kaliningrad served as a way station for Russian landing ships deployed from the Northern Fleet in 2022 in preparation for the invasion of Ukraine, an observation that alarmed Sweden,[113] and most recently highlighted the Arctic–Baltic strategic nexus.

[107] See Alexander Lott, 'The Baltic Sea Cable-Cuts and Ship Interdiction: The C-Lion1 Incident, Articles of War', Lieber Institute (26 November 2024), lieber.westpoint.edu/baltic-sea-cable-cuts-ship-interdiction-c-lion1-incident.

[108] Göran Swistek and Michael Paul, 'Geopolitics in the Baltic Sea Region', 9 SWP Comment 3 (2023).

[109] Anna Wieslander and Eric Adamson, 'A Glimpse of Sweden in NATO: Gotland Could be a Game-Changer for Baltic Defense', Atlantic Council (26 April 2023), www.atlanticcouncil.org/blogs/new-atlanticist/a-glimpse-of-sweden-in-nato-gotland-could-be-a-game-changer-for-baltic-defense.

[110] Zdzislaw Sliwa, Hans Helseth and Viljar Veeble, 'The Baltic Sea Islands and their Impact on the Regional Security', *Centrum Balticum* 4 (2022) (noting much Russian trade and half of Russia's imported food enter Russia from the Baltic Sea).

[111] Swistek and Paul, n 108, at 2. Strategists assert that Russia's principal tactic would be to deny NATO access to the Baltic Sea long enough for Russian ground forces to establish ground force dominance and seizure of Estonia, Latvia, and Lithuania through the Suwałki Gap (anti-access area denial capability). See Chang, n 84.

[112] John R Deni, 'NATO Must Prepare to Defend Its Weakest Point – the Suwalki Corridor' (3 March 2022), foreignpolicy.com/2022/03/03/nato-must-prepare-to-defend-its-weakest-point-the-suwalki-corridor (describing the 40-mile-wide corridor as a vulnerable 'chokepoint' for NATO and its most exposed Baltic state members).

[113] Swistek and Paul, n 108 (noting the alarming Swedish response of fortifying military installations on Gotland).

CONCLUSION

In contrast to Antarctica, which is sometimes described as a landmass surrounded by ocean, the Arctic is an ocean surrounded by landmass. With its maritime boundaries mostly settled, and its adjacent territorial boundaries secure, temptations arise to liken it to a lake, albeit a lake approximately the size of the continental United States. The lake-like comparison fails as a strategic analytic device in terms of the Arctic Ocean, and it fails in terms of the Baltic Sea. However, the two spatial zones are connected and indeed can be construed to constitute a strategic *Großraum*, one spatial galaxy that counterpoises the likemindedness of the NATO alliance against the historical geopolitical entanglements and entitlements of Russia's revolving presence in both spheres.

Chapter Eight

Russia's Security Dilemma

SINCE THE INVASION of Crimea in 2014, Russia has fortified its 24,140 km northern shore by adding 475 military sites and reactivating 50 Soviet outposts.[1] Major improvements have been made to its northernmost military installation, the Nagurskoye Air Base on the remote archipelago of Franz Josef Land, to Temp Air Base on Kotelny Island, and to key infrastructure projects on the Yamal Peninsula and the Russia's Arctic seaport of Sabetta.[2] In January 2021, Russia's Northern Fleet, headquartered on the Kola peninsula at Severomorsk, upgraded to the status of a military district.[3] This consolidation of power places its fleet on par with Russia's four other military districts and further instantiates the Northern Fleet as the largest and strategically most important of the four fleets of the Russian Navy.[4]

Russia has designed its Ivan Papanin-class icebreaking patrol vessels with the capability of carrying mobile Kalibr-K cruise missiles,[5] and has reinvigorated its 'Cold War-era marine mammal training program as a part of [its] broader shift toward polar region emphasis'.[6] In an unusual development, Chinese and Russian naval flotillas jointly patrolled international waters off Alaska in September 2022 and August 2023. Russia's regard for the Arctic's supreme national importance and its increasing cooperation with China, particularly as the war in Ukraine drags on, may indicate concessions to China that Russia would not ordinarily accept. China's willingness to cooperate militarily with

[1] Barry Gardiner, 'As the Ice Melts, a Perilous Russian Threat is Emerging in the Arctic', *The Guardian* (18 June 2023), www.theguardian.com/commentisfree/2023/jun/13/arctic-russia-nato-putin-climate.

[2] See Malte Humpert, *New Satellite Images Reveal Extent of Russia's Military and Economic Build-Up in the Arctic*, High North News (3 May 2019), www.highnorthnews.com/en/new-satellite-images-reveal-extent-russias-military-and-economic-build-arctic.

[3] See 'Putin Signs Decree to Transform Northern Fleet into Military District', Tass (21 December 2020), tass.com/defense/1238053.

[4] On the Northern Fleet and the heavily militarised Kola Peninsula, see generally Anne-Kristin Jørgensen and Geir Hønneland, *Integration vs. Autonomy: Civil-Military Relations on the Kola Peninsula* (2014).

[5] See Dorian Archus, 'Russia to Arm Icebreaking Patrol Ships with Kalibr Missile', *Naval Post* (16 October 2021), navalpost.com/russia-to-arm-icebreaker-with-kalibr (referencing a report by the *Tass* news agency).

[6] Ryan Burke and Jahara Matisek, 'The American Polar Pivot: Gaining a Comparative Advantage in Great Power Competition', 10 *Marine Corps Uni J* 70 (2019).

Russia may foster a 'strategic ambiguity about the extent to which that relationship may extend', making further military engagement in the high latitudes an area to watch.[7]

At the Rovaniemi Ministerial meeting of Arctic Council Foreign Ministers in 2019, the Trump Administration bluntly warned about Russia's and China's strategic intentions in the High North, declaring that the Arctic 'has become an arena for power and competition'.[8] That same year, the United States Coast Guard released its Arctic Strategic Outlook, which reflected a concern for geopolitical confrontation.[9] The United States Department of Defense recently established an Arctic Strategy and Global Resilience Office to coordinate its three geographic combatant commands in the Arctic to guard against its two strategic competitors, Russia and China.[10] Such competition reflects coming concerns of geopolitical confrontation, a security dilemma whereby actions by one state to enhance its security produce reactions from another state that decrease the security of the original state.

The result is a convoluted, perhaps triangulated, Thucydides Trap – a phrase coined by Graham Allison to describe a perilous situation in which a rising power inevitably threatens to displace a ruling power for hegemonic control. Allison attributed this 'collision course' to a circumstance identified by the ancient Greek historian and general Thucydides in his epic book, *History of the Peloponnesian War* (c fifth century BCE) where he explained: 'It was the *rise* of Athens and the *fear* that this instilled in Sparta that made war *inevitable*'.[11] The most likely (although not inevitable) outcome is war.[12]

[7] Melody Schreiber, 'A U.S. Coast Guard Ship Unexpectedly Encountered Chinese and Russian Warships Off Alaska', *Arctic Business J* (quoting Marisol Maddox).

[8] See Michael R Pompeo, 'Looking North: Sharpening America's Arctic Focus', US Department of State (6 May 2019), 2017–2021.state.gov/looking-north-sharpening-americas-arctic-focus (speech by the US Secretary of State raising doubts about China's and Russia's peaceful and transparent Arctic intentions). At the same meeting, the US generated 'widespread shock' by impeding the Council's ability to achieve consensus on climate change. Richard Milne, 'US Provokes Fury After Blocking Arctic Council Statement', *Financial Times* (7 May 2019), www.ft.com/content/f879ff9a-70ab-11e9-bf5c-6eeb837566c5.

[9] See 'Arctic Strategic Outlook', United States Coast Guard (2019), www.uscg.mil/Portals/0/Images/arctic/Arctic_Strategy_Book_APR_2019.pdf (noting that 'strategic competition drives more actors to look to the Arctic for economic and geopolitical advantages' and specifically citing Russia and China's 'persistent challenges to the rules-based international order … [and] continued peaceful stability of the Arctic region').

[10] See Jim Garamone, 'DOD Establishes Arctic Strategy and Global Resilience Office', US Department of Defence (27 September 2022), www.defense.gov/News/News-Stories/Article/Article/3171173/dod-establishes-arctic-strategy-and-global-resilience-office/#:~:text=The%20latest%20DOD%20strategy%20on,shared%20challenges%2C%22%20Ferguson%20said (announcing the new office as well as noting the newly created Arctic strategic education initiative housed at the Joint Base Elmendorf Richardson in Alaska (the Ted Stevens Center for Arctic Security Studies)).

[11] Graham Allison, *Destined for War: Can American and China Escape Thucydides's Trap?* (2017). ibid at vii (quoting Thucydides).

[12] Allison reviews 16 cases in history where a rising power challenged a dominant state, noting that 12 of the cases resulted in war.

Situating the Arctic within the framework of a security dilemma fomented by vulnerability and (mis)perception necessarily assimilates 'structural stress' brought on by the rising power of China and the declining power of the United States and Russia.[13] Well-discussed sub-fields of international relations theory compartmentalise this discussion under the rubrics of power cycle and power transition theory.[14] Here, and as distinguished from a static balance of power distribution, vertical and longitudinal dimensions of power are factored into the study of state relations, leading to a simultaneous consideration of the trajectories of power and changing relative capabilities of states.[15] The Arctic presents various nonlinear patterns of change that induce anxiety and affect power correlates, widening the prospect of springing such a trap. These variables include climate change, shifting alliances, emerging transit routes, migrating or unveiling living and mineral resources, concomitant and competing claims over such resources, and political turmoil in Ukraine, which unsettles an Arctic geopolitical course of dealing relatively frozen or understood for decades.

Amid this thaw has been the precipitous decline of Russian power in the world beginning with the rapid demise of the Soviet Union between 1989 and 1991. That event alone amounted to the 'most significant development for international relations of the last quarter of the twentieth century' and modern history's exemplar of great power decline during peacetime.[16] Historian John Lewis Gaddis correctly noted that the idea of (il)legitimacy caused the Soviet Union's undoing, not military defeat or economic crash.[17] Russia's turbulent nearer history continues to cast shadows over its place in the world. Although it remains 'by far' the richest country in the world in natural resources,[18] with established comparative advantages in the exports of wheat, corn, mineral fertilisers, natural gas, and 11 per cent of the world's global oil exports, its economy is only about '80 percent the size of the Italian economy',[19] and the added costs of the Ukraine invasion appear staggering although perversely advantageous to Russia's skewed authoritarian leadership.

[13] Graham Allison, 'Destined for War?', 149 *Nat Interest* 11 (2017).

[14] George Liska, 'Imperial America: The International Politics of Primacy' (1967) (discussing the cycle of a nation's foreign policy); Charles F Doran and Wes Parsons, 'War and the Cycle of Relative Power', 74 *Am Pol Sci Rev* 947 (1980) (articulating power cycle theory); George Modelski, *Long Cycles in World Politics* (1987) (charting regularities in the rise and decline of world powers); AFK Organski and Jacek Kugler, *The War Ledger* (1981) (developing power transition theory based on rate of growth and political capacity differentials).

[15] Young-Kwan Yoon, 'Introduction: Power Cycle Theory and Practice of International Relations', 24 *Int'l Pol Sci Rev* 6 and 8 (2003).

[16] Andrew C Kuchins, 'Foreword', in Thomas E Graham, Jr, *Russia's Decline and Uncertain Recovery* vi (2002).

[17] John Lewis Gaddis, *We Now Know: Rethinking Cold War History* 283 (1997).

[18] Thomas E Graham, Jr, *Russia's Decline and Uncertain Recovery* 75.

[19] Michael G Plummer, 'Johns Hopkins SAIS Faculty and Fellow Reflections: The War in Ukraine at One Year', *SAIS Rev* (2023), saisreview.sais.jhu.edu/sais-faculty-war-in-ukraine-one-year.

 Russia's Security Dilemma 146

The OECD estimated that the Russian economy shrank by 5.5 per cent in 2022 and another 4.5 per cent in 2023.[20] The IMF tabulated that global growth dropped from six per cent in 2021 to 3.2 per cent in 2002 with a further decline under three per cent predicted for the future.[21] This drag on the global economy, difficulties associated with replacing Russian products due to sanctions (which economists refer to as import substitution inelasticity), and war fatigue in Ukraine and the West appear as the few remaining advantages on which the Putin regime can rely.[22]

Russia's invasion of Ukraine comes at a great cost beyond contributing to NATO's newfound solidarity and Europe's invigorated status as a united military and ideological region. It has significantly drained Russian military equipment and forces from the European theatre of the High North, a redistribution estimated to 'take years' to rebuild.[23] It has reactivated the European Union enlargement process.[24] It has sparked a 'full-blown demographic crisis' in Russia, with upwards of 1.3 million young Russians fleeing the country in 2022 alone.[25] It has contributed to a diversification of foreign policy options among Central Asian powers and stimulated Chinese and United States efforts to weaken a distracted Russia's historic grip on Silk Road relations with Central Asia.

As an indication of Russia's loosening relations with Central Asia, China's President Xi hosted his first in-person regional summit in 2023 to bolster economic and political relationships with Kazakhstan, Kyrgyzstan, Tajikistan, Uzbekistan and Turkmenistan.[26] The summit followed United States Secretary of State Antony Blinken's first in-person trip to the so-called C5+1 Ministerial meeting to deepen bilateral relations with each country.[27] If Central Asian countries are emerging from the shadow of their relationship with Russia, so too is India. India's initial forbearance in condemning Russia's invasion of

[20] See ibid (quoting OECD estimates).

[21] ibid (quoting IMF estimates).

[22] See ibid 9 ('The global economy is … paying a price through … higher energy bills and supply-chain disruptions, and President Vladimir Putin is ostensibly counting on the associated economic costs to help erode popular support for Ukraine').

[23] 'Russian Security and the Effects of NATO Enlargement in the Arctic', Polar Geopolitics with Eric Paglia (6 October 2023), www.polargeopolitics.com/e/russia-security-and-the-effects-of-nato-enlargement-in-the-arctic/, time mark 3:28 (comment by Katarzyna Zysk).

[24] See 'Candidates to Join the European Union', Reuters (14 December 2023), www.reuters.com/world/candidates-join-european-union-2023-12-14 (reporting on the 2022 EU agreement to start accession talks with Ukraine and Moldova).

[25] Stacey Vanek Smith, 'She Had a Dream Job. Now, She's Part of a Massive Brain Drain Hammering Russia', NPR (31 May 2023), www.npr.org/2023/05/31/1176769042/russia-economy-brain-drain-oil-prices-flee-ukraine-invasion.

[26] See Ayjaz Wani, 'C+C5 Summit: Beijing's Increasing Shadow over Central Asia', Observer Research Foundation (29 May 2023), www.orfonline.org/expert-speak/cc5-summit-beijings-increasing-shadow-over-central-asia.

[27] See Toghrul Ali, 'Secretary Blinken's First Trip to Central Asia for C5+1 Meetings', *Caspian Pol'y Ctr* (28 February 2023), caspianpolicy.org/research/security-and-politics-program-spp/secretary-blinkens-first-trip-to-central-asia-for-c51-meetings.

Ukraine – abstaining on three United Nations resolutions – set it apart from its Quadrilateral Security Dialogue partners in the Indo-Pacific, the United States, Australia, and Japan. India's continuing engagement with Russia also complicated the effectiveness of a $60 per barrel price cap on seaborne Russian crude oil, which the G-7 cobbled together to balance Europe's needed supply of energy against Putin's ability to profit from such sale. Europe's overall reduction of consumption resulted in a discount on Indian purchases of Russian crude oil of 20 per cent, an amount that accounted for 27 per cent of the country's imports[28] and a 384 per cent surge in total imports from Russia.[29] Advantages have also accrued to China, which has replaced the European Union as Russia's key trading partner in the post-Ukraine invasion environment. China's exports to Russia have risen by over 121 per cent since 2021.[30] Western powers are paying an unintended mortgage on a sanctions policy meant to exact costs from Russia, with beneficial discounts accruing to India and China – an economic variant of evolving security dilemmas enveloping the war in Europe.

However, the discounts are not interest-free. The United States did not take issue with India over its circumvention of sanctions because Russia's engagement with India moderates what otherwise could result in strengthened ties with China.[31] This result would benefit neither the United States nor India, and already stokes concerns in Russia about its increasingly junior partner relationship with China. Such increasing economic reliance, coupled with China's sale of dual-use technology in support of Russia's war effort and diminished military industrial base,[32] creates its own Thucydides Trap with political leverage extending to the Arctic, where Asian-Pacific countries have long occupied Russia's pillion seat.

[28] See 'How India's Imports of Russian Oil Have Lubricated Global Markets', *The Economist* (11 April 2024), www.economist.com/asia/2024/04/11/how-indias-imports-of-russian-oil-have-lubricated-global-markets.

[29] Kiran Sharma, 'India's Russian Imports Soar 400% as US Offers Little Resistance', Nikkei Asia (17 February 2023), asia.nikkei.com/Economy/Trade/India-s-Russian-imports-soar-400-as-U.S.-offers-little-resistance#:~:text=NEW%20DELHI%20%2D%2D%20India%20appears,purchases%20of%20discounted%20crude%20oil.

[30] Niels Graham, 'Chinese Exports Have Replaced the EU as the Lifeline of Russia's Economy', Atlantic Council (22 February 2024), www.atlanticcouncil.org/blogs/econographics/chinese-exports-have-replaced-the-eu-as-the-lifeline-of-russias-economy/.

[31] See '"Not Looking to Sanction India, Our Relations are Most Consequential": U.S.', *The Hindu* (9 February 2023), www.thehindu.com/news/international/not-looking-to-sanction-india-our-relations-are-most-consequential-us/article66488650.ece (referencing comments from the US Assistant Secretary for European and Euroasian Affairs, Karen Donfried).

[32] Michael R Gordon, Waren P Strobel and Alan Cullison, 'China Has Helped Russia Boost Arms Production, U.S. Says', *Wall Street Journal* (12 April 2024), www.wsj.com/politics/national-security/china-russia-arms-production-help-c098c08b (noting China's delivery to Russia of non-lethal but militarily useful equipment such as drone engines, microelectronics, and optics); 'China Helping Moscow in Biggest Military Expansion Since Soviet Times, US Says', France24 (14 April 2024), www.france24.com/en/asia-pacific/20240412-china-helping-moscow-biggest-military-expansion-since-soviet-times-us-says (noting China's assistance with Russia's efforts to reconstitute its military industrial base).

Unlike Russia's recent rhetorical assertions toward all of Ukraine and indeed, the surrounding Black Sea region, which speak of reclaiming lost territory,[33] Russia's Arctic interests are paramount in terms of economics and defence and 'existential for [its] great power ambitions'.[34] Russia's mounting grievances and loosening, formerly presumed security relationships elsewhere in the world complicate its security dealings in the Arctic. The binary supposition at the base of the Thucydides Trap – the rising state challenging the ruling state – should broaden to include extra-regional factors that imprint relations in the Arctic. These factors also fuel great power calculations regarding perceived threats to their remaining domains of dominance.

STRIDENT RHETORIC OR EMBEDDED ANXIETY?

Following its invasion and annexation of Crimea in 2014, Russia's Deputy Prime Minister provocatively tweeted that 'The Arctic is [a] Russian Mecca', after an unannounced stopover in Norway's Arctic archipelago, Svalbard.[35] Russia persistently refuses to acknowledge Norway's place-naming effort to Norwegianise the historical name of the archipelago from Germanic Spitzbergen to the Old Norsk term, Svalbard. In commemorating the 100th anniversary of the signing of the Spitzbergen Treaty (1920; renamed Svalbard in 1925), Russia's foreign minister Sergey Lavrov repeatedly invited his Norwegian counterpart to respect perceived discriminatory restrictions targeting Russians on the archipelago, and invited 'our Norwegian *partners* … to lift the restrictions … on the archipelago'.[36]

When Norway announced in 1977 its attempt to territorialise the waters surrounding Svalbard, eschewing a pronouncement of an Exclusive Economic Zone in favour of a thinly disguised, quasi-legal, roundly contested Fisheries Protection Zone, Norway exempted Russian fishing vessels not only on historical

[33] 'Medvedev Made a "Bold" Proposal to the West: A Map of the Division of Ukraine is Shown', MKRU (5 March 2024), www.mk.ru/politics/2024/03/05/medvedev-sdelal-zhirnoe-predlozhenie-zapadu-pokazana-karta-razdela-ukrainy.html (quoting Dmityr Medvedev [in relation to Ukraine and the Black Sea region]: 'To put it quite simply: We are not seizing, but returning what is ours').

[34] Rolf Folland, 'Arctic Strategy, Deterrence and Détente', *J Indo-Pac Affs* (1022), www.airuniversity.af.edu/JIPA/Display/Article/3173373/arctic-strategy-deterrence-and-dtente.

[35] 'Norway in Arctic Dispute with Russia over Rogozin Visit', BBC News (20 April 2015), www.bbc.com/news/world-europe-32380101. Norway, the EU, and the US had banned Rogozin from visiting the West due to Russia's 2014 annexation of Crimea. ibid.

[36] Press Release on Foreign Minister Sergey Lavrov's Message to Norwegain Foreign Minister Ine Eiriksen Soreide on the Occasion of the 100th Anniversary of the Spitsbergen Treaty, The Ministry of Foreign Affairs of the Russian Federation (4 February 2020), archive.mibidru/ru/foreign_policy/news/-/asset_publisher/cKNonkJE02Bw/content/id/4019093?fbclid=IwAR0D1nXbaDl-Lv0kyW1_ZKBUXYe9fyD5w8SbRUn73xlz9q6jtPio0LL3Xh4&p_p_id=101_INSTANCE_cKNonkJE02Bw&_101_INSTANCE_cKNonkJE02Bw_languageId=en_GB.

grounds,[37] but also on political grounds.[38] It then evenly distributed quotas and licences for fishing in the zone, 'part of [Norway's] overall fisheries management of the Barents Sea, to Russian vessels.[39] Having sometimes turned a blind eye to Russian violations in the past, Norway tightened fisheries enforcement in the 1990s, prompting difficult encounters and interdictions of Russian vessels poaching in the zone.[40] Norwegian Coast Guard authorities and Russian fishing captains have more recently ritualised the functions of inspection and interdiction: Russian captains refuse to sign inspection protocols, but Norwegian inspectors are nevertheless allowed on board their vessels.[41]

When political relations fray behind this façade, Russia engages in other performative acts to unsettle Norwegian sovereignty interests. For instance, Russia periodically demands to discuss the status of the Fisheries Protection Zone in the Norwegian–Russian Joint Fishery Commission.[42] Following

[37] Norway exempted Russia from restricted access to the Fishing Protection Zone because it had been fishing in that maritime zone 10 years prior to its establishment. See Rossi, Christopher R Rossi, '"A Unique International Problem", The Svalbard Treaty, Equal Enjoyment, and Terra Nullius: Lessons of Territorial Temptation from History', 15 *Wash U Global Stud LR* 93, 106 (2016).

[38] See Andreas Østhagen, 'Analysis: How Norway and Russia Avoid Conflict Over Svalbard', High North News (22 June 2018), www.highnorthnews.com/en/analysis-how-norway-and-russia-avoid-conflict-over-svalbard (noting Norway 'avoided claiming an outright Exclusive Economic Zone [in 1977] fearing it would be challenged .... A dispute with Russia ... arose, although the two countries quickly agreed to disagree as long as Russian fishermen would have access to fisheries in the Zone').

[39] Amund Trellevik, 'Spitzbergen or Svalbard? The Answer Includes both Politics and History', High North News 13 February 2020), www.highnorthnews.com/en/spitsbergen-or-svalbard-answer-includes-both-politics-and-history.

[40] See Rachel Tiller and Elizabeth Nyman, 'Having the Cake and Eating It Too: To Manage or Own the Svalbard Fisheries Protection Zone', 60 *Mar Pol'y* 141, 146 (2015) (noting the issuance of warnings to Russian vessels by Norwegian Coast Guard authorities when other similar activity 'would lead to an arrest of other nationals'). Whether clarifying or not, Norwegian and Russian efforts to 'avoid escalation in crisis-scenarios' regarding fishing disputes in the Fisher Protection Zone has been explained in terms of 'mutual interests and the socializing effects of cooperative mechanisms'. Andreas Østhagen, 'Managing Conflict at Sea: The Case of Norway and Russia in the Svalbard Zone', 9 *Arctic RL & Pol* 100, 102 (2018). Serious instances of confrontation have occurred, however, involving the Russian fishing vessels *Novokuybyshevsk* in 1998, *Chernigov* in 2001, *Elektron* in 2005, *Sapphire II* in 2011. See ibid at 101. The *Novokuybyshevsk* was seized and towed by the Norwegian Coast Guard but released possibly due to the dispatchment of a Russian naval vessel and Russian warplanes. The *Elektron* was escorted toward Tromsø but changed course toward Russian waters with two Norwegian fisheries inspectors on-board, leading to a three-day chase and the *Elektron*'s escape, leading to charges that the incident was a conscious strategy on the part of Norwegian authorities not to escalate. See ibid at 108.

[41] Trellevik, n 39. See also Thomas Nilsen, 'Russia Threatens to Withdraw from Fishery Deal with Norway. Little to Worry about, Says Expert', Barents Observer (27 October 2023) (noting Geir Hønneland's opinion of Russian bluster regarding upending fisheries relations with Norway, given the fact that the 'biggest and best fish are found in the western parts of the Barents Sea, that is the Norwegian zone').

[42] See, eg, Trude Pettersen, 'Russia Wants to Discuss Svalbard Fisheries Protection Zone', Barents Observer (6 October 2011), barentsobserver.com/en/articles/russia-wants-discuss-svalbard-fisheries-protection-zone (underscoring Russia's displeasure with Norwegian surveillance in the Zone and noting that Russia does not acknowledge Norwegian jurisdiction in the waters unless jointly

Finland's accession to NATO, a Russian Orthodox prelate consecrated a seven-metre cross (adorned with the ribbon of Saint Georg[43]) on the 'holy lands' of Russia's abandoned mining town of Pyramiden, Svalbard.[44] This event followed symbolic but provocative military parades in the nearby Russian mining community and adjacent waters of Barentsburg.[45] Two weeks after Norway introduced its 2024 White Paper on Svalbard, Russia reintroduced 2023 plans to create a BRICS (Brazil, Russia, India, China, and South Africa)-styled international research centre in its mining ghost town of Pyramiden on the Svalbard Archipelago, with the possible inclusions of Turkey and Thailand.[46] This initiative directly contested the Norwegian policy decision to strengthen national control over the Archipelago and to consolidate higher education research within the confines of the state-owned University Centre of Svalbard (UNIS). Mindful of an international criticism of Norway's limitation of research to the hard sciences,[47] Russia's proposed research initiative included only natural science, but expanded research opportunities for social scientists, humanists, and ethnographers.[48]

Russian rhetoric and memory politics regarding the Arctic have appeared increasingly 'strident' since the annexation of Crimea, their tenor 'in sync'

approved). See also German Petelin, 'The Captain of Sapphire-2 Was *Left Without Documents*', IZ (11 October 2011), iz.ru/news/502646 (noting Russian Foreign Ministry demands that the vessel be released and Russia's Federal Agency for Fishery (*Rosrybolovstvo*) claim that such incidences create an unfavourable background for meetings of the Joint Fishery Commission) [trans from Russian].

[43] The bicolor black and orange ribbon of Saint Georg is a deeply significant Russian national and military symbol, commonly associated with the Red Army's contributions to victory in WWII, and more recently adapted to the military campaign in Ukraine and the projection of the sacredness of Russia's Motherland and borders (*Russkiy Mir*, Russian World). See Thomas Nilsen, 'Bishop Iyakov, Who Backs Putin's War, Raised Giant Cross at Svalbard Without Norway's Knowledge', Barents Observer (12 August 2023), thebarentsobserver.com/en/arctic/2023/08/russia-worlds-arctic-power-said-war-blessing-bishop-who-week-raised-giant-patriotic.

[44] ibid.

[45] See Atle Staalesen, 'Russia Stages Military-Style Propaganda Parade on Norway's Svalbard Archipelago', Barents Observer (9 May 2023), thebarentsobserver.com/en/security/2023/05/russia-stages-military-style-propaganda-parade-norways-svalbard-archipelago (commemorating Victory Day); Thomas Nilsen, 'Russian Officials Raised Navy Flags in Svalbard Waters', Barents Observer (15 October 2022) (commemorating Navy Day).

[46] See Thomas Nilsen, 'Moscow Continues to Push for BRICS Science Centre at Svalbard', Barents Observer (15 June 2024).

[47] Svalbard Meld St 26 (2023–2024), Melding til Stortinget, Svalbard, Art 5.4.1, at 65 (*Forskningsaktivitet og utdanningstilbud skal ta utgangspunkt i de naturgitte fortrinn som Svalbards beliggenhet gir, dvs. at klima, natur og miljø skal være fokusområder. Aktiviteten skal være av en slik art at den bare eller best kan utføres på Svalbard*) ['Research activity and educational provision must be based on the natural advantages that Svalbard's location provides, i.e. that climate, nature and the environment must be focus areas. The activity must be of such a nature that it can only or best be carried out on Svalbard']. See also 'Ny-Ålesund Research Station: Research Strategy Applicable from 2019', at 17 (2019) ('Research and monitoring activities in Ny-Ålesund are to be within the natural sciences,' although an exception is made for 'cultural heritage research').

[48] See Thomas Nilsen, 'Norway Aims to Upset the Apple Cart of Russia's Plans for Education Centre at Svalbard', Barents Observer (1 June 2024).

with an 'enhanced military posture and ambitious economic and infrastructure projects'.[49] The question is whether this rhetoric masks an increasing sense of insecurity with the possible understanding that Russia's tight grip over the Northern Sea Route will not satisfy projected investments and expectations.

THE NORTHERN SEA ROUTE'S UNFULFILLED DESTINY

President Putin called the Northern Sea Route – Russia's shipping lane(s) atop its Arctic coastal interior – the next rival to the Suez Canal.[50] When a dust storm grounded the giant container ship, *Ever Given*, in the single-lane northbound stretch of the Suez Canal in 2021, blocking billions of dollars of global trade for six days,[51] Russia's Ministry of Energy touted the safety and sustainability of its Northern Sea Route as a competitive and reliable alternative.[52] These claims strain credulity, certainly among seasoned mariners. They still regard the Northern Sea Route as a shifting assortment of treacherous, dangerously shallow, poorly demarcated, remote waterways riven with chokepoints.[53] This dangerous geomorphology creates underwater strictures that constrain the speed and size of transiting vessels, ultimately creating 'major obstacles' involving the overall economics of the route.[54] Key strictures include the Matochkin Strait, the Kara Gate, and the Yugorski Shar Straits in the Novaya Zemlya archipelago, which is the easternmost entry point from Europe along the Northeast Passage; the Long Strait (Proliv Long) off Wrangel Island, and the Dmitriya Laptev and Sannikov Straits separating the East Siberian Sea from the Laptev Sea en route from Alaska.

[49] Eugene Rumer, Richard Sokolsky and Paul Stronski, 'Russia in the Arctic – A Critical Examination', Carnegie Endowment for International Peace (29 March 2021), carnegieendowment.org/2021/03/29/russia-in-arctic-critical-examination-pub-84181.

[50] 'Russia Pushes Northern Sea Route As "Alternative" to Suez Canal', NDTV (26 March 2021), www.ndtv.com/world-news/russia-pushes-northern-sea-route-as-alternative-to-suez-canal-2399324.

[51] See Kit Chelle, Matthew Campbell and K Oanh Ha, 'Six Days in Suez: The Inside Story of the Ship that Broke Global Trade', Bloomberg (24 June 2021), www.bloomberg.com/news/features/2021-06-24/how-the-billion-dollar-ever-given-cargo-ship-got-stuck-in-the-suez-canal. First reports indicated a mechanical or engine failure. However, the Suez Canal Authority attributed the grounding to high winds and a dust storm. See Alex Longden, 'Were Bad Weather Conditions to Blame for the Grounding of the Ever Given?' *Meteorological Tech Int'l* (6 April 2021), www.meteorologicaltechnologyinternational.com/features/were-bad-weather-conditions-to-blame-for-the-grounding-of-the-ever-given.html.

[52] See 'Suez Canal Debacle Shows Value of Northern Sea Route, Russia Says', Reuters (30 March 2021), www.reuters.com/article/idUSKBN2BL0X0/.

[53] Christopher R Rossi, 'Russian Arctic Straits and the Temptation of *Uti Possidetis*', 24 *Trans L & Contemp Pblms* 19, 36 (2014).

[54] Jeroen FJ Pruyn, 'Will the Northern Sea Route Ever Be a Viable Alternative?', 43 *Mar Pol'y & Mgmt* 661, 662 (2016).

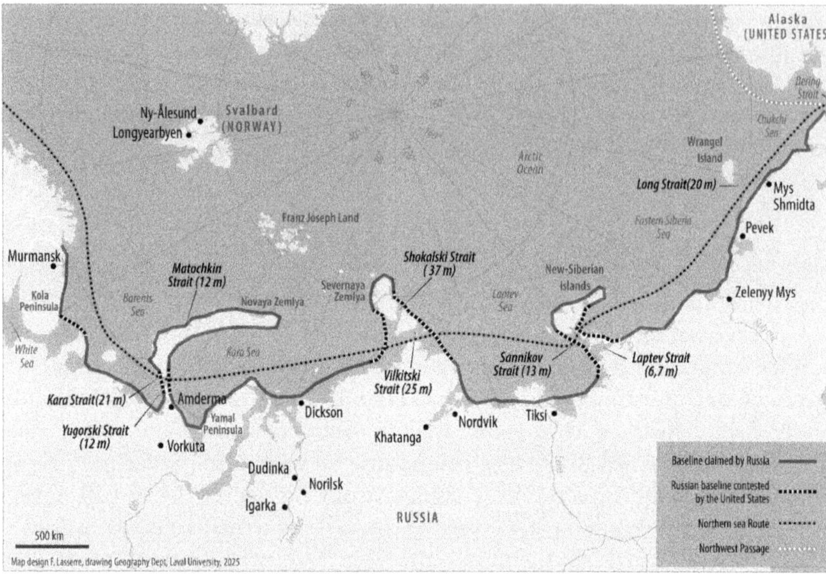

Figure 8.1 Straits along Northern Sea Route

The Vilkitski and Shokalski Straits, situated at the mid-point of the route, separating the Severnaya Zemlya archipelago from Siberia's Taymyr Peninsula (the northernmost point of the Eurasian land mass), are perhaps the key chokepoints along the entire Northeast Passage. Control over these short-cuts along the route, particularly the Vilkitski Strait, may affect the entire economic viability of the route.[55] The fluidity and flux of the Northern Sea Route, paradoxically matched by months of icebound rigidity, add confusion to assertions of its feasibility as a commercial artery and even about its geographical, environmental, and legal dimensions. However, the stark geostrategic reality of the region makes clear that control over the Northeast Passage depends on control over its chokepoints.

The presumption that an ice-free route necessarily yields a competitive route requires much more evidence in the High North than that provided by political bluster, particularly because the phenomenon of Arctic Oscillation may create rotational patters of wind and current that contribute to paralysing ice jams and ice keels.[56] Lawson Brigham, former captain of four United States Coast Guard (USCG) cutters including the *Polar Sea*, detailed myriad factors that mute 'hyped up, sensationalist arguments' on the future use of

[55] See Michael Byers, *International Law and the Arctic* 145 (2013); Eric Franckx, 'New Developments in the North-East Passage', 6 *Int'l J Estuarine & Coastal L* 33, 36 (1991).

[56] See generally 'Arctic Oscillation (AO)', NOAA (8 May 2024), www.ncei.noaa.gov/access/monitoring/ao.

the Arctic Ocean as a commercial shipping lane.[57] The seasonality of Arctic Ocean routes, compounded by 'the vagaries of Arctic weather and sea ice', 'the non-availability of marine infrastructure' and reliable communication and navigation charts coupled with the navigation challenges of operating in ice-covered (as opposed to ice-free) nocturnal environments only begin to complicate transit issues.[58]

Sometimes confused as the Northeast Passage, the Northern Sea Route comprises a portion of that fabled passageway. It started as a cabotage route for goods into and minerals out of Siberia,[59] and its strategic importance cemented during World War II. In 1984, the Supreme Soviet decree that the route extended from Novaya Zemlya in the west to the Bering Strait in the east, traversing four seas linked by 58 straits and three archipelagos (the Novaya Zemlya, Severnaya Zemlya and East Siberian Islands).[60] Some straits in the Laptev Sea are only eight metres deep; the minimum depth in the Sannikov section of the East Siberian Sea is 13 metres; portions of the Vilkitski Strait, the important conduit between the Kara and Laptev Sea, are 17 metres deep.[61]

However, the United States and Russia have long contested the legal status of the Northern Sea Route. The Soviet Union began considering the waters around its Siberian archipelagos as internal waters in the 1940s. In 1964 and 1965, the United States responded by sending the *USS Burton Island* into the East Siberian Sea and the *USCGC Northwind* into the Laptev Sea, 'ostensibly' on freedom of navigation 'oceanographic survey missions.[62] In 1967 the *USCGCs Edisto* and *East Wind* attempted a circumnavigation of the Arctic Ocean. They entered the Kara Sea, but encountered severe ice that blocked passage north of the Severnaya Zemlya archipelago. They redirected transit by charting southernly passage toward the Vilkitski Strait, which connects the Kara and Laptev Seas. That change in direction toward the Northern Sea Route caused a major Cold War incident that resulted in Soviet threats and a United States decision to terminate the mission.[63] Sporadic incidences have ensued, most recently in 2019, when the French Navy auxiliary ship, *BSAH Rhône* unexpectedly navigated the Northern Sea Route.[64] To date, the waters

[57] Lawson W Brigham, 'Governance and Economic Challenges for the Global Shipping Enterprise in a Seasonally Ice-Covered Arctic Ocean', in *The Arctic and World Order* 143.

[58] ibid at 146.

[59] E Franckx, 'New Developments in the North-East Passage', n 55, at 35.

[60] See Christopher R Rossi, 'The Northern Sea Route and the Seaward Extension of *Uti Possidetis (Juris)*', 83 *Nordic J Int'l L* 476, 480 (2014).

[61] See Rossi, 'Russian Arctic Straits', n 53 at 36 (quoting the research of R. Douglas Brubaker and Willy Østreng, Eric Franckx, and Alexandŕ Golts).

[62] See ibid at 39–40.

[63] See ibid at 41–42.

[64] See 'Russia Tightens Control over Northern Sea Route', The Maritime Executive (8 March 2019), maritime-executive.com/article/russia-tightens-control-over-northern-sea-route (prompting the Kremlin to formulate new advance limitation notice for warship voyages along the route). Russia responded to the *Rhône* transit with draft legislation requiring that foreign sovereign immune vessels (warships) comply with domestic, prior permission requirements, a violation of international

of the Northern Sea Route remain treacherous, particularly in the harshest Eastern icy waters of the Laptev Sea.

Given its geostrategic station, Russia stands as the Northeast Passage's undeniable gatekeeper at both eastern and western portals of entry. A lack of surface ice strengthened warships in the United States Navy fleet create significant operational risks relating to freedom of navigation claims quite apart from Russia's predictable response to a perceived intrusion of its sovereign territory. Consequently, such operations remain on hold.[65] Despite its freedom of navigation claim or its assertion of the *de jure* status of the Northern Sea Route as an international strait, the United States cannot contest Russia's de facto control over critical stretches of the route.

VOTING WITH RUDDERS

For these reasons, mega-container ships will likely never 'use the Arctic Ocean in a regular system … despite the opportunities afforded by increases in marine access'.[66] Large container ships also will steer clear of the Northern Sea Route due to a host of 'practical geographical and navigational limitations' relating to shallower draft. With a draft of over 15 metres and nearly as long as the Empire State Building is high, 'the world's largest and most cost-effective cargo ships' like the *Ever Clear* cannot navigate the Northern Sea Route.[67]

It is most likely that any future seasonal, summer trans-Arctic navigation across the Northern Sea Route will create a 'niche market' for liquified natural gas transported in smaller container ships.[68] Brigham posed the interesting problem of whether international shipping companies would venture into such waters aware that the Kremlin would have 'complete control of this shipping enterprise', including factors relating to the assumption of risk and assessment of responsibility for accidents. His conclusion: 'A strong argument can be made that the [Northern Sea Route] is moving in the direction of a more domestic (internal) rather than an international waterway.'[69]

legal requirements. See Cornell G Overfield, 'FONOP in Vain: The Legal Logics of a U.S. Navy FONOP in the Canadia or Russian Arctic', *Arctic YB* 2021, 1, 11 (2021). In August 2021, the *USCGC Healy* made a rare transit through the Northwest Passage, which Canada claims as internal water. US authorities made it explicitly clear to Canada that the passage was not part of a Freedom of Navigation Operation.

[65] See Andrey Todorov, 'Dire Straits of the Russian Arctic: Options and Challenges for a Potential US FONOP in the Northern Sea Route', 139 *Mar Pol'y* 105020 (2022).

[66] ibid at 147.

[67] James Foggo and Rachael A Gosnell, 'Building a Trans-Polar Bridge', CEPA (21 May 2021), cepa.org/comprehensive-reports/building-a-trans-polar-bridge (noting the route 'is simply [too] poorly suited' to accommodate such traffic).

[68] ibid.

[69] ibid at 152–53.

No foreign-owned commercial vessel has transited the route since the invasion of Ukraine, 'a first in almost fifteen years'.[70] Non-Russian vessels have voted with their rudders and have completely abandoned the Northern Sea Route, wary of United States and European sanctions.[71] Nevertheless, Russia has committed to $35 billion in investments until 2035 in developing the Northern Sea Route and creating a commercial Arctic waterway from Vladivostok to Murmansk.[72] Russia has now constructed 17 deep-water ports along its 17,500 km Arctic coastline, including a new multi-billion dollar *entrepôt* at Sabetta on the Yamal Peninsula.[73] In contrast, the prospect of the United States creating its first deep-water Arctic port with an expanded $600 million port facility at Nome, Alaska is not expected to be operational until the end of the decade.[74] The operational United States polar icebreaking fleet consists of one heavy polar icebreaker, *Polar Star*, and one medium vessel, *Healy*. The *Polar Star*'s condition has been described as 'precarious'.[75] A second heavy polar icebreaker, *Polar Sea*, has been dry-docked due to engine failure since 2010.[76] The aging United States fleet, commissioned for polar service covering two oceans in 1976 and 1978, had an estimated service life of 30 years.[77] Moreover the *Polar Star* can crack through ice up to six feet thick at a continuous speed of three knots.[78] Russian icebreakers can navigate ice up to 13 feet thick, providing Russia access to 99 per cent of Arctic winter ice coverage as opposed to 59 per cent for the United States.[79]

[70] Malte Humpert, 'International Shipping on Northern Sea Route Collapses as Foreign Companies Stay Away', High North News (12 September 2022), www.highnorthnews.com/en/international-shipping-northern-sea-route-collapses-foreign-companies-stay-away [hereinafter Humpert, 'International Shipping'].

[71] See Eytan Goldstein, 'Eclipsed, Again: Russia's Northern Sea Route Will Have to Wait', *Harv Int'l Rev* (24 February 2023), hir.harvard.edu/eclipsed-again-russias-northern-sea-route-will-have-to-wait. Arctic cargo shipping volume along the Northern Sea Route did, however, register an increase of 34 metric tons in 2022 despite the Ukraine war, largely due to Russian oil and gas deliveries from the Russian Arctic to Asia and Europe. See Malte Humpert, 'Russia's Northern Sea Route Sees More Traffic Despite War and Sanctions', High North News (18 Jan. 2023), www.highnorthnews.com/en/russias-northern-sea-route-sees-more-traffic-despite-war-and-sanctions. Even during the record-breaking year of 2021, the Northern Sea Route recorded only 86 international transits. See Humpert, 'International Shipping', n 70.

[72] Conor McCann, 'Moscow is Betting Big on its Arctic Shipping Route as the Costs of Invading Ukraine Continue to Mount', Australian Broadcasting Corporation (10 March 2023), www.abc.net.au/news/2023-03-11/russias-northern-sea-route-gamble-vladimir-putin/102020368.

[73] See Atle Staalesen, 'Russian Arctic Ports Have Best Year Ever', Barents Observer, 16 January 2017, thebarentsobserver.com/en/industry-and-energy/2017/01/russian-arctic-ports-have-best-year-ever.

[74] 'Cruising to Nome: The First U.S. Deep Water Port for the Arctic to Host Cruise Ships, Military', AP (18 June 2023), www.usnews.com/news/business/articles/2023-06-18/cruising-to-nome-the-first-u-s-deep-water-port-for-the-arctic-to-host-cruise-ships-military.

[75] Ronald O'Rourke, 'Coast Guard Polar Security Cutter (Polar Icebreaker) Program: Background and Issues for Congress', CRS (updated 27 March 2024) at 4.

[76] ibid at 3–4.

[77] See ibid at 4. ('*Polar Star* and *Polar Sea* entered service in 1976 and 1978, respectively, and are now well beyond their originally intended 30-year service lives').

[78] Burke and Matisek, n 6, at 75.

[79] ibid (noting that Russia can navigate 269,958 km^2 of the Arctic's total winter ice coverage of 271,304 km^2 in contrast to the United States' capability of 159,426 km^2).

A MELTING SPATIAL DEVELOPMENT STRATEGY AND THE IDEA OF A TRANSPOLAR ROUTE

Russia has cultivated the expectation that the Northern Sea Route will secure its supreme position over a central component of Arctic affairs. It forms a central part of its spatial development strategy, which identifies the Northern Sea Route as 'a key logistics and transport hub of the planet … a truly global, competitive transport artery'.[80] Russia has depended on the rules-based order in the Arctic to further its position of historical dominance, and yet, ironically, has undermined that dominance by denuding itself of authority among the regional institutions and arrangements that uphold that order.[81] But what implications will there be for Russia of a transpolar route, a route that in important ways circumvents the advantages that mastery over its 24,000 km Arctic coastline provides?

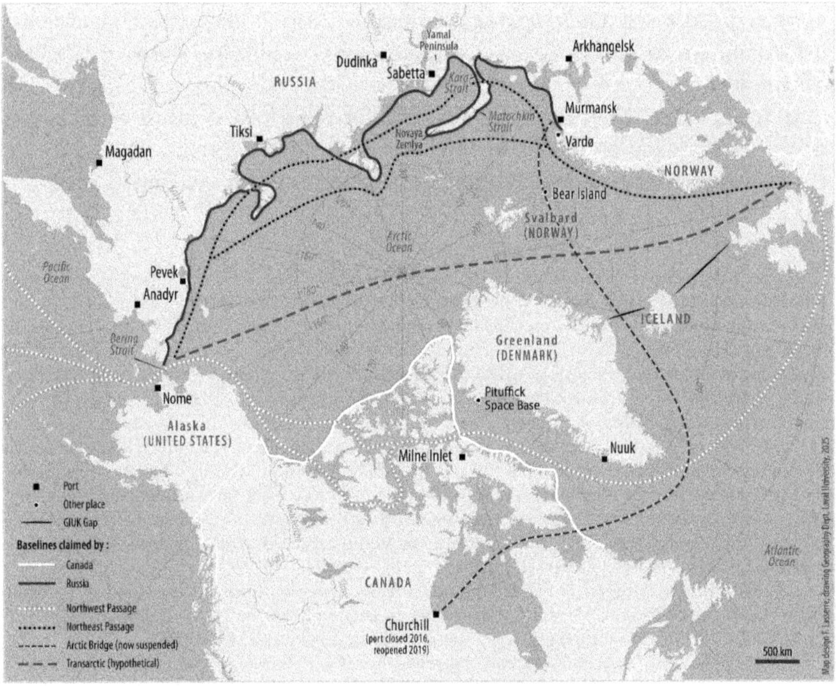

Figure 8.2 Geopolitics of Imagined and Extant Arctic Routes

[80] Marina Martynova, E'U, Russia and China Arctic Strategies: Comparative Analysis, 45th International Scientific Conference on Economic and Social Development 773, 774 (2019), www-proquest-com.mime.uit.no/docview/2317565816/fulltextPDF/3A73578A1ABB4D75PQ/1?accountid=17260&sourcetype=Conference%20Papers%20&%20Proceedings.

[81] See generally Torbjørn Pedersen and Beate Steinveg, 'Russia's Clashing Ambitions: Arctic Status Quo and World-Order Revision', 12 *Pol & Gov* (2024), doi.org/10.17645/pag.i377 (noting the tensions involved in Russia's dismantling of world order while seeking to maintain the status quo in the Arctic).

Discussions regarding projected Arctic transpolar shipping routes began to appear in the early 2000s.[82] Despite recognised uncertainties associated with charting such a route, even a more southerly route (closer to the Northern Sea Route) would lie 'outside any coastal state's Exclusive Economic Zone' and therefore be considered high seas. '[N]either the coastal state's powers as stipulated in UNCLOS and other marine agreements, nor Article 234, the Convention's 'Arctic [ice-covered] Exceptions clause' would apply.'[83] Polar class, ice-resistant ships, mandated by insurance companies and the International Maritime Organization's Polar Code, created regulatory restrictions based on ice-covered transit surface, not open water.[84] Indeed the once-futuristic technology of icebreaking, introduced in its 'modern variant in 1897', is a technology threatened to be overtaken by history.[85] A transpolar route would likely 'redistribute[] transits away from the Russian-administered Northern Sea Route',[86] and toward the bluer waters of the Central Arctic Ocean, where bathymetric limitations are not of concern. Likely transshipment port beneficiaries would be Svalbard, more so than Iceland (due to proximity to Europe's largest port, Rotterdam) and Nome, Alaska more so than Provideniya, Russia near the Bering Strait (given Russia's emphasis on Northern Sea Route port development in its western section).[87] Interestingly, Mia Bennett noted that 'The only country that seems to be ready for that reality is China', which began factoring into its 2018 Arctic Policy the dual idea that a transarctic passage would avail, and that it would become an part of China's Polar Silk Road.[88]

[82] See, eg, 'Breaking the Ice: Arctic Development and Maritime Transportation, Prospects of the Transarctic Route – Impact and Opportunities', Government of Iceland (2007), library.arcticportal.org/333/1/Breaking_The_Ice_Conference_Report.pdf; Scott R Stephenson, Laurence C Smith and John A Agnew, 'Divergent Long-Term Trajectories of Human Access to the Arctic', 1 *Nature Climate Change* 156 (2011); Malte Humpert and Andreas Raspotnik, 'The Future of Arctic Shipping Along the Transpolar Sea Route', *Arctic YB* 281 (2012).

[83] Humpert and Raspotnik, n 82, at 288.

[84] See Mia Bennett, 'The Arctic Shipping Route No One's Talking About', Maritime Executive (8 May 2019), maritime-executive.com/editorials/the-arctic-shipping-route-no-one-s-talking-about. The Polar Code is mandatory under both the International Convention for the Safety of Life at Sea (SOLAS) and the International Convention for the Prevention of Pollution from Ships (MARPOL). Ships intending to operate in defined waters of the Antarctic and Arctic must apply for certification based upon stringent functional requirements regarding watertight and weathertight integrity, machine installations, operational safety, voyage planning, pollution prevention and the like. See generally 'International Code for Ships Operating in Polar Waters (Polar Code)', IMO, www.imo.org/en/OurWork/Safety/Pages/polar-code.aspx.

[85] Bennett, 'The Arctic Shipping Route No One's Talking About', n 84.

[86] Xueke Li and Amanda H Lynch, 'New Insights Into Projected Arctic Sea Road: Operational Risks, Economic Values, and Policy Implications', 176 *Climate Change* 30 (2023). According to Mia Bennett et al: 'As ice avoidance becomes less of a concern with climate change, shipping lines may select routes that minimise distance rather than ice avoidance, possibly making routes north of the [Northern Sea Route] and eventually the TSR more attractive. The Russian government could then encounter difficulties in attracting transit shipping to the [Northern Sea Route]. Mia M Bennett et al, 'The Opening of the Transpolar Sea Route: Logistical, Geopolitical, Environmental, and Socioeconomic Impacts', *Mar Pol'y* § 4.2 (2020).

[87] Bennett et al, n 86, §§ 3.3.1–3.3.2. See also Nyman et al, 'The Svalbard Archipelago: An Exploratory Analysis of Port Investment in the Context of the New Arctic Routes', 19 *Mar Stud*.at 5 ('The archipelago of Svalbard is uniquely placed to service the hypothetical future Trans-Arctic Route').

[88] Bennett, 'The Arctic Shipping Route No One's Talking About', n 84.

Chapter Nine

China's Polar Pivot

Animated by the Svalbard Treaty's non-discrimination provisions and its historical encounters with and opposition to unequal treaties, China became an early 1925 signatory to the Svalbard Treaty.[1] The treaty discordantly conferred full and absolute sovereignty over the archipelago on Norway while extending equal enjoyment and liberty of access rights to nationals of signatories to the treaty. Although China sources this treaty as evidence of its 'long history of engagement in Arctic affairs', subsequent polar encounters more often focused on Antarctica, to the extent that China focused on polar issues at all. China only began 'paying more attention to the Arctic' in the 1990s when climate change prompted a series of Arctic expeditions.[2]

Recently, Chinese President Xi Jinping expressed China's ambition to become a 'polar great power' (极地强 国, *jidi qiangguo*) by 2030,[3] describing the Arctic as 'one of the world's new strategic frontiers'.[4] According to Elizabeth Economy, Xi 'has signalled his intention to lead in the development of norms in areas where they are not yet fully established', including the Arctic where China 'has already moved aggressively'.[5] In the 10 years ending in 2023, China invested more than '$90 billion in Arctic energy and mineral projects, primarily in Russia'.[6] Between 2008 and 2018, Chinese scholars added more than 300 articles on Arctic affairs to a national academic registry.[7]

[1] See Tianbao Qin, 'Dispute Over the Applicable Scope of the Svalbard Treaty: A Chinese Lawyer's Perspective', *J East Asia & Int'l L* 149, 151 (2015).

[2] Kai Sun, 'Beyond the Dragon and the Panda: Understanding China's Engagement in the Arctic', Asia Pol'y (21 July 2014), www.nbr.org/publication/beyond-the-dragon-and-the-panda-understanding-chinas-engagement-in-the-arctic.

[3] P Whitney Lackenbauer, Adam Lajeunesse and Ryan Dean, 'Why China Is Not a Peer Competitor in the Arctic', *J Indo-Pac Affs* 80, 81 (September–October 2022).

[4] Rush Doshi, Alexis Dale-Huang and Gaoqi Zhang, 'Northern Expedition: China's Arctic Activities and Ambitions', Brookings 1 (April 2021), www.brookings.edu/articles/northern-expedition-chinas-arctic-activities-and-ambitions.

[5] Elizabeth Economy, 'Xi Jingping's New World Order', 101 *For Affs* 52, 64–65 (2022) (hereinafter Economy, 'Xi Jingping's New World Order').

[6] Malte Humpert, 'Putin and Xi Discuss Further Deepening of Arctic Partnership', High North News (23 March 2023), www.highnorthnews.com/en/putin-and-xi-discuss-further-deepening-arctic-partnership#:%7E:text=Over%20the%20past%20decade%20China,figure%20to%20surpass%20%24200bn.

[7] Nengye Liu and Qi Xu, 'The Predicates of Chinese Legal Philosophy in the Polar Regions', in *Philosophies of Polar Law* 131, 135 (2020) (discussing over 300 Arctic papers of 350 polar papers in the China National Knowledge Infrastructure database).

Some of these *moves* reflect China's strident global rhetoric. Its former Vice Minister for Foreign Affairs, He Yafei, declared that the end to the *Pax Americana* was in sight. Fudan University's Shen Dingli characterised China's future as occupying the 'high moral ground'. Xi himself described China's rejuvenation as 'a historic inevitability'. As the world's largest trading power, its greatest source of global lending, its largest military, second largest population, and record of technological accomplishments, there is support for China's claims.[8]

Perhaps Western interpretations of these aforementioned speech acts colour some of China's more tactile Arctic ventures. China opened its Arctic Yellow River Research Station in Ny-Ålesund in 2004,[9] and petitioned for observer status with the Arctic Council in 2007, achieving that designation in 2013.[10] China has invested heavily in Track II regional efforts to elevate its Arctic profile, establishing 'a China-Russia Arctic Forum and the China-Nordic Arctic Research Center to deepen relations with governments and sub-national actors'.[11] China now operates three research icebreakers,[12] which are equipped with deep-sea submersibles to carry out crewed missions in the Arctic water column and seabed.[13] Such vessels may be deployed for wide-ranging scientific purposes, but most if not all such vessels harbour a dual-purpose military capability. China's development of a polar subglacial hydroacoustic buoy monitoring system,[14] a squadron of polar-capable aircraft,[15] and its high-altitude balloon launches have raised concerns about its military surveillance interests in the Arctic and

[8] Economy, 'Xi Jingping's New World Order', n 5, at 66.

[9] See Arctic Yellow River Station, Polar Research Institute of China (operating at 78°55'N).

[10] See Anders Christoffer Edstrøm, Iselin Stensdal and Gørild M Heggelund, 'The "New Superpower": What Are China's Intentions in the Arctic', in *Norway's Arctic Policy: Geopolitics, Security and Identity in the High North* 95 (Andreas Østerhagen ed, 2023). On observer status in the Arctic Council, see Arctic Council Rules of Procedure, Pt.V: Other Matters, 36–38, and Annex 2 (1998), oaarchive.arctic-council.org/server/api/core/bitstreams/6e73a734-2f8b-40f6-849a-245ef9942790/content.

[11] Doshi et al, n 4. The China-Nordic Arctic Research Center was established in Shanghai in 2013. For more, see CNARC, www.cnarc.info/organization. The China-Russia Arctic Forum began as an informal set of seminars at St Petersburg University in 2011. See Maxim Gutenev, ML Lagutina and Alexander Sergunin, 'Russian Universities as Actors of Arctic Science Diplomacy', 32 *Higher Ed. in Russia* 70 (2023) [Russian trans]. See also 11th China-Russia Arctic Forum Held at OUC, Ocean University of China (2022), eweb.ouc.edu.cn/2022/1114/c892a382392/page.htm.

[12] Polina Leganger Bronder, 'China to Build Its Third Icebreaker', Barents Observer (10December2021),thebarentsobserver.com/en/arctic/2021/12/china-build-its-third-arctic-icebreaker (discussing the construction of the PRC's three icebreakers – the Xue Long, Xue Long 2, and Zhong Shan Da Xue Ji Di).

[13] Ameya Paleja, 'China to Build Icebreaker with Submersible to Reach Arctic Seabed', *Interesting Engineering* (28 June 2023).

[14] See Stephen Chen, 'China Plans Massive Listening Programme at the North Pole After Declaring Success in Arctic Test of Underwater Devise', *South China Morning Post* (9 July 2023), www.scmp.com/news/china/science/article/3226755/china-plans-massive-listening-programme-north-pole-after-declaring-success-arctic-test-underwater (noting the development of field testing by the Polar Research Institute of China).

[15] Ryan Burke and Jahara Matisek, 'The American Polar Pivot: Gaining a Comparative Advantage in Great Power Competition', 10 *MCU J* 70, 71 (2019).

North America.[16] If China is trying to supplant the United States as the dominant force in the Asia-Pacific region, with initiatives to lead the free-trade Regional Comprehensive Economic Partnership[17] and join the Comprehensive and Progressive Agreement for TransPacific Partnership ((CPTPP), which was created to counter growing Chinese influence)[18] is it now positioning itself to claim greater space in the Arctic?

SECURITISATION AND THE POLAR SILK ROAD

Connections between Asia and Europe across the polar North underscore the strategic and commercial interests of China's Polar Silk Road,[19] which is part of its grander Belt and Road Initiative that is the centerpiece of Xi's foreign policy bid to elevate China to a global leadership position.[20] This latter massive global

[16] See Sakshi Tiwari, 'Canada Discovers "Chinese Buoys" in the Arctic That Could Be Tracking US Nuclear Submarines in the Region – Media', EurAsian Times (14 August 2023), www.eurasiantimes.com/canada-discovers-chinese-buoys-in-the-arctic-that-could-be-tracking (noting the Canadian military's recovery of a Chinese monitoring buoy in the Arctic Ocean days after the United States shot down an alleged Chinese high-altitude balloon that had entered American airspace after traversing the Canadian Arctic); Jim Garamone, 'F-22 Safely Shoots Down Chinese Spy Balloon Off South Carolina Coast', US DoD News (2023), www.defense.gov/News/News-Stories/Article/Article/3288543/f-22-safely-shoots-down-chinese-spy-balloon-off-south-carolina-coast (asserting that the Chinese balloon was attempting 'to surveil strategic sites in the continental U.S.' after first traversing US and Canadian airspace near the Aleutian Islands).

[17] See generally The Regional Comprehensive Economic Partnership (RCEP), ASEAN (2024), asean.org/our-communities/economic-community/integration-with-global-economy/the-regional-comprehensive-economic-partnership-rcep/ (presenting an overview of the economic partnership of the 10 ASEAN Member States and six ASEAN freee trad agreement partners).

[18] See 'China Applies to Join Pacific Trade Pact to Boost Economic Clout', Reuters (17 September 2021), www.reuters.com/world/china/china-officially-applies-join-cptpp-trade-pact-2021-09-16; Lucy Craymer and Joe Cash, 'Biggest Hurdles to China Entry Into Trans-Pacific Trade Pact are Political', Reuters (31 July 2023), www.reuters.com/world/biggest-hurdles-china-entry-into-trans-pacific-trade-pact-are-political-2023-07-31 (describing the creation of the CPTPP as a means to contain China).

[19] China's 2018 White Paper on Arctic Policy introduced the phrase 'Polar Silk Road'. See 'China's Arctic Policy' State Council, The People's Republic of China (26 January 2018), english.www.gov.cn/archive/white_paper/2018/01/26/content_281476026660336.htm. The phrase has been defined to mean 'a series of cooperative international ventures among Russia, the Nordic Countries and certain East Asian countries': Jian Yang, *Arctic Governance and China's Engagement* 105 (2024). Projects connected to the Polar Silk Road initiative include energy projects, primarily in Russia's Arctic, shipping and commercialisation networks involving the Northern Sea Route, proposals for an Arctic Corridor project connecting Rovaniemi, Finland with the Norwegian port of Kirkenes, followed by railway connections in Scandinavia on through to Helsinki and then to undersea rail connections to Tallinn and Central Europe, and other forms of technological and scientific cooperation. See ibid at 108–16.

[20] See Elizabeth C. Economy, *The Third Revolution: Xi Jinping and the New Chinese State* 2–3 and 190–93 (2018). See also 'The Five Main Projects of the Belt and Road Initiative', *S China Morning Post* (May 2017), multimedia.scmp.com/news/china/article/One-Belt-One-Road/pakistan.html [perma.cc/J3VB-T4MM]; Guo Peiqing and Chen Huiwen, 'Chinese Perspective on the Arctic and its Implications for Nordic Countries', Arctic Inst (20 June 2023), www.thearcticinstitute.org/chinese-perspective-arctic-implication-nordic-countries.

development initiative incorporates plans to construct railways to London, Iran and Kazakhstan, an Asian gas pipeline, a super link to the Gwadar Port in Pakistan's Baluchistan province (thus accessing the Arabian Sea and Arabian/Persian Gulf), and the development of Arctic commercial routes, the so-called Polar Silk Road. The Belt and Road initiative has been described as a modern equivalent of *huairou* (怀柔), the ancient Chinese soft power equivalent of 'winning hearts of foreigners through tributary trade'.[21] To reposition itself as the centre of the international system, China's intends to develop six corridors – three over land, three maritime – to connect China to Asia, Europe and the Middle East.[22]

China is well motivated to develop Arctic commercial pathways given extant geopolitical dependencies it faces with energy and trade needs. Ninety per cent of Chinese trade transits maritime routes and much of that trade requires imports of foreign oil and liquefied natural gas.[23] More than 60 per cent of China's maritime trade moves through the Strait of Malacca, a 65 km-wide chokepoint, which is less than 3 km wide at its narrowest point. It separates Malaysia and Singapore from Indonesia and connects the South China Sea and the Indian Ocean.[24] In 2003, Chinese President Hu Jintao called China's predicament the 'Malacca Dilemma', owing to China's dependence on the route, the rising pelagic power of India, and the nearby presence of the United States Navy's Seventh and Fifth fleets, which operate in the Indo-Pacific and Middle East regions.[25] This vulnerability feeds Chinese encirclement fears and allegations of its construction of a string of pearls maritime infrastructure around the Indian Ocean[26] to offset Western defences. These Western defences were revived with the Trump Administration's Quadrilateral Security Dialogue with Australia, India, and Japan, and have been fortified by the Biden Administration's creation of trilateral security partnerships with Australia and the United Kingdom (AUKUS), and Japan and the Philippines (JAPHUS), as well as longstanding monitoring stations dotting the Korean peninsula, Japan, Okinawa, Taiwan, and the Philippines.

[21] Economy, *The Third Revolution*, n 20, at 222.

[22] See Economy, 'Xi Jingping's New World Order', n 5, at 57.

[23] See Lucas Myers, 'China's Economic Security Challenge: Difficulties Overcoming the Malacca Dilemma', *Georgetown J Int'l Affs* (22 March 2023), gjia.georgetown.edu/2023/03/22/chinas-economic-security-challenge-difficulties-overcoming-the-malacca-dilemma.

[24] See Zahra Ahmed, '10 Things about Malacca Strait You Might Not Know', Marine Insight (22 February 2023), www.marineinsight.com/environment/malacca-strait.

[25] See Paweł Paszak, 'China and the "Malacca Dilemma"', (28 February 2021), warsawinstitute.org/china-malacca-dilemma/.

[26] See generally Virginia Marantidou, 'Revisiting China's "String of Pearls" Strategy: Places "with Chinese Characteristics" and their Security Implications', 14 Pacific Forum, CSIS (2014), pacforum.org/wp-content/uploads/2019/02/140624_issuesinsights_vol14no7.pdf (discussing the western description of Chinese port investments along the Indian Ocean beginning in the early 2000s).

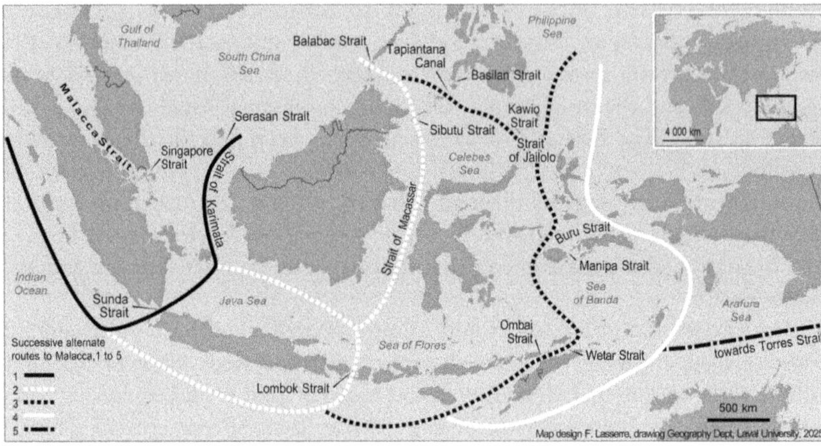

Figure 9.1 Indian Ocean to Pacific Ocean maritime chokepoints
Source: US Energy Information Administration.

Alleviating China's vulnerability by creating additional pathways for trade explains development projects such as the China–Pakistan Economic Corridor linking Gwadar Port in Pakistan to Xinjiang Province in China, the Myanmar Oil Pipeline to Kunming, and the centuries-old dream of building a canal or land bridge across Thailand's Kra Isthmus, thus bypassing the Strait of Malacca and shortcutting by two to three days access to the Indian Ocean via the Gulf of Thailand.[27] An alternative route across the top of the world presents logical commercial and strategic advantages to China's global outlook.

A MUTED RECORD OF ARCTIC ACHIEVEMENT, DEBT TRAP DIPLOMACY, AND SECURITISATION

China's success in establishing its Polar Silk Road and elevating its presence as a regional Arctic power have proven far less successful than Beijing advertises.[28]

[27] See Shaun Cameron, 'By Land or Sea: Thailand Perseveres With the Kra Canal', The Interpreter (22 September 2021), www.lowyinstitute.org/the-interpreter/land-or-sea-thailand-perseveres-kra-canal (invigorating discussion of a Chinese-financed circumvention of the Malacca Dilemma).

[28] P. Whitney Lackenbauer, Adam Lajeunesse and Ryan Dean, 'Why China Is Not a Peer Competitor in the Arctic', *J Indo-Pacific Affs* (3 October 2022), www.airuniversity.af.edu/JIPA/Display/Article/3172586/why-china-is-not-a-peer-competitor-in-the-arctic (describing China's Arctic geopolitical accomplishments as 'overinflated' and 'far more tenuous [] than Beijing advertises'); Marc Lanteigne, 'The Rise (and Fall?) of the Polar Silk Road', The Diplomat (29 August 2022), thediplomat.com/2022/08/the-rise-and-fall-of-the-polar-silk-road (noting that 'many original components of the PSR [Polar Silk Road] across the Arctic … have been delayed or scrapped'); *Nordic-China Cooperation: Challenges and Opportunities* (Andreas Bøje Forsby ed, 2019) (summarising 'the rather limited measures taken by Nordic countries to adopt a joint approach to China').

Plans to turn Kirkenes, Norway into China's first European port of call, with a Chinese-funded rail link to Finland and farther southward, gathered some non-Indigenous Norwegian boosters but never materialised.[29] China's efforts to develop commercial relations in Iceland began with a promising 2013 Free Trade Agreement, the first among European countries. It fell flat shortly thereafter when a massive Chinese land acquisition deal raised suspicions in Reykjavik.[30] The Norwegian Government blocked China's purchase of the last available privately owned land in Svalbard on extrapolated grounds of national security law that protect 'stability' and 'Norwegian interests'.[31] The land, about the size of Manhattan, is located on the remote Sore Fagerfjord, a peninsula devoid of infrastructure and protected from development and motorised transport. China's regard as a 'deep-pocketed investor' for Greenland and huge consumer market for its mining, fishing, and tourism industries awakened national security concerns in Brussels, Copenhagen, and Washington.[32] Its bids to invest in iron mining, airport refurbishment, an abandoned Danish naval base at Kangilinngut, and the potential Kuannersuit (Kvanefjeld) rare earth project prompted a Cold War-like resecuritisation campaign.[33]

China's engagement with Greenland suggested to Western powers an attempt to forge local political allegiances based on enticements of Chinese engineering and infrastructure projects.[34] China's global development policies have long been criticised as debt-trap diplomacy – a means of employing financial leverage to increase economic dependence to secure political or military advantage. China's practice and its motivation have been debated in the Indian Ocean region,[35]

[29] *cf* Atle Staalesen, 'Kirkenes Port Developers Put Their Faith in the Chinese', Barents Observer (7 June 2019), thebarentsobserver.com/en/node/5478, with Thomas Nilsen, 'Lapland Regional Council Rejects Arctic Railway', Barents Observer (17 May 2021), thebarentsobserver.com/en/industry-and-energy/2021/05/lapland-regional-council-rejects-arctic-railway (noting strong objections from the Norwegian and Finnish Sámi parliaments).

[30] See generally Helgi Steinar Gunnlaugsson, *Explaining the Economic Inconsistencies of China-Iceland Relations: Examining the Success of the China-Iceland Free Trade Agreement and the Failure of Huang Nubo's Land Acquisition Deal* (2017) (discussing the geopolitical suspicions and incentives affecting Chinese–Icelandic relations).

[31] 'Norway Blocks Sale of Last Private Land on Svalbard after Chinese Interest', *The Guardian* (1 July 2024), www.theguardian.com/world/article/2024/jul/01/norway-blocks-sale-last-private-land-svalbard-china-interest (quoting Norwegian Trade and Industry minister, Cecilie Myrseth).

[32] Chuan Chen, 'China's Engagement in Greenland: Mutual Economic Benefits and Political Non-interference', 41 *Polar Res* (2022), polarresearch.net/index.php/polar/article/view/7706/14451.

[33] Patrick Andersson and Jesper W Zeuthen, 'How China Left Greenland: Mutually Reinforcing Securitization Policies and Chinese Mining Plans in Greenland', in *Greenland in Arctic Security: (De)securitization Dynamics under Climactic Thaw and Geopolitical Freeze* 175 (Marc Jacobsen, Ole Wæver and Ulrik Pram Gad eds, 2024) [hereinafter *Greenland in Arctic Security*].

[34] On claims of Chinese wedge politics in High North latitudes and elsewhere, see Jeff D Colgan and Nicholas L Miller, 'The Rewards of Rivalry: U.S.-Chinese Competition Can Spur Climate Progress', 101 *For Affs* 108 (November/December 2022).

[35] Mohit Choudhary, 'China's Malacca Bluff: Examining China's Indian Ocean Strategy and Future Security Architecture of the Region', *J Indo-Pac Affs* 99, 100 (2023) (criticising ostensibly

South Asia,[36] Africa,[37] Oceana,[38] and Latin America.[39] Its appropriateness as a strategy to penetrate capital intensive Europe, even in commercially underdeveloped Greenland, seems less convincing or concerning.

In the Arctic context, Patrick Andersson and Jesper Zeuthen argued that a fundamental misperception of China's intentions accompanied its political bargaining process, as China tended to frame state interests in terms of national objectives rather than in terms of poverty alleviation and food security.[40] This policy orientation serves as Western evidence of China's Arctic securitisation intent, when from a Chinese perspective it less threateningly serves domestic political objectives.[41] The authors also noted a type of mirror-imaging from China's vantage point, where 'certain forms of engagement with the West are regarded as problematic in the Chinese system' due to Western political sensitivities.[42] In a growing awareness of such sensitivities, the authors wrote that China decided to adopt for external translation the term Belt and Road Initiative to avoid Western suspicions that it was masking a grander Arctic 'strategy', 'agenda', 'project', or 'program'.[43] Even the term Polar Silk Road has been suggested as too politically sensitive for Scandinavian countries to endorse because of poor relations between Europe and Russia.[44]

Recognition of these sensitivities expands the field of securitisation studies. It subjects securitisation theory to a broader interrogation of the nature of the threat. It views the types of political systems beyond the framework of democracies, where the theory has been applied most intensively, and enlarges the geographic scope of its application.[45] However, the immediacy of the threat remains at this expanded core of securitisation theory.

anti-imperialist China for increasing economic dependence of vulnerable countries to secure political leverage in the Indian Ocean region).

[36] See Cissy Zhou, 'Sri Lanka's China "Debt Trap" Fears Grow as Beijing Keeps Investing', NikkeiAsia (2 January 2024), asia.nikkei.com/Spotlight/Asia-Insight/Sri-Lanka-s-China-debt-trap-fears-grow-as-Beijing-keeps-investing (discussing China's role in Sri Lanka's sovereign debt crisis).

[37] Compare Deborah Brautigam and Meg Rithmire, 'The Chinese 'Debt Trap' Is a Myth', The Atlantic (6 February 2021), www.theatlantic.com/international/archive/2021/02/china-debt-trap-diplomacy/617953/ (describing the claim as wrongful) and *The Elements of the China Challenge, Policy Planning Staff, U.S. Secretary of State* 23–24 (2020) (holding: 'Largely debt-financed, China's projects in Africa often fail to meet reasonable international standards of sustainability and transparency, and burden local economies with heavy debt and other problems').

[38] See Joanne Wallis et al, 'Ordering the Islands? Pacific Responses to China's Strategic Narratives', 16 *Chinese J Int'l Pol* 457 (2023) (focusing on case studies involving Fiji, Solomon Islands, and Samoa).

[39] See Diana Roy, 'China's Growing Influence in Latin America', *Council on For Rel* (15 June 2023) (noting China's rising hemispheric presence and specifically Venezuela's outstanding loans from China).

[40] Andersson and Zeuthen, n 33, at 190.

[41] ibid at 188.

[42] ibid at 190.

[43] ibid at 188.

[44] ibid.

[45] See Juha A Vuori, 'Illocutionary Logic and Strands of Securitization: Applying the Theory of Securitization to the Study of Non-Democratic Political Orders', 14 *Eur J Int'l Rel* 65, 65–66,

Here, a Schmittian logic of the political, framed around the friend–enemy binary, coincides with securitisation theory. It emphasises the need for the sovereign to take extralegal measures to confront exigencies. This idea of the state of exception (*Ausnahmenzustände*) pivoted security studies toward the study of broader political systems.[46] This line of reasoning developed with securitisation studies' Copenhagen School expositors,[47] who interpreted securitisation to mean the process through which non-politicised or politicised issues 'are elevated to security issues that need to be dealt with urgency, and that legitimate the bypassing of public debate and democratic procedures'.[48] This critical approach to security studies focused on why things become existential threats, bypassing discussion of whether such threats objectively exist.

In Greenland's case, China's development interests stimulated strong Western resistance. Although Greenland is a self-governing, autonomous territory of Denmark,[49] 50 per cent of its government budget derives from Denmark's annual block grant and Greenland's defence remains completely under and NATO's security umbrella. These postcolonial dependencies breed a strong and intensifying independence movement among Greenland's armyless 58,0000 people and poses a serious question for a resource-rich territory of about Alaska's size.[50] What would an independent Greenland mean for the Arctic? The answer, apart from a diminishment of Danish identity in global affairs, remains oblique.

Already, it means a clear separation from Denmark. In 2024, Greenland's Inatsisartut (Parliament) issued its own White Paper on Arctic strategy.

and 68 (democracies and legitimacy) (2008). See also Ole Wæver, Security the Speech Act: Analysing the Politics of a Word, Working Paper no 19. Copenhagen: Centre for Peace and Conflict research (1989).

[46] See Matt McDonald, 'Securitization and the Construction of Security', 14 *Eur J Int'l Rel* 563, 579–80 (2008) (noting that 'the securitization framework is based' on the logic of Schmitt's articulation of the nature of threat).

[47] See generally Ole Wæver, 'Securitization and Desecuritization', in *On Security* 46 (Ronnie D Lipschutz ed, 1995) (introducing the concept primarily as a speech act that frames a particular issue as an existential issue); Barry Buzan, Ole Wæver and Jaap de Wilde, *Security: A New Framework for Analysis* (1998) (developing the theory of a regional security complex and fortifying role of audiences and constituencies in constructing the speech act); Jef Huysmans, 'Revisiting Copenhagen: Or, On the Creative Development of a Security Studies Agenda in Europe', 4 *Eur J Int'l Rel* 479 (1998) (exploring the grammar and chronology of securitisation).

[48] Rens van Munster, 'Securitization', Oxford Bibliographies (2012), www.oxfordbibliographies.com/display/document/obo-9780199743292/obo-9780199743292-0091.xml.

[49] Act on Greenland Self-Government, Act. No 473 (12 June 2009) [trans], wwwex.ilo.org/dyn/natlex2/natlex2/files/download/110442/DNK110442%20Eng.pdf.

[50] See Joseph Wehmeyer, 'What Would Greenland's Independence Mean for the Arctic?' Council on Foreign Relations (2023) (noting Greenland's parliament, the Inatsisartut created its first draft constitution for independence in April 2023). See also Shen Shiwei, 'Greenland FM Aims to Strengthen Cooperation with China on Week-Long Visit', CGTN (25 October 2023), news.cgtn.com/news/2023-10-25/Greenland-FM-aims-to-strengthen-cooperation-with-China-on-week-long-visit-1obkvqWp1aU/index.html (noting the opening of Greenland's Representative Office in Beijing).

Dispositively titled, 'Nothing About Us Without Us', the document asserts Greenland's primacy as Denmark's only connection to the Arctic, its interest in stronger collaborations with North-to-North political parliaments in Alaska, the Yukon, the Northwest Territories, Nunavut, and Nunavik, its leadership in the Arctic Council, and its prioritised engagement with East Asia.[51]

However, Western reactions regarded China's ventures in Greenland as a security threat. The European Union upgraded its presence there and the United States reopened its consulate. Denmark pressured the Inatsisartut to disengage with China, and the United States warned Denmark by characterising China as a 'less trustworthy' interloper attempting to shape Greenlandic values.[52] Andersson and Zeuthen described China's Greenlandic overtures as stimulating 'a process of mutually reinforcing securitization policies',[53] which may one day result in greater competition for access to Greenland.[54] Currently, no further Chinese investments appear in the making in Greenland.[55]

CHINA'S ENGAGEMENT WITH RUSSIA

Engagement with Russia comprises an essential component of China's ambition, as well as a perceptible component of Russian policy. While a rapprochement seems apparent and increasingly necessary in the wake of Russia's invasion of Ukraine, the relationship appears more squarely centred around pragmatic short- and medium-term interests rather than a long-term alignment of strategic interests. China's non-Arctic status necessitates mindful cooperation with circumpolar states. However, any deepening cooperation with Russia engenders more cautious responses from other Arctic powers, which in turn requires China to balance its economic and security gains with Russia against its costs in

[51] See Greenland in the World: Nothing About Us Without Us, Greenland's Foreign, Security and Defense Policy 2024–2033–An Arctic Strategy 31, Naalakkersuisut/Gov, Greenland (February 2024), naalakkersuisut.gl/Publikationer?types=&subjects=&page=1&dates=2024&sc_lang=da.

[52] See Sou-Jie van Brunnersum, 'China Failed its Arctic Ambitions in Greenland', Politico (22 October 2022), www.politico.eu/article/china-arctic-greenland-united-states (noting European Commission decision to set up a formal presence in Greenland in 2023); Marc Jacobsen and Signe Lyngholm Lindbjerg, 'Denmark's Security Perspectives on USA, China, and Russia in Greenland: How Great Power Threats Made Danish Politicians Talk about Independent Greenland Agency', in *Greenland in Arctic Security*, n 33, at 196, 219 (noting that the Government of Denmark engaged with the Government of Greenland in 'extraordinary means' … 'having accepted American securitizations' to counter Chinese commercial endeavours in Greenland); Statement by US Ambassador to Denmark, Carla Sands, 'Wake Up to the Arctic's Importance', US Embassy & Consulate in the Kingdom of Denmark (20 April 2020), dk.usembassy.gov/wake-up-to-the-arctics-importance/?fbclid=IwAR1MgkaTBYuNJga25sK7UTFI7sze00lIuxhEvnPyABtUKDcakGmZ9WAqAeE ('less than trustworthy').

[53] Andersson and Zeuthen, n 33, at 188.

[54] ibid at 177.

[55] ibid at 190.

terms of fortifying relations with the Arctic 7. And behind China's reversal of status with Russia, which feeds Russian anxiety of assuming a vassal status with China, is the awareness of China's growing influence in formerly Soviet Central Asia and Russia's serving as the only remaining possessor of territory seized from the Qing empire during its Century of Humiliation.[56]

In 2013, Russian President Putin's announced a 'pivot to Asia', which followed the Obama Administration's 2011 slow turn,[57] and, incidentally, China's efforts to gain formal observer status in the Arctic Council. Russia's pivot evidenced an increasing acknowledgment of the growing economic power of North-East Asia and a need to keep closer tabs on China's emerging Arctic intentions.[58] Bobo Lo and Fiona Hill argued that Russia's 'pivot [was] driven as much by its anxiety about the vulnerability of its sparsely populated eastern flank as by its desire to project influence'.[59] From an historical perspective, Lo noted elsewhere that Moscow and Beijing's practical cooperation 'is hamstrung by historical suspicions, cultural prejudices, geopolitical rivalry, and competing priorities', leaving 'lingering doubt' about the sustainability of any 'multifaceted' or strategic partnership.[60] As an indication of this suspicion, China has slow-walked the Kremlin's interest in building the Power of Siberia 2 gas pipeline to compensate for its gas glut due to the 80 per cent decline in gas exports to Europe following the Ukraine invasion. Russia's pivot to the East to secure this export channel demonstrates a dependence on China, and China's ability to bargain for terms it deems most suitable to its needs.[61] Another slow-walked project involved the only cross-border bridge spanning the 2,000-km section of the Amur River separating China and Russia. The agreement to build the 2.5 km railway bridge concluded in 1995. It opened in 2022.[62]

[56] See Stephen Kotkin, 'The Five Futures of Russia', *For Affs* 64, 71 (May/June 2024).

[57] See generally Robert Blackwill and Richard Fontaine, *Lost Decade, The US Pivot to Asia and the Rise of Chinese Power* (2024) (assessing the historical evolution of the shift of American foreign policy toward putting Asian issues at the forefront). See also Andrew J Nathan, 'What Exactly Is America's China Policy?', *For Pol'y* 33, 34 (Spring 2022) (noting that 'the Obama Administration was tied up in wars in Iraq and Afghanistan and negotiations over the Iranian nuclear program, and the attempted pivot brought little more than a heightened diplomatic presence in the region').

[58] See Radityo Dharmaputra, 'Russia's Pivot to the East: Between China, the US and the Other Asia', International Centre for Defence and Security (24 October 2019), icds.ee/en/russias-pivot-to-the-east-between-china-the-us-and-the-other-asia (noting Russia's pivot to Asia involve a 'diversified and multi-vectored foreign policy to balance China's dominant position in Asia').

[59] Bobo Lo and Fiona Hill, 'Putin's Pivot: Why Russia is Looking East', Brookings (31 July 2013), www.brookings.edu/articles/putins-pivot-why-russia-is-looking-east.

[60] Bobo Lo, *Axis of Convenience: Moscow, Beijing, and the New Geopolitics* 2 (2008).

[61] See Tatiana Mitrova, 'Preliminary Outlines of the New Russian Gas Export Strategy', Centre on Global Energy Pol'y/SIPA (20 November 2023), iea.blob.core.windows.net/assets/46b64b95-0cfe-4751-ad5d-46e74d79ea71/TatianaMitrova_PreliminaryoutlinesofthenewRussiangasexportstrategy.pdf (discussing and charting the proposed gas route from the Yamal peninsula south-eastward through Ulan Bator to China).

[62] Lilit Marcus, 'First Cross-River Railway Bridge between China and Russia Completed', CNN (20 August 2021), edition.cnn.com/travel/article/tongjiang-china-russia-bridge-complete-intl-hnk/

Nengye Liu and Jan Solski noted similarities in China's and Russia's coastal state practice. Both countries tend to maximise exclusive authority, delimit such authority by use of straight baselines, employ domestic regulations to route, report, and pilot activity in the Exclusive Economic Zone, and maintain, like all coastal states, vigilance regarding foreign shipping proximate to their coasts.[63] However, Liu and Solski noted that 'careful and vague statements' condition the two countries' Arctic legal relationship regarding the 'elephant in the room' – a divergence of interests regarding the breadth of UNCLOS Article 234's 'ice-covered area'.[64] Russia has pliably used Article 234 to support its international claims of jurisdiction over the Northern Sea Route, an interpretation that China has neither affirmed nor confronted in a wait-and-see-styled strategy to maximise future freedom of navigation interests involving its own the Polar Silk Road initiative.[65]

Generally, China has followed an incremental policy based on bilateral engagements rather than disruptive general assertions. It has eschewed references to Arctic or global governance in official Chinese government documents and has emphasised instead bilateral ventures and 'intergovernmental mechanisms rather than multi-stakeholder approaches'.[66] The question remains whether China is cultivating a wait-and-see economic schema for the High North or a strategy for marine plunder that violates the rule of law.[67] NATO's focus on Russia and Ukraine runs a risk of drawing general Western attention away from China and its major foreign policy objectives.

CHINA'S ENGAGEMENT WITH INTERNATIONAL LAW

Congyan Cai added texture to China's Arctic engagement with international law. He argued that China's ascendancy to great power status necessitated an

index.html; 'China-Russia Rail Bridge is Finally Open', RailFreight.com (17 November 2022), www.railfreight.com/railfreight/2022/11/17/china-russia-rail-bridge-is-finally-open/?gdpr=accept.

[63] Nengye Liu and Jan Jakub Solski, 'The Polar Silk Road and the Future Governance of the Northern Sea Route', 35 *Leiden J Int'l L* 853, 865–66 (2022).

[64] ibid at 866.

[65] See ibid (adding: 'Russia and China may be expected to tolerate, though not essentially accept, each other's security concerns' and that 'the lack of complete satisfaction with the status quo' may be the preferable modality for mutually confronting Western Westphalianism rather than highlighting their own points of future contention'). See also Negyre Liu and Kamrul Hossain, 'China and The Development of International Law on Arctic Shipping', in *Arctic Law and Governance: The Role of China, Finland and the EU* 233, 251(Timo Koivurova et al, eds, 2017) (contending that China's wait and see approach to Art 234 may allow for an interpretation 'in favour of international rules and standards for shipping rather than more stringent unilateral legislation').

[66] Yang, n 19, at 158. For an example of bilateral ventures, see China's and Iceland's 2012 Framework Agreement on Arctic Cooperation, library.arcticportal.org/2447/1/China%20Iceland%20Agreement%202012.pdf.

[67] For a moderate, wait-and-see perspective on China and its relative inability to alter operations of the Arctic regime complex controlled by the Arctic Council, see generally Mariia Kobzeva and Andrey Todorov, 'Can China Change the Arctic Regime?' 59 *Polar Record* 1 (2023).

adaptation of the extant international legal frame, which was not in place during the previous ascendant periods accompanying the rise of Great Britain and the United States. Consequently, China's engagement with international law moved first through a period of little engagement (1949–1970s), followed by a period of reformation, opening up, and emphasis on consent and compliance in relation to lawmaking (late 1970s–1990s), to the present period. This present period witnesses China more actively shaping international law through norm entrepreneurship and strategic engagement with international institutions such as the Shanghai Cooperation Organization, the New Development Bank, and the Asian Infrastructure Investment Bank.[68] This orientation marks China both as a stabilising force within international law, and as a builder of a new brand of exceptionalism – an 'Eastphalia' as opposed to a 'Westphalia' – which shifts the geographic centre of international legal gravity geographically eastward and substantively toward a normative system that advances Chinese values and interests.

To suspicious observers mindful of China's poor ecological record, this strategy appears to be a stalking horse for coming competition over Arctic resources.[69] To others, this strategy already represents a Trojan Horse. It is a way for China to 'calibrate external perceptions'[70] in favour of its rhetorical support for multilateralism while surreptitiously fragmenting the closed 'rules-based' governance structure of Western powers. China is thought to fine-tune this discursive strategy through the deployment of cooperative narratives that 'operate beneath the threshold of overt strategic challenge' to cloak its aggressive ambition.[71] Isaac Kardon concluded that 'China is not so much changing the rules as it is reducing their importance.'[72] Alternatively, China subscribes to the rule by law, but not the rule of law.[73] As an example, China has invoked UNCLOS as supportive of the proposition that the Arctic Ocean is a global shipping commons, a view more generally cast by Rear Admiral Yin Zhou as a region 'belong[ing] to all the people around the world, as no nation has sovereignty over it'.[74] The logic seems to apply with regard to China's commercial and strategic interests, except when it does not,[75] as in the cases of China's spurious historic entitlement claims to the South China Sea or to the rapacious illegal, unreported and unregulated takings

[68] Congyan Cai, *The Rise of China and International Law: Taking Chinese Exceptionalism Seriously* (2019).

[69] Doshi et al, n 4.

[70] ibid.

[71] Elizabeth Buchanan, 'China's Hybrid Arctic Strategy', Concordiam (8 September 2021), perconcordiam.com/chinas-hybrid-arctic-strategy/.

[72] Isaac B Kardon, *China's Law of the Sea: The New Rules of Maritime Order* 257 (2023).

[73] See ibid at 59.

[74] Economy, *The Third Revolution*, n 20, at 227 (noting China's view of the Law of the Sea Convention and quoting Admiral Zhou).

[75] See Peter Alan Dutton, 'Oceans Under Pressure: China's Challenge to the Maritime Order', Council on Geostrategy (23 January 2024), www.geostrategy.org.uk/britains-world/oceans-under-pressure-chinas-challenge-to-the-maritime-order (criticising China's undermining of UNCLOS's foundational elements defining maritime boundaries, balancing coastal state rights with international freedoms, protecting the marine environment, and stabilising the dispute resolution process).

of its long-distance fishing fleet. China's alignment with international law draws heavily from interests related to coastal state authority. Where littoral proximity is more attenuated, as in the Arctic, a more global Third World-oriented perspective appears, but framed loosely enough to admit to future layered interpretations while never admitting of a reversal in position or orientation.

WOLF WARRIOR DIPLOMACY

Chinese discursive practice has shifted to confront these suspicious Western characterisations, in what has been termed wolf warrior diplomacy (战狼外交, *zhanlang waijiao*), a diplomatic fight to control language power and the international narration geopolitics.[76] This practice has been critiqued as a debasement of the Chinese diplomacy tradition established by China's first foreign minister, Zhou Enlai (1898–1976) to reflect more assertive expressions associated with Xi's regime,[77] and it has raised securitisation concerns that cloud an assessment of Chinese intentions.

Mathieu Boulègue has argued that 'China has demonstrated a willingness to change the norms and the governance facts in the Arctic. It wants a free-for-all global common', where, if unchecked, such a classification could 'coalesce' specific states around China's lead to 'push for different norms … that would fit the Chinese agenda'.[78] Elana Wilson Rowe noted that China's periodic framing of the Arctic as a global commons intends to create political space for it in an area 'already managed under international ocean law frameworks as well as national sovereignty'.[79] By weaponising the 'effort[] to craft the Arctic as a global "commons"',[80] the argument is that China attempts to divert attention from its goal of advancing an alternative governance mechanism modelled along Arctic-themed relationships with the China-Nordic Arctic Research Center (CNARC),[81] the BRICS (Brazil, Russia, India, China, and South Africa) group

[76] See Lai Fu, 'Growling Back at the West', China Media Project (8 August 2021), chinamediaproject.org/2021/08/08/growling-back-at-the-west (referring to wolf warrior diplomacy as a 'diplomatic strategy of assertiveness' and a 'fight for international discourse power').

[77] See generally Peter Martin, *China's Civilian Army: The Making of Wolf Warrior Diplomacy* (2021) (borrowing the term from a popular Chinese Rambo-styled action movie).

[78] Statement by Wilson Center Polar Institute global fellow, Mathieu Boulègue, International Relations and Defence Committee, House of Lords, 3 May 2023, committees.parliament.uk/oralevidence/13111/html.

[79] Statement by Norwegian Institute of International Affairs Research Professor Elana Wilson Rowe, International Relations and Defence Committee, House of Lords, 24 May 2023, committees.parliament.uk/oralevidence/13230/html.

[80] Buchanan, n 71.

[81] CNARC is a consortium of research institutes from China and Nordic countries. Chinese members include the Polar Research Institute of China, the Shanghai Institutes for International Studies, Ocean University of China, Shanghai Jiao Tong University, Tongji University, Salian Maritime University, Center for Polar Issues Studies, and Shanghai Ocean University. Nordic members include the Icelandic Centre for Research (RANNIS), the University of Lapland Arctic

of nations, and the Shanghai Cooperation Organization.[82] Its purpose would be to secure its geopolitical status as co-equal Great Power to the United States and assert for itself an Arctic if not worldwide[83] self-judging jurisdictional claim over matters it deems of national interest.

Mia Bennett framed China's regional narrative regarding the Arctic as in fact two spatially inconsistent 'but ultimately mutually reinforcing narratives', a closed narrative based on territorial stakeholders and China's proximity to Arctic natural resources, and a global commons rendering 'whose environmental dynamics affect the entire planet'.[84] The pursuit of both narratives intends to gain legitimacy as an intra-regional actor among circumpolar powers and extra-regional champion of a globalist perspective in order to 'diminish[] the prerogative that the Arctic's intraregional states draw from having territory of the Arctic Circle'.[85]

China's Arctic ambitions are more established than its intentions. China will present itself as an Arctic actor, inasmuch as its Japanese and South Korean competitors have already done so. Its presence will be felt more intentionally in the Arctic Council, in shipping and global commerce given its economic throw weight, in the formation of legal characterisations of the global commons, and in the evolving geopolitical policy frameworks involving Greenland, Iceland, and emerging transpolar transit possibilities. Wolf warrior diplomacy to distract from its poor ecological and human rights records, particularly given its objectional treatment of Indigenous and minority populations it is own country, will

Centre, Fridtjof Nansen Institute, Nord University, Nordic Institute of Asian Studies, Norwegian Polar Institute, Swedish Polar Research Secretariat, UiT (The Arctic University of Norway), Umeå University, and the University of Akureyri. See CNARC, www.cnarc.info/members#nordic.

[82] See eg, Pavel Devyatkin, Can Cooperation Be Restored? 2022 *Arctic YB* 1 (2022), arcticyearbook.com/images/yearbook/2022/Briefing-Notes/2BN_AY2022_Devyatkin.pdf (noting increasing cooperation between the Shanghai Cooperation Organization and Russia as part of a global trend especially noticeable since Russia's invasion of Ukraine); 'Russia to Engage BRICS, SCO Partners in Arctic Projects – Foreign Ministry', Tass (14 May 2023), tass.com/russia/1617145 (noting 'a number of Arctic-themed contracts with BRICS and SCO countries' under active development): 'Arctic Continues to Attract Interest of BRICS and SCO Countries as a Space for Cooperation', *China Daily* (24 March 2023) global.chinadaily.com.cn/a/202303/24/WS641d71f7a31057c47ebb66d4.html; Atle Staalesen, 'Chinese Bank Invests in Russia's Northern Sea Route', Eye on the Arctic (12 June 2018), www.rcinet.ca/eye-on-the-arctic/tag/shanghai-cooperation-organisation/ (noting Chinese-led Shanghai Cooperation Organization Arctic contracts with Russia).

[83] See generally Xiaoli Guo, 'Explaining China's Central Asia Pivot', Lowy Institute Interpreter (26 May 2023), www.lowyinstitute.org/the-interpreter/explaining-china-s-central-asia-pivot (noting apprehensions relating to China's increasing economic partnerships with Central Asian nations due to Russia's weakened influence since the war in Ukraine); Lucy Stevenson-Yang and Henry Tugendhat, 'China's Engagement in Latin America: Views from the Region', United States Institute of Peace (8 August 2022), www.usip.org/publications/2022/08/chinas-engagement-latin-america-views-region (reviewing informed opinions on China's increasingly complex relationships with Latin American countries); Deborah Bräutigam, *The Dragon's Gift: The Real Story of China in Africa* (2008) (presenting a nuanced interpretation of China's rising economic engagement with African countries and African elites).

[84] Mia M Bennett, 'How China Sees the Arctic: Reading Between Extraregional and Intraregional Narratives', 20 *Geopolitics* 645, 646 (2015).

[85] ibid at 662.

apply in the Arctic, but China will first seek to diplomatically minimise its use through its commonplace practices of avoidance, word-slicing, and backsliding.

China's major geopolitical challenge in the Arctic will be with Russia. Russia maintains its great power status there and serves as China's gatekeeper. Managing this relationship requires sensitivity to Russia's increasingly uncomfortable status as China's vassal. Assertions of Arctic dominance by Russia due to its dwindling great power presence elsewhere should be expected. Reliance on China's capital and assistance along its Northern tier and its support of aggression against Ukraine benefit and moderate relations with both countries in the near term. Certainly, China's rhetoric and military build-up to invade Taiwan and its expanding presence in the Indo-Pacific region create headwinds for Western defence strategists. They drain and divert Western attention from Russia's gambit in Ukraine and act as indirect assets that subsidise Russia's war. However, the implications of China's Belt and Road Initiative and its Polar Silk Road tributary, potentially discordant foreign policies issues relating to Russia's taking of Qing dynasty territory in Far East Asia, and China's strengthening relationship with Central Asian post-Soviet, feed Russian anxiety and sense of national identity. They remain as fissures at the base of Sino-Russian relations that will hamper Chinese Arctic interests and future relations between the two countries.

Chapter Ten

The Arctic Omnipresence

THIS BOOK ATTEMPTS to reacquaint geopolitics explicitly with international relations and international law and to think specifically about the Arctic in these reconnected ways. A broader dialogue about the Arctic is needed in light of Russia's 2022 invasion of Ukraine, and indeed, in light of the second coming of the Trump Administration in 2025. Since that invasion, policy makers have increasingly compartmentalised the region in military terms and through events remote and proximate to the invasion. Even before Trump's second inauguration, his brooding rhetoric on the necessity of owning Greenland, more properly conceived as a wedge initiative to separate Indigenous economic engagement from Danish dominance and control, nevertheless contributed to the resurrection of traditionally narrow themes of geopolitics as a form of power politics separated from values.

Stoked by media hype, analysts revisit national security perceptions arising from the history of the national security state, the idea of *raison d'état*, and the Cold War. This understanding of security, however, tends to react to events *du jour*, whether they involve sliced underwater cables, Russian intelligence operatives posing as Brazilian Arctic researchers, high-altitude balloons floating across Arctic North America, Chinese bids to secure Arctic port access, or other events that present a tincture of pretext cross-referenced as hybrid warfare.

This episodic hopscotching betrays a regard for the spatial and historical context of the Arctic and sometimes subjects strategic policy planning to whimsical interpretation. For example, merely hours after Trump expressed the 'absolute necessity' of owning Greenland, Denmark announced a 'huge boost' in the island's defence spending, including fighter aircraft upgrades to three civilian airports, the purchase of two new inspection ships, two long-range drones, and two dog sled teams to cover a geographic area more than three times the size of Texas.[1] Amid the growing furore following Trump's extended demand to control Greenland, the whimsy directed toward Denmark's surveillance capability of its

[1] Robert Greenal and Paul Kirby, 'Denmark Boosts Greenland Defence after Trump Repeats Desire for US Control', BBC (24 December 2024), www.bbc.com/news/articles/ckgzl19n9eko (noting as well that the timing of Denmark's announcement amounted to an 'irony of fate').

former colony shifted to a more serious announcement of a 14.6 billion Danish kroner ($2.05 billion) upgrade to its Arctic defence.[2]

The poet Delmore Schwartz reportedly said that even paranoids have real enemies. So, too, do Arctic security observers. One need not embrace the anxiety of perceived threats to accept the idea that Arctic geopolitics is much larger than its traditional geospace, however variously defined. A current round of Arctic introspection traces directly from Russia's invasion of Ukraine, to be sure. This very association needs to present the Arctic as a *Großraum* (or *Großräume*) extending beyond the concentrated security studies framework to include dialogues of ideology, law, culture, climate, and history.

To expand the Arctic geopolitical frame of reference, this book returns to the emphasis provided by the spatial scale suggested by Carl Schmitt, but with a caveat necessarily important to repeat. Schmitt influentially expanded the vocabulary of international relations, connected it to the intersections of international law, history, geography, and spatial hegemony, and invigorated discussions regarding decision-making during exigencies and states of exception. However, he darkly deviated from an analytical mindset through projections of his abhorrent advocacy. He hit upon a proper consideration of the importance of spatial studies and geopolitics, but contributed to its easily discarded application among mainstream security paradigms of today. His legacy occludes spatial studies' pre-Schmittian history and contributes to its continuing undertheorised status. Mere mention of the term *Großraum* generates side-eyed slights tracing from Schmitt's omnipresent association with the term. *Großraum*'s visceral but well-earned connection to *Lebensraum* presents enough of a third rail to electrocute other adaptations of *Großraum*, again a testament to Schmitt's lingering dark legacy.

Perhaps this derision inadvertently supports mainstream policy approaches that orient toward topical problems at the expense of their placement within a greater historical, spatial or theorised context. Schmitt's advocacy approach injected race, anti-Semitism, a hatred of liberalism and modernity, nostalgic and authoritarian visions of conservatism, and a warped justification for territorial aggrandisement into the mix. His stew of derision generated a false equivalency reminiscent of the legal defence of *tu quoque* (you [did it] too) proffered at Nuremburg to excuse war criminality or mitigate punishment. If the United States could base its spatial security on the large-scale nineteenth century hemispheric application of the Monroe Doctrine, why should Nazi Germany not be able to do the same over twentieth-century Central Europe? (And why should China not be able to do the same over twenty-first century South-East Asia?). If the United States did it, so may they (*illi quoque*).

[2] Billy Stockwell, James Frater and Eve Brennan, 'Denmark Boosts Arctic Defense Spending by $2 Billion after Trump's Greenland Interest', CNN (27 January 2025), dition.cnn.com/2025/01/27/europe/denmark-greenland-trump-defense-latam-intl/index.html.

However, a more appropriate sense of equivalency applies in the history of the Arctic. A sense of Manifest Destiny scripted Western forays into the High North, first in search of pathways to Eastern emporia, with whaling and sealing activities in support, and then fortified by the application of a Western standard of civilisation, with its inbred *mission civilisatrice*.[3] Culturally formed perspectives on the High North, similar to Frederick Jackson Turner's seminal essay on *The Significance of the Frontier in American History* (1893),[4] also appeared with Muscovy's version of Manifest Destiny over Eurasia. It broods today over Russia's complicated domestication of Siberia and the hauntology of its suffering throughout World War II. It informs its Slavic Middle Kingdom thesis and pulls at Russian national identity as surely as the Ural Mountains divide West from East.

Russia's invasion of Ukraine presents another brooding question about Russia's Manifest Destiny in the Arctic. How best should one characterise it in this great and increasingly significant space? Will it divide into multipolar contests over *Großräume* given emerging global and regional interests? Will the management of its mineral and living resources conform to the precepts of the rule of law, rational use, Indigenous perspectives, and sustainable development, or to the opportunistic excesses of extractive capitalism or authoritarianism? Has Russia's invasion of Ukraine turned the Arctic from a sphere of confluence into a sphere of influence? An enlarged vision of the Arctic may not provide the answer, but it provides the necessary framework to approach answers.

An important but imperfect parallel can be drawn between the invasion of Ukraine and the Arctic. Russia's internalised attachment to the Arctic is no less pronounced than its historical and cultural attachment to Ukraine, which Putin hyperbolically described in 2021 as encompassing 'one people'.[5] If the

[3] The etymology of the anachronistic term Eskimo partially evokes stereotyped association of the peoples now more commonly referred to as Yup'ik, Inupiat, Natives, and more. Poignant other examples include the live human exhibitions of Esquimaux villagers showcased at the World's Columbian Exposition's Midway exhibit (the Chicago World's Fair) in 1893 (see Chicago History Museum, images.chicagohistory.org/asset/4658), and at the 1897 American Museum of Natural History basement summer exhibit of six Native Greenlanders, who were dressed in full Arctic furs. The New York exhibit, facilitated by Arctic explorer Robert Peary and anthropologist Franz Boas, resulted in deaths due to sickness, which also occurred at the former exhibit and at other such exhibits. Even the Inughuit death rituals became an object of fascination for the museum scientists and 'prying western eyes'. Shari M Huhndorf, 'Nanook and His Contemporaries: Imagining Eskimos in American Culture, 1897–1922', 27 *Crit Inq* 122–123 (2000). One of their skeletons, of Qisuk, became a museum display item after a mock burial had been arranged to appease but deceive the family. Their remains were repatriated for proper burial to Greenland in1993. See Kenn Harper, *Give me my Father's Body: The Life of Minik, the New York Eskimo* 86–90 (2000). See also Kenn Harper, *Minik: The New York Eskimo: An Arctic Explorer, a Museum and the Betrayal of the Inuit People* (2017) (revising and updating the earlier work).

[4] Jackson presented his thesis at the meeting of the American Historical Association on 12 July 1893, held during the World Columbian Exposition (the Chicago World's Fair). See also n 1.

[5] Vladimir Putin, On the Historical Unity of Russians and Ukrainians, President of Russia (12 July 2021), en.kremlin.ru/events/president/news/66181 (stating additionally, 'Russians and Ukrainians were one people – a single whole. These words were not driven by some short-term considerations or prompted by the current political context. It is what I have said on numerous occasions and what I firmly believe').

Arctic does not present itself as a unitary whole, or even as a far-fetched Russian Mecca, then, like Russia's assertions of Western Ukraine and Crimea, it cannot be completely separated from Russia, either. And what of the still substantial areas of the Arctic beyond the limits of national jurisdiction? What part of the Arctic global commons will remain global?

These kinds of questions arise frequently during periods of turmoil, when geopolitical rather than international legal perspectives tend to predominate the consideration of solutions. Schmitt's Realpolitik perspective reinforces this ordering given his famous concept of the state, which presupposes the concept of the political and his influential decisionist reduction of the true sovereign to the person who decides when the state of exception exists and what actions to take when the exception arises. His perspective resembles a long line of criticisms about the subordinate role of international law and feeds rather incongruously postcolonial perspectives, which associate international legal frameworks with hegemony birthed first by the discovery doctrine, then imperialism, then colonialism, and now corporatism.

Periods of turmoil also tend to expose international law's deficiencies and inabilities to maintain the precepts it purports to uphold. 'What went wrong' thinking takes hold and reexaminations arise. These reflections spawn reverse engineering projects akin to those employed by hospitals when they trace infection outbreaks on hospital wards.[6] Here, Schmitt's influence remains strong and conventional.[7]

Sceptics of international law have long identified the source of international law's infection. They say it is not a truly mature legal system because it does not have a sovereign capable of enforcing its edicts.[8] It is a system mired in infancy. It cannot prevent aggression and it lacks antibiotics and effective autoimmune (internal) mechanisms to deal with attacks from powerful intruders, except perhaps through recourse to the original home remedy, self-help.

Russia's attack against international law's rule-oriented world prompts yet another set of re-examinations, nowhere more evident than in the Arctic. Russia's invasion of Ukraine has had major repercussions there, notwithstanding Kiev's 1665 km distance from the Polar Circle. This observation again implicates the Arctic as a *Großraum*. It also reflects on the raft of criticism attaching to the Arctic platitude of exceptionalism, which critics now claim either never existed or existed only as a chimera in the wishful mind of liberal internationalists.

[6] Utrecht international law professor AHA Soons frequently posed the question to his students, not conceding that much in the main was ever wrong with it. For assessments, see Cedric Ryngaert, Erik J Molenaar and Sarah MH Nouwen eds, *What's Wrong with International Law?* Liber Amicorum AHA Soons (2015).

[7] See generally Martti Koskenniemi, 'Carl Schmitt and International Law', in *Oxford Handbook of Carl Schmitt* 592 (Jens Meierheinrich and Oliver Simons eds, 2015).

[8] See John Austin, *The Province of Jurisprudence Determined* 5 (famously contending: 'Every law or rule (taken with the largest signification which can be given to the term properly) is a command. Or, rather, laws or rules, properly so called, are a species of commands').

As recently as 2020, the geopolitical landscape of the Arctic seemed significantly different. It was described as a 'significant departure from the great power politics of the Cold War era', a place where superpower rivalry 'had been replaced by multiple political interests of the eight Arctic States'.[9] A slightly less sanguine assessment, proffered shortly before Russia's invasion, offered up a new paradigm of the Arctic as a zone of peaceful competition.[10] These are optimistic and familiar refrains,[11] as familiar as the official 2022 Western pronouncements that the Kremlin's war of choice against Ukraine has made the alliance 'more unified and resolute' than ever.[12] But conditions changed quickly.[13]

The shibboleths of cooperation and low tension or friendly competition misjudged the Arctic's connection to less pristine politics in lower latitudes. Certainly, the Arctic Council has now been rebalanced, if rebalance is the right word. It now splits the advanced democracies of the Arctic 7 from the largely shunned illiberal behemoth of Russia, with China now roaming the northern latitudes as an Asiatic Flying Dutchman in search of a home port.

Trump's virulent populism and his hostility toward internationalism indicate that balancing democracy's Arctic Western vision against the authoritarian world may not be placed on a secure fulcrum, or perhaps not as bolted to the ground as the idea of NATO solidarity suggests and the United States' pledge of republican allegiance propounds. Russia's invasion of Ukraine has re-established NATO's policy of enhanced containment, but stirred European suspicions about the United States' Atlantic alliance resolve. Again, conditions can change quickly. If it cannot be concluded with assurance that Russia's political landscape will change for the better once Putin's era ends, neither can it be concluded that the West's resolve will remain steadfast in view of pronounced political cleavages emerging in the United States and as problematically exposed by Trump's nationalist and unilateralist legacy, still in the making.

Arctic geopolitical discussions should rest on a firmer foundation, one mindful of, but not overly driven by, the vicissitudes of contemporary politics or event-driven machinations. This book's reimagination employs an already imagined

[9] Nong Hong, *China's Role in the Arctic: Observing and Being Observed* 1 (2020).

[10] Oran R Young, Jian Yang and Andrei Zagorski, 'The "New" Arctic as a Zone of Peaceful Competition', 11 *Polar Perspectives* (2022), www.wilsoncenter.org/sites/default/files/media/uploads/documents/Polar%20Perspectives%20No.%2011_NewArcticPeacefulCompetition.pdf.

[11] George HW Bush, Address Before a Joint Session of the Congress on the Persian Gulf Crisis and the Federal Budget Deficit, 11 September 1990, bush41library.tamu.edu/archives/public-papers/2217.

[12] Lisa Ferdinando, 'NATO Unified, Resolute in Face of Russia's "Illegal" Ukraine Invasion, Austin Says', U.S. Department of Defense (13 October 2022), www.defense.gov/News/News-Stories/Article/Article/3188194/nato-unified-resolute-in-face-of-russias-illegal-ukraine-invasion-austin-says (quoting the United States Secretary of Defense Lloyd J Austin III).

[13] See President-elect Trump on Greenland and Panama Canal, C-SPAN (7 Jan. 2025), www.c-span.org/video/?c5148065/president-elect-trump-greenland-panama-canal (noting Trump's refusal to rule out military or economic coercion against NATO ally Denmark to obtain ownership of Greenland); and Joshua Posaner et al, 'Europe Splits on Trump's Call to Dramatically Boost Defense Spending, Politico (8 January 2025) (discussing NATO member resistance to Trump's argument that members must increase defence spending to 5% of GDP).

concept, *Großraum*, but not in terms of its coopted political formulation by Schmittian enthusiasts, or by twenty-first-century internationalists seeking to make the world safe for democracy. It broadens the discussion of *Großraum* and includes ideological and cultural extracts, which were present at the creation of the Monroe Doctrine, magnified by Teddy Roosevelt's imperialist Caribbean policy, and adulterated by the importation of geospatial analyses by the likes of Schmitt.

Such adulterations require a recasting of the idea of *Großraum* but not its abandonment or banishment from international relations discourse. Importantly, Schmitt understood the characterisation of large spaces in terms of constitutive parts. His *Nomos of the Earth* – the *jus publicum europaeum* – nostalgically tried to assert a regional European *nomos* specifically in opposition to an Anglo-American universal *nomos*. Aside from the parochial competition, his abstract interest in regions, or *Großräume* hints at a more proper analytical framing of the Arctic of today, a more comprehensive understanding than security analysts envision.

And an important analytical framing of the Arctic as a sphere of confluence still exists. It is politically centred around the democratic ethos of the Arctic 7 and a tightened bond of NATO unity, notwithstanding rhetorical tensions and burden sharing strains raised by the Trump Administration. However, it is also framed around Russia's general rule orientation with regard to UNCLOS. Its pariah status in Europe nevertheless necessitates a more pragmatic approach in the vast Arctic, because its own self-interest requires a workable and stable Arctic environment in order to maintain and fully benefit from its substantial financial and security investments there. From Russia's perspective, China's emerging interest in the Arctic may eventually unsettle the Kremlin's security interests as much as a Western threat. For this reason, Russia maintains tight control over its Arctic Zone particularly in terms of licensing joint ventures and allowing foreign controlling interests over its energy resources. These domestic strictures tamp down China's energy diversification efforts in the Arctic as much as they shield Russia from concerns about Beijing's debt-trap diplomacy. Russia has prospected foreign capital markets in Saudi Arabia, India, and Asia to diversify development of its Arctic Zone resources. Such diversification ironically lessens Russia's insecurity about Chinese penetrations that may problematise Western interests as much as Russian interests.

These considerations involve a more spatial understanding of Arctic relations, not simply in terms of geography, but in terms of culture and ideology. Reimagining the framework of the Arctic in terms of spatiality has long been the object of international law, another aspect of Schmitt's geopolitical orientation. Indeed, regimes have long been the province of international law before international relations specialists turned attention to them.[14] And much of the Arctic *Großraum* reflects this the rule of law.

[14] Hugo Grotius conceptualised the law of the sea with the publication of *Mare Liberum* in 1609. International relations specialists invigorated discussions about regimes in the 1980s. See, eg, Robert Keohane, 'The Demand for International Regimes', 36 *Int'l Org* 325 (1982); John Ruggie, 'International Regimes, Transactions, and Change: Embedded Liberalism in the Postwar Economic Order', 36 *Int'l Org* 379 (1983); Stephen Krasner ed, *International Regimes* (1983).

Consider the great geographical and conceptual spaces brought under international law's umbrella. The OSPAR Convention (1998) provides the international framework for protecting the marine environment of the North-East Atlantic. It replaced or modernised the 1972 and the 1974 Paris Convention on Pollution of the North Sea and Adjacent Areas from Land-Based Sources.[15] It set up a committee and working groups to create six strategies to address a wide range of environmental challenges. The London Convention and MARPOL, established under the IMO, regulate Arctic marine environments pertaining to fishing, shipping, pollution, and resource extraction. UNCLOS and its implementing agreements regulate the high seas, the Area, the continental shelf, the extended continental shelf, the EEZ, contiguous zone, and territorial sea. Five regional fisheries management organisations (RFMOs) protect tuna,[16] seven RFMOs cover non-tuna arrangements,[17] four regional fisheries management arrangements (RFMAs) address the Central Arctic Ocean, pollock resources in the Central Bering Sea, Russian–Norwegian fisheries, and Southern Indian Ocean fisheries, and the United Nations Fish Stocks Agreement.[18] There are species-specific regulations for polar bears and fish, and regional seas agreements, multilateral cooperative ventures such as the Arctic Council and the Barents Euro Arctic Council, numerous bilateral cooperative agreements, established maritime zones and delimitation agreements, additional agreements on biodiversity, seals, whales, caribou, and birds and Memoranda of Understanding on the protection of Indigenous peoples.

International law touches numerous and vibrant spatial arrangements not blown off course by the post-Ukraine invasion securitisation framework that understandably occupies much Arctic discussion today. The Arctic *Großraum* remains a valid conceptual and analytical frame for deepening the understanding of the Arctic. Modern political geography, with sensitivity to human geography, history, and culture, has reclaimed it and high-north latitudes from the securitisation discourse that has tended to singularly define the nature of the threat as a competitive struggle among great and regional powers over an icy landscape that Dante described as more inhospitable than the infernal ring of fire.

[15] See Lilly Weidemann, *International Governance of the Arctic Marine Environment: With Particular Emphasis on High Seas Fisheries* 98 (2014).

[16] See generally the Commission for the Conservation of Southern Bluefin Tuna, the Inter-American Tropical Tuna Commission, the International Commission on the Conservation of Atlantic Tunas, the Indian Ocean Tuna Commission, and the Western and Central Pacific Fisheries Commission.

[17] See generally the Commission for the Conservation of Antarctic Marine Living Resources, General Fisheries Commission for the Mediterranean, Northwest Atlantic Fisheries Organization, North-East Atlantic Fisheries Commission, North Pacific Fisheries Commission, South East Atlantic Fisheries Organisation, and the South Pacific Regional Fisheries Management Organisation.

[18] See generally Erik J Molenaar, 'Participation in the Central Arctic Ocean Fisheries Agreement', in *Emerging Legal Orders in the Arctic* 132 (reviewing numerous agreements pertaining to the breadth of international fisheries regulations).

Bibliography

BOOKS

Agamben, Giorgio. *State of Exception*. Keven Attell translation. University of Chicago Press, 2005.

Agnew, John. *Hidden Geopolitics: Governance in a Globalized World*. Roman & Littlefield, 2023.

Agnew, John A and Luca Muscarà, *Making Political Geography*. 2nd edn. Rowman & Littefield, 2012.

Akerman, James R, ed. *The Imperial Map: Cartography and the Mastery of Empire*. University of Chicago Press, 2009.

Albro, Robert, George Marcus, Laura A McNamara and Monica Schoch-Spana. *Anthropologists in the Securityscape: Ethics, Practice, and Professional Identity*. Routledge, 2012.

Aleinikoff, T Alexander and Douglas Klusmeyer, eds. *Citizenship Today: Global Perspectives and Practices*. Carnegie Endowment for International Peace, 2001.

Allison, Graham. *Destined for War: Can American and China Escape Thucydides's Trap?* Houghton Mifflin Harcourt, 2017.

Anaya, S James. *Indigenous Peoples in International Law*. Oxford University Press, 1996.

Anghie, Antony. *Imperialism, Sovereignty and the Making of International Law*. Cambridge University Press, 2012.

Arendt, Hannah. *Origins of Totalitarianism*. Harcourt, Brace and World, 1966 [1951].

Aristotle. *Metaphysics*. WD Ross translation. Nuvision Publisher, 2009.

——. *Nichomachean Ethics*. FH Peters translation. 5th edn. Kegan Paul, Trench, Truebner & Co, 1893.

——. *Politics*. Translated and with an Introduction, Notes, and Glossary by Carnes Lord. 2nd edn. University of Chicago Press, 2013.

Armitage, David. *The Ideological Origins of the British Empire*. Cambridge University Press, 2000.

Austin, John. *The Province of Jurisprudence Determined*. Burt Franklin, 1861 [1832].

Baker, Gideon, ed. *Hospitality and World Politics*. Springer, 2013.

Baker, Peter and Susan Glasser. *The Divider: Trump in the White House, 2017–2021*. Penguin Random House, 2022.

Barns, Justin, Heather Exner-Pirot, Lassi Heininen and P Whitney Lackenbauer, eds. *China's Arctic Engagement: Following the Polar Silk Road to Greenland and Russia*. Arctic Yearbook, 2021.

Bassin, Mark and Gonzalo Pozo, eds. *The Politics of Eurasianism: Identity, Popular Culture and Russia's Foreign Policy*. Rowman & Littlefield International Ltd, 2017.

Beiser, Frederick C. *The German Historicist Tradition*. Oxford University Press, 2011.

Bellamy, Richard and Madeleine Kennedy-Macfoy, eds. *Citizenship*. Routledge, 2014.

Bendersky, Joseph J *Carl Schmitt: Theorist for the Reich*. Princeton University Press, 1983.

Beneyto, José María and Ignacio de la Rasilla, eds. *Francisco de Vitoria and the Shadow of Carl Schmitt in International Law: Crossroads in History and Political Theology*. Brill/Nijhoff, forthcoming.

Bickel, Lennard. *Mawson's Will: The Greatest Polar Survival Story Ever Written*. Steerforth, 2000.

Blackwill, Robert and Richard Fontaine. *Lost Decade, The US Pivot to Asia and the Rise of Chinese Power*. Oxford University Press, 2024.

Bobrick, Benson. East of the Sun: The Epic Conquest and Tragic History of Siberia. Poseidon Press/ Simon & Schuster, 1992.

Bolívar, Simón. *Carta de Jamaica. Contestación de un Americano Meridional a un Caballero de esta Isla*. Instituto Nacional de Estudios Históricos de las Revoluciones de México (2021) [1815].

Bond, Martyn. *Hitler's Cosmopolitan Bastard: Count Richard Coudenhove-Kalergi and His Vision of Europe*. McGill-Queen's University Press, 2021.

Boyd, Julian P, ed, Lyman H Butterfield and Mina R Bryan associated eds. *Papers of Thomas Jefferson: October 1780 to February 1781, Vol IV*. Princeton University Press, 1950.

Bräutigam, Deborah. *The Dragon's Gift: The Real Story of China in Africa*. Oxford University Press, 2008.

Brunhes, Jean and Camile Vallaux. *La géographie de l'historie: Géographie de la paix et de la guerre sur terre et sur mer*. F Alcon, 1921.

Buchanan, Elizabeth. *Red Arctic: Russian Strategy Under Putin*. Brookings, 2023.

Buchstein, Hubertus. *Enduring Enmity: The Story of Otto Kirchheimer and Carl Schmitt*. Translated by Sandra H Lustig. Verlag, Bielefeld, 2024.

Bunikowski, Dawid and Alan D Hemmings, eds. *Philosophies of Polar Law*. Routledge, 2021.

Butler, Chris and Edward Mussawir, eds. *Spaces of Justice, Peripheries, Passages, Appropriations*. Routledge, 2017.

Buzan, Barry and Ole Wæver. *Regions and Powers: The Structure of International Security*. Cambridge University Press, 2003.

Buzan, Barry, Ole Wæver and Jaap de Wilde. *Security: A New Framework for Analysis*. Lynne Rienner Publishers, 1998.

Buzan, Barry and Lene Hansen. *The Evolution of International Security Studies*. Cambridge University Press, 2009.

Byers, Michael. *International Law and the Arctic*. Cambridge University Press, 2013.

Cai, Congyan. *The Rise of China and International Law: Taking Chinese Exceptionalism Seriously*. Oxford University Press, 2019.

Cameron, Garth. *Umberto Nobile and the Arctic Search for the Airship Italia*. Fonthill Media, 2017.

Cherry-Garrard, Apsley. *The Worst Journey in the World*. Picador Travel Classics, 1994 [1922].

Christaller, Walter. *Central Places in Southern Germany*. Carlisle W Baskin translation. Prentice-Hall, 1966 [1933]).

Clark, Wesley, Jüri Luik, Egon Ramms and Richard Shirreff. *Closing Nato's Baltic Gap*. International Centre for Defense and Security, 2016.

Clover, Charles. *Black Wind, White Snow: The Rise of Russia's New Nationalism*. Yale University Press, 2016.

Cohen, Felix. *Handbook of Federal Indian Law. 2012 Edition*. LexisNexis, 2012.

Cohen, Saul Bernard. *Geopolitics of the World System*. Rowman & Littlefield, 2003.

Cornell, Drucilla, Michael Rosenfeld and David Gray Carlson, eds. *Deconstruction and the Possibility of Justice*. Routledge, 1992.

Cotty, Andrew, ed. *Subregional Cooperation in the New Europe: Building Security, Prosperity and Solidarity from the Barents to the Black Sea*. Palgrave Macmillan, 1999.

Crandall, Brita H and Russell C Crandall. '*Our Hemisphere'? The United States in Latin America, from 1776 to the Twenty-First Century*. Yale University Press, 2021.

Dalby, Simon. *Creating the Second Cold War: The Discourse of Politics*. Bloomsbury, 2016.

de la Rasilla del Moral, Ignacio. *In the Shadow of Vitoria: A History of International Law in Spain, 1770–1953*. Brill/Nijhoff, 2017.

De Lucia, Vito, Alex Oude Elferink and Lan Ngoc Nguyen, eds. *International Law and Marine Areas Beyond National Jurisdiction: Reflections on Justice, Space, Knowledge and Power*. Brill, 2022.

de Montaigne, Michael. *Essays Bk 1*. Charles Cotton translation. Ballantyne Press 1877 [1686].

de Poncins, Gontran. *Kabloona*. Reynal & Hitchcock, 1941.

Derrida, Jaques. *Specters of Marx: The State of the Debt, the Work of Mourning, and the New International*. Routledge, 1994.

——. *The Politics of Friendship*. George Collins translation. Verso Books, 2005 [1994].

Dodds, Klaus and David Atkinson, eds. *Geopolitical Traditions: A Century of Geopolitical Thought*. Routledge, 2000.

Dugin, Aleksandr. *Foundations of Geopolitics*. Lawless translation. Arktogea, 1997.
——. *The Fourth Political Theory*. Nina Kurpianova, Maria Tokmakova, Olga Schief, Vaan Maas, Valentin Cherednikov, Zhirayr Ananyan, Fedor Smirnov, Cyrill Lazareff, Ivan Fedorov, translation. Eurasian Movement, 2012.
Dunphy, Graeme and Andrew Gow, eds. *Encyclopedia of Early Modern History Online*. Brill, 2015.
Durov, IM. *The Dictionary of the Living Pomor Language in its Everyday and Ethnographic Use,* Slovar' zhivogo pomorskogo yazyka v ego bytovom i etnograficheskom primenenii. Karelian Research Center of the Russian Academy of Sciences, 2011.
Economy, Elizabeth C. *The Third Revolution: Xi Jinping and the New Chinese State*. Council on Foreign Relations, 2018.
Elden, Stuart. *The Birth of Territory*. University of Chicago Press, 2013.
Emmerson, Charles. *The Future History of the Arctic*. Hachette Book Group, 2010.
Erokhin, Vasili, Gao Tianming and Xiuhua Zhang, eds. *Handbook of Research on International Collaboration, Economic Development, and Sustainability in the Arctic*. IGI Global, 2018.
Etkind, Alexander. *Russia Against Modernity*. Wiley, 2023.
Fasolt, Constantin. *The Limits of History*. University of Chicago Press, 2004.
Finger, Matthias and Gunnar Rekvig, eds. *Global Arctic: An Introduction to the Multifaceted Dynamics of the Arctic*. Springer International Publishing, 2022.
Finger, Matthias and Lassi Heininen, eds. *The GlobalArctic Handbook*. Springer International Publishing, 2019.
Fleure, HJ *Human Geography in Western Europe: A Study in Appreciation*. Legare Street Press, 2022 [1918].
Forsby, Andreas Bøje, ed. *Nordic–China Cooperation: Challenges and Opportunities*. University of Chicago Press, 2019.
Fris, Karsten, Elana Wilson Rowe, Ulf Svederup, Mike S Fraga, Pavel K Baev, Troy J Bouffard, Marc Lanteigne, Marisol Maddox and Jan-Gunnar Winther, eds. *Navigating Breakup: Security Realities of Freezing Politics and Thawing Landscapes in the Arctic*. NUPI/Wilson Center, 2023.
Fukuyama, Francis. *The End of History and the Last Man*. Free Press, 2006.
Gaddis, John Lewis. *We Now Know: Rethinking Cold War History*. Clarendon Press, 1997.
Gamarra Chopo, Y, ed. *La idea de América en el pensamiento ius internacionalista del siglo XXI; Estudios a propósito de los bicentenarios de las independencies de las repúblicas latinoamericanas*. Institución Fernando el Católico, 2010.
Giaccaria, Paolo and Claudio Minca, eds. *Hitler's Geographies, The Spatialities of the Third Reich*. University of Chicago Press, 2016.
Gilpin, Robert. *War and Change in World Politics*. Cambridge University Press, 1981.
Graham, Jr, Thomas E. *Russia's Decline and Uncertain Recovery*. Carnegie Endowment for International Peace, 2002.
Grotius, Hugo. *Mare Liberum 1609–2009*. Robert Feenstra ed, with a general introduction by Jeroen Vervliet. Brill, 2009 [1609].
Gruchmann, Lothar. *Nationalsozialistische Großraumordnung. Die Konstruktion einer 'deutschen Monroe-Doktrin'*. Institut für Zeitgeschichte, 1962.
Gunnlaugsson, Helgi Steinar. *Explaining the Economic Inconsistencies of China-Iceland Relations: Examining the Success of the China-Iceland Free Trade Agreement and the Failure of Huang Nubo's Land Acquisition Deal*. Lambert Academic Publishing, 2017.
Hahn, Hans-Werner. *Wirschaftliche Integration im 19. Jahrundert: die hessichen Staaten und der Deutsche Zollverein*. Vandenhoeck & Ruprecht, 1982.
Halberstam, David. *The Best and the Brightest*. Random House, Inc, 1972.
Harper, Kenn. *Give Me My Father's Body; The Life of Minik, the New York Eskimo*. Steerforth Press, 2000.
——. *Minik: The New York Eskimo: An Arctic Explorer, a Museum, and the Betrayal of the Inuit People*. Steerforth Press, 2017.
Harreld, Donald J, ed. *A Companion to the Hanseatic League*. Brill, 2015.

Hartshorne, Richard. *The Nature of Geography: A Critical Survey of Current Thought in Light of the Past*. The Association Lancaster, 1939.

Harvey, David. *Spaces of Global Capitalism: A Theory of Uneven Geographical Development*, 2006.

Haslam, Jonathan. *The Spectre of War: International Communism and the Origin of World War II*. Princeton University Press, 2021.

Haushofer, Karl. *Geopolitik des Pazifischen Ozeans: Studien Über die Wechselbeziehungen zwischen Geographie und Geschichte*. Kurt Vowinckel Verlag, 1924.

Haushofer, Karl, Erich Obst, Hermann Lautensach and Otto Maul. *Bausteine zur Geopolitik*. Kurt Vowinckel Verlag, 1928.

Heller, Kevin John and Gerry Simpson, eds. *The Hidden Histories of War Crimes Trials*. Oxford University Press, 2013.

Henderson, WO. *The Zollverein*. 2nd edn. Routledge, 1959.

Henson, Matthew. *A Negro Explorer at the North Pole: The Autobiography of Matthew Henson*. Invisible Cities Press, 2001 [1912].

Herf, Jeffrey. *Reactionary Modernism: Technology, Culture, and Politics in Weimar and the Third Reich*. Cambridge University Press, 1984.

Herrero, Montserrat. *The Political Discourse of Carl Schmitt: A Mystic of Order*. Rowman & Littlefield, 2015.

Herrmann, Thora Martina and Thibault Martin, eds. *Indigenous Peoples' Governance of Land and Protected Territories in the Arctic*. Springer, 2016.

Holger, H Herwig, *The Demon of Geopolitics: How Karl Haushofer Educated Hitler and Hess*. Rowman & Littlefield, 2016.

Hessler, John W and Chet Van Duzer, eds. *Seeing the World Anew: The Radical Vision of Martin Waldseemüller's 1507 and 1516 World Maps*. Levenger Press in association with the Library of Congress, 2012.

Hill, Fiona and Clifford G Gaddy. *The Siberian Curse: How Communist Planners Left Russia Out in the Cold*. Brookings Institution Press, 2003.

Hinrichsen, Simon. *When Nations Can't Default: A History of War Reparations and Sovereign Debt*. Cambridge University Press, 2023.

Hønneland, Geir. *Russia and the Arctic: Environment, Identity and Foreign Policy*. 2nd edn. Bloomsbury Publishing, 2020.

Higginbotham John and Jennifer Spence. *The North American Arctic: Energizing Regional Collaboration and Governance*. Center for International Governance Innovation, 2018.

Hitler, Adolf. *Mein Kampf*. Translated by Ralph Manheim. Introduction by Abraham Foxman. Houghton Mifflin 1999 [1927].

Hogan, Michael J. *A Cross of Iron: Harry S. Truman and the Origins of the National Security State*, 1945–1954. Cambridge University Press, 1998.

Hohendahl, Peter Uwe. *Perilous Futures: On Carl Schmitt's Late Writings*. Cornell University Press, 2018.

Holtsmark, Sven G. *The Limits to Soviet Influence: Soviet Strategic Interests in Norway and Denmark 1944–1947*. Institutt for forsvarsstudier, 1994.

Hong, Nong, *China's Role in the Arctic: Observing and Being Observed*. Routledge, 2020.

Hooker, William. *Carl Schmitt's International Thought: Order and Orientation*. Cambridge University Press, 2009.

Huntford, Roland. *The Last Place on Earth: Scott and Amundsen's Race to the South Pole*. Introduction by Paul Theroux, revised and updated. Random House, 1999.

Huntington, Samuel P. *The Clash of Civilizations and the Remaking of World Order*. Simon & Schuster, 1996.

Indian Affairs, Laws and Treaties, Vol II, 439–449. Compiled and edited by Charles J Kappler. Government Printing Office, Washington, DC, 1904.

Jacobsen, Marc, Ole Wæver and Ulrik Pram Gad, eds. *Greenland in Arctic Security: (De)securitization Dynamics under Climactic Thaw and Geopolitical Freeze*. University of Michigan Press, 2024.

Janz, Bruce B, ed. *Place Space and Hermeneutics*. Springer, 2017.
Jensen, Bent. *Den Lange Befrielse: Bornholm Besat og Befriet 1945–1946*. Odense University Slavic Studies Series, 2020.
Joerges, Christian and Navraj Singh Ghaleigh, eds. *Darker Legacies of Law in Europe: The Shadow of National Socialism and Fascism over Europe and its Legal Traditions*. With a Prologue by Michael Stolleis and an Epilogue by JHH Weiler. Hart Publishing, 2003.
Jørgensen, Anne-Kristin and Geir Hønneland. *Integration vs. Autonomy: Civil-Military Relations on the Kola Peninsula*. Routledge Revivals, 2014.
Josephson, Paul R. *The Conquest of the Russian Arctic*. Harvard University Press, 2014.
Kant, Immanuel. *Perpetual Peace: A Philosophical Essay*. Translation and introduction by M Campbell Smith. George Allen & Unwin Ltd, 1903 [1795].
Kaplan, Robert D. *The Coming Anarchy: Shattering the Dreams of the Post Cold War*. Random House, 2001.
Käpylä, Juha and Harri Mikkola. *On Arctic Exceptionalism: Critical Reflections in the Light of the Arctic Sunrise Case and the Crisis in Ukraine*. Finnish Institute of International Affairs, 2015.
Karlsson, Gunnar. *The History of Iceland*. University of Minnesota Press, 2000.
Katzenstein, Peter J, ed. *Civilizations in World Politics: Plural and Pluralist Perspectives*. Routledge, 2010.
Kjellén, Rudolf. *Der Staat als Lebensform*. S Hirzel, 1917.
Koenen, Andreas. *Der Fall Carl Schmitt: Sein Aufstieg zum 'Kronjuristen des Dritten Reiches'*. Wissenschaft Buchgesellschaft, 1995.
Koivurova, Timo, Tianbao Qin, Sébastien Duyck and Tapio Nykänen, eds. *Arctic Law and Governance: The Role of China, Finland and the EU*. Bloomsbury, 2017.
Kouri, EI and Jens E Olesen, eds. *The Cambridge History of Scandinavia, Vol II, 1520–1870*. Cambridge University Press, 2016.
Krakauer, Jon. *Into the Wild*. Anchor Books, 1996.
Krasner, Stephen, ed. *International Regimes*. Cornell University Press, 1983.
Lansing, Alfred. *Endurance: Shackleton's Incredible Voyage*. McGraw-Hill Book Company, 1959.
Lantzeff, George V. *Siberia in the Seventeenth Century: A Study of the Colonial Administration*. University of California Press, 1943.
las Casas, Bartolomé de. *Brevísima relación de la destruición de las Indias*. (1542).
——. *Historia de las Indias*. [posthumously published, 1875].
Legg, Stephen, ed. *Spatiality, Sovereignty and Carl Schmitt: Geographies of the* Nomos. Translated by Mathew Hanna. Routledge 2011.
Lehti, Marko, Henna-Riikka Pennanen and Jukka Jouhki, eds. *Contestations of Liberal Order: The West in Crisis?* Palgrave Macmillan, 2020.
Lewis, David G. *Russia's New Authoritarianism: Putin and the Politics of Order*. Edinburgh University Press, 2020.
Lilla, Mark. *The Reckless Mind: Intellectuals in Politics*. New York Review of Books, 2001.
Lipschutz, Ronnie D, ed. *On Security*. Columbia University Press, 1995.
Liska, George. *Imperial America: The International Politics of Primacy*. The Johns Hopkins Press, 1967.
Liu, Nengye, Elizabeth A Kirk and Tore Henriksen. *The European Union and the Arctic*. Brill, 2017.
Lo, Bobo. *Axis of Convenience: Moscow, Beijing, and the New Geopolitics*. Brookings Institution Press, 2008.
Locke, John. *An Essay Concerning Human Understanding in Four Books*. Project Gutenberg EBook 2010 [1690].
——. *Second Treatise of Government*. Project Gutenberg EBook 2012 [1690].
Lucretius. *De Rerum Natura. The Latin Text of Lucretius*. William Ellery Leonard and Stanley Barney Smith, eds. University of Wisconsin Press, 2008 [1921].
Mackinder, HJ. *Britain and the British Seas*. D Appleton & Company, 1902.

Martin, Peter. *China's Civilian Army: The Making of Wolf Warrior Diplomacy*. Oxford University Press, 2021.

McCannon, John. *A History of the Arctic: Nature, Exploration and Exploitation*. University of Chicago Press, 2012.

——. *Red Arctic: Polar Exploration and the Myth of the North in the Soviet Union, 1932–1939*. Oxford University Press, 1988.

Mahan, Alfred Thayer. *The Influence of Sea Power Upon History, 1660–1783*. Dover Publications, 1987 [1890].

Marchal, Kai and Carl KY Shaw, eds. *Carl Schmitt and Leo Strauss in the Chinese-Speaking World: Reorienting the Political*. Rowman & Littlefield, 2017.

Marrus, Michael R. *The Unwanted: European Refugees in the Twentieth Century*. Oxford University Press, 1985.

Mearsheimer, John J. *The Tragedy of Great Power Politics*. WW Norton, 2001.

Mehring, Reinhard. *Carl Schmitt: A Biography*. Wiley, 2014.

Meierhenrich, Jens and Oliver Simons, eds. *The Oxford Handbook of Carl Schmitt*. Oxford University Press, 2015.

Mikkelsen, Ejnar. *Two Against the Ice*. Rupert Hart-Davis, 1957.

Milun, Kathryn. *The Political Uncommons: The Cross-Cultural Logic of the Global Commons*. Routledge, 2011.

Minca, Claudio and Rory Rowan, *On Schmitt and Space*. Routledge, 2016.

Mineral Resources in the Arctic: An Introduction. Geological Survey of Norway, 2016.

Misiunas, Romuald J and Rein Taagepera. *The Baltic States: Years of Dependence: 1940–1990*. University of California Press, 1993.

Modelski, George. *Long Cycles in World Politics*. Palgrave Macmillan, 1987.

Mouffe, Chantal, ed. *The Challenge of Carl Schmitt*. Verso, 1999.

Müller, Jan-Werner. *A Dangerous Mind: Carl Schmitt in Post-War European Thought*. Yale University Press, 2003.

Murphy, Alexander B. *National Claims to Territory in the Modern State System*. Geopolitics Publisher, 2002.

Nail, Thomas. *Theory of the Earth*. Stanford University Press, 2021.

Nansen, Fridtjof. *Farthest North: Being a Record of a Voyage of Exploration of the Ship 'Fram' 1893–1896 and of a Fifteen Months' Sleigh Journey With an Appendix in Two Volumes*. Macmillan and Co/Copp Clark Co, 1897.

Nelson, Drew S, ed. *NSC-68: Forging the Strategy of Containment with Analyses by Paul H Nitze*. National Defense University, 1994.

Newton, Isaac. *Principia*. Andrew Motte translation. Daniel Adee Publisher, 1846.

Nielsen, Jens Petter and Edwin Okhuizen, eds. *From Northeast Passage to Northern Sea Route: A History of the Waterway North of Eurasia*. Brill, 2022.

Nissen, Henrik S, ed. *Scandinavia During the Second World War*. Henrik S Nissen, Thomas Munch-Petersen translation. University of Minnesota, 1983.

Nordquist, Myron H, ed. *IV Center for Oceans Policy, University of Virginia, United Nations Convention on the Law of the Sea 1982: A Commentary*. Martinus Nijhoff Publishers, 1982.

Nunan, Timothy, ed. *Carl Schmitt, Writings on War*. Polity Press, 2011.

Núñez, Jorge E. *Sovereignty Conflicts and International Law and Politics: A Distributive Justice Issue*. Routledge, 2017.

Ó Tuathail, Gearóid and Simon Dalby, eds. *Rethinking Geopolitics*. Routledge, 1998.

Odysseos, Louiza and Fabio Petito, *The International Political Thought of Carl Schmitt: Terror, Liberal War and the Crisis of Global Order*. Routledge, 2007.

Onuf, Nicholas Greenwood. *The Republican Legacy in International Thought*. Cambridge University Press, 1998.

Onuf, Peter, ed. *Jeffersonian Legacies*. University of Virginia Press, 1993.

Onuf, Peter and Nicholas Onuf, *Federal Union, Modern World: The Law of Nations in an Age of Revolutions 1776–1814*. Rowman & Littlefield Publishers, 1994.
Orford, Anne. *International Law and the Politics of History*. Cambridge University Press, 2021.
Organski, AFK and Jacek Kugler, *The War Ledger*. University of Chicago Press, 1981.
Østhagen, Andreas, ed. *Norway's Arctic Policy: Geopolitics, Security and Identity in the High North*. Edgar Elgar Publishing, 2023.
Pagden, Anthony. *The Fall of Natural Man: The American Indian and the Origins of Comparative Ethnology*. Cambridge University Press, 1982.
Pardo, Arvid. *The Common Heritage of Mankind: Selected Papers on Oceans and World Order 1967–1974*. Malta University Press, 1975.
Parker, Kunal M. *Making Foreigners: Immigration and Citizenship Law in America, 1600–2000*. Cambridge University Press, 2015.
Parland, Thomas. *The Extreme Nationalist Threat in Russia: The Growing Influence of Western Rightist Ideas*. Routledge, 2005.
Patrikeeff, Felix and Harold Shukman. *Railways and the Russo-Japanese War: Transporting War*. Routledge, 2007.
Pearcy, George Etzel. *A 38 States U.S.A*. Plycon Press, 1973.
Peirce, Benjamin Mills. *A Report on the Resources of Iceland and Greenland*. US State Department, Government Printing Office, 1868.
Petrow, Richard. *The Bitter Years: The Invasion and Occupation of Denmark and Norway, April 1940–May 1945*. William Morrow, 1974.
Plessner, Helmuth. *Levels of Organic Life and the Human: An Introduction to Philosophical Anthropology*. Translated by Millay Hyatt. Introduction by JM Bernstein. Fordham University Press, 2019 [1928].
Powell, Richard C and Klaus Dodds, eds. *Polar Geopolitics? Knowledges, Resources and Legal Regimes*. Edward Elgar Publishing, 2014.
Pye, Michael. *The Edge of the World: How the North Sea Made Us What We Are*. Penguin Books, 2014.
Ratzel, Friedrich. *Anthropo-Geographie: Oder Grundzüge der Anwendung der Erdkunde Auf die Geschichte*. Verlag von J Engelhorn, 1882.
——. *Der Lebensraum: Eine Biogeographishe Studie*. H Laupp, 1901.
——. *Politische Geographie*. R Oldenbourg, 1897.
Rekvig, Gunnar and Matthias Finger, eds. *GlobalArctic: The New Dynamics of Arctic Governance*. Palgrave Macmillan, 2025.
Ritter, Carl. *Die Erdkunde im Verhältnis zur Natur und zure Geschichte des Menschen*. Reimer, 1847 [1817].
Rossi, Christopher R. *Broken Chain of Being: James Brown Scott and the Origins of Modern International Law*. Kluwer Law International, 1998.
——. *Equity and International Law*. Transnational Publishers, 1991.
——. *Remoteness Reconsidered: The Atacama Desert and International Law*. University of Michigan Press, 2021.
——. *Sovereignty and Territorial Temptation: The Grotian Tendency*. Cambridge University Press, 2017.
——. *Whiggish International Law: Elihu Root, the Monroe Doctrine, and International Law in the Americas*. Brill/Nijhoff, 2019.
Rothwell, Donald R. *The Polar Regions and the Development of International Law*. Cambridge University Press, 1996.
Routledge, Paul. *Space Invaders: Radical Geographies of Protest*. Pluto Press, 2017.
Russett, Bruce and Harvey Starr. *World Politics: The Menu for Choice*. 3rd edn. WH Freeman, 1989.
Ryngaert, Cedrik, Erik J Molenaar and Sarah MH Nouwen, eds. *What's Wrong with International Law? Liber Amicorum AHA Soons*. Brill, 2015.

Scarfi, Juan Pablo. *The Hidden History of International Law in the Americas: Empire and Legal Networks*. Oxford University Press, 2017.
Schechtman, Joseph B. *European Population Transfers: 1939–1945*. Oxford University Press, 1946.
Scheuerman, William. *Carl Schmitt: The End of Law*. Rowman & Littlefield, 1999.
Schlögel, Karl. *In Space We Read Time: On the History of Civilization and Geopolitics*. Gerrit Jackson translation. Bard Graduation Center, 2016.
——, ed. *Mastering Russian Spaces: Raum und Raumbewältigung als Probleme der russischen Geschichte*. Oldenbourg Verlag, 2011.
Schmitt, Carl. *Land and Sea: A World-Historical Meditation*. Translated by Samuel Garrett Zeitlin. Edited and with Introductions by Russell A Berman and Samuel Garrett Zeitlin. Telos Press, 2015.
——. *Legality and Legitimacy*. Jeffrey Seitzer translation, John P McCormick introduction. Duke University Press, 2004 [1932].
——. *Roman Catholicism and Political Form*. Translated and annotated by GL Ulmen, Bloomsbury Publishing, 1996.
—— *The Concept of the Political*. George Schwab translation and introduction. University of Chicago Press, 2007.
——. *The* Nomos *of the Earth in the International Law of the* Jus Publicum Europaeum. GL Ulman translator. Telos Press Publishing, 2003 [1974].
——. *Theory of the Partisan*. GL Ulman translation. Telos Press Publishing, 2007.
——. *Völkerrechtliche Großraumordnung mit Interventionsverbot für raumfremde Mächte. Ein Beitrag zum Reichsbegriff im Völkerrecht*. Duncker & Humblot, 1941.
Sedgwick, Mark, ed. *Key Thinkers of the Radical Right: Behind the New Threat to Liberal Democracy*. Oxford University Press, 2019.
Sellheim, Nikolas, Yulia V Zaika and Ilan Kelman, eds. *Arctic Triumph, Northern Innovation and Persistence*. Springer, 2019.
Serreze, Mark C. *Brave New Arctic: The Untold Story of the Melting North*. Princeton University Press, 2018.
Shibata, Akiho, Leilei Zou, Niklas Sellheim and Marzia Scopelliti, eds. *Emerging Legal Orders in the Arctic: The Role of Non-Arctic Actors*. Routledge, 2019.
Simms, Brendan. *Die Rückkehr des* Großraums? Duncker & Humblot, 2023.
Solzhenitsyn, Aleksandr I. *Lenin in Zürich*. HT Willotts translation. Farar, Straus, Giroux, 1976.
——. *The First Circle*. Northwestern University Press, 1997 [1968].
——. *The Gulag Archipelago 1918–1956: An Experiment in Literary Investigation*. Thomas P Whitney translation. Harperrerennial, 2007.
Spohr, Kristina and Daniel S Hamilton, eds. Jason C Moyer, assoc ed. *The Arctic and World Order*. Brookings Institution Press, 2020.
Spykman, Nicholas John. *The Geography of the Peace*. Helen R Nicholl, ed., Harcourt, Brace, 1944.
Stefansson, Vilhjalmur. *The Friendly Arctic: The Story of Five Years in Polar Regions*. 1921.
Steinberg, John W, Bruce Menning, David Schimmelpenninck van der Oye, David Wolff and Shinji Yokote, eds. *The Russo-Japanese War in Global Perspective: World War Zero*. Brill, 2005.
Steinveg, Beate. *Arctic Governance Through Conferencing: Actors, Agendas and Arenas*. Springer, 2023.
Stuart, Douglas T. *Creating the National Security State: A History of the Law That Transformed America*. Princeton University Press, 2008.
The Bible. (New King James Version).
Thrift, Nigel and Rob Kitchin, eds. *International Encyclopedia of Human Geography*. Elsevier Ltd, 2009.
Thucydides. *The War of the Peloponnesians and the Athenians*. Jeremy Mynott ed. Cambridge University Press, 2013.
Toman, Jindřich. *The Magic of a Common Language, Jakobsen, Mathesius, Trubetzkoy, and the Prague Linguistic Circle*. MIT Press, 2003.

Trubetzkoy, Nikolai Sergeyevich. *Europe and Mankind.* Alexandr (Sasha) Trubetskoy translation. 2023 [1920].
van Baak, Joost. *The House in Russian Literature: A Mythopoetic Exploration.* Brill Academic Publisher, 2009.
Van Tol, Jan, Christopher Bassler, Katherine Kjellström Elgin and Tyler Hacker, eds. *Deterrence and Defense in the Baltic Region: New Realities.* Center for Strategic and Budgetary Assessments, 2022.
Voigt, Rudiger, ed. *Großraum-Denken: Carl Schmitts Kategorie der Großaumordnung.* Franz Steiner Verlag, 2008.
Vitoria, Francisci, *De Indis et de Iure Belli Relectiones.* Edited by Ernest Nys. Carnegie Institution of Washington, 1917 [1557].
Vylegzhanin, AN and VK ZilaNovember *Spitsbergen: Legal Regime of Adjacent Maritime Areas.* WE Butler editor and translator. Eleven International Publishing, 2007.
Walker, RBJ. *Inside/Outside: International Relations as Political Theory.* Cambridge University Press, 1992.
Waltz, Kenneth. *Man, the State, and War.* Columbia University Press, 2001 [1959].
——. *Theory of International Politics.* Waveland Press, Inc, 1979.
Ware, Edith. *The Study of International Relations in the United States.* Columbia University Press, 1934.
Watson, Paul. *Ice Ghosts-The Epic Hunt for the Lost Franklin Expedition.* WW Norton & Co, 2018.
Weber, Joachim, ed. *Konfliktraum Arktis: Die Großmächte und der Hohe Norden.* MilesVerlag, 2021.
Weidemann, Lilly. *International Governance of the Arctic Marine Environment: With Particular Emphasis on High Seas Fisheries.* Springer, 2014.
Weigert, Hans W. *Principles of Political Geography.* Appleton-Century-Crofts, 1957.
Wood, Alan, ed. *The History of Siberia: From Russian Conquest to Revolution.* Routledge, 1991.
Wu, Shicun and Keyuan Zou, eds. *Arbitration Concerning the South China Sea: Philippines versus China.* Routledge, 2016.
Yadrintsev, Nikolai Mikhailovich. *Siberia as a Colony: Geographically, Ethnographically and Historically* [Sibir, kak koloniya v geograficheskom, etnograficheskom I istoricheskom otnoshenii]. M Stasyulevych, 1882.
Yang, Jian Yang. *Arctic Governance and China's Engagement.* Shanghai Institutes for International Affairs, 2024.
Young, Oran R. *Arctic Politics: Conflict and Cooperation in the Circumpolar North.* University of Chicago Press, 1992.
Young, Oran R and Jong-Deog Kim eds, *North Pacific Perspectives on the Arctic.* Elgar, 2024.
Zarakol, Ayşe. *After Defeat: How the East Learned to Live with the West.* Cambridge University Press, 2011.
Zolo, Danilo. *Invoking Humanity: War, Law and Global Order.* Bloomsbury Publishers, 2002.

ARTICLES AND BOOK CHAPTERS

'90 Billion Barrels of Oil and 1,670 Trillion Cubic Feet of Natural Gas Assessed in the Arctic', US Geological Survey, 23 July 2008.
'A Trillion-Rouble Plan', Arctic Russia, 11 December 2022. arctic-russia.ru/en/article/a-trillion-rouble-plan.
Abbas, Shahzada Rahim. 'Russia's Eurasian Union Dream: A Way Forward Towards Multipolar World Order', 9(1) *Journal of Global Faultlines* 33–42, 2022.
Abdel-Malek, Anouar. 'Geopolitics and National Movements: An Essay on the Dialectics of Imperialism', 9(1) *Antipode* 28–35, 1977.
About the Sámi Parliament, Sámediggi. sametinget.no/about-the-sami-parliament.
About Us, Council of the Baltic Sea States. cbss.org.

About Us, Seabed 2030. seabed2030.org/about.

Abrahamsson, C. 'On the Geneology of Lebensraum', 68 *Geographica Helvetica* 37–44, 2013.

Acharya, Amitav. 'After Liberal Hegemony: The Advent of a Multiplex World Order', 31(3) *Ethics and International Affairs* 271–85, 2017.

Ackrén, Maria. 'Diplomacy and Paradiplomacy in the North Atlantic and the Arctic – A Comparative Approach'. In *The GlobalArctic Handbook* 235–49. Edited by Matthias Finger and Lassi Heininen. Springer International Publishing, 2019.

Agnew, John. 'Representing Space: Space, Scale and Culture in Social Science'. In *Place/Culture/Representation* 251–72. Edited by James Duncan and David Law. Routledge, 1993.

——. 'The Territorial Trap: The Geographical Assumptions of International Relations Theory', 1(1) *Review of International Political Economy*, 53–80, 1994.

Ahmed, Zahra. '10 Things about Malacca Strait You Might Not Know', Marine Insight, 22 February 2023.

Albert, Eleanor. 'South Korea's Chaebol Challenge', Council on Foreign Relations, 4 May 2018.

Ali, Toghrul. 'Secretary Blinken's First Trip to Central Asia for C5+1 Meetings', Caspian Policy Center, 28 February 2023.

Allemandou, Ségolène. 'The Chilling Global Impact of Siberia's Record Heatwave', France24, 16 July 2020.

Allison, Graham. 'Destined for War?' 149 *National Interest* 9–21. May/June 2017.

Andaur, Karoline. 'Norway's Deep Sea Mining Plans Risk the Arctic's Future', The Circle, April 2023.

Anderson, Albin T. 'Origins of the Winter War: A Study of Russo-Finnish Diplomacy', 6(2) *World Politics* 169–89, 1954.

Andersson, Patrick and Jesper W Zeuthen. 'How China Left Greenland: Mutually Reinforcing Securitization Policies and Chinese Mining Plans in Greenland'. In *Greenland in Arctic Security: (De)securitization Dynamics under Climactic Thaw and Geopolitical Freeze* 175–196. Edited by Marc Jacobsen, Ole Wæver and Ulrik Pram Gad. University of Michigan Press, 2024.

Andriole, Stephen J. 'The Levels of Analysis Problems and the Study of Foreign International, and Global Affairs: A Review Critique, and Another Final Solution', 5(2–3) *International Interactions* 113–33, 1979.

Aniskov, Yevgeny. 'The Ice Is Not Broken', 87 *Environment and Rights* 4–11, 2023.

Antaki, Mark. 'Carl Schmitt's Nomos of the Earth', 42(2) *Osgood Hall Law Journal* 317–334, 2004.

Archus, Dorian. 'Russia to Arm Icebreaking Patrol Ships with Kalibr Missile', Naval Post, 16 October 2021.

'Arctic Continues to Attract Interest of BRICS and SCO Countries as a Space for Cooperation', *China Daily*, 24 March 2023.

'Ask Dr. Pauly: What Are Distant Water Fleets, and How Do They Affect Overfishing?' Oceana, 21 October 2013.

'Association of the Indigenous Minorities and the Far East of the Russian Federation Came Out in Support of the President of Our Country V.V. Putin', RAIPON, 1 March 2022.

Atkinson, David and Klaus Dodds. 'Introduction to Geopolitical Traditions: A Century of Geopolitical Thought'. In *Geopolitical Traditions: A Century of Geopolitical Thought* 1–24. Edited by Klaus Dodds and David Atkinson. Routledge, 2000.

Åtland, Kristian. 'Mikhail Gorbachev, the Murmansk Initiative, and the Desecuritization of Interstate Relations in the Arctic', 43(3) *Cooperation and Conflict* 289–311, 2008.

Auer, Stefan. 'What Carl Schmitt Reveals About Putin', UnHerd, 27 August 2022.

Ayadin, Eda. 'The Arctic Council, A Strengthening Descent from Pantheon to Agora', High North News, 22 May 2023.

Backman, Jussi. 'A Russian Radical Conservative Challenge to the Liberal Global Order: Aleksandr Dugin'. In *Contestations of Liberal Order: The West in Crisis?* 298–314. Edited by Marko Lehti, Henna-Riikka Pennanen and Jukka Jouhki. Palgrave Macmillan, 2020.

Baker, Betsy. 'Beyond the Northern Sea Route: Enhancing Russian–United States Cooperation in the Bering Strait Region', *Polar Perspectives* No 8, November 2021.

Baldwin, David A. 'Security Studies and the End of the Cold War', 48 *World Politics* 117–41, 1995.

Balton, David. 'Advancing US Diplomacy in the Arctic', *Foreign Service Journal*, May 2021.

Barbashin, Anton and Hannah Thoburn. 'Putin's Brain: Alexander Dugin and the Philosophy Behind Putin's Invasion of Crimea', Foreign Affairs, 31 March 2014.

Barnes, Richard. 'The Construction of Ocean Space in Areas Beyond National Jurisdiction: A Fisheries Perspective'. In *International Law and Marine Areas beyond National Jursidiction: Reflections on Justice, Space, Knowledge, and Power* 275–315. Edited by Vito De Lucia, Alex Oude Elferink and Lan Ngoc Nguyen. Brill/Nijhoff, 2022.

Barnes, Trevor J. 'A Morality Tale of Two Location Theorists in Hitler's Germany: Walter Christaller and August Lösch. In Hitler's Geographies', *The Spatialities of the Third Reich* 198–217. Edited by Paolo Giaccaria and Claudia Minca. University of Chicago Press, 2016.

Barnes, Trevor J and Claudio Minca, 'Nazi Spatial Theory: The Dark Geographies of Carl Schmitt and Walter Christaller'. 103(3) *Annals of the Association of American Geographers* 669–87, 2013.

Bassin, Mark. 'Between Realism and the "New Right": Geopolitics in Germany in the 1990s', 28(3) *Transactions of the Institute of British Geographers* 350–66, 2003.

——. 'Eurasian Visions of Russian Nationhood in Space'. In *Mastering Russian Spaces: Raum und Raumbewältigung als Probleme der Russichen Geschichte* 47–64. Edited by Karl Schlögel. De Gruyter Oldenbourg, 2011.

——. 'Inventing Siberia: Visions of the Russian East in the Early Nineteenth Century', 96(3) *The American Historical Review* 763–94, 1991.

Bassin, Mark and Gonzalo Pozo. 'Introduction'. In *The Politics of Eurasianism: Identity, Popular Culture and Russia's Foreign Policy* 1–16. Edited by Mark Bassin and Gonzalo Pozo. Rowman & Littlefield International Ltd, 2017.

Baumert, Kevin A. 'Article 76 of the UN Convention on the Law of the Sea: Parties and Non-Parties', 99 *International Law Studies* 963–90, 2022.

Baxter, RR. 'International Law in "Her Infinite Variety"', 29(4) *International and Comparative Law Quarterly* 549–66, 1980.

Beake, Nick and Kate Vandy. 'Svalbard: The Race to Save the Fastest-Warming Place on Earth', BBC News, 27 October 2022.

Beichman, Arnold. 'Roosevelt's Failure at Yalta', Hoover Digest, 6 October 2004.

Bendersky, Joseph. 'The Expendable Kronjurist: Carl Schmitt and National Socialism', 1933–36, 14(2) *Journal of Contemporary History* 309–28, 1979.

Bennett, Mia. 'How China Sees the Arctic: Reading Between Extraregional and Intraregional Narratives', 20 *Geopolitics* 645–68, 2015.

——. 'The Arctic Shipping Route No One's Talking About', Maritime Executive, 8 May 2019.

Bennett, Mia M, Scott R Stephenson, Kang Yang, Michael T Bravo and Bert De Jonghe. 'The Opening of the Transpolar Sea Route: Logistical, Geopolitical, Environmental, and Socioeconomic Impacts', Marine Policy 104178 [1–15], 2020.

Benshoff, Laura. 'The Nord Stream Pipelines Have Stopped Leaking. But the Methane Emitted Broke Records', NPR, 4 October 2022.

Bermudez Jr, Joseph S. 'Ice Curtain: Protecting the Arctic Motherland', Center for Strategic and International Studies (CSIS), 25 March 2020.

Bergseth, Brock and Jon C Day. 'Compliance – The "Achilles Heel" of Protected Areas', 155 105728 [1–3], 2023.

Bertelsen, Rasmus Gjedssø. 'Jackie Fisher's Missing Key: The Northern Sea Route in Geoeconomics and Geostrategy'. In *Konfliktraum Arktis: Die Großmächte und der Hohe Norden* 43–76. Edited by Joachim Weber. Miles Verlag, 2021.

Bertram, GCL and David Lack. 'Bear Island', 81 *Geographical Journal* 43–52, 1933.

Bertuzzi, Luca. 'EU Eyes Arctic Internet Cable to Connect Europe to Asia via Alaska', Euractiv, 14 October 2022.

Bethlehem, Daniel. 'The End of Geography: The Changing Nature of the International System and the Challenge to International Law', 25(1) *European Journal of International Law* 9–24, 2014.

Bhambry, Tul'si (Tuesday) trans Friedrich Ratzel, 'Lebensraum: A Biogeographical Study', [1901] 61 *Journal of Historical Geography* 59–80, 2018.

Bjøl, Erling. 'NATO and Denmark', 3(2) *Cooperation and Conflict* 93–107, 1968.

Black, JL. 'Opening up Siberia: Russia's "Window on the East"'. In *The History of Siberia: From Russian Conquest to Revolution* 57–68. Edited by Alan Wood. Routledge, 1991.

Borrell, Josep. 'The Arctic, A Key Region for the EU and Global Security', European Union, External Action, 3 February 2021.

Bouffard, Troy J. 'Overview of US Arctic Strategies: National and Geopolitical Perspectives. In Navigating Breakup: Security Realities of Freezing Politics and Thawing Landscapes in the Arctic', 37–43. Edited by Karsten Friis, Elana Wilson Rowe, Mike Sfraga and Ulf Sverdrup. With Pavel K Baev, Troy J Bouffard, Marc Lanteigne, Marisol Maddox and Jan-Gunnar Winther. Norwegian Institute of International Affairs, 2023.

Braudel, Fernand. 'Histoire et Sciences sociales: La longue durée', 13 *Annales Économies, Sociétés, Civilisations* 725–53, 1958.

Brautigam, Deborah and Meg Rithmire. 'The Chinese "Debt Trap" Is a Myth', The Atlantic, 6 February 2021.

Breese, J. 'Interpretation of the Anglo-Russian Treaty of 1825 and Establishment of the Alaska-Canada Boundary], 33(257) *Survey Review* 161–76, 2013.

Brembo, Frida, Sondre Skjelvik and Elvind Molde. 'Flertall for å lete etter mineraler på havbunnen', NRK, 5 December 2023.

Brenna, David. '"NATO Lake" Vital in Long-Term Russia Conflict: Estonia FM', Newsweek, 14 May 2023.

Brenner, Samuel, Luc Rainville, Jim Thomson and Craig Lee. 'The Evolution of a Shallow Front in the Arctic Marginal Ice Zone', 8(17) *Elementa: Science of the Anthropocene* [1–17], 2020.

Brigham, Lawson W. 'Governance and Economic Challenges for the Global Shipping Enterprise in a Seasonally Ice-Covered Arctic Ocean'. In *The Arctic and World Order* 143–60. Edited by Kristina Spohr and Daniel S Hamilton, Jason C Moyer associate editor. Brookings Institution Press, 2020.

Bronder, Polina Leganger. 'China to Build Its Third Icebreaker', Barents Observer, 10 December 2021.

Brunnstrom, David and Trevor Hunnicutt. 'Biden Says U.S. Forces Would Defend Taiwan in the Event of a Chinese Invasion', Reuters, 19 September 2022.

Buchanan, Elizabeth. 'China's Hybrid Arctic Strategy', Concordiam, 8 September 2021.

——. 'Russia and China in the Arctic: Assumptions and Realities', The Strategist, 25 September 2020.

Bugos, Shannon. 'Russia Suspends New START', Arms Control Association, March 2023.

Bunikowski, Dawid. 'The Philosophy of Law in the Arctic'. In *Philosophies of Polar Law* 30–45. Edited by Dawid Bunikowski and Alan D Hemmings. Routledge, 2021.

Burke, Ryan and Jahara Matisek. 'The American Polar Pivot: Gaining a Comparative Advantage in Great Power Competition', 10(2) *Marine Corps University Journal* 70–91, 2019.

Bye, Hilde-Gunn. 'Denmark Wants to Prioritize Arctic Defense and Put the Baltic Sea Second', High North News, 3 May 2023.

Calbérac, Yann. 'Close Reading Michel Foucault's and Yves Lacoste's Concepts of Space Through Spatial Metaphors', 7(1) *Le foucaldien* [1–21], 2021.

Cameron, Shaun. 'By Land or Sea: Thailand Perseveres with the Kra Canal', The Interpreter, 22 September 2021.

Campana, Steven E, Ragnhildur B Stefánsdóttir and Jón Sólmundsson. 'Shifting Fish Distributions in Warming Sub-Arctic Oceans', 10 *Science Reports* 16448, 2020.

'Carl Schmitt and Copenhagen School Security Studies', 4 *Western Balkans Security Observer*, 2009.

Carrington, Damian. 'Too Late Now to Save Arctic Summer Ice, Climate Scientists Find', *The Guardian*, 6 June 2023.

Cartwright, Mark. 'The Seven Voyages of Zheng He', *World Historical Encyclopedia*, 7 February 2019.

Carty, Andrew. 'Carl Schmitt's Critique of Liberal International Legal Order Between 1933 and 1945', 14(1) *Leiden Journal of International Law* 25–76, 2001.

Casimir, Nicholas and Baron de Bogoushevsky. 'The English in Muscovy During the Sixteenth Century', 7 *Transactions of the Royal Historical Society* 58–129, 1878.
Cattelan, Stefano. 'Mare Clausum in Legal Argumentation: Claiming the Seas in the Early Modern Age' (PhD dissertation, Aarhus University, 2020).
Chadick, Wayne L. 'Naval Tradition–A Russian Heritage', 22(6) *Naval War College Review*, 26–44, 1969.
Chakrabarty, Dipesh. 'The Climate of History: Four Theses', 35 *Critical Inquiry* 197–204, 2009.
Chang, Felix K. 'Crowded Pond: NATO and Russian Maritime Power in the Baltic Sea', Foreign Policy Research Institute, 14 December 2021.
Charlton, Guy C. 'Aboriginal Rights and Constitutional Conflict: The Marshall Court, State and Federal Sovereignty, and Native American Rights under the 1789 Constitution', 8(1) *American Indian Law Journal* 149–219, 2019.
Charron, Andrea. 'NATO and the Geopolitical Future of the Arctic', *Arctic Yearbook* 2020 [1–8], 2020.
Chelle, Kit, Matthew Campbell and K Oanh Ha. 'Six Days in Suez: The Inside Story of the Ship that Broke Global Trade', Bloomberg, 24 June 2021.
Chen, Chuan. 'China's Engagement in Greenland: Mutual Economic Benefits and Political Non-interference', 41 *Polar Research* 2022, 7706 [1–7], 2022.
Chen, Duanhong. 'National Security and the Constitution', Reading the China Dream. Introduction and trans by David Ownby, 4 December 2020.
Chen, Stephen. 'China Plans Massive Listening Programme at the North Pole After Declaring Success in Arctic Test of Underwater Devise', *South China Morning Post*, 9 July 2023.
Chiacchia, Benjamin. 'The Case for an Arctic Treaty', 146 US Naval Institute Proceedings, 2020.
Chiappa, Claudia and Pierre Emmanuel Ngendakumana. 'Everything Indicates' Chinese Ship Damaged Baltic Pipeline on Purpose, Finland Says', Politico, 1 December 2023.
'China Applies to Join Pacific Trade Pact to Boost Economic Clout', Reuters, 17 September 2021.
'China Helping Moscow in Biggest Military Expansion Since Soviet Times, US Says', France24, 14 April 2024.
'China-Russia Rail Bridge is Finally Open', RailFreight.com, 17 November 2022.
'China's Expanding Investment in Global Ports, Iceland', Economist Intelligence, 11 October 2017.
Choudhary, Mohit. 'China's Malacca Bluff: Examining China's Indian Ocean Strategy and Future Security Architecture of the Region', *Journal Indo-Pacific Affairs* 99–108, 2023.
Cinciripini, Luca. 'The Arctic within EU Strategies: A Renewed Centrality', IAI, 28 July 2023.
Claval, P. 'National Schools of Geography'. In *International Encyclopedia of Human Geography* 236–41. Edited by Nigel Thrift and Rob Kitchin. Elsevier Ltd, 2009.
Clark, Colin. 'New Chinese 10-Dash Map Sparks Furor across Indo-Pacific: Vietnam, India, Philippines, Malaysia', Breaking Defense, 1 September 2023.
Claval, Paul. 'Hérodote and the French Left'. In *Geographical Traditions: Critical Histories of a Century of Geopolitical Thought* 239–67. Edited by Klaus Dodds and David Atkinson. Routledge, 2000.
Clayton, Andrew RL. 'The Debate over the Panama Congress and the Origins of the Second American Party System', 47 *The Historian* 219–38, 1985.
Clover, Charles. 'The Unlikely Origins of Russia's Manifest Destiny: How an Obscure Academic and a Marginalized Philosopher Captured the Minds of the Kremlin and Helped Forge the New Russian Nationalism', Foreign Policy, 27 July 2016.
Coggins, Shaugn, James D Ford, Lea Berrang-Ford, Sherilee Harper, Keith Hyams, Jouni Paavolva, Ingrig Arotoma-Rojas and Poshendra Satyal. 'Indigenous Peoples and Climate Justice in the Arctic', *Georgetown Journal of International Affairs*, 23 February 2021.
Colgan, Jeff D and Nicholas L Miller. 'The Rewards of Rivalry: U.S.-Chinese Competition Can Spur Climate Progress', 101 *Foreign Affairs* 108, November/December 2022.
Commager, Henry Steele. 'The Defeat of America', *The New York Review*, 5 October 1972.
Conley, Heather A, Sophie Arts, Bonnie S Glaser, Kristine Berzina and Jaine Archambeau. 'A New Era of Arctic Geopolitics'. German Marshall Fund Report, 18 July 2024.

Cordes, Miłosz Jeromin. 'Bornholm, Russia and the Politics of Memory', Lossi 36, 8 May 2022.

Cornwall, Warren. '"We Are Cut off." Tensions with Russia are Hobbling Arctic Research', *Science*, 3 May 2023.

Covey, Nicole. 'Legitimization of the Arctic Coastal States (A5) through the Central Arctic Ocean (CAO) Fisheries Agreement', NAADSN Policy Primer 1–9, 28 October 2021.

Cox, Kevin R. '"Rescaling the State" in Question', 2 *Cambridge Journal of Regions, Economy and Society* 107–121, 2009.

Cox, Robert W. 'Social Forces, States and World Orders: Beyond International Relations Theory', 10(2) *Millennium: Journal of International Studies* 126–28, 1981.

Craymer, Lucy and Joe Cash. 'Biggest Hurdles to China Entry into Trans-Pacific Trade Pact are Political', Reuters, 31 July 2023.

'Cruising to Nome: The First U.S. Deep Water Port for the Arctic to Host Cruise Ships, Military', Associated Press, 18 June 2023.

Cuningham, Alan. 'Underneath the Ice: Undersea Cables, the Arctic Circle, and International Security', Arctic Institute, 29 March 2022.

Dalby, Simon. 'The Environment as Geopolitical Threat: Reading Robert Kaplan's "Coming Anarchy"', 3(4) *Ecumene* 472–76, 1996.

Dankov, Artem. 'The Paradoxes of Social and Economic Development in Central Asia', Russian International Affairs Council, 31 January 2020.

Davies, Maia. 'Norway Suspends Controversial Deep-Sea Mining Plans', BBC, 2 December 2024.

Day, Alan J. 'Back to the Finland Station, International Boundaries Research Unit [IBRU]' *Boundary and Security Bulletin* 60–64, 1993.

de Buitrago, Sybille Reinke. 'Risk Representations and Confrontational Actions in the Arctic', 12(3) *Journal of Strategic Studies* 13–36, 2019.

Delaney, David and Helga Leitner. 'The Political Construction of Scale', 16(2) *Political Geography* 93–97, 1997.

De Lucia, Vito and Philipp Peter Nickels. 'Reflecting on the Role of the Arctic Council vis-à-vis a Future International Legally Binding Instrument on Biodiversity in Areas Beyond National Jurisdiction', 11 *Arctic Review on Law and Politics* 189–214, 2020.

Dempsey, Caitlin. 'Arctic Circle', Geographyrealm, 2022.

Deni, John R. 'Is the Baltic Sea a NATO Lake? Carnegie Endowment International Peace', 18 December 2023.

——. 'NATO Must Prepare to Defend Its Weakest Point – the Suwalki Corridor', 3 March 2022.

'Deploying US Rocket System at Bornholm to Lead to Escalation with Russia, Envoy Says', Tass, 2 June 2022.

Derrida, Jacques. 'Force of Law: The "Mystical Foundation of Authority"'. In *Deconstruction and the Possibility of Justice* 3–67. Edited by Drucilla Cornell, Michel Rosenfeld and David Gray Carlson. Routledge, 1992.

Devyatkin, Pavel. 'Can Cooperation Be Restored?' *Arctic Yearbook*, 2022.

'Did the Unipolar Moment Ever End? Foreign Affairs Asks the Experts', Foreign Affairs, 23 May 2023.

Dharmaputra, Radityo. 'Russia's Pivot to the East: Between China, the US and the Other Asia', International Centre for Defense and Security, 24 October 2019.

Dickie, Gloria. 'Russian Officials Call Arctic Council Boycott "Regrettable"', Reuters, 4 March 2022.

Digges, Charles. 'War Puts Cleanup of Russia's Radioactive Wrecks on Ice', Bulletin of the Atomic Scientists, 28 November 2022.

Dodds, Klaus and Chih Yuan Woon. 'Triumphant Geopolitics? Making Space of and For Arctic Geopolitics in the Arctic Ocean'. In *Arctic Triumph, Northern Innovation and Persistence* 163–80. Edited by Nikolas Sellheim, Yulia V Zaika and Ilan Kelman. Springer, 2019.

D'Odorico, Paolo, Yufei He, Scott Collins, Stephan FJ De Wekker, Vic Engel and Jose D Fuentes. 'Vegetation-Microclimate Feedbacks in Woodland-Grassland Ecotones', 22 *Global Ecology and Biogeography* 364–79, 2013.

Doran, Charles F and Wes Parsons. 'War and the Cycle of Relative Power', 74(4) *American Political Science Review* 947–965, 1980.

Doshi, Rush, Alexis Dale-Huang and Gaoqi Zhang. 'Northern Expedition: China's Arctic Activities and Ambitions', Brookings 1–68, 2021.
Dmytryshyn, Basil. 'The Administrative Apparatus of the Russian Colony in Siberia and Northern Asia, 1581–1700'. In *The History of Siberia: From Russian Conquest to Revolution* 17–36. Edited by Alan Wood. Routledge, 1991.
Dorough, Dalee Sambo. 'Our homeland: Arctic Indigenous Peoples' Perspectives on Non-Arctic States'. In *Emerging Legal Orders in the Arctic: The Role of Non-Arctic Actors* 69–90. Edited by Akiho Shibata, Leilei Zou, Nikolas Sellheim and Marzia Scopelliti. Routledge, 2019.
Duenow, Victor. 'Baltic Sea Mining as an Extension of the Russian Gray Zone', Foreign Policy Resource Institute, 18 April 2022.
Dugin, Alexander. 'Carl Schmitt's 5 Lessons for Russia', Eurasianist-Archive.com. Jafe Arnold translation, 12 October 2016.
Dullien, Sebastian. 'Wer ein Energieembargo fordert, muss die Gefahren kennen', Spiegel Wirtschaft, 12 March 2022.
Dusik, Jan. 'Norway Undermines the High Seas Treaty by Rushing Deep Sea Mining Authorization', WWF, 28 June 2024.
Dutton, Peter Alan. 'Oceans Under Pressure: China's Challenge to the Maritime Order', Council on Geostrategy, 23 January 2024.
Easton, Adam and Tom Spender. 'Kaliningrad: Russian Fury as Poland Body Recommends Renaming Exclave', BBC News, 10 May 2023.
Economy, Elizabeth. 'Xi Jingping's New World Order', 101 *Foreign Affairs* 52–67, January/February 2022.
Edstrøm, Anders Christoffer, Iselin Stensdal and Gørild M Heggelund. 'The "New Superpower": What Are China's Intentions in the Arctic'. In *Norway's Arctic Policy: Geopolitics, Security and Identity in the High North* 95–108. Edited by Andreas Østerhagen. Edgar Elgar Publishing, 2023.
Edvardsen, Astri. 'Norway and Russia Reached a Fisheries Agreement for 2023', High North News, 28 October 2022.
——. 'Russia: "The Risk of Weakening the Arctic Council Should Not Be Underestimated"', High North News, 12 May 2023.
——. 'Russian Fishing Vessels Now Only Allowed Access to Three Northern Norwegian Ports – And Will Be Controlled at Each Docking', High North News, 7 October 2022.
——. 'Svalbard Gets Exemptions from New Sanctions against Russia', High North News, 5 May 2022.
Eisenhower, Dwight D. 'Address to the American Society of Newspaper Editors', American Rhetoric, 16 April 1953.
Eiterjord, Trym. 'What the 14th Five-Year Plan Says About China's Arctic Interests', Arctic Institute, 23 November 2023.
Elden, Stuart. 'Reading Schmitt Geopolitically: Nomos, Territory and Großraum', 161 *Radical Philosophy* 18–26, 2010.
——. 'Terrain, Politics, History', 11(2) *Dialogues in Human Geography* 170–89, 2020.
'Effects of Recent Developments on Arctic Regional Governance', NAADSN, 3 March 2022.
'Estonia as an Aspiring Arctic Council Observer State: The Arctic's Inventive Neighbour', Embassy of Estonia (Oslo), 1 January 2025.
Exner-Pirot, Heather and Robert W Murray. 'Regional Order in the Arctic: Negotiated Exceptionalism', 20(3) *Politik* 47–64, 2017.
Fago, Jason. 'Neil Freeman's Alternative Geography', *The New Yorker*, 25 March 2013.
Fellows, Grant Scott. 'The Foundations of Alexandr Dugin's Geopolitics: Montage Fascism and Eurasianism as Blowback'. MA thesis, Josef Korbel School of International Studies, University of Denver, 2018.
Ferdinando, Lisa. 'NATO Unified, Resolute in Face of Russia's "Illegal Ukraine Invasion", Austin Says', U.S. DOD News, 13 October 2022.

Finger, Matthias and Gunnar Rekvig. 'Introduction'. In *GlobalArctic: An Introduction to the Multi-faceted Dynamics of the Arctic* 1–20. Edited by Matthias Finger and Gunnar Rekvig. Springer International Publishing, 2022.

Fish, Tim. 'Eastern European Navies Expand as Russian Occupation of Ukraine Drags On', USNI News, 20 July 2023.

Flint, Colin. 'Structure, Agency, and Context: The Contributions of Geography to World-Systems Analysis', 66(4) *Sociological Inquiry* 496–508, 1996.

Fløistad, Brit and Lars Lothe. 'Indigenous Peoples Rights in the Arctic', Arctis, www.arctis-search.com/Indigenous+Peoples+Rights+in+the+Arctic (no date).

Foggo, James and Rachael A Gosnell. 'Building a Trans-Polar Bridge', Center for European Policy Analysis (CEPA), 21 May 2021.

Folland, Rolf. 'Arctic Strategy, Deterrence and Détente, *Journal of Indo-Pacific Affairs*, 30 March 2021.

Forsyth, James. 'The Siberian Native Peoples Before and After the Russian Conquest'. In *The History of Siberia: From Russian Conquest to Revolution* 69–91. Edited by Alan Wood. Routledge, 1991.

Forsyth, Michael J. 'Why Alaska and the Arctic are Critical to the National Security of the United States', *Military Review* 113–19, January–February 2018.

Franckx, Eric. 'New Developments in the North-East Passage', 6(1) *International Journal of Estuarine and Coastal Law* 33–40, 1991.

Frank, VS. 'The Territorial Terms of the Sino-Russian Treaty of Nerchinsk', 1689, 16 *Pacific Historical Review* 265–70, 1947.

Freeman, Neil. 'Electoral College Reform (Fifty States with Equal Population)', Fake is the New Real, 2012.

Friedrichs, Jörg. 'Defining the International Public Enemy: The Political Struggle behind the Legal Debate on International Terrorism', 19(1) *Leiden Journal of International Law* 69–91, 2006.

Fukuyama, Francis. 'The End of History?' 16 *National Interest* 3–18, 1989.

Galli, Carlo and Elisabeth Fay. 'Carl Schmitt and the Global Age', 10(2) *New Centennial Review* 1–25, 2010.

Garamone, Jim. 'DOD Establishes Arctic Strategy and Global Resilience Office', US Department of Defense, 27 September 2022.

——. 'F-22 Safely Shoots Down Chinese Spy Balloon Off South Carolina Coast', US Department of Defense News, 4 February 2023.

Gardiner, Barry. 'As the Ice Melts, a Perilous Russian Threat is Emerging in the Arctic', *The Guardian*, 18 June 2023.

'Gas Pipelines on the Norwegian Continental Shelf', Arkiv for utskrift, Norwegianpetroleum.no, www.norskpetroleum.no/en/utskrift.

Gibson, James R. 'Russian Expansion in Siberia and America', 70(2) *Geographical Review* 127–36, 1980.

Gilderhus, Mark T. 'The Monroe Doctrine: Meanings and Implications', 36(1) *Presidential Studies Quarterly* 5–16, 2006.

Gladkiy, Yu N, VD Sukhorukov, S Yu Kornekova, SV Kulik and NV Kaledin. '"Polar Silk Road": Project Implementation and Geo-Economic Interests of Russia and China', *IOP Conference Series: Earth and Environmental Science* 012009 [1–7], 2021.

Glebov, Sergei. 'A Life with Imperial Dreams: Petr Nikolaevich Savitsky, Eurasianism, and the Invention of "Structural" Geography', 3 *Ab Imperio* 299–329, 2005.

Goldstein, Etyan. 'Eclipsed, Again: Russia's Northern Sea Route Will Have to Wait', *Harvard International Review*, 24 February 2023.

Goldstein, Lyle J. 'What Does China Want with the Arctic?' *National Interest*, 2 September 2019.

Gordon, Michael R, Waren P Strobel and Alan Cullison. 'China Has Helped Russia Boost Arms Production, U.S. Says', *Wall Street Journal*, 12 April 2024.

Górski, Jędrzej. 'Northern Sea Route: International Law Perspectives'. In *International Collaboration, Economic Development, and Sustainability in the Arctic* 292–313. Edited by Vasilii Erokhin, Gao Tianming, Zhang Xiuhua. IGI Global, 2018.

Gourevitch, Peter. 'The Second Image Reversed: The International Sources of Domestic Politics', 32(4) *International Organization* 881–912, 1982.
Graham, Niels. 'Chinese Exports Have Replaced the EU as the Lifeline of Russia's Economy', Atlantic Council, 22 February 2024.
Gray, Alexander B. 'NATO's Northern Flank Has Too Many Weak Spots', Foreign Policy, 7 August 2023.
Grdovic, Mark and Marius Kristiansen. 'Why USSOCOM Should Develop an Arctic Strategy', Strategem, 17 January 2022.
Greaves, Wilfrid. 'Arctic Break Up: Climate Change, Geopolitics, and the Fragmenting Arctic Security Region', *Arctic Yearbook 2019*, 1–17, 2019.
Greenall, Robert and Paul Kirby. 'Denmark Boosts Greenland Defence after Trump Repeats Desire for US Control', BBC, 24 December 2024.
'Greenland Raises Hemisphere Issue; Monroe Doctrine to be Applied If It Is Necessary – Danish Envoy Sees Roosevelt', *New York Times*, 11 April 1940.
Guiterrez, Miren and Guy Jobbins. 'China's Distant-Water Fishing Fleet: Scale, Impact and Governance', Overseas Development Institute, 2 June 2020.
Guo, Peiqing and Hiuwen Chen Huiwen. 'Chinese Perspective on the Arctic and Its Implication for Nordic Countries', Arctic Institute, 20 June 2023.
Guo, Xiaoli. 'Explaining China's Central Asia Pivot', The Interpreter, Lowy Institute, 26 May 2023.
Gustafson, Milton O. 'Seward's Bargain: The Alaska Purchase from Russia', 26 *Prologue Magazine*, National Archives, 1994.
Gutenev, Maxim, ML Lagutina and Alexander Sergunin. 'Russian Universities as Actors of Arctic Science Diplomacy', 32 *Higher Education in Russia* [Vysshee Obrazovanie v Rossii] 70–88, 2023 [Russian translation].
Gwladys, Fouche and Nerijus Adomaitis. 'Norway Moves To Open Its Waters to Deep-Sea mining', Reuters, 20 June 2023.
Haavisto, Pekka. 'Review of the Arctic Council Structures', Finnish Institute of International Affairs 1–55, 2001.
Hajianpour, Hamid and Khalil Salehi. 'Investigating the Causes and Failure of the English Company of Muscovy in Safavid Iran', 15(1) *Historical Sciences Studies* 23–43, 2023.
Hamilton, Alexander. 'The Federalist Papers: No. 11, Avalon Project' [23 November 1787].
Halecki, Oscar. 'Polish-Russian Relations–Past and Present', 5(3) *Review of Politics* 322–38, 1943.
Hannikainen, Lauri. 'Finland's Continuation War (1941-1944): War of Aggression or Defence? War of Alliance or Separate War', 17(1) *Baltic Year Book of International Law Online* 77–121, 2020.
Hansson, Michael. 'Nansen International Office for Refugees Nobel Lecture', The Nobel Prize, 10 December 1938.
Hao, Jiansheng, Xueqin Zhang, Peng Cui, Lanhai Li, Yan Wang, Guotao Zhang and Chaoyue Li. 'Impacts of Climate Change on Snow Avalanche Activity Along a Transportation Corridor in the Tianshan Mountains', 14 *International Journal of Disaster Risk Science* 510–22, 2023.
Hartshorne, Richard. 'Political Geography in the Modern World', 4(1) *Journal of Conflict Resolution* 52–66, 1960.
Harvey, Chelsea. 'The Arctic Is Warming Four Times Faster Than the Rest of the Planet', Scientific American, 12 August 2022.
Harvey, David. 'Reshaping Economic Geography: The World Development Report 2009', 40(6) *Development and Change* 1269–77, 2009.
Hasin, Gershon. 'Ocean Governance in the 21st Century: A "New Package-Deal" to Balance Mare Liberum and Mare Clausum', 48 *Yale Journal of International Law* 223–87, 2023.
Heininen, Lassi. '"Comprehensive Security" – A Prerequisite for Sustainable Development'. In *Towards a Sustainable Arctic: International Security, Climate Change and Green Shipping* 25–48. Edited by Michael Goodsite and Niklas Swanström. World Scientific Publishing Company, 2023.

——. 'The Post-Cold War Arctic. In Global Arctic: An Introduction to the Multifaceted Dynamics of the Arctic' 109–28. Edited by Matthias Finger and Gunnar Rekvig. Springer International Publishing, 2022.

——. 'Special Features of Arctic Geopolitics – A Potential Asset for World Politics'. In *The Global Arctic Handbook* 215–34. Edited by Matthias Finger and Lassi Heininen, Springer International Publishing, 2019.

Heffernan, Michael. 'Fin de siècle, fin du monde? On the Origins of European Geopolitics, 1980–1920'. In *Geopolitical Traditions: A Century of Geopolitical Thought* 27–51. Edited by Klaus Dodds and David Atkinson. Routledge, 2000.

——. 'Historical Geography, Making History', Institute of Historical Research, 2008.

——. 'Mapping Schmitt'. In *Spatiality, Sovereignty and Carl Schmitt: Geographies of the Nomos* 234–243. Edited by Stephen Legg. Routledge, 2011.

Heininen, Lassi, Heather Exner-Pirot and Justin Barnes. 'Introduction – The Russian Arctic: Economic, Politics and Peoples', *Arctic Yearbook* 2023.

Heleniak, Timothy. 'The Future of the Arctic Populations', 44(2) *Polar Geography* 136–52, 2021.

Heng, Calvin and Eyck Freymann. 'Outsiders Wanting In: Asian States and Arctic Governance', Belfer Center, June 2023.

Herbertson, AJ. 'The Natural Regions of the World', 3(3) *Geographical Teacher* 104–13, 1905.

Herz, John H. 'Idealist Internationalism and the Security Dilemma', 2(2) *World Politics* 157–180, 1950.

Hilpold, Peter.' Justifying the Unjustifiable: Russia's Aggression against Ukraine, International Law, and Carl Schmitt's "Theory of the Greater Space" ("Großraumtheorie")', 22(3) *Chinese Journal of International Law* 409–33, 2019.

Hoag, Hannah. 'Sea Ice Retreat Could Lead to Rapid Overfishing in the Arctic', The Atlantic, 17 March 2017.

Hobson, John and Shizhi Zhang. 'The Return of the Chinese Tribute System? Re-viewing the Belt and Road Initiative', 2(4) *Global Studies Quarterly* 1–11, 2022.

Hoel, Alf Håkon. 'Do We Need a New Legal Regime for the Arctic Ocean?' 24 *International Journal of Marine and Coastal Law* 443–56, 2009.

——. 'Sea, Fish, and Resource Management in the High North'. In *Norway's Arctic Policy: Geopolitics, Security and Identity in the High North* 65–76. Edited by Andreas Østhagen. Edgar Elgar Publishing, 2023.

Holm, Arne O. 'Barely Anyone Talks of Low Tension in the Arctic Anymore', High North News, 17 March 2023.

——. 'The Arctic Council is Dead. Long Live the Arctic Council', High North News, 28 March 2023.

Holtsmar, Sven G. 'Russia and the Svalbard Treaty, Artica' [no date].

Hosch, Gilles, Nathan A Miller, Yann Yvergniaux, Elaine Young and Tim Huntington. ''IUU Safe Havens or PSMA Ports: A Global Assessment of Port State Performance and Risk, 155 Marine Policy 105751 [1–20], 2023.

'How India's Imports of Russian Oil Have Lubricated Global Markets', *The Economist*, 11 April 2024.

Huh, Sookyeon. 'Title to Territory in the Post-Colonial Era: Original Title and Terra Nullius in the ICJ Judgments on Cases Concerning Ligitan/Sipadan (2002) and Pedra Branca (2008)', 26(3) *European Journal of International Law* 709–25, 2015.

Huhndorf, Shari M. 'Nanook and His Contemporaries: Imagining Eskimos in American Culture, 1897–1920', 27(1) *Critical Inquiry* 122–48 (2000).

Humpert, Malte. 'EU Received 300 Shipments of LNG from Russia Since Beginning of Ukraine War', High North News, 29 June 2023.

——. 'International Shipping on Northern Sea Route Collapses as Foreign Companies Stay Away', High North News, 12 September 2022.

——. 'New Satellite Images Reveal Extent of Russia's Military and Economic Build-Up in the Arctic', High North News, 3 May 2019.

——. 'Nord Stream Pipeline Sabotage Mirrors Svalbard Cable Incident', High North News, 29 September 2022.

——. 'Putin and Xi Discuss Further Deepening of Arctic Partnership', High North News, 23 March 2023.

——. 'Russia Amends Arctic Policy Prioritizing "National Interest" and Removing Cooperation Within Arctic Council', High North News, 23 February 2023.

——. 'Russia Inks Deal with Dubai's DP World to Develop Arctic Container Shipping', High North News, 23 October 2023.

——. 'Russia's Northern Sea Route Sees More Traffic Despite War and Sanctions', High North News, 18 January 2023.

Humpert, Malte and Andreas Raspotnik. 'The Future of Arctic Shipping Along the Transpolar Sea Route', *Arctic Yearbook* 281–307, 2012.

Huntington, Samuel P. 'The Clash of Civilizations?' 72(3) *Foreign Affairs* 22–49, 1993.

Huysmans, Jef. 'Revisiting Copenhagen: Or, On the Creative Development of a Security Studies Agenda in Europe', 4(4) *European Journal of International Relations* 479–505, 1998.

Ingram, Alan. 'Alexander Dugin: Geopolitics and Neo-Fascism in Post-Soviet Russia', 20(8) *Political Geography* 1029–51, 2001.

Inman, Samuel Guy. 'The Monroe Doctrine and Hispanic America', 4(4) *Hispanic American Historical Review* 635–76, 1921.

Irwin, Douglas A and Oliver Ward. 'What is the "Washington Consensus?"', Peterson Institute for International Economics, 8 September 2021.

Ištok, Robert and Dominika Plavčanová. 'Russian Geopolitics and Geopolitics of Russia. Phenomena of Space', 1 *European Journal of Geopolitics* 61–94, 2013.

Jacobsen, Marc and Signe Lyngholm Lindbjerg. 'Denmark's Security Perspectives on USA, China, and Russia in Greenland: How Great Power Threats Made Danish Politicians Talk about Independent Greenland Agency'. In *Greenland in Arctic Security: (De)securitization Dynamics under Climactic Thaw and Geopolitical Freeze* 196–226. Edited by Marc Jacobsen, Ole Wæver and Ulrik Pram Gad. University of Michigan Press, 2024.

Jarrett. Isabel. 'Most Long-Distance Fishing in Foreign Waters Dominated by Only a Few Governments', Pew, 27 May 2022.

Jensen, Bent. 'Soviet Occupation of a New Type: The Long Liberation of the Danish Island of Bornholm 1944–1946', 25(3) *Scandinavian Journal of History* 219–237, 2000.

Jiang, Shigong. 'Empire and World Order. Reading the China Dream'. Introduction and translation by David Ownby, 2019.

Joerges, Christian. 'Europe a Großraum? Shifting Legal Conceptualisations of the Integration Project'. In *Darker Legacies of Law in Europe: The Shadow of National Socialism and Fascism over Europe and Its Legal Traditions* 167–91. Edited by Christian Joerges and Navraj Singh Ghaleigh. Prologue by Michael Stolleis, epilogue by JHH Weiler. Bloomsbury, 2003.

Joenniemi, Pertti. 'The Barents Euro-Arctic Council'. In *Subregional Cooperation in the New Europe: Building Security, Prosperity and Solidarity from the Barents to the Black Sea* 23–45. Edited by Andrew Cottey. Springer, 1999.

Jonassen, Trine. 'Far North Fiber One Step Closer to Pan-Arctic Connectivity', High North News, 12 April 2023.

——. 'The Arctic Council: The Arctic 7 Resume Limited Work Without Russia', High North News, 8 June 2022.

Jones, David Martin. 'Putin's Geopolitical Brain', CIEO, 23 August 2022.

Jones, Stan. 'Northern Sea Route Beckons LNG Shippers', Alaska Natural Gas Transportation Projects. Office of the Federal Coordinator, October 2013.

Joppke, Christian. 'Citizenship between De- and Re-Ethnicization', 44 Archives Européennes de Sociologie, 429–58, 2003.

Jurkevics, Anna. '*Hannah Arendt Reads Carl Schmitt's The* Nomos *of the Earth: A Dialogue on Law and Geopolitics from the Margins*', 16(3) *European Journal of Political Theory* 345–66, 2017.

Kachaturian, Rafael. 'The Specter of Russian Nationalism', 56(1) *Dissent* 19–24, 2009.

Kampmark, Ginoy. 'AI Giant Palantir on a Quest to Help the West', Green Left, 31 December 2023.

Kankaanpää, Paula and Oran R Young. 'The Effectiveness of the Arctic Council', 31(1) *Polar Research* 17176, 2012.

Kaplan, Robert D. 'The Coming Anarchy: How Scarcity, Crime, Overpopulation, Tribalism, and Disease are Rapidly Destroying the Social Fabric of our Planet', The Atlantic, February 1994.

Kapoor, Nivedita. 'Russia and the Future of the Arctic', ORF Occasional Paper No 336, October 2021.

Käpylä, Juha and Harri Mikkola. 'Contemporary Arctic Meets World Politics: Rethinking Arctic Exceptionalism in the Age of Uncertainty'. In *The Global Arctic Handbook* 153–70 Edited by Matthias Finger and Lassi Heininen. Springer International Publishing, 2019.

Kardaś, Szymon. 'Conscious Uncoupling: Europeans' Russian Gas Challenge in 2023', European Council on Foreign Relations, 13 February 2023.

Kass, Stephen L. 'Obligatory Negotiations in International Organizations', 1965 *Canadian Yearbook of International Law* 36–72, 1965.

Katzenstein, Peter J. 'A World of Plural and Pluralist Civilizations: Multiple Actors, Traditions, and Practices'. In *Civilizations in World Politics: Plural and Pluralist Perspectives* 1–41. Edited by Peter Katzenstein. Routledge, 2010.

Kauranen, Anne. 'What Can Finland's Armed Forces and Arsenal Offer NATO?' Reuters, 4 April 2023.

Kennedy-Pipe, 'Caroline and Chris Bellamy. Stalin's Danish Mystery', *History Today*, 5 March 2020.

Keohane, Robert. 'The Demand for International Regimes', 36(2) *International Organization* 325–55, 1982.

Kertysova, Katarina and Akash Ramnath. 'How Permafrost Thaw Puts the Russian Arctic at Risk', IPI Global Observatory, 22 November 2021.

Kessler, Glenn, Salvador Rizzo and Meg Kelly. 'Trump's False or Misleading Claims Total 30,573 over 4 Years', *Washington Post*, 24 January 2021.

Kessler, Sabrina. 'A Secret Services' Darling Goes Public', DW, 30 September 2020.

Kim, Yeon-Hee, Nathan P. Gillett, Dirk Notz and Elizaveta Malinina. 'Observationally-Constrained Projections of an Ice-Free Arctic Even under a Low Emission Scenario', 14 *Nature Communications* 1–8, 2023.

Kjellén, Rudolf. 'Studier ofver Sveriges politiska gränser', 19 *Ymer* 183–331, 1899.

Klein, Margarete. 'Myths and Misconceptions Around Russian Military Intent', Chatham House, 14 July 2022.

Kleinschmidt, Jochen. 'Politische Räume, Grossräume und Weltgesellschaft'. In *Großraum-Denken: Carl Schmitts Kategorie der Großaumordnung* 71–98. Edited by Rüdiger Voigt. Steiner, 2008.

Klimenko, Ekaterina. 'Russia's New Arctic Policy Document Signals Continuity Rather than Change', SIPRI, 6 April 2020.

Knutsen, Jan Normann. 'Norway in the First World War', 5 *Folia Scandinavica Poznan* 43–58, 1999.

Kobzeva, Mariia and Andrey Todorov. 'Can China Change the Arctic Regime?' 59 *Polar Record* 1–10, 2023.

Koivurova, Timo. 'Is this the End of the Arctic Council and Arctic Governance as we Know it?' Polar Connection, 11 December 2019.

Kökerer, Can Mert. 'The Sine Qua Non of Carl Schmitt's Political Thinking: The Issue of Interstate Relations', 47(10) *Philosophy and Social Criticism* 1137–53, 2020.

Konyshev, Valery. 'Arctic Science Diplomacy: With or Without Russia', Geneva Centre for Security Policy 1–14, 2023.

Koopman, Sara. 'Alter-geopolitics: Other Securities are Happening', 42(3) *Geoforum* 274–84, 2011.

Korobeinikov, Aleksandr. 'Non-Russian Intellectuals of Siberia: Regionalism and the Transformation of the Russian Empire', Peripheral Histories, 1 December 2021.

Koskenniemi, Martti. 'Carl Schmitt and International Law'. In *The Oxford Handbook of Carl Schmitt* 592–611. Edited by Jens Meierhenrich and Oliver Simons. Oxford University Press, 2015.

——. 'Colonization of the "Indies": The Origin of International Law?' In *La idea de América en el pensamiento ius internacionalista del siglo XXI; Estudios a propósito de los bicentenarios de las independencies de las repúblicas latinoamericanas* 43–63. Edited by Y Gamarra Chopo. Institución Fernando el Católico, 2010.
——. 'International Law as Political Theology: How to Read Nomos der Erde?', 11(4) *Constellations* 492–511, 2004.
Kotkin, Stephen. 'The Five Futures of Russia', Foreign Affairs, May/June 2024.
Kovacs, Kit M, Christian Lydersen, Jade Vacquiè-Garcia, Olga Shpak, Dmitry Glazov and Mads Peter Heide-Jørgensen. 'The Endangered Spitsbergen Bowhead Whales' Secrets Revealed After Hundreds of Years in Hiding', 16 *Biology Letters* 1–6, 2020.
Kraikovski, Alexei. 'Profits from Under the Water: The International Blubber Market, Russian Monopolistic Companies and the Idea of Whaling Development in the Eighteenth Century', 31(1) *International Journal of Maritime History* 34–49, 2019.
Krasner, Stephen D. 'Problematic Sovereignty. In Problematic Sovereignty: Contested Rules and Political Possibilities' 10–11. Edited by Stephen D' Krasner. Columbia University Press, 2000.
Kratz, Jessie. 'Mystery of the Arctic Ice: Who Was First to the North Pole', National Archives, 6 April 2022.
Krauthammer, Charles. 'The Unipolar Moment', 70 *Foreign Affairs* 23–33, 1990/1991.
Krawietz, Werner. 'Völkerrechtliche Großraumordnung mit Interventionsverbot für raumfremde Mächte', 34 *Rechtstheorie* 284, 2004.
'Kremlin calls Poland's Decision to Rename Kaliningrad a "Hostile Act"', *The Guardian*, 10 May 2023.
Kristof, Ladis KD. 'The Origins and Evolution of Geopolitics', 4(1) *Journal of Conflict Resolution* 15–51, 1960.
Kroll, Charlotte. 'Reading the Temperature Curve: Sinophone Schmitt-fever in Context and Perspective'. In *Carl Schmitt and Leo Strauss in the Chinese-Speaking World: Reorienting the Political* 103–19. Edited by Kai Marchal and Carl KY Shaw. Lexington Books, 2017.
Kronvall, Olof, Magnus Petersson, Charles Silva and Kjetil Skogrand. 'Comments on Ola Tunander's Article "The Uneasy Imbrication of Nation-State and NATO: The Case of Sweden"', 35(4) *Cooperation and Conflict* 417–29, 2000.
Kuchins, Andrew C. 'Foreword'. In Thomas E Graham, Jr, *Russia's Decline and Uncertain Recovery* vi–vii. Carnegie Endowment for International Peace, 2002.
Kullerud, Lars and Oran R Young. 'Adding a Gakkel Ridge Regime to the Evolving Arctic Ocean Governance Complex', GRID, 26 October 2020.
Lackenbauer, P Whitney and Ryan Dean. 'Arctic Exceptionalism'. In *The Arctic and World Order* 327–56. Edited by Kristina Spohr and Daniel S Hamilton, Jason C Moyer associate editor. Brookings Institution Press, 2020.
Lackenbauer, P Whitney, Adam Lajeunesse and Ryan Dean. 'Why China is not a Peer Competitor in the Arctic', *Journal of Indo-Pacific Affairs*, 3 October 2022.
Lacoste, Yves. 'Geography, Geopolitics, and Geographical Reasoning', 146–47(3–4) *Hérodote* 14–44, 2012.
Lai, Fu. 'Growling Back at the West', China Media Project, 8 August 2021.
Lakhtine, W. 'Rights over the Arctic', 24(4) *American Journal of International Law* 703–17, 1930.
Lalonde, Suzanne. 'The U.S.-Canada Northwest Passage Disagreement: Why Agreeing to Disagree Is More Important Than Ever'. In *The Arctic and World Order* 267–94. Edited by Kristina Spohr and Daniel S. Hamilton, Jason C Moyer associate editor. Brookings Institution Press, 2020.
Lambach, Daniel. 'Space, Scale, and Global Politics: Towards a Critical Approach to Space in International Relations', 48(2) *Review of International Studies* 282–300, 2022.
Landauer, Carl. 'Regionalism, Geography, and the International Legal Imagination', 11(2) *Chicago Journal of International Law* 557–95, 2011.
Langlet, Arne and Alice BM Vadrot, 'Not "Undermining" Who? Unpacking the Emerging BBNJ Regime Complex', 147 Marine Policy 105372 [1–10], 2023.

Lansing, Robert. 'A Unique International Problem', 11(4) *American Journal of International Law*, 763–71, 1917.

Lanteigne, Marc. 'The Rise (and Fall?) of the Polar Silk Road,' The Diplomat, 29 August 2022.

Lasserre, Frédéric. 'The Geopolitics of the Northwest Passage in an International Relations Perspective', 170(2) *Relations internationals* 107–24, 2017.

Last, John. 'Future of Arctic Council in Doubt After End of Russian Chairship', CBC News. 11 May 2023.

Laurell, Marlene. 'Alexander Dugin and Eurasianism'. In *Key Thinkers of the Radical Right* 155–69. Edited by Mark Sedgwick. Oxford University Press, 2019.

——. 'When Eurasia Looks East: Is Eurasianism Sinophile or Sinophobe?' In *The Politics of Eurasianism: Identity, Popular Culture and Russia's Foreign Policy* 145–60. Edited by Mark Bassin and Gonzalo Pozo. Rowman and Littlefield International Ltd, 2017.

Lauterpacht, Hersch. 'The Grotian Tradition in International Law', 23 *British Year Book of International Law* 1–53 1946.

Lebel, Julien and Annika E Nilsson. 'EU Engagement in the Arctic: Challenges to Achieving Ambitions in an Area Outside Its Jurisdiction', 15 *Arctic Review of Law and Politics* 47–71, 2024.

LeFeber, Walter. 'Jefferson and an American Foreign Policy'. In *Jeffersonian Legacies* 370–91. Edited by Peter S Onuf. University of Virginia Press, 1993.

Leffler, Melvyn P. 'Adherence to Agreements: Yalta and the Experiences of the Early Cold War', 11(1) *International Security* 88–123, 1986.

Lehto, Essi and Andrius Sytas. 'Finland Boards Oil Tanker Suspected of Causing Internet, Power Cable Outages', Reuters, 26 December 2024.

Lempinen, Hanna and Marjo Lindroth. 'Fear and Hoping in the Arctic: Charting the Emotional Fabric of Resource Extraction', 8(2) *Extractive Industries and Society* 100872 [1–7], 2021.

Thomas Jefferson to George Rogers Clark, 25 December 1780. In *4 Papers of Thomas Jefferson: October 1780 to February 1781*, 237–38. Edited by Julian P Boyd, associated editors Lyman H Butterfield and Mina R Bryan. Princeton University Press, 1950.

Li, Xueke and Amanda H Lynch. 'New Insights into Projected Arctic Sea Road: Operational Risks, Economic Values, and Policy Implications', 176(30) *Climate Change* 1–16, 2023.

Lind, Jennifer. 'Back to Bipolarity: How China's Rise Transformed the Balance of Power', 49(2) *International Security* 7–55, 2024.

Linnainmäki, Joel. 'An Alliance of Strategic Divergencies: Contextualizing Northern Europe and Finland in Nato Decision-making'. In *NATO's New Northern Direction: The Evolving Role of the Alliance* 18–30. Edited by Matti Pesu. Finnish Foreign Policy Paper 11, 2024.

Lipin, Michael. 'China Begins to Revive Arctic Scientific Ground Projects After Setbacks', VOA, 5 December 2022.

Lipunov, Nikita and Pavel Devyatkin. 'The Arctic in the 2023 Russian Foreign Policy Concept', Arctic Institute, 30 May 2023.

Lisaerde, Margaux. 'Scandinavian Universities to Suspend Ties with Russia', ResearchProfessional News, 7 March 2022.

Liu, Nengye and Qi Xu. 'The Predicates of Chinese Legal Philosophy in the Polar Regions'. In *Philosophies of Polar Law* 131–55. Edited by Dawid Bunikowski and Alan D Hemmings. Routledge, 2021.

Liu, Nengye and Jan Jakub Solski. 'The Polar Silk Road and the Future Governance of the Northern Sea Route', 35 *Leiden Journal of International Law* 853–66, 2022.

Liu, Nengye and Kamrul Hossain. 'China and The Development of International Law on Arctic Shipping'. In *Arctic Law and Governance: The Role of China, Finland and the EU* 233–52. Edited by Timo Koivurova, Tianbao Qin, Sébastien Duyck and Tapio Nykänen. Bloomsbury Publishers, 2017.

Liu, Niwen, Megat Al Imran Yasin, Syed Agil Alsagoff, Chwee Fang Ng and Mengyu Li. 'A Community of Shared Future for Mankind: A Study on the News Discourse of Environmental Cooperation in Countries along the Belt and Road Initiative', Plos One, 23 October 2023.

Liu, Xiaofeng. 'New China and the End of American "International Law"', 3(3) *American Affairs Journal*, 2019.
Llanque, Marcus and Herfried Münkler. 'Vorwort von 1963'. In *Carl Schmitt: Der Begriff des Politischen: Ein Kooperativer Kommentar* 9–20. Edited by Reinhard Mehring. Akademie Verlag, 2003.
Lo, Bobo and Fiona Hill. 'Putin's Pivot: Why Russia is Looking East', Brookings, 31 July 2013.
Longden, Alex. 'Were Bad Weather Conditions to Blame for the Grounding of the Ever Given?' Meteorological Technology International, 6 April 2021.
Lösch, August. 'The Nature of Economic Regions', 5(1) *Southern Economic Journal* 71–78, 1938.
Lott, Alexander. 'The Baltic Sea Cable-Cuts and Ship Interdiction: The C-Lion1 Incident, Articles of War', Lieber Institute, West Point, 26 November 2024.
Luce, Henry. 'The American Century', *Life Magazine*, 17 February 1941.
Lustig, Sandra H. 'Translator's Preface'. In Hubertus Buchstein, *Enduring Enmity: The Story of Otto Kirchheimer and Carl Schmitt* 15–23. Translated by Sandra H Lustig. Verlag, Bielefeld, 2024.
Mackenzie, Lucia, with Joshua Posaner, Hanne Cokelaere and Giovanna Coi. 'What Sweden Brings to NATO', Politico, 7 March 2024.
Mackinder, HJ. 'The Geographical Pivot of History', 23(4) *Geographical Journal* 421–37, 1904.
Maddox, Marisol and Lyston Lea. 'The Intelligence Community Must Evolve to Meet the Reality of Arctic Change', 13 *Polar Perspectives* 2023.
Madison, James. The Federalist Papers: No 10, 23 November 1787.
——. The Federalist Papers: No. 14, 30 November 1787.
Marantidou, Virginia. 'Revisiting China's "String of Pearls" Strategy: Places "with Chinese Characteristics" and their Security Implications', 14(7) *Pacific Forum, Center for Strategic and International Studies (CSIS)* 1–39, 2014.
Marcus, Lilit. 'First Cross-River Railway Bridge between China and Russia Completed', CNN, 20 August 2021.
Martinez, Luis R, Jonas Jessen and Guo Xu. 'A Glimpse of Freedom: Allied Occupation and Political Resistance in East Germany', IZA Institute of Labor Economics 1–67, 2020.
Martinussen, Birgitte Annie Molid. 'Researcher: "New Svalbard White Paper Affirms Norwegian Jurisdiction on Svalbard"', High North News, 20 June 2024.
Martynova, Marina. 'EU, Russia and China Arctic Strategies: Comparative Analysis', 45th International Scientific Conference on Economic and Social Development 773–78, 2019.
Massey, Doreen. "Questions of Locality', 78 *Geography* 142–49, 1993.
Masters, Jonathan. 'The Thawing Arctic: Risks and Opportunities', Council on Foreign Relations, 17 December 2013.
Mattingly, Garrett. 'No Peace Beyond What Line?' 13 *Transactions of the Royal Historical Society* 145–62, 1963.
McCann, Conor. 'Moscow is Betting Big on its Arctic Shipping Route as the Costs of Invading Ukraine Continue to Mount', Australian Broadcasting Company, 10 March 2023.
McCormick, John P. 'Carl Schmitt's Europe: Cultural, Imperial and Spatial, Proposals for European Integration, 1923–1955'. In *Darker Legacies of Law in Europe: The Shadow of National Socialism and Fascism over Europe and Its Legal Traditions* 133–141. Edited by Christian Joerges and Navraj Singh Ghaleigh. Prologue by Michael Stolleis, epilogue by JHH Weiler. Bloomsbury, 2003.
McDonald, Matt. 'Securitization and the Construction of Security', 14(4) *European Journal of International Relations* 563–87, 2008.
'Medvedev Made a "Bold" Proposal to the West: A Map of the Division of Ukraine is Shown', MKRU, 5 March 2024.
Megoran, Nick. 'For Ethnography in Political Geography: Experiencing and Re-Imagining Ferghana Valley Boundary Closures', 25(6) *Political Geography* 622–40. 2006.
Menning, Bruce W. 'Neither Mahan nor Moltke: Strategy in the War'. In *The Russo-Japanese War in Global Perspective: World War Zero* 129–56. Edited by John W Steinberg, Bruce W Menning, David Schimmelpenninck van der Oye, David Wolff and Shinji Yokote, 2005.

Mersheimer, John J. 'Why the Ukraine Crisis Is the West's Fault: The Liberal Delusions That Provoked Putin', 93(5) *Foreign Affairs* 77–84, 2014.
Miller, Steven E. 'The Return of the Strategic Arctic', Arctic Yearbook 2022, 1–8 (2023).
Milne, Richard. 'US Provokes Fury After Blocking Arctic Council Statement', *Financial Times*, 7 May 2019.
Milne, Richard and Max Seddon. 'Sweden Joins "NATO Lake" on Moscow's Doorstep', *Financial Times*, 7 March 2024.
'Minister of Foreign Affairs: In 2022, Latvia is Preparing to Apply for the Role of an Observer in the Arctic Council', Ministry of Foreign Affairs of Latvia, 11 November 2021.
Mitchell, Ryan Martinez. 'Chinese Receptions of Carl Schmitt Since 1929', 8(1) *Penn State Journal of Law and International Affairs* 181–263, 2020.
Mitrova, Tatiana. 'Preliminary Outlines of the New Russian Gas Export Strategy, Center on Global Energy Policy/SIPA', 20 November 2023.
Molenaar, Erik J. 'Participation in the Central Arctic Ocean Fisheries Agreement'. In *Emerging Legal Orders in the Arctic: The Role of Non-Arctic Actors* 132–70. Edited by Akiho Shibata, Leilei Zou, Nikolas Sellheim and Marzia Scopelliti. Routledge, 2019.
Molin, Karl. 'Winning the Peace: Vision and Disappointment in Nordic Security Policy, 1945-1949'. In *Scandinavia During the Second World War* 324–382. Edited by Henrik S Nissen, Thomas Munch-Petersen translation. Universitetsforlaget, University of Minnesota Press, 1983.
Montecalvo, Isabella, Philippe Le Billon, Chris Arsenault and Milko Schvartzman. 'Ocean Predators: Squids, Chinese Fleets and the Geopolitics of High Seas Fishing', 152 *Marine Policy* 105584 [1–11], 2023.
Moon, Woosok, Baek-Min Kim, Gun-Hwan Yang and John S Wettlaufer. 'Wavier Jet Streams Driven by Zonally Asymmetric Surface Thermal Forcing', 119 *PNAS* e2200890119, 2022.
Moore, David Chioni. 'Colonialism, Eurasianism, Orientalism: N.S. Trubetzkoy's Russian Vision', 41(2) *Slavic and East European Journal* 321–40, 1997.
Mouffe, Chantal. 'Schmitt's Vision of a Multipolar World Order', 104(2) *South Atlantic Quarterly* 245–51, 2020.
Mounk, Yascha. 'After Trump, Is American Democracy Doomed by Populism?' Council on Foreign Relations, 14 January 2021.
Mouritzen, Hans. 'Security Communities in the Baltic Sea Region: Real and Imagined', 32(3) *Security Dialogue* 297–98, 2001.
Muhammad, Ali and Sugeng Riyanto. 'International Security Studies: Origins, Development and Contending Approaches', 10(20) *Austral: Brazilian Journal of Strategy and International Relations* 230–49, 2021.
Murphy, Tara. 'Security Challenges in the 21st Century Global Commons', 5(2) *Yale Journal of International Affairs* 28–43, 2010.
Myers, Lucas. 'China's Economic Security Challenge: Difficulties Overcoming the Malacca Dilemma', *Georgetown Journal of International Affairs*, 22 March 2023.
Nail, Thomas. 'Forum 1: Migrant Climate in the Kinocene', 14(3) *Mobilities* 375–80, 2019.
——. 'The Climate Industrial Complex'. The Philosophy of Movement, November 2019.
Nathan, Andrew J. 'What Exactly Is America's China Policy?' Foreign Policy, 14 April 2022.
Naval Gun Battery Vara, Battlefieldsww2.com [no date].
Nefedova, TG, AI Treivish and AV Sheludkov. 'Spatially Uneven Development in Russia', 12(1) *Regional Research of Russia* 4–19, 2022.
Nepal, Santosh and Arun Bhakta Shrestha. 'Impact of Climate Change on the Hydrological Regime of the Indus, Ganges and Brahmaputra River Basins: A Review of the Literature', 31(2) *International Journal of Water Resources Development* 201–18, 2015.
Netzloff, Mark. 'Lines of Amity: The Law of Nations in the Americas'. In *Cultures of Diplomacy and Literary Writing in the Early Modern World* 54–68. Edited by Tracey A Sowerby and Joanna Craigwood. Oxford University Press, 2019.

Nilsen, Thomas. 'Bishop Iyakov, Who Backs Putin's War, Raised Giant Cross at Svalbard Without Norway's Knowledge', Barents Observer, 12 August 2023.
——. 'Lapland Regional Council Rejects Arctic Railway', Barents Observer, 17 May 2021.
——. 'Moscow Continues to Push for BRICS Science Centre at Svalbard', Barents Observer, 15 June 2024.
——. 'Norway Aims to Upset the Apple Cart of Russia's Plans for Education Centre at Svalbard', Barents Observer, 1 June 2024.
——. 'Russia Announces Multiple Missiles Towards Bear Gap as US Air Force Bombers Deploy to Norway for First Time', Barents 'Observer, 17 February 2021.
——. 'Russia Threatens to Withdraw from Fishery Deal with Norway. Little to Worry about, Says Expert', Barents Observer, 27 October 2023.
——. 'Russian Officials Raised Navy Flags in Svalbard Waters', Barents Observer, 15 October 2022.
Nguyen, Lan Ngoc. 'Principled Challenges: Between Collective Interest and Individual Freedom'. In *International Law and Marine Areas Beyond National Jurisdiction: Reflections on Justice, Space, Knowledge and Power* 114–47. Edited by Vito De Lucia, Alex Oude Elferink and Lan Ngoc Nguyen. Brill, 2022.
Northam, Jackie. 'In a Remote Arctic Outpost, Norway Keeps Watch on Russia's Military Buildup', NPR, 3 November 2019.
'Norway in Arctic Dispute with Russia over Rogozin Visit', BBC News, 20 April 2015.
'Norway Blocks Sale of Last Private Land on Svalbard after Chinese Interest', *The Guardian*, 1 July 2024,
"'Not Looking to Sanction India, Our Relations are Most Consequential': U.S.", *The Hindu*, 9 February 2023.
Nyman, Elizabeth, Cassia Bomer Galvao, Joan Mileski and Rachel Tiller. 'The Svalbard Archipelago: An Exploratory Analysis of Port Investment in the Context of the New Arctic Routes', 19 *Maritime Studies* 1–13, 2020.
Ó Tuathail, Gearóid. 'Present at the (Dis)integration: Deterritorialization and Reterritorialization in the New Wor(l)d Order', 84(3) *Annals of the Association of American Geographers* 381–98, 1994.
Ó Tuathail, Gearóid and Simon Dalby. 'Introduction: Rethinking Geopolitics: Towards a Critical Geopolitics'. In *Rethinking Geopolitics* 1–16. Edited by Gearóid Ó Tuathail and Simon Dalby. Routledge, 1998.
Obregón, Liliana. 'Between Civilization and Barbarism: Creole Interventions in International Law', 27(5) *Third World Quarterly* 815–32, 2006.
'Ocean Governance: Who Owns the Ocean', Heinrich Böll Stiftung, 2 June 2017.
Olesen, Jens E. 'The Struggle for Supremacy in the Baltic between Denmark and Sweden, 1563–1721'. In *The Cambridge History of Scandinavia*, Vol II, 1520–1870, 246–267. Edited by EI Kouri and Jens E Olesen. Cambridge University Press, 2016.
Oliphant, Craig. 'Russia's Role and Interests in Central Asia', Saferworld 1–13, 2013.
Olsvig, Sara and Miriam Cullen. 'Arctic Indigenous Peoples and International Law', 93 *Nordic Journal of International Law* 152–69, 2024.
Onuf, Nicholas. 'Relative Strangers: Reflections on Hospitality, Social Distance and Diplomacy'. In *Hospitality and World Politics* 173–96. Edited by G Baker. Springer, 2013.
——. 'Friendship and Hospitality: Some Conceptual Preliminaries', 5(1) *Journal of International Political Theory* 1–21, 2009.
——. 'Levels', 1(1) *European Journal of International Relations* 35–58, 1995.
Orford, Anne. 'Regional Orders, Geopolitics, and the Future of International Law', 74(1) *Current Legal Problems* 149–94, 2021.
O'Rourke, Ronald. 'Coast Guard Polar Security Cutter (Polar Icebreaker) Program: Background and Issues for Congress', Congressional Research Service 1–76, 2020.
Orsi, Roberto. 'On the Relevance of Carl Schmitt's Concept of Großraum in Contemporary International Relations'. 17(3) *Journal of International Political Theory* 295–315, 2019.

Orsini, Amandine, Amandine, Jean-Frédéric Morin and Oran Young. 'Regime complexes: A Buzz, a Boom, or a Boost for Global Governance?' 19(1) *Global Governance* 27–39, 2013.

Østhagen, Andreas. 'The New Geopolitics of the Arctic: Russia, China and the EU', 18(2) *European View* 259, 2019.

——. 'Analysis: How Norway and Russia Avoid Conflict Over Svalbard', High North News, 22 June 2018.

——. 'Managing Conflict at Sea: The Case of Norway and Russia in the Svalbard Zone', 9 *Arctic Review of Law and Politics* 100–23, 2018.

Østhagen, Andreas and P Whitney Lackenbauer. 'Security Dynamics In, Through, and Over the Arctic "Region"'. In *Towards a Sustainable Arctic: International Security, Climate Change and Green Shipping* 1–24. Edited by Michael Goodsite and Niklas Swanström. World Scientific Publishing Company, 2023.

Østhagen, Andreas and Svein Vigeland Rottem. 'Geopolitics and Increased Tension? Differentiating between Political Dynamics in the Arctic'. In *Norway's Arctic Policy: Geopolitics, Security and Identity in the High North* 23–37. Edited by Andreas Østhagen. Edgar Elgar Publishing, 2023.

Overfield, Cornell G. 'FONOP in Vain: The Legal Logics of a U.S. Navy FONOP in the Canadia or Russian Arctic', Arctic Yearbook, 1–18, 2021.

Oxman, Bernard H. 'The Territorial Temptation: A Siren Song at Sea', 100(4) *American Journal of International Law* 830–51, 2006.

Paglia, Eric. 'Not a Proper Crisis', 2(3) *Anthropocene Review* 247–61, 2015.

——. 'The Northward Course of the Anthropocene: Transformation, Temporality and Telecoupling in a Time of Environmental Crisis' 19 (doctoral dissertation (CRISMART), Swedish Defence University, 2016.

Pakhalyuk, Konstantin. 'When Did the First World War End for Russia? Marking the Centenary of the Treaty of Brest-Litovsk', Russian International Affairs Council, 5 March 2018.

Paleja, Ameya. 'China to Build Icebreaker with Submersible to Reach Arctic Seabed', Interesting Engineering, 28 June 2023.

Papanicolopulu, Irini. 'The Land Dominates the Sea (Dominates the Land Dominates the Sea)', 47 *Questions of International Law* 39–48, 2018.

Park, Young Kil. 'South Korea's Interests in the Arctic', 18 *Asia Policy* 59–65, 2014.

Paszak, Paweł. 'China and the "Malacca Dilemma"', Warsaw Institute, 28 February 2021.

Paul, Michael. 'Arctic Repercussions of Russia's Invasion', Stiftung Wissenschaft und Politik, 10 June 2022.

Paul, Michael and Göran Swistek. 'Russia in the Arctic: Development Plans, Military Potential, and Conflict Prevention', Stiftung Wissenschaft und Politik Research Paper 3, February 2022.

Pawlak, Julian. 'No, Don't Call the Baltic a "NATO Lake"', RUSI, 5 September 2022.

Pearcy, G Etzel and Lewis M Alexander. 'Pattern of Air Service Availability in the Eastern Hemisphere', 29(1) *Economic Geography* 74–78, 1953.

Pedersen, Torbjørn. 'The Politics of Presence: The Longyearbyen Dilemma', 8 *Arctic Review of Law and Politics* 95–108, 2017.

Pedersen, Torbjørn and Beate Steinveg. 'Russia's Clashing Ambitions: Arctic Status Quo and World-Order Revision', 12 *Politics and Governance* 1–12, 2024.

Pedersen, Torbjørn and Odd Gunnar Skagestad. 'Norway's Flawed Nordområdene Policy'. In *Norway's Arctic Policy: Geopolitics, Security and Identity in the High North* 55–63. Edited by Andreas Østhagen. Edgar Elgar Publishing, 2023.

Peet, Elizabeth. 'The Rise of Siberian Nationalism', Wilson Quarterly, 1 July 2015.

Peimani, Hooman. 'Melting of the Arctic Sea Ice: Significance for the APEC Economies' Energy Security'. APEC Oil and Gas Security Studies, Series 6, November 2015.

Perdue, Peter C. 'Boundaries and Trade in the Early Modern World: Negotiations at Nerchinsk and Beijing', 43(3) *Eighteenth-Century Studies* 341–56, 2010.

Pesu, Matti. 'NATO in the North: The Emerging Division of Labour in Northern European Security', Finnish Institute of International Affairs Briefing Paper 370, 1–8, 2023.

Petelin, German. 'The Captain of Sapphire-2 Was Left Without Documents', IZ, 11 October 2011.

'Peter the Great: How did England help Russia to Establish its Navy in the Early 18th Century?' Royal Museums Greenwich, www.rmg.co.uk/stories/topics/peter-great [no date].

Petsko, Emily. 'Why Does So Much of the Ocean Remain Unexplored and Unprotected?' Oceana, 8 June 2020.

Pettersen, Trude. 'Russia Wants to Discuss Svalbard Fisheries Protection Zone', Barents Observer, 6 October 2011.

Philippopoulos-Mihalopoulos, Andreas. 'Spatial Justice in a World of Violence'. In *Spaces of Justice, Peripheries, Passages, Appropriations* 21–36. Edited by Chris Butler and Edward Mussawir. Routledge, 2017.

Pincus, Rebecca. 'Points of Clarity: US-Russian Arctic Identities', Wilson Center, 29 January 2024.

——. 'The Indo-Pacific Dimension in US Arctic Strategy'. *Journal of Indo-Pacific Affairs*, 25 October 2021.

Ploecki, Florian. 'A Novel Institution: The Zollverein and the Origins of the Customs Union'. University of Adelaide Discussion Paper No 2019-05 (November 2019).

Plummer, Michael G. 'Johns Hopkins SAIS Faculty and Fellow Reflections: The War in Ukraine at One Year', SAIS Review, 2023.

Pompeo, Michael R. 'Looking North: Sharpening America's Arctic Focus', US Department of State, 6 May 2019.

Posaner, Joshua, Laura Kayali, Julius Brinkmann and Oliver Noyan. 'Europe Splits on Trump's Call to Dramatically Boost Defense Spending', Politico, 8 January 2025.

Posner, Eric A and Adrian Vermeule. 'Demystifying Schmitt'. In *The Oxford Handbook of Carl Schmitt* 612–26. Edited by Jens Meierhenrich and Oliver Simons. Oxford University Press, 2015.

Potz, Richard. 'Cuius regio, eius religio'. In *Encyclopedia of Early Modern History Online*. Edited by Graeme Dunphy and Andrew Gow. Brill, 2015.

Pounds, Norman JG. 'The Origin of the Idea of Natural Frontiers in France', 41(2) *Annals of the Association of American Geographers* 146–57, 1951.

Powell, Richard C and Klaus Dodds. 'Polar Geopolitics'. In *Polar Geopolitics? Knowledges, Resources and Legal Regimes* 3–19. Edited by Richard C Powell and Klaus Dodds. Edward Elgar Publishing, 2014.

Poynting, Mark. 'World's First Year-Long Breach of Key 1.5C Warming Limit', BBC, 8 February 2024.

'President-elect Trump on Greenland and Panama Canal', C-SPAN, 7 January 2025.

'President Trump Eyes a New Real-Estate Purchase: Greenland', *Wall Street Journal*, 16 August 2019.

Pruyn, Jeroen FJ. 'Will the Northern Sea Route Ever Be a Viable Alternative?' 43(6) *Maritime Policy and Management* 661–75, 2016.

Pu, Wei. 'How the Eleven-Dash Line Became a Nine-Dash Line, and Other Stories', Radio Free Asia, 16 July 2015.

'Putin Signs Decree to Transform Northern Fleet into Military District', Tass, 21 December 2020.

'Putin Urges to Preserve Arctic as Territory of Dialogue', Tass, 30 March 2017.

Putin, Vladimir. 'On the Historical Unity of Russians and Ukrainians', President of Russia, 12 July 2021.

Putnam, Robert D. 'Diplomacy and Domestic Politics: The Logic of Two-Level Games', 42(3) *International Organization* 427–460, 1988.

Qin, Tianbao. 'Dispute Over the Applicable Scope of the Svalbard Treaty: A Chinese Lawyer's Perspective', 8 *Journal of East Asia and International Law* 149–70, 2015.

Quinn, Eilís. 'Arctic Council Charting Way Forward to Resume Work Says Norwegian SAO', Barents Observer, 6 September 2023.

Roach, J. Ashley. 'Freedom of the Seas in the Arctic Region'. In *The Arctic and World Order* 219–50. Edited by Kristina Spohr and Daniel S Hamilton, Jason C Moyer associate editor. Brookings Institution Press, 2020.

Robic, M-C. 'Friedrich Ratzel, géographie et sciences sociales en France (1890–1918)–Centralité et distanciations', 78(1) *Geographica Helvetica* 157–67, 2023.

Rocha Martins, António. 'The Zoon Politikon: Medieval Aristotelian Interpretations', 75(3) *Revista Portuguesa de Filosofia* 1539–74, 2019.

Rossi, Christopher R. 'A Case Ill Suited for Judgment: Constructing "A Sovereign Access to the Sea" in the Atacama Desert', 48(2) *University of Miami Inter-American Law Review* 28–86, 2017.

——. 'A Particular Kind of Dominium: The Grotian Tendency and the Global Commons in a Time of High Arctic Change', 11(1) *Journal International Law and International Relations*. 1–60, 2015.

——. '"A Unique International Problem": The Svalbard Treaty, Equal Enjoyment, and Terra Nullius: Lessons of Territorial Temptation from History', 15(1) *Washington University Global Studies Law Review* 93–136, 2016.

——. 'Arctic Anadromy and Congested Regime Governance', 52 *Environmental Law Reporter* 10193–210, 2022.

——. 'Hauntings, Hegemony, and the Threatened African Exodus from the International Criminal Court', 40(2) 369–405, 2018.

——. 'Interstitial Space and the High Himalayan Dispute between China and India', 62 *Harvard International Law Journal* 429–68, 2021.

——. 'Russian Arctic Straits and the Temptation of Uti Possidetis', 24(1) *Transnational Law and Contemporary Problems* 19–68, 2014.

——. 'The Blind Eye: Jus Soli, and the "Pretended" Treaty of New Echota', 9(2) *American Indian Law Journal* 402–33, 2021.

——. 'The Club within the Club: The Challenge of a Soft Law Framework in a Global Arctic Context', 5(1) *Polar Journal* 8–34, 2015.

——. 'The Extravagant Pretension: Schmitt,Vitoria, the Discovery Doctrine, and the Trail of Tears'. In *Francisco de Vitoria and the Shadow of Carl Schmitt in International Law: Crossroads in History and Political Theology*. Edited by José María Beneyto and Ignacio de la Rasilla. Brill/Nijhoff, forthcoming.

——. 'The Gulf of Fonseca and International Law: Condominium or Anti-Colonial Imperialism?' 3(1) *Jus Gentium: Journal of International Legal History* 115–53, 2018.

——. 'The Nomos of Climate Change and the Sociological Refugee in a Sinking Century', 50(3) *George Washington University International Law Review* 613–52, 2018.

——. 'The Rotating Wheel: A New Cycle of Pacific Relations in the Emerging Arctic and the Role of the Middle Powers'. In *The GlobalArctic: The New Dynamics of Arctic Governance* __–__. Edited by Gunnar Rekvig and Matthias Finger. Palgrave Macmillan, 2025.

——. 'The Widening Gyre: Legal Formalism and International Law's Sense of Place', 11(1) *Notre Dame Journal International and Comparative Law* 107–37, 2021.

——. 'Treaty of Tordesillas Syndrome: Sovereignty ad Absurdum and the South China Sea Arbitration', 50(2) *Cornell International Law Journal* 231–83, 2017.

Rottem, Svein Vigeland. 'The Arctic Council in Danger', High North News, 28 March 2023.

Rowe, Elana Wilson. 'Analyzing Frenemies: An Arctic Repertoire of Cooperation and Rivalry', 76 *Political Geography* 102072 [1–10], 2020.

Roy, Diana. 'China's Growing Influence in Latin America', Council on Foreign Relations, 15 June 2023.

Rudels, Bert and Edy Carmack. 'Arctic Ocean Water Mass Structure and Circulation', 35(3–4) *Oceanography* 52–65, 2022.

Rudolf, Peter. 'The Sino-American World Conflict', Stiftung Wissenschaft und Politik, 2020.

Ruggie, John. 'International Regimes, Transactions, and Change: Embedded Liberalism in the Post-war Economic Order', 36(2) *International Organization* 379–415, 1983.

Rumer, Eugene, Richard Sokolsky and Paul Stronski. 'Russia in the Arctic – A Critical Examination', Carnegie Endowment for International Peace 1–23, 2021.

Russell, Emily. 'US, Russia Agree on Shipping Standards for Bering Strait', Alaska Public Media, 6 June 2018.

'Russia is Considering Withdrawing from the UN Convention on the Law of the Sea in the Arctic', IZ, 18 March 2024.

'Russia Pushes Northern Sea Route As "Alternative" to Suez Canal', NDTV, 26 March 2021.

'Russia Tightens Control over Northern Sea Route', The Maritime Executive, 8 Marh 2019.

'Russia to Engage BRICS, SCO Partners in Arctic Projects – Foreign Ministry', Tass, 14 May 2023.

'Russia to Quit Arctic Council in Case of West's Destructive Behavior – Diplomat', Tass, 14 May 2023.

'Russian Security and the Effects of NATO Enlargement in the Arctic', Polar Geopolitics with Eric Paglia, 6 October 2023.

'Russisk statsborger evakuert fra fartøy nær Nordpolen', NRK, 7 June 2023. www.nrk.no/tromsog-finnmark/russisk-statsborger-evakuert-fra-fartoy-1.16436054.

Sacks, Benjamin J, Marigold Black and Peter Dortmans. 'Arctic Governance Is In Trouble. The Antarctic Could Be Next'. RandBlog, 7 December 2022.

'Sailing Through the Ice'. Arctic Russia, 16 March 2022, arctic-russia.ru/en/article/sailing-through-the-ice.

Sakwa, Richard. 'The Age of Eurasia? In The Politics of Eurasianism: Identity, Popular Culture and Russia's Foreign Policy' 201–220. Edited by Mark Bassin and Gonzalo Pozo. Rowman and Littlefield International Ltd, 2017.

Saldžiūnas, Vaidas. 'Kaliningrad: A Useless Sliver of Russia or the Cause of a New Fulda Gap?' International Center for Defence and Security, 12 February 2016.

Sarnowsky, Jürgen. 'The "Golden Age" of the Hanseatic League'. In *A Companion to the Hanseatic League* 64–100. Edited by Donald J Harreld. Brill, 2015.

Savitsky, Peter [Petr] Nikolaevich. 'Eurasia Middle Earth'. In *Foundations of Geopolitics* 71–80. Edited by Aleksandr Dugin, Lawless translation. Arktogeja, 1997.

——. 'The Geographical and Geopolitical Foundation of Eurasianism', Eurasianist-Archive.com. Edited by Jafe Arnold, John Stachelski translation. 2016.

Schlögel, Karl. 'Raum und Raumbewältigung als Probleme der russischen Geschichte, Zur Einführung'. In *Mastering Russian Spaces: Raum und Raumbewältigung als Probleme der russischen Geschichte* 1–27. Edited by Karl Schlögel. De Gruyter Oldenbourg, 2011.

Schreiber, Melody. 'A U.S. Coast Guard Ship Unexpectedly Encountered Chinese and Russian Warships Off Alaska', *Arctic Business Journal*, 26 September 2022.

Shackelford, Scott J. 'Was Selden Right? The Expansion of Closed Seas and its Consequences', 47(1) *Stanford Journal of International Law* 1–50, 2011.

Sharma, Kiran. 'India's Russian Imports Soar 400% as US Offers Little Resistance', NikkeiAsia, 17 February 2023.

Shen, Shiwei. 'Greenland FM Aims to Strengthen Cooperation with China on Week-Long Visit', CGTN, 25 October 2023.

Simmons, Beth A and Hein E Goemans. 'Built on Borders: Tensions with the Institution Liberalism (Thought It) Left Behind', 75 *International Organization* 387–410, 2021.

Simpson, Brett. 'Scandinavia Is Preparing for War', Foreign Policy, 9 February 2024.

Singer, J David. 'The Level-of-Analysis Problem in International Relations', 14(1) *World Politics* 77–92, 1961.

Singleton, Tom. 'Stay Ahead in AI Race, Tech Boss Urges West', BBC News, 8 June 2023.

Sipes, Katie, Raegan Paul, Aubrey Fine, Peibo Li, Renxing Liang, Julia Boike, Tullis C Onstott Tatiana A Vishnivetskaya, Sean Schaeffer and Karen G Loyd. 'Permafrost Active Layer Microbes from Ny Ålesund, Svalbard (79°N) Show Autotrophic and Heterotrophic Metabolisms with Diverse Carbon-Degrading Enzymes', 12 *Frontiers in Microbiology* 1–14 2022.

Schmitt, Carl. '*Großraum* versus Universalism: The International Legal Struggle over the Monroe Doctrine' ['Großraum gegen Universalismus: der völkerrechtliche Kampf um die Monroedoktrin']. In *Spatiality, Sovereignty and Carl Schmitt: Geographies of the Nomos* 46–54. Edited by Stephen Legg, Matthew Hanna translation. Routledge, 2011 [1939]).

——. 'The *Großraum* Order of International Law with a Ban on Intervention for Spatially Foreign Powers: A Contribution to the Concept of Reich in International Law' (1939–1941). In *Carl Schmitt: Writings on War*. Edited and translated by Timothy Nunan, 75–125. Polity, 2011.

——. 'The Turn to the Discriminating Concept of War' (1937). In *Carl Schmitt: Writings on War*. Edited and translated by Timothy Nunan, 30–74. Polity, 2011.

Schulman, Alex. 'Carl Schmitt and the Clash of Civilizations: The Missing Context', 17(2) *Journal of Political Ideologies* 147–67, 2012.

Sharapova, Anna, Sara Seck, Sarah MacLeod and Olga Koubrak. 'Indigenous Rights and Interests in a Changing Arctic Ocean', 13 *Arctic Review of Law and Politics* 286–311, 2022.

Shevtsov, Viacheslav, Iraida Nam and Elena Khakhalkina. 'Siberian Identity in the Historical Perspective and at Present', 28 SHS Web of Conferences 01092 [1–4], 2016.

Simpson, Brett. 'The Rise and Sudden Fall of the Arctic Council', Foreign Policy, 31 May 2023.

Skordas, Achilles. 'Russia's Eurasian *Großraum* and its Consequences', Verfassungsblog, 31 March 2022.

Sliwa, Zdzislaw, Hans Helseth and Viljar Veeble. 'The Baltic Sea Islands and their Impact on the Regional Security', Centrum Balticum, BSR Policy Briefing Series 1–14, 2022.

Smith, Stacey Vanek. 'She Had a Dream Job. Now, She's Part of a Massive Brain Drain Hammering Russia', NPR, 31 May 2023.

Smith, Timothy William James. 'Search and Rescue in the Arctic: Is the U.S. Prepared?' PhD dissertation, Pardee RAND Graduate School, 2017.

Snoeijs-Leijonmalm, Pauline, Hauke Flores, Serdar Sakinan, Nicole Hildebrandt, Anders Svenson, Giulia Castellani, Kim Vane, Felix C Mark, Céline Heuzé and the EFICA-Mosaic Team. 'Unexpected Fish and Squid in the Central Arctic Deep Scattering Layer', 8(7) *Science Advances* [1–17], 2022.

Solski, Jan Jakub. 'The Northern Sear Route in the 2010s: Development and Implementation of Relevant Law', 11 *Arctic Review of Law and Politics* 383–410, 2020.

Sorokina, Sorokina. 'Who Are the Pomors and How Did They Create the Civilization of the Russian North?' Russia Beyond, 17 November 2022.

Spohr, Kristina and Daniel S Hamilton. 'From Last Frontier to First Frontier: The Arctic and World Order'. In *The Arctic and World Order* 1–46. Edited by Kristina Spohr and Daniel S Hamilton, Jason C Moyer associate editor. Brookings Institution Press, 2020.

Spring, DW. 'The Soviet Decision for War against Finland', 30 November 1939, 38(2) *Soviet Studies* 207–26, 1986.

Staalesen, Atle. 'Chinese Bank Invests in Russia's Northern Sea Route', Eye on the Arctic, 12 June 2018.

——. '"Human Activity" Behind Svalbard Cable Disruption', Barents Observer, 11 February 2022.

——. 'Kirkenes Port Developers Put Their Faith in the Chinese', Barents Observer, 7 June 2019.

——. 'More than 60% of Russian Territory is Permafrost. Now it is Melting', Barents Observer, 14 May 2021.

——. 'Russia Stages Military-Style Propaganda Parade on Norway's Svalbard Archipelago', Barents Observer, 9 May 2023.

——. 'Russian Arctic Ports Have Best Year Ever', Barents Observer, 16 January 2017.

'State of the Cryosphere 2023: Two Degrees is Too High', International Cryosphere Climate Initiative 1–62, 2023.

Stephenson, Scott R, Laurence C Smith and John A Agnew. 'Divergent Long-Term Trajectories of Human Access to the Arctic', 1 *Nature Climate Change* 156–60, 2011.

Stevenson-Yang, Lucy and Henry Tugendhat. 'China's Engagement in Latin America: Views from the Region', US Institute of Peace, 8 August 2022.

Stirk, Peter. 'Carl Schmitt's "Völkerrechtliche Grossraumordnung"', 20(2) *History of Political Thought* 357–74, 1999.

Stockwell, Billy, James Frater and Eve Brennan, 'Denmark Boosts Arctic Defense Spending by $2 Billion after Trump's Greenland Interest', CNN, 27 January 2025.

Stone, Mike. 'White House Huddles with Industry on Tech Innovation for Ukraine', Reuters, 8 January 2024.

Storå, Nils. 'Russian Walrus Hunting in Spitsbergen', 11(2) *Études/Inuit/Studies* 117–37, 1987.

Storey, Ed. 'Bolting for the Baltic', *Legion: Canada's Military History Magazine*, 3 May 2022.
Struzik, Ed. ''How Tensions with Russia are Jeopardizing Key Arctic Research', YaleEnvironment360, 7 February 2023.
Suchoples, Jarosław. 'In the Shadow of the Eastern Neighbor. Finland in the Security Policy of Russia and the Soviet Union from Peter the Great to Contemporary Times', 26(4) *Studies in European Affairs* 9–38, 2022.
Suciu, Peter. 'Why China's 10-Dash Line Map is a Clear Threat', National Interest, 16 November 2023.
'Suez Canal Debacle Shows Value of Northern Sea Route, Russia Says', Reuters, 30 March 2021.
Sukhorukov, VD, Yu N Gladkiy and SV Kulik. 'The Russian Arctic World as a "Cultural Circle" and an Object of Development', 816 IOP Conference Series: Earth and Environmental Science 012010 [1–8], 2021.
Sun, Kai. 'Beyond the Dragon and the Panda: Understanding China's Engagement in the Arctic', Asia Policy, 21 July 2014.
Sunderland, Willard. 'Russians into Iakuts? "Going Native" and Problems of Russian National Identity in the Siberian North, 1870s–1914', 55(4) *Slavic Review* 806–25, 1996.
Sundet, Jan H and Alf Håkon Hoel. 'The Norwegian Management of an Introduced Species: The Arctic Red King Crab Fishery', 72 *March Policy* 278–84, 2016.
Suryanarayanan, Kanagavalli. 'Third Pole's View on the North Pole – India's Arctic Policy', Polar Connection, 12 April 2022.
Swistek Göran and Michael Paul. 'Geopolitics in the Baltic Sea Region', 9 *Stiftung Wissenschaft und Politik* 1–8, 2023.
'Taiwan Supports Global Treaty Against Illegal Fishing', Department of Information Service, 29 July 2016.
'Taiwan's Distant-Water Fleet Still on Troubled Waters', European Values Center for Security Policy, 19 September 2023.
Tallgren, Immi. 'The Finnish War-Responsibility Trial in 1945–6: The Limits of Ad Hoc Criminal Justice?' In *The Hidden Histories of War Crimes Trials* 430–454. Edited by Kevin John Heller and Gerry Simpson. Oxford University Press, 2013.
Taylor, Peter. 'Geographical Scales within the World-Economy Approach', 5(1) *Review* 3–11, 1981.
Teschke, Benno. 'Geopolitics', 14(1) *Historical Materialism* 327–35, 2006.
Teschke, Benno Gerhard. 'Fatal Attraction: A Critique of Carl Schmitt's International Political and Legal Theory', 3(2) *International Theory* 179–227, 2011.
'"The Baltic Sea Will Become a NATO Lake" – Interview with Gen. Major Pekka Toveri, Former Intelligence Chief of the General Staff of the Finnish Defense Forces', GeorgiaToday, 19 May 2022.
'The Elements of the China Challenge, Policy Planning Staff', US Secretary of State, 2020.
'The Five Main Projects of the Belt and Road Initiative', *South China Morning Post*, May 2017.
'The High Seas, An Undisclosed World', Océans Connectés [no date].
'The Latest Arctic Explorations – The Remarkable Escape of the Polaris Party', Scientific American, 7 June 1873.
'The Muscovy Company: World's First Joint Stock Company', Business Standard, 25 July 2021.
'The Nuclear Legacy of the Arctic: Cleaning It Up Without International Assistance Will Be Tough, Environment and Rights N° 87', *Bellona Arctic* 26–34, 2023.
'The Pomors', Svalbard Musuem, svalbardmuseum.no/en/the-pomors.
Thompson, Felix. 'JBIC Halts Financing for Russian LNG Project', Global Trade Review, 14 June 2022.
Tickler, David, Jessica J Meeuwig, Maria-Lourdes Palomares, Daniel Pauley and Dirk Zeller. 'Far From Home: Distance Patterns of Global Fishing Fleets', 4(8) *Science Advances* [1–6], 2018.
Tiller, Rachel and Elizabeth Nyman. 'Having the Cake and Eating It Too: To Manage or Own the Svalbard Fisheries Protection Zone', 60 *Marine Policy* 141–48, 2015.
Titley, David W and Courtney St' John. Arctic Security Considerations and the US Navy's Roadmap for the Arctic', 63(2) *Naval War College Review* 35–48, 2010.
Tiwari, Sakshi. 'Canada Discovers "Chinese Buoys" in the Arctic That Could Be Tracking US Nuclear Submarines in the Region – Media', EurAsian Times, 14 August 2023.

Tjoflot, Gunn Kristin. 'GoNorth Heads for the Gakkel Ridge in the Arctic Ocean', UiO, 10 July 2023.

Todorov, Andrey. 'Dire Straits of the Russian Arctic: Options and Challenges for a Potential US FONOP in the Northern Sea Route', 139 *Marine Policy* 105020 [1–8], 2022.

Toscano, Alberto. 'Carl Schmitt in Beijing: Partisanship, Geopolitics and the Demolition of the Eurocentric World', 11(4) *Postcolonial Studies* 417–33, 2008.

Trellevik, Amund. 'Spitzbergen or Svalbard? The Answer Includes both Politics and History', High North News, 13 February 2020.

Treves, Tullio. 'Piracy, Law of the Sea, and Use of Force: Developments off the Coast of Somalia', 20(2) *European Journal of International Law* 399–414, 2009.

Troell, Max, Arne Eide, John Isaksen, Øystein Hermansen and Anne-Sophie Crépin. 'Seafood from a Changing Arctic', 46 (suppl 3) *Ambio* S368–S386, 2017.

'Trump: "We Need Greenland for National Security Purposes"', Forbes Breaking News, 7 January 2025.

Tschudi, Felix H. 'Time Equals Money: Developing a Profitable Shipping System Using the Northern Sea Route', 70 *Proceedings* 17–21, 2013.

Tsiouvalas, Apostolos. 'Law of the Sea in the Kinocene: Lessons from the Piniatorsuaq' (doctoral dissertation, UiT NCLOS).

Tsiouvalas, Apostolos and Endalew Lijalem Enyew. 'The Legal Implications of the 2022 Canada-Denmark/Greenland Agreement on Hans Island (Tartupaluk) for the Inuit Peoples of Greenland and Nunavut', Arctic Institute, 24 January 2023.

Tsiouvalas, Apostolos and Jan Jakub Solski. '"One Map to Rule Them All?" Revisiting Legalities Through Cartographic Representations of the Northwest Passage', 54(4) *Ocean Development and International Law* 393–420, 2023.

Tsiouvalas, Apostolos and Jen Evans, 'From "Common Pools" to "Fish Pools": Shifting Property Institutions in Traditional Waters of Norway and Canada', 54(2) *Ocean Development. and International Law* 135–62, 2023.

'Top Risks 2023', *Eurasia Group* 1–30, 2023.

Tunander, Ola. 'A Criticism of Court Chroniclers: A Response from Tunander', 35(4) *Cooperation and Conflict* 431–40, 2000.

——. 'The Uneasy Imbrication of Nation-State and NATO: The Case of Sweden', 34(2) *Cooperation and Conflict* 169–203, 1999.

'Ukrainian Attacks Increasingly Sap the Power of Russia's Black Sea Fleet', Associated Press, 6 March 2024.

Ulmen, GL. 'The Sociology of the State: Carl Schmitt and Max Weber', 1(2) *State, Culture, and Society* 3–57, 1985.

——. 'Translator's Introduction'. In *Carl Schmitt,* Nomos *of the Earth in the International Law of the* Jus Publicum Europaeum 9–34. Translated and annotated by GL Ulmen. Telos Press Publishing, 2006.

Urbina, Ian. 'How China's Expanding Fishing Fleet Is Depleting the World's Oceans', YaleEnvironment360, 17 August 2020.

'U.S. Purchase of Alaska Ridiculed as "Seward's Folly"', History, 3 March 2010.

Vakulenko, Sergey. 'Shock and Awe: Who Attacked the Nord Stream Pipelines?' Carnegie Endowment for International Peace, 30 September 2022.

Vamvakeros, Katarina. 'A Brief Description over Human Geography', 12(1) *Journal Geography and Natural Disaster* 240, 2022.

van Brunnersum, Sou-Jie. 'China Failed its Arctic Ambitions in Greenland', Politico, 22 October 2022.

van Munster, Rens. 'Securitization', Oxford Bibliographies, 2012.

Vaughn, Bruce, Ben Dolven, Tomás F Husted, Caitlin Keating-Bitonti, Katarina C O'Regan, Liana W Rosen, Michael D Sutherland and Liana Wong. 'China's Role in the Exploitation of Global Fisheries'. Congressional Research Service, 12 April 2022.

Vázquez, Gonzalo. 'NATO Should Mind the Gap', Center for Maritime Strategy, 28 March 2023.

Vec, Miloš. 'The Last World: 150 Years of Franz Josef Land', Völkerrechtsblog, 14 July 2023.

Verhoosel, Gaetan. 'Beyond the Unsustainable Rhetoric of Sustainable Development: Transfering Environmentally Sound Technologies', 11(1) *Georgetown International Environmental Law Review* 49–76, 1988.

Vidal de la Blache, P. 'Les genres de vie dans la géographie humaine', 20(111) *Annales de Géographie* 193–212, 1911.

Volpe, Marco. 'The Tortuous Path of China's Win-Win Strategy in Greenland', Arctic Institute, 24 March 2020.

von Bernstorff, Jochen. 'The Use of Force in International Law before World War I: On Imperial Ordering and the Ontology of the Nation-State', 29(1) *European Journal of International Law* 233–60, 2018.

von Leesen, Gotje, Bjarte Bogstad, Einars Hjörleifsson, Ulysses S Ninnemann and Steven E Campana. 'Temperature Exposure in Cod Driven by Changes in Abundance', 79(4) *Canadian Journal of Fisheries and Aquatic Sciences* 587–600, 2022.

Vuori, Juha A. 'Illocutionary Logic and Strands of Securitization: Applying the Theory of Securitization to the Study of Non-Democratic Political Orders', 14(1) *European Journal of International Relations* 65–99, 2008.

Wæver, Ole. 'Securitization and Desecuritization'. In *On Security* 46–24. Edited by Ronnie D Lipschutz. Columbia University Press, 1995.

——. 'Security the Speech Act: Analysing the Politics of a Word', Working Paper No 19. Centre for Peace and Conflict Research, 1989.

Wall, Colin. 'Invisible and Vital: Undersea Cables and Translatlantic Security', Center for Strategic and International Studies (CSIS), 11 June 2021.

Wall, Colin and Njord Wegge. 'The Russian Arctic Threat: Consequences of the Ukraine War', Center for Strategic and International Studies (CSIS), 25 January 2023.

Wall, Mike. 'Russian Space Officials Jettison the Bluster After Rogozin's Departure', Space.com, 6 October 2022.

Wallis, Diana and Stewart Arnold. 'Governing Common Seas: From a Baltic Strategy to an Arctic Policy', 42(1) *Journal of Baltic Studies*, 103–07, 2011.

Wallis, Joanne, Geyi Xie, William Waqavakatoga, Priestley Habru and Maima Koro. 'Ordering the Islands? Pacific Responses to China's Strategic Narratives', 16(4) *Chinese Journal International Politics* 457–81, 2023.

Walsh, Nick Paton and Sarah Dean. 'Russia's Militarization of the Arctic Shows No Sign of Slowing Down', CNN, 22 December 2023.

Walt, Stephen. 'Liberal Illusions Caused the Ukraine Crisis', Foreign Policy, 19 January 2022.

Waltz, Kennith N. 'The Origins of War in Neorealist Theory', 18(4) *Journal of Interdisciplinary History* 615–28, 1988.

Wani, Ayjaz. 'C+C5 Summit: Beijing's Increasing Shadow over Central Asia', Observer Resource Foundation, 29 May 2023.

Weber, Bob. 'Canada Pledges to Work with U.S. Over Competing Claims to Arctic Sea Floor', CBC News, 3 January 2024.

Wegge, Njord. 'Arctic Security Strategies and the North Atlantic States', 11 *Arctic Review of Law and Policy* 360–82, 2020.

Weil, Patrick. 'Access to Citizenship: A Comparison of Twenty-Five Nationality Laws'. In *Citizenship Today: Global Perspectives and Practices* 17–35. Edited by T Alexander Aleinikoff and Douglas Klusmeyer. Carnegie Endowment for International Peace, 2001.

Wenande, Christian. 'Russia Alarmed about Foreign Troops on Bornholm', *Copenhagen Post*, 18 February 2022.

Wendt, Alexander and Daniel Friedheim. 'Hierarchy under Anarchy: Informal Empire and the East German State'. In *State Sovereignty as Social Construct* 240–77. Edited by Thomas Biersteker and Cynthia Weber. Cambridge University Press, 1996.

Werber, Niels. 'Zweimal Großraum: Netzwerke und Raumordnung bei Carl Schmitt', 61(2–3) *Archiv des Völkerrechts* 248–58, 2023.

Wehmeyer, Joseph. 'What Would Greenland's Independence Mean for the Arctic?' Council on Foreign Relations, 2023.

Westgaard, Katrine. 'The Baltic Sea Region: A Laboratory for Overcoming European Security Challenges', Carnegie Endowment for International Peace, 21 December 2023.

'What is the Arctic', Barents Watch, 1 October 2015.

Whetton, Cris. 'Remember Bengtskar!', 125 US Naval Institute Proceedings, March 1999.

White, Edward. 'China's Fishing Fleet Embroiled in Rising Tensions with US', *Financial Times*, 23 May 2023.

Wieslander, Anna and Eric Adamson. 'A Glimpse of Sweden in NATO: Gotland Could be a Game-Changer for Baltic Defense', Atlantic Council, 26 April 2023.

Wilcox, Francis O. 'The Monroe Doctrine and World War II', 36(3) *American Political Science Review* 433–53, 1942.

Wilkins, Henry. 'Gulf of Guinea Countries Agree to Stop Illegal Chinese Fishing', VOA, 9 December 2022.

Willassen, Silje. 'The Great Power Competition in the North Atlantic', Strategem, 15 May 2021.

Williams, Michael C. 'Words, Images, Enemies: Securitization and International Politics', 47(4) *International Studies Quarterly* 511–31, 2003.

Wills, Steve. 'Kaliningrad: Impregnable Fortress or "Russian Alamo"?' CNAindepth, 15 May 2023.

Wofsy, Cody and Hannah Schoen Steinberg. 'Trump's Remarks on Birthright Citizenship, Explained'. ACLU, 13 December 2024.

Wolfers, Arnold. '"National Security" as an Ambiguous Symbol', 67(4) *Political Science Quarterly* 481–502, 1952.

Wolin, Richard. 'Carl Schmitt: The Conservative Revolution and the Aesthetics of Horror', 20(3) *Political Theory* 424–47 (1993).

Wood, Alan. 'Introduction: Siberia's Role in Russian History'. In *The History of Siberia: From Russian Conquest to Revolution* 1–17. Edited by Alan Wood. Routledge, 1991.

Wood, Steve. 'Change in the Baltic Sea Region: Geopolitics, Identity, and the Russian Negative Integration Factor', 32(3) *Journal of Contemporary European Studies* 787–802, 2024.

Wright, John K. 'The Open Polar Sea', 43(3) *Geological. Review* 338–65, 1953.

Xiaofeng, Liu. 'New China and the End of American "International Law"', 3 *American Affairs*, Fall 2019.

Xie, Libin and Haig Patapan. 'Schmitt Fever: The Use and Abuse of Carl Schmitt in Contemporary China', 18(1) *International Journal of Constitutional Law* 130–46, 2020.

Xing, Li and Rasmus Gjedssø Bertelsen. 'The Drivers of Chinese Arctic Interests: Political Stability and Energy and Transportation Security'. In *China's Arctic Engagement: Following the Polar Silk Road to Greenland and Russia* 15–37. Edited by Justin Barns, Heather Exner-Pirot, Lassi Heininen and P Whitney Lackenbauer. Arctic Yearbook, 2021.

Yoon, Young-Kwan. 'Introduction: Power Cycle Theory and Practice of International Relations', 24(1) *International Political Science Review* 5–12, 2003.

Young, Oran R. 'The Age of the Arctic', 61 *Foreign Policy* 160–79, 1985–1986.

Young, Oran R, Jian Yang and Andrei Zagorski. 'The "New" Arctic as a Zone of Peaceful Competition', 11 *Polar Perspectives* 2022 [no page numbers].

Yu, Ji. 'China's Alignment with Putin is Uneasy. But Its Rivalry with the US Makes Him Too Useful to Abandon', Chatham House, 17 May 2024.

Zarmanian, Thalin. 'Carl Schmitt and the Problem of Legal Order: From Domestic to International', 19(1) *Leiden Journal of International Law* 41–67, 2006.

Zhou, Cissy. 'Sri Lanka's China "Debt Trap" Fears Grow as Beijing Keeps Investing', NikkeiAsia, 2 January 2024.

Zou, Keyuan and Liu Xinchang. 'The U-Shaped Line and Historic Rights in the Philippines v. China Arbitration Case'. In *Arbitration Concerning the South China Sea: Philippines versus China* 127–32. Edited by Wu Shicun and Zou Keyuan. Routledge, 2016.

DOCUMENTS

14th Amendment to the U.S. Constitution: Civil Rights (1868), Milestone Documents, National Archives, updated 6 March 2024.

2021 Assessment of Undiscovered Technically Recoverable Oil and Gas Resources of the Nation's Outer Continental Shelf Region, Bureau of Ocean Energy Management (BOEM), US Department of the Interior, October 2021. www.boem.gov/2021-assessment-undiscovered-oil-and-gas-resources-nations-outer.

2023 Report to Congress: Improving International Fisheries Management, National Oceanagraphic and Atmospheric Administration (NOAA) Fisheries, 2023. www.fisheries.noaa.gov/s3/2023-08/2023.ReportSummary.ImprovingIFManagement.pdf.

ACGF, The Arctic Coast Guard Forum. About the ACGF: ACGF (arcticcoastguardforum.com).

Act on Greenland Self-Government, Act No 473, Statsministeriet, 12 June 2009. english.stm.dk/media/10522/gl-selvstyrelov-uk.pdf.

Adapting to Change: UK Policy Towards the Arctic, HM Government, 2013. assets.publishing.service.gov.uk/media/5a757c1ded915d731495a53a/Adapting_To_Change_UK_policy_towards_the_Arctic.pdf.

AR6 Synthesis Report, Climate Change 2023, Intergovernmental Panel on Climate Change (IPCC), 2023. www.ipcc.ch/report/ar6/syr.

Agreement on Cooperation on Aeronautical and Maritime Search and Rescue in the Arctic, Search and Rescue Agreement, 12 May 2011. oaarchive.arctic-council.org/items/9c343a3f-cc4b-4e75-bfd3-4b318137f8a2.

Agreement on Cooperation on Marine Oil Pollution Preparedness and Response in the Arctic, 15 May 2013. oaarchive.arctic-council.org/items/ee4c9907-7270-41f6-b681-f797fc81659f.

Agreement on Enhancing International Arctic Scientific Cooperation, 2018. oaarchive.arctic-council.org/items/9d1ecc0c-e82a-43b5-9a2f-28225bf183b9.

Agreement on Port State Measures to Prevent, Deter and Eliminate Illegal, Unreported and Unregulated Fishing, 22 November 2009. www.wto.org/english/tratop_e/rulesneg_e/fish_e/2009_psma.pdf.

Ambassador in Norway (Bay) to the Secretary of State (10 January 1947). Foreign Relations of the United States, 1947, The British Commonwealth; Europe, Vol III.

Ambassador in Norway (Bay) to the Secretary of State (17 January 1947). Foreign Relations of the United States, 1947, The British Commonwealth; Europe, Vol III.

Ambassador in Norway (Bay) to the Secretary of State (11 March 1947). Foreign Relations of the United States, 1947, The British Commonwealth; Europe, Vol III.

Ambassador in Norway (Bay) to the Secretary of State (28 March 1947). Foreign Relations of the United States, 1947, The British Commonwealth; Europe, Vol III.

Ambassador in the Soviet Union (Smith) to the Secretary of State (16 January 1947). Foreign Relations of the United States, 1947 The British Commonwealth; Europe, Vol III.

An Introduction To: The International Agreement to Prevent Unregulated High Seas of the Central Arctic Ocean, Arctic Council, 25 June 2021. arctic-council.org/news/introduction-to-international-agreement-to-prevent-unregulated-fishing-in-the-high-seas-of-the-central-arctic-ocean.

Announcement of U.S. Extended Continental Shelf Outer Limits, Department of State, 19 December 2023. www.state.gov/announcement-of-u-s-extended-continental-shelf-outer-limits.

Arctic: Agreement to Prevent Unregulated Fishing Enters into Force, European Commission, 25 June 2021. oceans-and-fisheries.ec.europa.eu/news/arctic-agreement-prevent-unregulated-fishing-enters-force-2021-06-25_en.

Arctic and Northern Policy Framework, Government of Canada, 2019. cdn.prod.website-files.com/645b173b42ee12d72d1885cc/6462ffd561d8a317478acffa_nth-arctic_northern_policy_framework_1662642171557_eng.pdf.

Arctic Climate Impact Assessment, Arctic Council, 2005. oaarchive.arctic-council.org/handle/11374/2453?show=full.

Arctic Council Rules of Procedure, 17–18 September 1998. oaarchive.arctic-council.org/server/api/core/bitstreams/50b5ff78-382d-4425-aaaa-72af1a787e94/content.

Arctic Environmental Protection Strategy, 14 June 1991. library.arcticportal.org/1542/1/artic_environment.pdf.

Arctic Oscillation (AO), NOAA, 8 May 2024. www.ncei.noaa.gov/access/monitoring/ao.

Arctic Peoples, Arctic Council, arctic-council.org/explore/topics.

Arctic Research and Policy Act, 15 USC Ch 67 § 4111.

Arctic Security Forces Roundtable, Center for Arctic Security and Resilience (CASR), 2022. www.uaf.edu/casr/projects/asfr.php.

Arctic Strategic Outlook, United States Coast Guard, 2019. www.uscg.mil/Portals/0/Images/arctic/Arctic_Strategy_Book_APR_2019.pdf.

Arctic Task Force, Conference of Peripheral and Maritime Regions (CPMR), Baltic Sea Commission, 2024. cpmr-baltic.org/policy-work/arctic.

Arctic Tree Line, Polarpedia. polarpedia.eu/en/arctic-tree-line.

Arctic Yellow River Station, Polar Research Institute of China. en.pric.org.cn/index.php?c=category&id=98.

Baltic Countries to Build Defensive Installations on their Borders, Ministry of Defence, Republic of Estonia, 19 January 2024. www.kaitseministeerium.ee/en/news/baltic-countries-build-defensive-installations-their-borders.

Barents Euro-Arctic Cooperation: Joint Statement of the European Union, Finland, Denmark, Iceland, Norway and Sweden on suspending activities with Russia, European Union External Action, 3 March 2022. www.eeas.europa.eu/eeas/barents-euro-arctic-cooperation-joint-statement-european-union-finland-denmark-iceland-norway-and_en.

Barents Euro-Arctic Council, BEAC, barents-council.org/#:~:text=The%20Barents%20Euro%2DArctic%20Councilandtext=The%20Barents%20Council%20is%20the,by%20working%20on%20their%20own.

Blue Mining, European Commission, 2023. bluemining.eu (detailing the background and objectives of the Blue Mining consortium).

Breaking the Ice: Arctic Development and Maritime Transportation, Prospects of the Transarctic Route – Impact and Opportunities, Government of Iceland, 2007. www.stjornarradid.is/media/utanrikisraduneyti-media/media/mfa_pdf/dagskra_-_breaking_the_ice.pdf.

Conservation of Arctic Flora and Fauna (CAFF), Arctic Biodiversity Report, Arctic Circle 2014. YouTube, www.youtube.com/watch?v=MCXtLxIzqwE.

Candidates to Join the European Union, Reuters, 14 December 2023. www.reuters.com/world/candidates-join-european-union-2023-12-14.

Changes in the Arctic: Background and Issues for Congress, Congressional Research Service (updated 2023). sgp.fas.org/crs/misc/R41153.pdf.

Chicago History Museum, images.chicagohistory.org/asset/4658.

China: Democracy That Works, PRC State Council Information Office, 4 December 2021. www.news.cn/english/2021-12/04/c_1310351231.htm.

China's Arctic Policy, Xinhua News Agency, 26 January 2018. www.gov.cn/xinwen/2018-01/26/content_5260891.htm.

China's Arctic Policy, St Council, PRC, January 2018. english.www.gov.cn/archive/white_paper/2018/01/26/content_281476026660336.htm.

Climate Change Indicators: Arctic Sea Ice, United States Environmental Protection Agency, July 2022. climatechange.chicago.gov/climate-indicators/downloads-indicators-report.

Collection DOC 438-British Government Protocol Respecting New Hebrides: Signed at London on August 6, 1914, by representatives of the British and French.

Finland and Sweden Submit Applications to Join Nation, NATO, 18 May 2022. www.nato.int/cps/en/natohq/news_195468.htm.

Governments[Ratification], Pacific Manuscripts Bureau, British Government Protocol respecting the New Hebrides: signed at London on August 6, 1914, by representatives of the British and French Governments [Ratification] – Pacific Manuscripts Bureau.

Communiqué Issued at the End of the Yalta Conference [No 1417] Foreign Relations of the United States Diplomatic Papers, The Conference of Berlin (The Potsdam Conference), 1945, Volume II, 740.0011 EW/2–1145.

Conference of Parliamentarians of the Arctic Region, treaties.un.org/doc/source/events/PD/arctic_council.pdf.

Cooperation in the Barents Euro-Arctic Region, Barents Euro-Arctic Region, barents-council.org/about-us/cooperation-in-the-barents-euro-arctic-region.

Cooperation with Russian Side on Hold, Sáámiráđđi, 10 April 2022. www.saamicouncil.net/news-archive/cooperation-with-russian-side-on-hold.

Danish Minister (Kauffmann) to the Secretary of State (13 April 1941), Foreign Relations of the United States Diplomatic Papers, 1941, Europe, Vol II, 859B.7962/123.

Data Capable Crossroad or Circumpolar Chokepoint: The Geopolitics of Subsea Infrastructure in the Arctic, Polar Geopolitics, 10 November 2023.

Declaration on the Establishment of the Arctic Council. Joint Communique of the Government of the Arctic Countries on the Establishment of the Arctic Council, Ottawa, Canada, 19 September 1996. library.arcticportal.org/1270/1/ottawa_decl_1996-3.pdf.

Decree on Approval of the Foreign Policy Concept of the Russian Federation, 31 March 2023. www.kremlin.ru/events/president/news/ [English trans].

de L'Isle, Guillaume. Carte de Tartarie. Library of Congress. 1706. www.loc.gov/item/99446168.

Deutsche Gesellschaft für Geographie (DGfG) and Goethe University, *Großraum* from Carl Schmitt to Aleksandr Dugin: Unpacking the Persistence of a Classical Geopolitical Trope, 20 September 2023 (paper abstract, Mark Bassin). dkg2023.de/papers/gro%C3%9Fraum-from-carl-schmitt-to-87862.

Deutsche Gesellschaft für Geographie (DGfG) and Goethe University, Greater Area and Border Fringe: Continuities and Breaks in Geopolitics after 1945, 20 September 2023. dkg2023.de/sitzungen/gro%C3%9Fraum-und-grenzsaum-kontinuit%C3%A4ten-und-90601 (paper abstracts of Niels Werber, Ulrike Jureit and Patricia Chiantera).

Diplomatic Dialogue, Geneva Centre for Security Policy (GCSP). www.gcsp.ch/gcsp-activities#diplomatic-dialogue.

Dmitry Rogozin (@Rogozin), 19 April 2015.

EU Position in World Trade, European Commission, 2 October 2014. ec.europa.eu/trade/policy/eu-position-in-world-trade.

EU Council 11508/24, 30, 25 June 2024.

Evolution of NATO Cooperation with Its Partners: Opportunities and Challenges, Polish Institute of International Affairs (PISM: Polski Instytut Spraw Międzynarodowych), 21 August 2020. pism.pl/publications/Evolution_of_NATO_Cooperation_with_Its_Partners_Opportunities_and_Challenges.

Expeditions, Fram Polar Exploration Museum. frammuseum.no/polar-history/expeditions.

eorge HW Bush, Address Before a Joint Session of the Congress on the Persian Gulf Crisis and the Federal Budget Deficit, 11 September 1990. bush41library.tamu.edu/archives/public-papers/2217.

Geographical Coverage, Arctic Monitoring and Assessment Program (AMAP), 2023. www.amap.no/about/geographical-coverage.

Greenland in the World: Nothing About Us Without Us, Greenland's Foreign, Security and Defense Policy 2024-2033–An Arctic Strategy, Naalakkersuisut/Government of Greenland, February 2024. vivian.gl/wp-content/uploads/2024/03/greenlands_foreign_-security_and_defense_policy_2024_2033.pdf.

Gun Battery Dueodde, Battlefieldsww2.com, www.battlefieldsww2.com/gun-battery-dueodde.html.

From Moscow to the Very Outskirts: The Problems of Flooded Objects Were Discussed at an International Conference, Комплексная утилизация АПЛ, 24 December 2019.

Full Text of President Xi Jinping's 2024 New Year Message, PRC Ministry of Foreign Affairs, 31 December 2023. www.mfa.gov.cn/eng/zxxx_662805/202312/t20231231_11215608.html.

The Future Tasks of the Alliance, NATO, 14 December 1967 [Harmel Report]. www.nato.int/cps/en/natohq/official_texts_26700.htm.

Heidegger, Schmitt, Dugin: Exploring Intellectual Sources of Illiberalism, Institute for European, Russian, and Eurasian Studies, George Washington University, 20 October 2023. YouTube, ieres.elliott.gwu.edu/project/heidegger-schmitt-dugin-exploring-intellectual-sources-of-illiberalism.

Himadri Station, National Centre for Polar and Ocean Research (NCPOR), Ministry of Earth Sciences, Government of India. National Centre For Polar And Ocean Research (Ncpor), GOA.

Joint Communication on a Stronger EU Engagement for a Peaceful, Sustainable and Prosperous Arctic, EU External Action, 13 November 2021. www.eeas.europa.eu/eeas/joint-communication-stronger-eu-engagement-peaceful-sustainable-and-prosperous-arctic-0_en.

IASC Council, International Arctic Science Committee (IASC). iasc.info/about/organisation/council.

ILO Convention No. 169, Indigenous and Tribal Peoples Convention, 1989. normlex.ilo.org/dyn/normlex/en/f?p=NORMLEXPUB:55:0::NO::P55_TYPE,P55_LANG,P55_DOCUMENT,P55_NODE:REV,en,C169,/Document.

Ilulissat Declaration, Arctic Ocean Conference, Ilulissat, Greenland, 27–28 May, 2008. www.regjer-ingen.no/globalassets/upload/ud/080525_arctic_ocean_conference-_outcome.pdf.

Impacts of a Warming Arctic, Arctic Climate Impact Assessment, 2004. www.amap.no/documents/doc/impacts-of-a-warming-arctic-2004/786.

India's Arctic Policy: Building a Partnership for Sustainable Development. Government of India, 2022. www.moes.gov.in/sites/default/files/2022-03/compressed-SINGLE-PAGE-ENGLISH.pdf.

Interactive Map, Association of Indigenous Peoples of the North, Siberia and the Far East, RAIPON, raipon.info.

Intergovernmental Conference on Marine Biodiversity of Areas Beyond National Jurisdiction, UN. www.un.org/bbnj.

International American Conference, Reports of Committees and Discussions Thereon. Vol IV, Historical Appendix. The Congress of 1826, at Panama and Subsequent Movements Toward a Conference of American Nations, Ex Doc 232, 1890. tile.loc.gov/storage-services/public/gdcmassbookdig/congressof1826at00inte/congressof1826at00inte.pdf.

International Agreement to Prevent Unregulated Fishing in the High Seas of the Central Arctic Ocean, 2018. vlab.noaa.gov/documents/22926311/0/AGREEMENT+TO+PREVENT+UNREGULATED+HIGH+SEAS+FISHERIES+IN+THE+CENTRAL+ARCTIC+OCEAN.pdf/b33ec030-17f1-20d5-7c73-a50f84cf6712?t=1685588546248.

International Code for Ships Operating in Polar Waters (Polar Code), International Maritime Organization (IMO), 1 January 2017. International Code for Ships Operating in Polar Waters (Polar Code) (imo.org).

Japan's Arctic Policy [Provisional Translation], Cabinet Office, 16 October 2015. www8.cao.go.jp/ocean/policies/arcticpolicy/arcticpolicy.html.

Joint Statement between the People's Republic of China and the Russian Federation on Deepening the Comprehensive Strategic Partnership of Coordination for a New Era on the Occasion of the 75th Anniversary of the Establishment of Diplomatic Relations between the Two Countries (Full Text), Xinhua News Agency. 16 May 2024.

Joint Statement by the Arctic 7 on the Limited Resumption of Arctic Council Cooperation – Without Russia!, Arctic Portal.org. 9 June 2022. arcticportal.org/ap-library/news/2855-joint-statement-by-the-arctic-7-on-the-limited-resumption-of-arctic-council-cooperation-without-russia.

Joint Statement of the Russian Federation and the People's Republic of China on the International Relations Entering a New Era and the Global Sustainable Development, President of Russia. 4 February 2022. www.en.kremlin.ru/supplement/5770.

Key Aspects of the Paris Agreement, UN. unfccc.int/most-requested/key-aspects-of-the-paris-agreement#:~:text=The%20Paris%20Agreement's%20central%20aim,further%20to%201.5%20degrees%20Celsius.

Letter from R. J. Walker to William H. Seward, Washington, 24 April 1868, 1–5. In *A Report on the Resources of Iceland and Greenland compiled by Benjamin Mills Peirce*. Washington: Government Printing Office, 1868.

Limits of Oceans and Seas. Draft, 4th ed. International Hydrographic Bureau, 1986. docs.iho.int/mtg_docs/com_wg/S-23WG/S-23WG_Misc/Draft_1986/Draft_1986.htm.

Lov om rettsforhold og forvaltning av grunn og naturressurser i Finnmark (Finnmarksloven), LOV-2005-06-17-85, Lovdata. lovdata.no/dokument/NL/lov/2005-06-17-85.

Maddox, Maddox. Arctic Security and the Urgency of Understanding Actorless Threats, Dickey Center for International Understanding, Dartmouth University, YouTube, 1 April 2024. www.youtube.com/watch?v=WZrajuzT1tI.

Memorandum by the Director of the Office of European Affairs (Matthews) to the Secretary of State (23 December 1946), Foreign Relations of the United States, 1947, The British Commonwealth; Europe, Vol. III (1947).

Memorandum of Conversation, by the Assistant Secretary of State (Berle) (20 April 1940), Foreign Relations of the United States Diplomatic Papers, 1940, General and Europe, Vol II, B59B.01/152.

Mercator, Gerardus. *Nova et Aucta Orbis Terrae Descriptio ad Usum Navigantium Emendate Accommodata*. 1569 [planisphere of spherical earth].

Mer pukkellaks kan skyldes høyere temperatur, Statsforvalteren.no, 5 November 2021.

Mikhail Gorbachev's Speech in Murmansk at the Ceremonial Meeting on the Occasion of the Presentation of the Order of Lenin and the Gold Star to the City of Murmansk, 1 October 1987. Barentsinfo.org, www.barentsinfo.fi/docs/Gorbachev_speech.pdf.

Mitchell, Ryan. Carl Schmitt and the Development of Conservative State Theory in China, YouTube, 9 October 2020. www.youtube.com/watch?v=PBO9W5oqKK8

Moll, Herman. A New and Correct Map of the Whole World. Library of Congress Online Catalog [1719].

Minister: Russia Will Develop International Scientific Station on Spitsbergen, Tass, 6 April 2023. tass.com/economy/1600365.

Monitoring Polar Bears, Arctic Council, 8 March 2011. arctic-council.org/news/monitoring-polar-bears.

Nansen International Office for Refugees, History. The Nobel Prize, www.nobelprize.org/prizes/peace/1938/nansen/history.

National Intelligence Estimate, Climate Change and International Responses Increasing Challenges to US National Security Through 2040, National Intelligence Estimate, 2021. oeab.noaa.gov/wp-content/uploads/2022/04/NIE_Climate_Change_and_National_Security.pdf.

National Strategy for the Arctic Region, The White House. October 2022. www.whitehouse.gov/wp-content/uploads/2022/10/National-Strategy-for-the-Arctic-Region.pdf.

NATO's Forward Presence, NATO, June 2022. www.nato.int/nato_static_fl2014/assets/pdf/2022/6/pdf/2206-factsheet_efp_en.pdf.

Nordic Response 2024, Forsvaret, 5 March 2024. www.forsvaret.no/en/exercises-and-operations/exercises/nr24.

North American Aerospace Defense Command (NORAD), www.norad.mil/About-NORAD.

Northern Dimension Policy Framework: Joint Statement by the European Union, Iceland and Norway on Suspending Activities with Russia and Belarus. European Union External Action, 8 March 2022. www.eeas.europa.eu/eeas/northern-dimension-policy-joint-statement-european-union-iceland-and-norway-suspending-activities_en.

Nunavut Act. SC 1993, c 28, Government of Canada.

Ny-Ålesund Research Station: Research Strategy Applicable from 2019. www.forskningsradet.no/siteassets/publikasjoner/2019/ny-alesund-research-station-research-strategy2.pdf.

Official Records of the General Assembly, Twenty-Second Session, Agenda Item 92, Doc A./6695.

Ortelius, Abraham. *Tartariae sive Magni Chami Regni tÿpus*. Library of Congress Online Catalog [1603].

Our Story, U.S. Northern Command. www.northcom.mil/About.

Our Friends in the North: UK Strategy Towards the Arctic, UK Parliament, 29 November 2023. publications.parliament.uk/pa/ld5804/ldselect/ldintrel/8/805.htm.

Outline of the People's Republic of China 14th Five-Year Plan for National Economic and Social Development and Long-Range Objectives for 2035, Xinhua News Agency, 12 March 2021. Reprinted and translated in CSET, cset.georgetown.edu/wp-content/uploads/t0284_14th_Five_Year_Plan_EN.pdf [China's 14th Five-Year Plan].

Payer, Julius. Nie zurück! (1892).
Peace Treaty of Brest Litovsk, 3 March 1918. avalon.law.yale.edu/20th_century/brest.asp.
Permafrost: Everything You Need to Know, Natural Resources Defense Council (NRDC), 26 June 2018. www.nrdc.org/stories/permafrost-everything-you-need-know#sec-whatis.
Permanent Participants, Arctic Council. arctic-council.org/about/permanent-participants.
Press Release on Foreign Minister Sergey Lavrov's Message to Norwegain Foreign Minister Ine Eiriksen Soreide on the Occasion of the 100th Anniversary of the Spitsbergen Treaty, Ministry of Foreign Affairs Russian Federation, 4 February 2020. norway.mid.ru/en/embassy/press-centre/news/press_release_on_foreign_minister_sergey_lavrov_s_message_to_norwegian_foreign_minister_ine_eriksen_.
Prime Meridian, National Geographic. education.nationalgeographic.org/resource/prime-meridian.
Protecting Greenland: The American Consulate at Godthab, 1940–42, ADST, 2024. adst.org/2017/07/protecting-greenland-american-consulate-godthab-1940-42.
Recent Developments in the Arctic, CIA/SC/RR 82, 13 October 1954. www.cia.gov/readingroom/docs/DOC_0000496064.pdf.
Regaining Arctic Dominance – The U.S. Army in the Arctic, Department of the Army, 2021. www.army.mil/e2/downloads/rv7/about/2021_army_arctic_strategy.pdf.
The Regional Comprehensive Economic Partnership (RCEP), ASEAN. asean.org/our-communities/economic-community/integration-with-global-economy/the-regional-comprehensive-economic-partnership-rcep.
REPowerEU Plan, SWD (2022) 230 final, EUR-Lex, 18 May 2022. eur-lex.europa.eu/legal-content/EN/TXT/?uri=COM%3A2022%3A230%3AFIN&qid=1653033742483.
Rio Declaration on Environment and Development, 1992. www.iau-hesd.net/sites/default/files/documents/rio_e.pdf.
Roosevelt, Franklin D. First Inaugural Address to Congress, March 4, 1933. Avalon Project, Yale Law School, avalon.law.yale.edu/20th_century/froos1.asp.
Rovaniemi Process, www.rovaniemiarcticspirit.fi/EN/Our-Story.
Russia Facts/Figures, The Arctic Institute, 1 August 2022. www.thearcticinstitute.org/country-backgrounders/russia.
Russian Federation Naval Doctrine Approved, President of Russia, 31 July 2022. en.kremlin.ru/events/president/news/69084.
Russia's Chairmanship of the Arctic Council 2021-2023, Responsible Governance for a Sustainable Arctic, arctic-council-russia.ru/en.
Russland med I kampen mot fremmede arter i Arktis, Sysselmesteren på Svalbard, 20 April 20 2021. www.sysselmesteren.no/nyheter/2021/04/russland-med-i-kampen-mot-fremmede-arter-i-arktis.
Sea Ice, National Snow and Ice Data Center, 2018. nsidc.org/learn/parts-cryosphere/sea-ice.
Secretary of State [Byrne] to the Legation in Denmark (2 January 1947), Foreign Relations of the United States, 1947, The British Commonwealth; Europe, Vol III.
Secretary of State [Marshall] to the Secretary of the Navy (Forrestal) (18 February 1947), Foreign Relations of the United States, 1947, The British Commonwealth; Europe, Vol III, 811.24559B/1–247: Telegram.
Secretary of State [Hull] to the Consul at Gothaab (Penfield) (17 February 1941), Foreign Relations of the United States Diplomatic Papers, 1941, Europe, Volume II, 859B.7962/3: Telegram.
Secretary of War (Patterson) and the Secretary of the Navy (Forrestal) to the Secretary of State (4 February 1947), Foreign Relations of the United States, 1947, The British Commonwealth; Europe, Vol III.
Socnorth (Special Operations Command North), 19 September 2023. www.socom.mil/socnorth/Pages/Special-Operations-Command-North-deploys-Special-Operations-Forces-to-the-Arctic-during-Operation-Polar-Dagger.aspx.
Statement by U.S. Ambassador to Denmark, Carla Sands, Wake Up to the Arctic's Importance, U.S. Embassy and Consulate in the Kingdom of Denmark, 20 April 2020. dk.usembassy.gov/wake-up-to-the-arctics-importance.
Statement by Norwegian Institute of International Affairs Research Professor Elana Wilson Rowe, International Relations and Defence Committee, House of Lords, 24 May 2023.

Statement by Wilson Center Polar Institute Global Fellow, Mathieu Boulègue, International Relations and Defence Committee, House of Lords, 3 May 2023.

Statement of Klaus Dodds, International Relations and Defence Committee, House of Lords [UK], 19 April 2023, Q3, committees.parliament.uk/oralevidence/13105/html.

Statement from ICES Council, ICES, 20 March 2022. www.ices.dk/news-and-events/news-archive/news/Pages/TemporarySuspension.aspx.

Statement of Arctic Economic Council executive director, Mads Qvist Frederiksen, International Relations and Defence Committee, House of Lords [UK], 7 June 2023, Q 76.

Strategic Competition in the Arctic, Transportation and Maritime Security Subcommittee Hearing, Homeland Security Committee (comment of Mr O'Rourke), www.youtube.com/live/hE8CGxMOR0I?app=desktop.

Summary of Proceedings, Seminar on Arctic Cooperation in Difficult Times, 15–17 November 2023). www.svs.is/static/files/Arctic_Days_2023/arctic.impressions-and-participants.final.pdf.

Svalbard Meld. St 26 (2023–2024), Melding til Stortinget, Svalbard. www.regjeringen.no/no/dokumenter/meld.-st.-26-20232024/id3041130.

Ted Stevens Center for Arctic Security Studies, tedstevensarcticcenter.org.

Telegram, The Charg[é] in the Soviet Union (Kennan) to the Secretary of State (22 February 1946) [Long Telegram]. National Security Archive, nsarchive.gwu.edu/document/21043-long-telegram-transcript.

The EU in the Arctic, EEAS, 2021. The EU in the Arctic | EEAS (europa.eu).

The European Green Deal, European Commission, commission.europa.eu/strategy-and-policy/priorities-2019-2024/european-green-deal_en.

The Final Liberation of Bornholm, Det KGL.Bibliotek, www.kb.dk/en/inspiration/liberation/final-liberation-bornholm.

The Russian Federation, Arctic Council, arctic-council.org/about/states/russian-federation.

Treaty of New Echota [Treaty with the Cherokee], 1835. In *Indian Affairs, Laws and Treaties, Vol II*, 439–449. Compiled and edited by Charles J. Kappler. Government Printing Office, 1904.

Treaty of Non-Aggression between Germany and the Union of Soviet Socialist Republics [Molotov-Ribbentrop Pact/ Hitler-Stalin Pact]. Avalon Project, avalon.law.yale.edu/20th_century/nonagres.asp.

Speech by Prime Minister Ulf Kristersson at Folk och Försvars Annual National Conference 2024, Government of Sweden, 8 January 2024. www.government.se/speeches/2024/01/speech-by-prime-minister-ulf-kristersson-at-folk-och-forsvars-annual-national-conference-2024.

United Nations Convention on the Law of the Sea, 1982. treaties.un.org/doc/publication/CTC/Ch_XXI_6_english_p.pdf.

United States Department of Defense 2024 Arctic Strategy, 21 June 2024. media.defense.gov/2024/Jul/22/2003507411/-1/-1/0/DOD-ARCTIC-STRATEGY-2024.PDF.

Unpacking the 2022 US National Strategy for the Arctic Region, Wilson Center, 25 October 2022. www.youtube.com/watch?v=B-gDTEuap48.

Unrivaled Speed, Security, And Diversity Linking Asia, North America and Europe through the Arctic, Far North Fiber. www.farnorthfiber.com.

Utvalgte Tableller of Figurer fra denne Statistikken, Offentlig Sektor på Svalbard, Statistisk Sentralbyrå, 17 October 2023. www.ssb.no/en/offentlig-sektor/offentlig-forvaltning/statistikk/offentlig-sektor-pa-svalbard.

Waldseemüller, Martin. Universalis Cosmographia secundum Ptholomaei traditionem et Americi Vespucii alioru[m]que lustrationes (1507), Library of Congress, www.loc.gov/resource/g3200.ct000725/?r=-0.292,0.011,1.111,0.677,0.

Index

www.ingramcontent.com/pod-product-compliance
Ingram Content Group UK Ltd.
Pitfield, Milton Keynes, MK11 3LW, UK
UKHW020809290926
15470UKWH00003B/1049

9 781509 988327